Longing for Egmond

Gari Melchers and George Hitchcock: Their Years in the Netherlands

Marjan van Heteren

With the assistance of
Olga Kruisbrink

Stedelijk Museum Alkmaar
Waanders Publishers, Zwolle

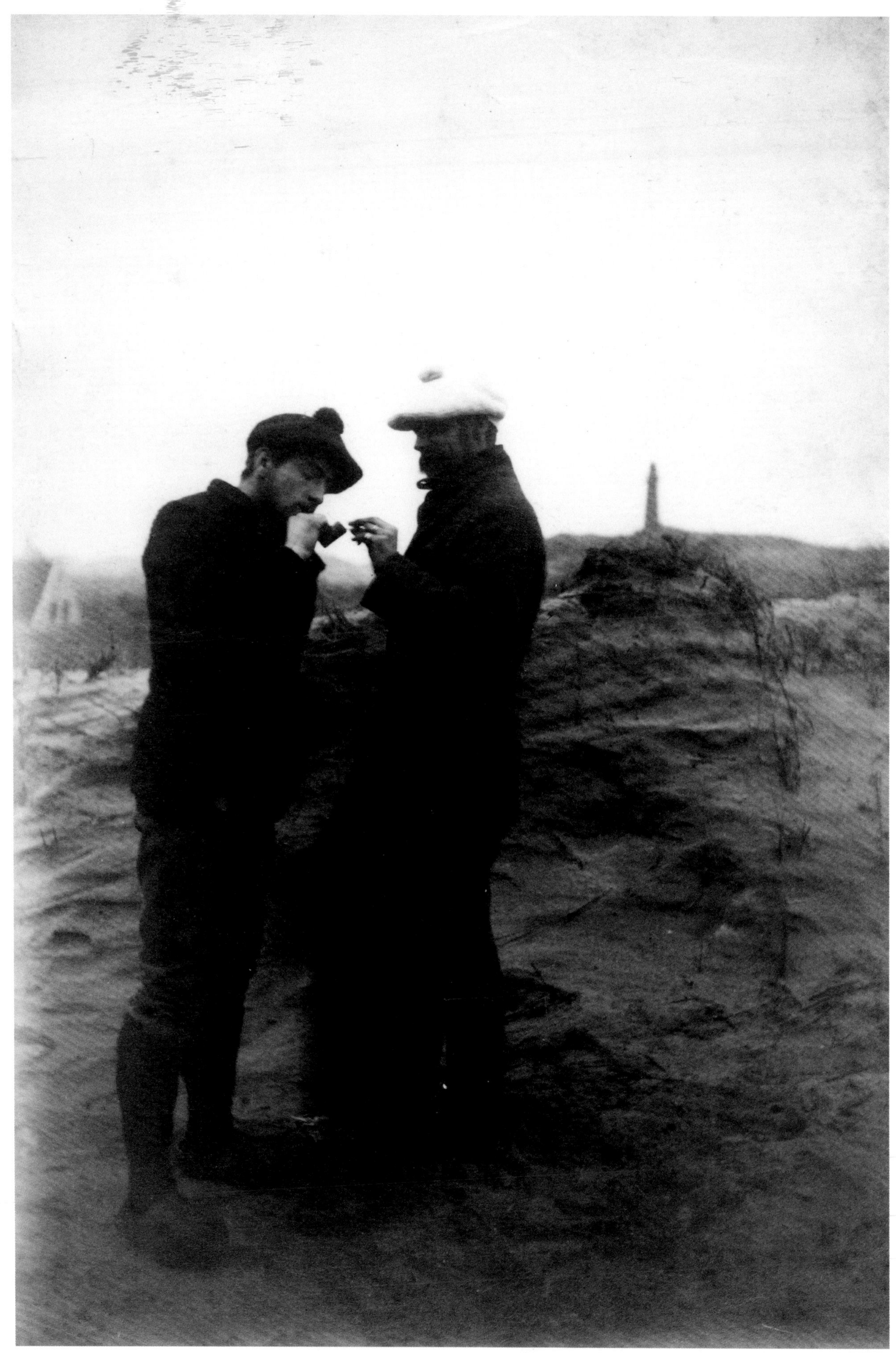

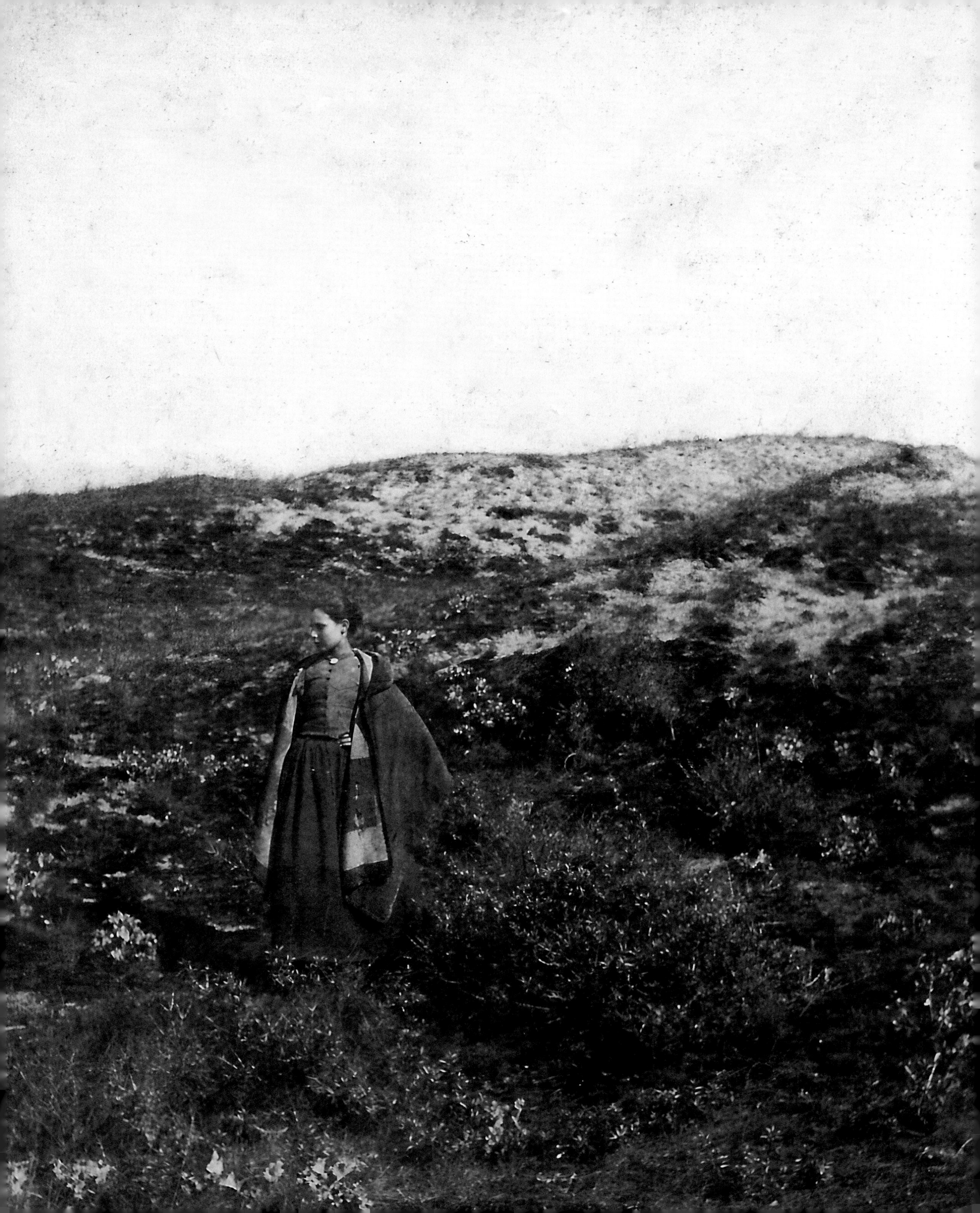

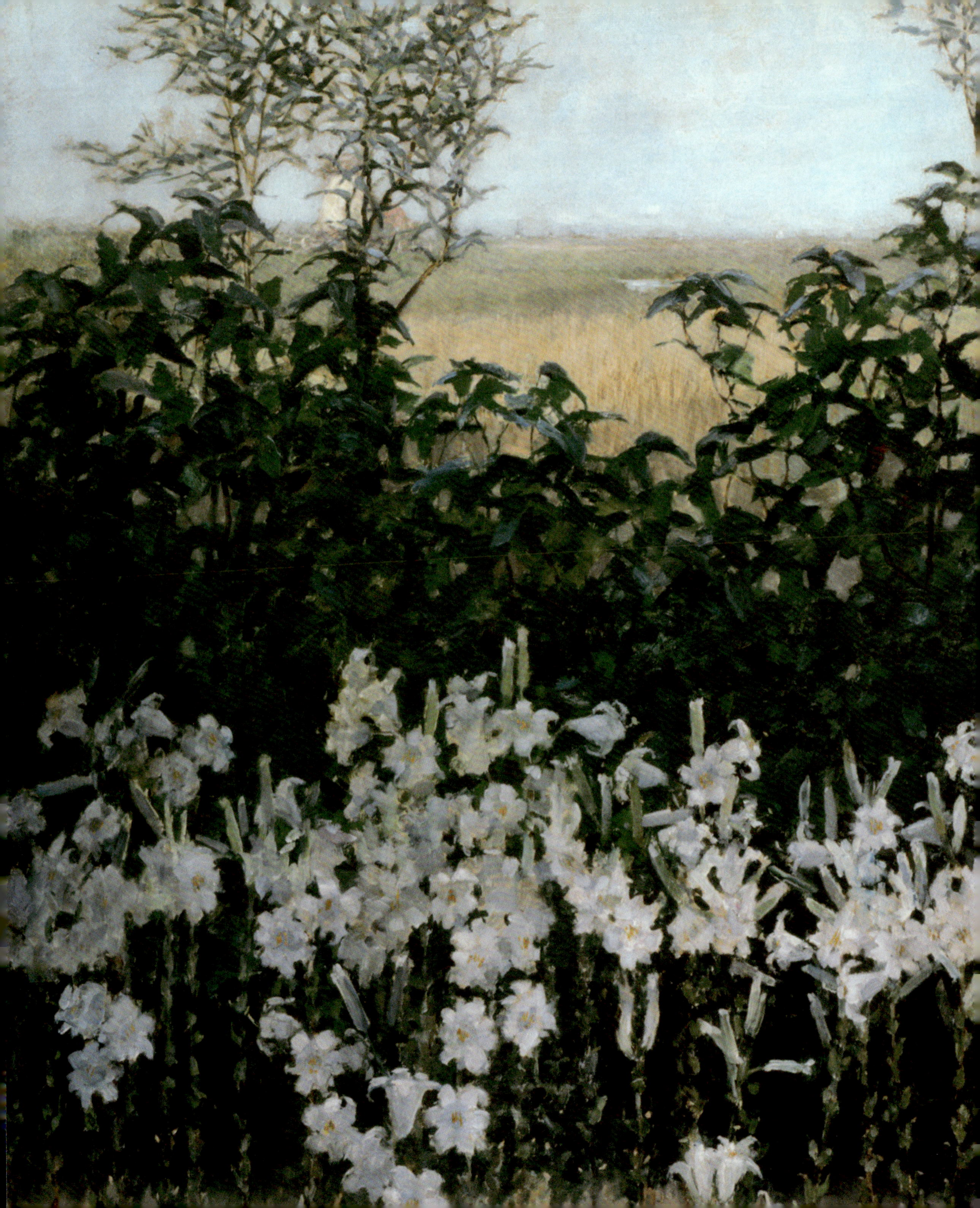

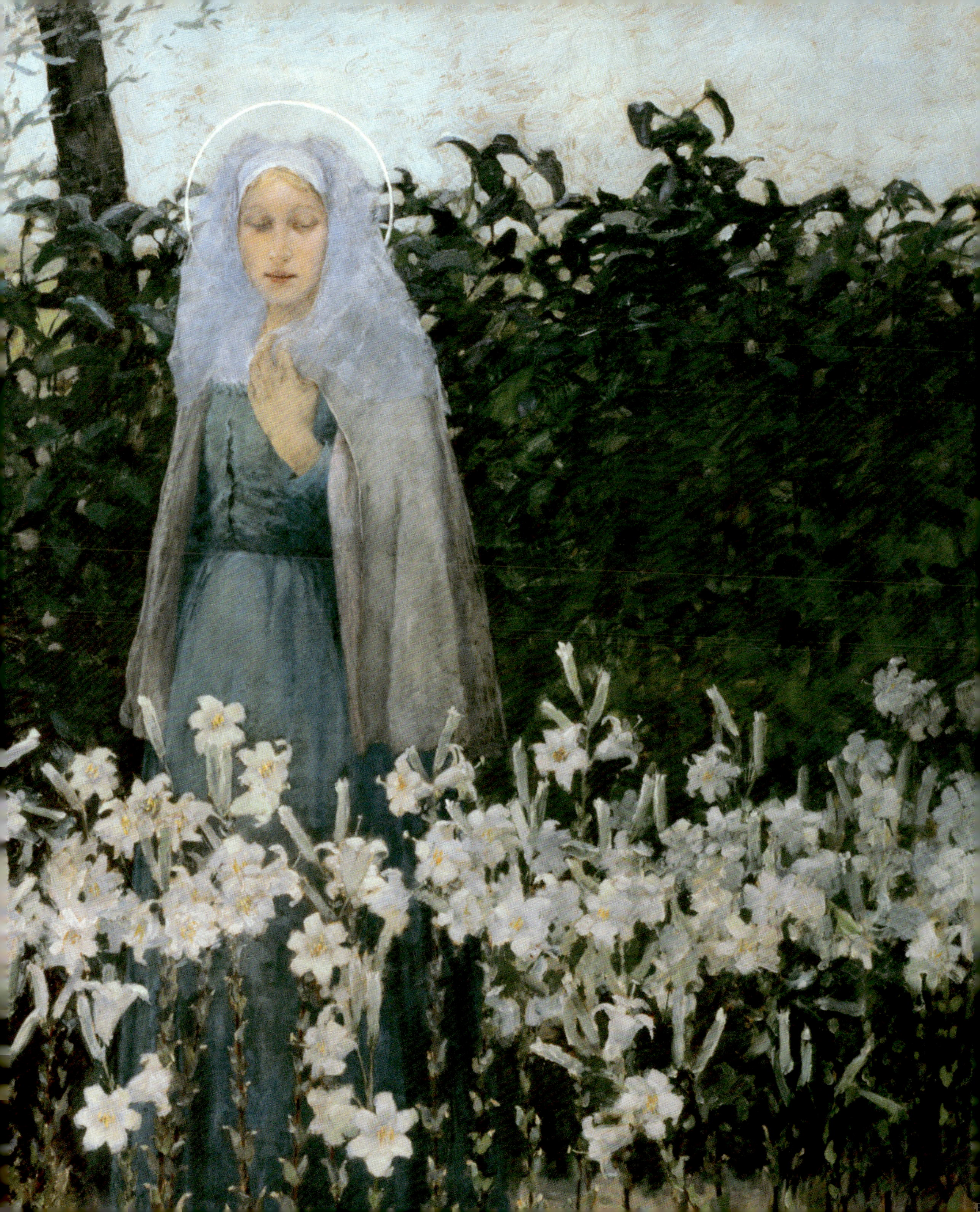

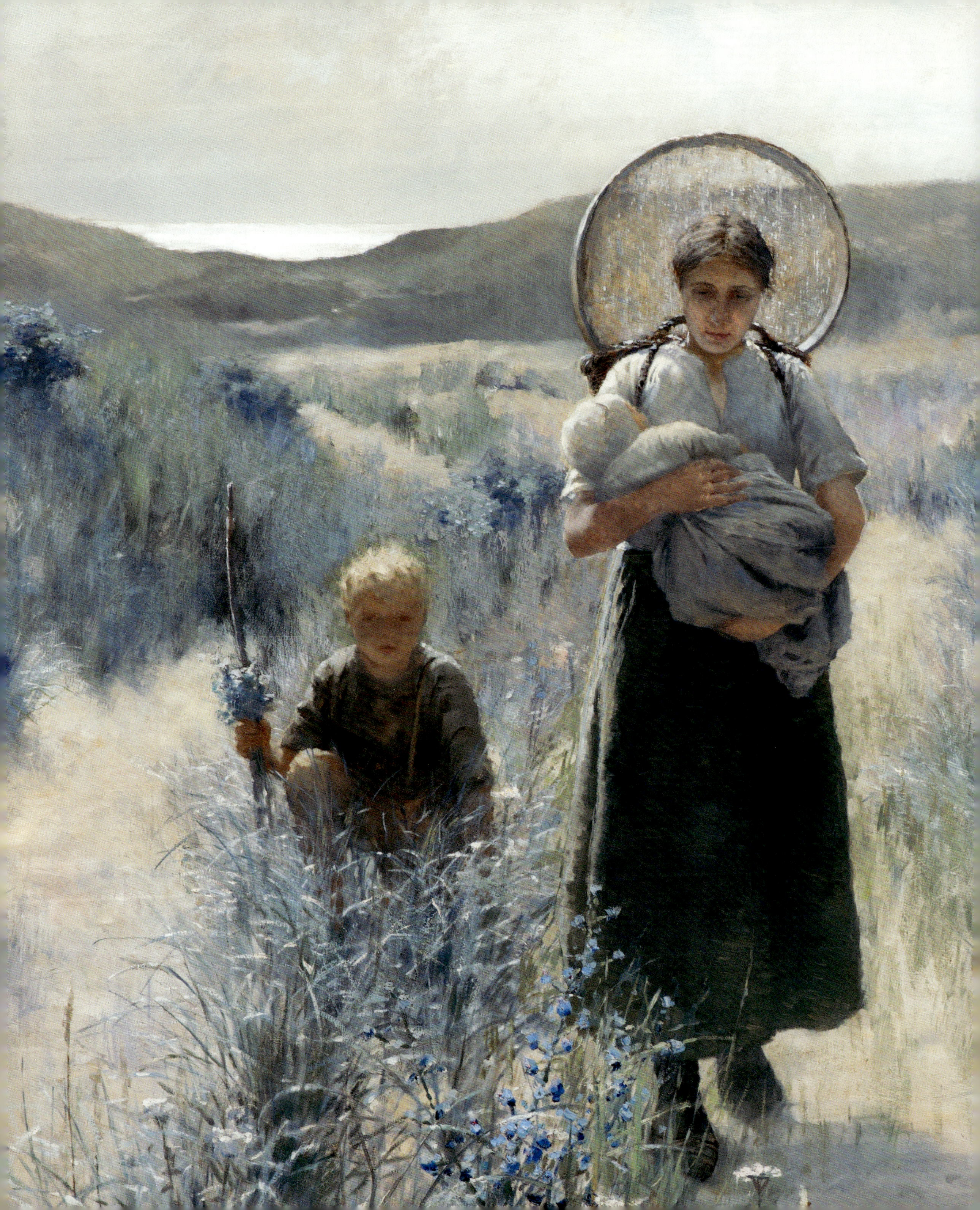

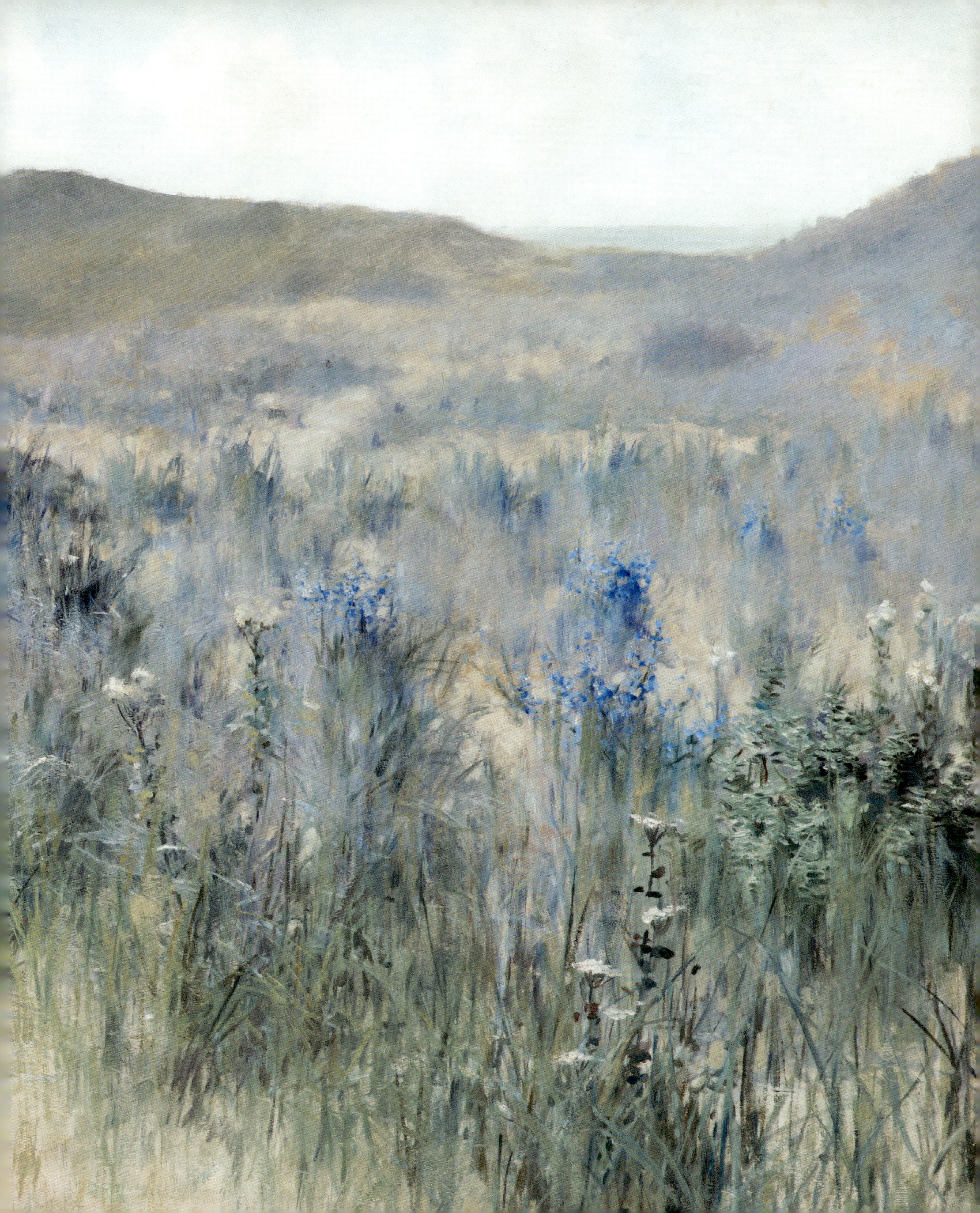

Longing

Gari Melchers and George Hitchcock: Their Years in the Netherlands

for
Egmond

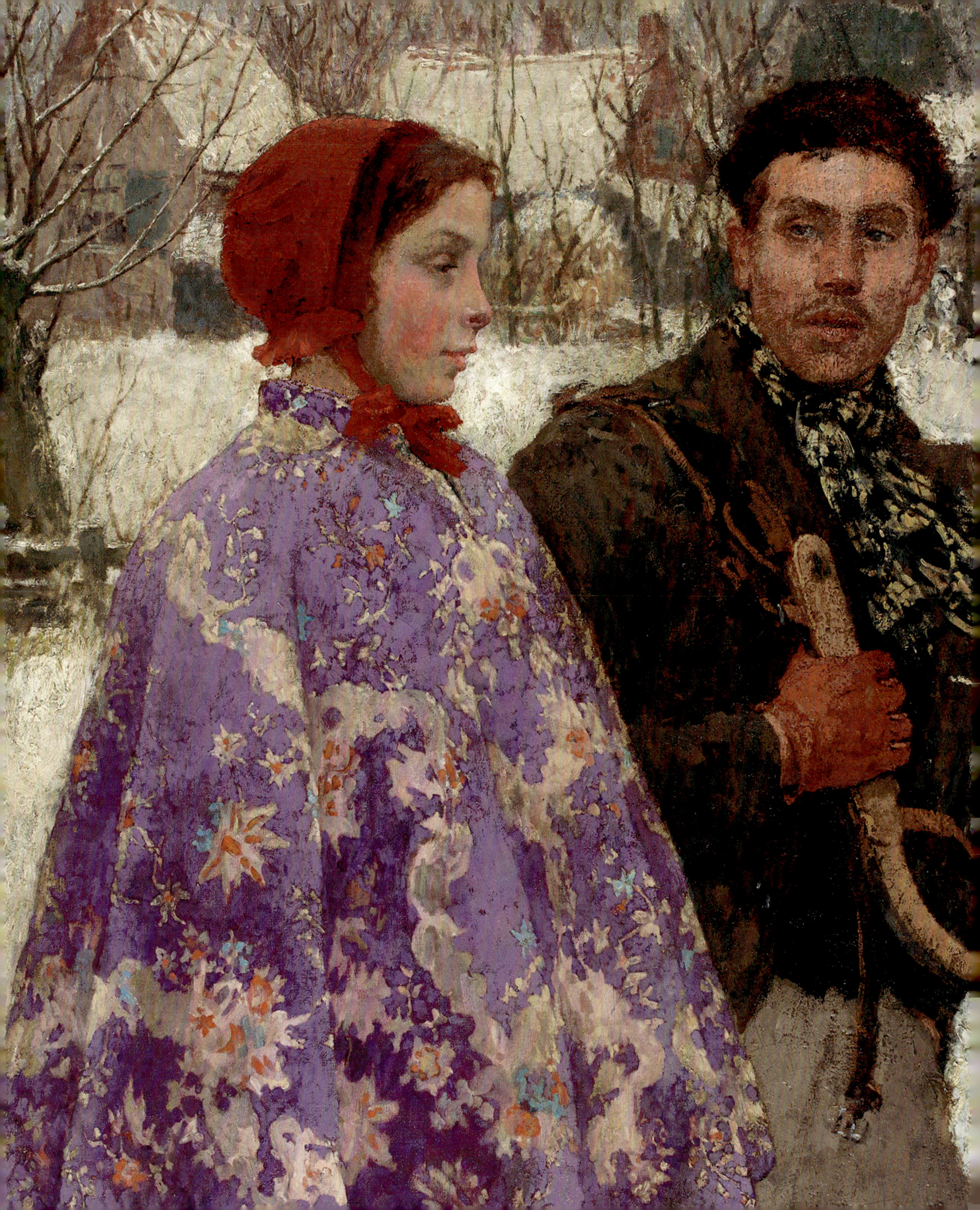

Contents

12   Foreword
Marrigje Rikken

16   Longing for Egmond

22   The Years of Training and Their Encounter

38   Holland Mania

62   "For Art's Sake": The Art Summer School

74   The Success Consolidated

108   The Final Years in Egmond

124   Longing for Egmond – In Conclusion

126   Appendix: Artists in Egmond
Olga Kruisbrink

132   Notes
140   Bibliography
142   Photo Credits
142   Lenders

Foreword

Holland attracts me more than any other country. Convinced that to truly excel at something, one must know it thoroughly, I settled permanently a few years ago in Egmond aan Zee, with a colleague [Hitchcock] who shares my passion for this country

Gari Melchers (1886) [1]

For centuries, the three Egmond villages – Egmond aan Zee, Egmond-Binnen and Egmond aan den Hoef – have held a strong appeal for artists. In the seventeenth century, Dutch masters such as Jacob van Ruisdael (1628/29-1682) and Jan van Goyen (1596-1656) were drawn to these rustic places. They captured the serene coastal landscape with its rolling dunes, the ruins of the influential abbey, and the imposing castle and church at the edge of the beach. In doing so, they often took artistic liberties. The surroundings were presented as grander or more picturesque than they were in reality. During that time, in general, the less pleasant realities – whether in cities where workers toiled in filthy conditions or in villages where fishermen and farmers earned meager wages for long days of labor – are noticeably absent. These painted landscapes offered an escape from that reality, presenting an idealized world that served, in a way, as a sanctuary for those who viewed them.

The situation was little different in the nineteenth century. With the advent of industrialization, the cities and the surrounding villages and countryside changed. Artists deliberately sought out more remote venues, portraying the landscape as just a little more idyllic than it truly was – leaving out smokestacks and rough edges. This was also true for the American painters George Hitchcock and Gari Melchers, the central figures of this publication accompanying the exhibition *Longing for Egmond. From Inspiration to Artists' Village* (2025). Both artists settled in Egmond for prolonged periods of time, immortalizing not only the landscape but also its inhabitants. They too portrayed life at its finest, with dazzling fields of flowers, radiant mothers with children, and peaceful everyday scenes. Hitchcock even attracted a new wave of international artists to Egmond with his Art Summer School.

Their seventeenth-century predecessors opted for low horizons, affording the Dutch cloudscapes free rein and underscoring mankind's puniness in the great outdoors. Melchers and Hitchcock, by contrast, raised the horizon line, allowing their Egmond models to take center stage. This shift – both literally and figuratively – reveals a changing view of the landscape and the role of people therein. Awareness of the landscape remains just as relevant today. Nature is under increasing pressure from human intervention. Wind turbines now mark the coastline of Egmond aan Zee – symbols of the necessary transition to sustainable energy, which will undoubtedly continue to reshape the landscape in the future. This evolving context also changes how we view the work of Melchers and Hitchcock. Although not widely known as innovators, their Egmond paintings – now the subject of scholarly research for the first time as part of this exhibition and publication – offer fresh perspectives and new insights.

Moreover, the study of art history should not be limited to the great innovators alone. An inclusive approach must also acknowledge artists who, while not part of the avant-garde, nonetheless garnered recognition and success. For a long time, American artists who trained and worked in Europe at the end of the nineteenth century were considered "inferior" to their European contemporaries, largely because their works lacked a distinct American character of their own. Yet it is precisely their outsider's perspective that invites us to see our familiar Dutch surroundings in a new light. Hitchcock and Melchers embraced the Netherlands – Egmond in particular – with deep affection. It is time we return that embrace.

Marrigje Rikken
Director, Stedelijk Museum Alkmaar

Acknowledgments

Egmond's timeless appeal to artists comes to life in this richly illustrated publication and the accompanying exhibition *Longing for Egmond: From Inspiration to Artists' Village*. A project of this scale would not have been possible without the generous support and collaboration of numerous individuals and institutions.

We thank all of the museums and art dealers who kindly loaned works for the exhibition: Rijksmuseum, Amsterdam; Dordrechts Museum; Fondation Custodia, Paris; The National Gallery, London; Gari Melchers Home and Studio, University of Mary Washington, Fredericksburg; Telfair Museums, Savannah; National Gallery of Art, Washington; Smithsonian American Art Museum, Washington; Museum van Egmond; Lawrence Steigrad Fine Arts, New York; and The Thomas H. and Diane DeMell Jacobsen Ph.D. Foundation, Florida.

We also extend our sincere thanks to the private collectors who entrusted us with their works of art. Our appreciation likewise goes to the Municipality of Alkmaar and all the foundations that supported the exhibition or this publication: The Netherland-America Foundation, BPD Cultuurfonds, Pieter Haverkorn van Rijsewijk Foundation and Gifted Art Foundation.

Finally, we acknowledge the many individuals who provided information, advice, and essential support. We are especially indebted to Susan Martis (Gari Melchers Home and Studio), Rob Leijen (Egmond Historic Association), and Peter van den Berg (who very generously made his entire archive available). We would also like to warmly thank the following individuals for their valuable contributions: Stephen Bartley (Archivist, Chelsea Arts Club Archive / Heatherley's), Heike Biedermann (Albertinum Dresden), Lisette Blokker (Alkmaar Regional Archives), Mark Cole (The Cleveland Museum of Art), Caroline Corbeau-Parsons (Musée d'Orsay), Sebastian Grigo (Stadtarchiv Düsseldorf), Stephanie Herdrich (The Metropolitan Museum of Art), Jacco Hooikammer (Open Air Museum Arnhem), Sunny Jansen, Mayken Jonkman (Rijksmuseum), Jeroen Kapelle (RKD), Christi Klinkert (Frans Hals Museum), Erik van Koeveringe, Sarah Kohn (Flint Institute of Arts), Ken Myers (Detroit Institute of Arts), Adrienne Quarles van Ufford (Panorama Mesdag Museum), Frans Smeding (Smeding Consultancy), Michael Stech (Naturalis), Renske Suijver (The Mesdag Collection), Djalma Taihuutu (Van Gogh Museum), Kate Weinstein (Art Institute of Chicago), Hoang Tran (PAFA), and Andrew Weislogel (Herbert F. Johnson Museum of Art | Cornell University).

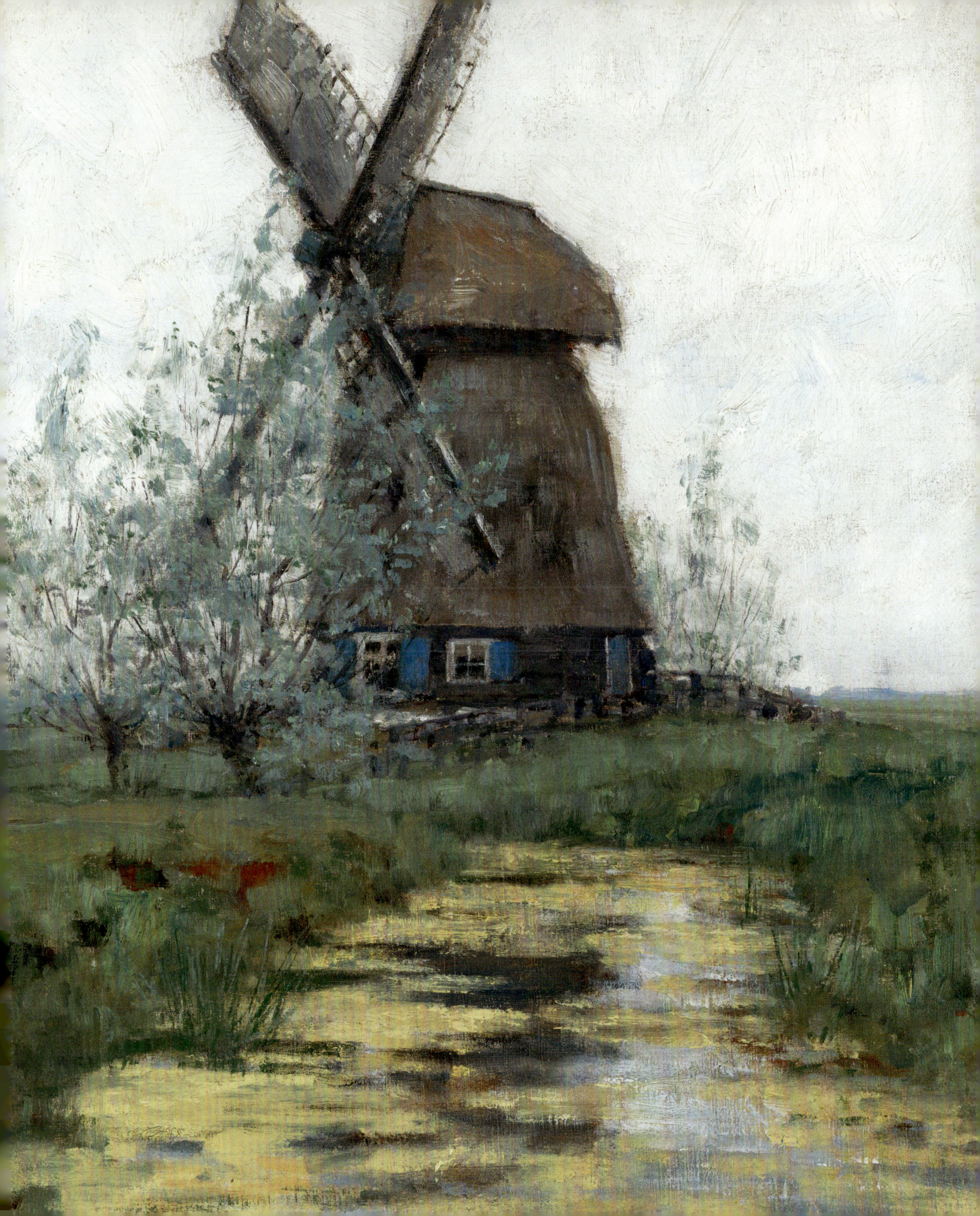

Longing for Egmond

From Egmond commenced a career.
[...] 'There's where it all began'

Henrietta Lewis-Hind (1928)[2]

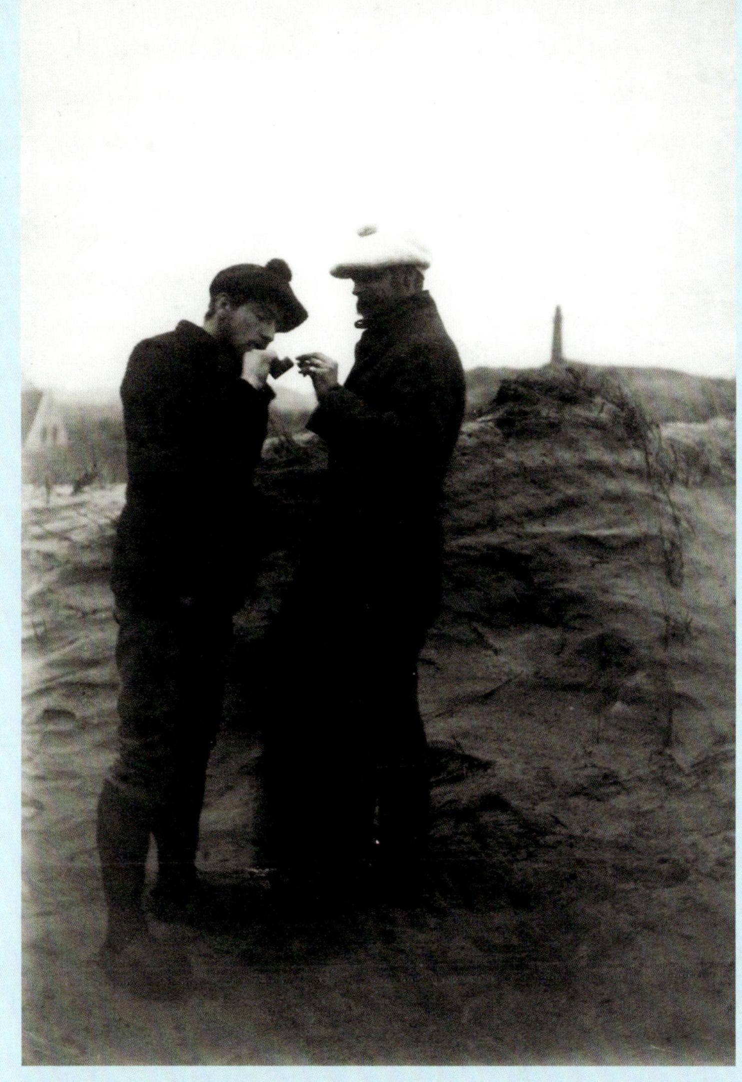

In October 1884, two American artists exhibited their work in the Netherlands for the first time at the Amsterdam artists' society Arti et Amicitiae.[3] Both of these men, Gari Melchers (Detroit 1860–Fredericksburg 1932) and George Hitchcock (Providence, Rhode Island 1850–Marken 1913), reported residing in Egmond aan Zee. One of the works Hitchcock exhibited featured a typical Egmond subject: *Egmond "Pinks"* (flat-bottom fishing vessels). Whether Melchers' submission, *The Grandfather,* and the painting with the rather curious title *Looking at the Neighbor Woman* were also painted in Egmond is unfortunately unknown.[4]

Less than a month after the opening, George Hitchcock, his wife Henrietta Hitchcock-Richardson (1862–1938), and Gari Melchers purchased a plot of land on the Torensduin in Egmond aan Zee, where they immediately had a house with a studio built.[5] The village on the North Sea coast was more than just a temporary source of inspiration for them. To carry out their plans, Hitchcock borrowed 900 guilders from the ten-year-younger Melchers, who included a clause in the agreement stating that he could cancel the loan at any time, for example, if their friendship were to end. Additionally, Melchers had it stipulated in the deed that he could always stay in the studio.[6] Evidently, the house on the dune was intended primarily to be home to the Hitchcocks and Melchers planned to visit regularly [fig. 1].

Who were these American artists now known only to a few in the Netherlands? Why did they travel from Detroit and Chicago to Europe and later to the Netherlands, eventually finding their way to Egmond aan Zee? It is remarkable that they discovered this then small, insignificant fishing village, which was only accessible by a horse-drawn omnibus that traveled twice a day from Alkmaar to Egmond.

Less than a decade before their arrival, the three neighboring Egmond villages – Egmond aan Zee, Egmond-Binnnen, and Egmond aan den Hoef – had been chronicled by the Mennonite pastor Jacobus Kraandijk, who made walking tours throughout the Netherlands.[7] He described Egmond aan Zee "at the foot of the dunes, with their gleaming white tops, their drab green slopes sharply contrasting with the clear blue sky," as a smelly maze of dead-end streets and alleys. On the beach near the lighthouse, he saw the hustle and bustle around some forty fishermen's pinks.[8] Formerly home to one of Holland's most influential abbeys, Egmond-Binnen had declined from a thriving and important place to "a small and rather dilapidated village" [fig. 2].[9] And even Egmond aan den Hoef, with its

   1 Gari Melchers (left) and George Hitchcock, Egmond aan Zee, Holland, ca. 1890. Photo Gari Melchers Home and Studio, University of Mary Washington, Fredericksburg

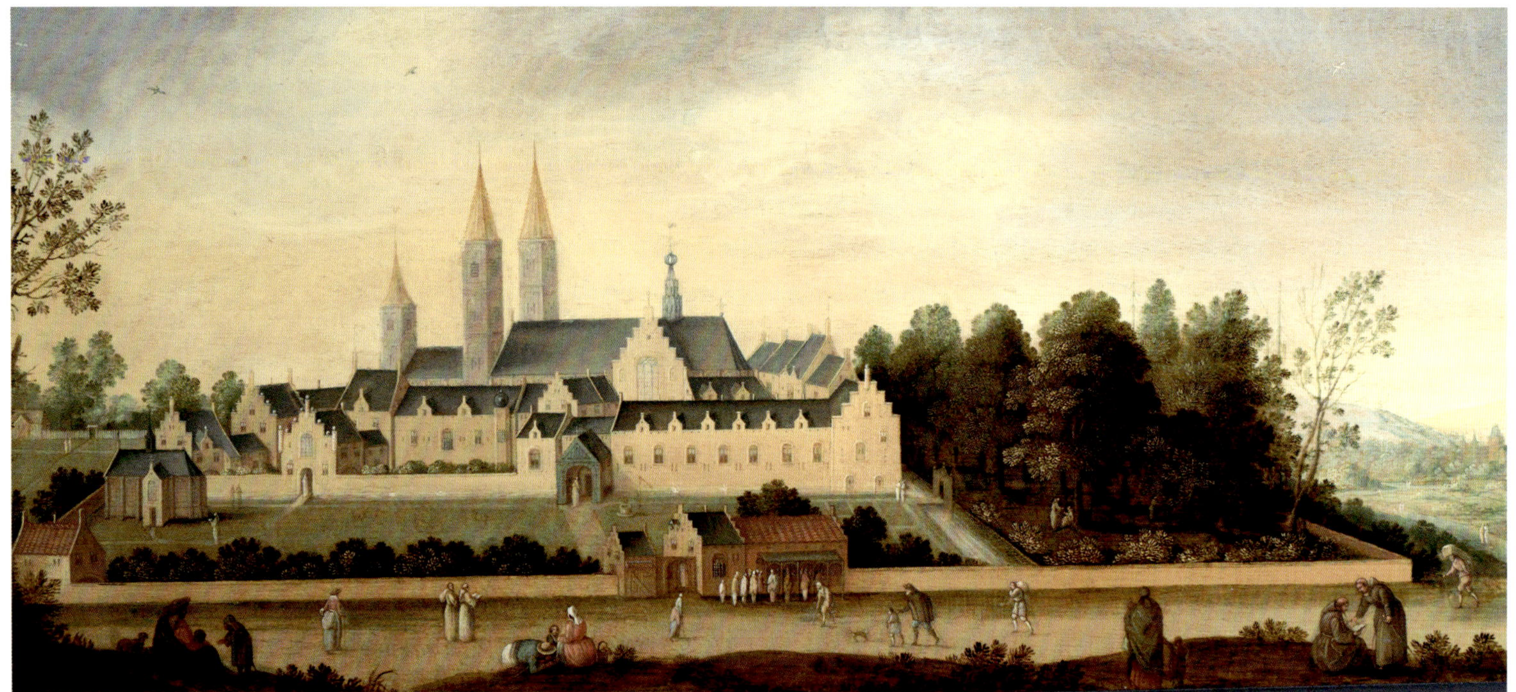

expansive, fertile meadows, was still only a shadow of the prosperous village where once stood the mighty castle of the Counts of Egmond [fig. 3].[10] In short, none of the three Egmonds had any particular appeal to travelers like Kraandijk in the nineteenth century. And yet, it was in Egmond "where it all began."

The explanation for Hitchcock's and Melchers' interest in Egmond lies partly in the phenomenon of American artists who traveled to Europe in the last quarter of the nineteenth century for their education. Most aspiring young artists studied for years in Paris, London, Munich, or Düsseldorf, at academies or in the studios of renowned masters. During the summer months, many artists – and students – took study trips to other countries in Europe, which certainly included the Netherlands. The Netherlands was an attractive destination for American artists because of its seventeenth-century masters, who were internationally regarded as the pinnacle of painting. As a result, most Americans visited the Rijksmuseum (housed in the Trippenhuis until 1885) in Amsterdam and the Stedelijk Museum in Haarlem, where since 1862 the work of Frans Hals, among others, was displayed.

Moreover, resting on the foundations of the rich artistic legacy of Rembrandt, Ruisdael, and Hobbema, a new school of contemporary masters had arisen, also garnering international recognition: the painters of The Hague School. The brothers Jacob (1837-1899), Matthijs (1839-1917) and Willem Maris (1844-1910), Anton Mauve (1838-1888), Willem Roelofs (1822-1897), and Constant Gabriël (1828-1903) glorified the pristine Dutch polder landscape. Artists such as Jozef Israëls (1824-1911) and Hendrik Willem Mesdag (1831-1915) depicted the daily lives of farmers and fishermen [fig. 4]. Sought after worldwide, works by The Hague School masters were shipped by the dozens in large crates across the North Sea and the North Atlantic, to be eagerly snapped up for high sums by industrialists such as James Staats Forbes, Edward Drummond Libbey, and Frank Frick for their collections [fig. 5].[11] American artists, such as William Merritt Chase (1849-1916), enjoyed visiting the studios of their Dutch confreres during their summer travels through the Low Countries. In 1903, for example, Chase visited the studios of Mesdag and Israëls, describing the latter as "a very charming little man (he does not stand as high as my shoulder)."[12] Hitchcock and Melchers were personally acquainted with Mesdag, and presumably also visited exhibitions and studios in the Netherlands.[13]

Hitchcock and Melchers spent many years in the three Egmonds, from 1884 to 1905 and 1914, respectively. They painted the landscape, the people, and their rituals on large and small canvases in bright colors. In their style, they were more aligned with their French contemporaries, who celebrated the sensation of color and light, rather than with the Dutch painters of The Hague School, also known as "the gray school." Due to the presence of these American painters, ever more artists were drawn to Egmond, and during the summer months, a vibrant artist colony began to form.

[...] the Mighty Castle of Egmond aan den Hoef

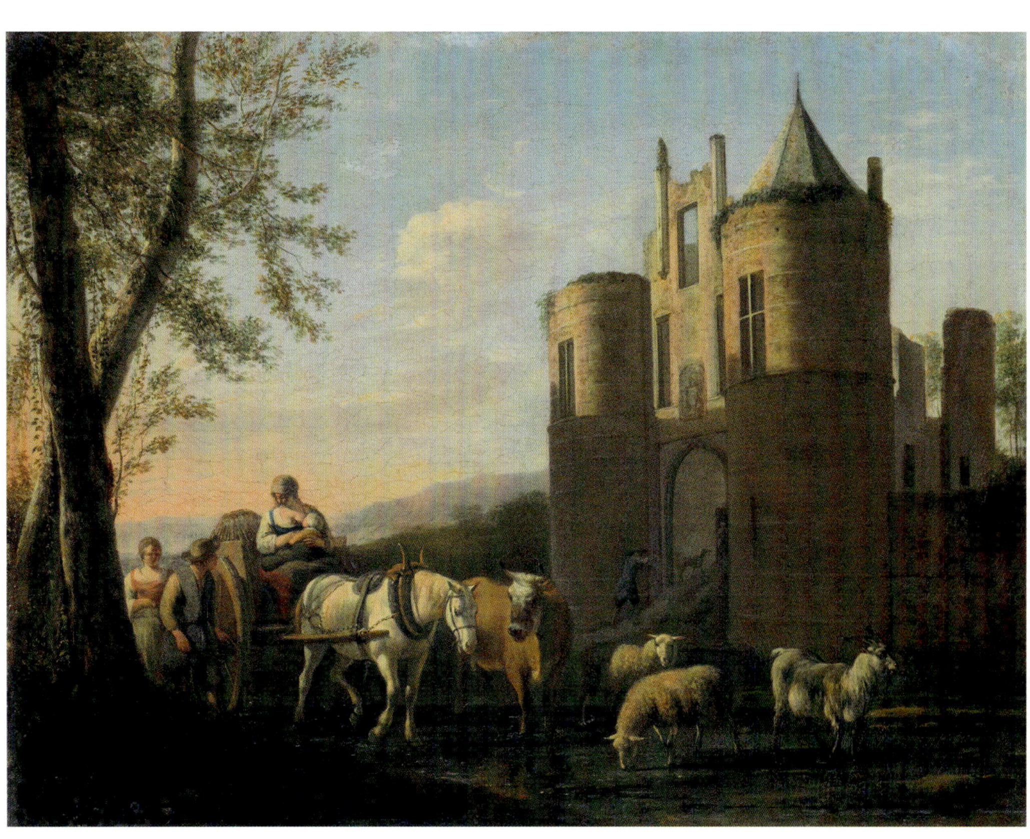

   3 G.W. Berckhout, *Egmond Castle*, 1653, oil on canvas, 96 x 160 cm. Rijksmuseum, Amsterdam

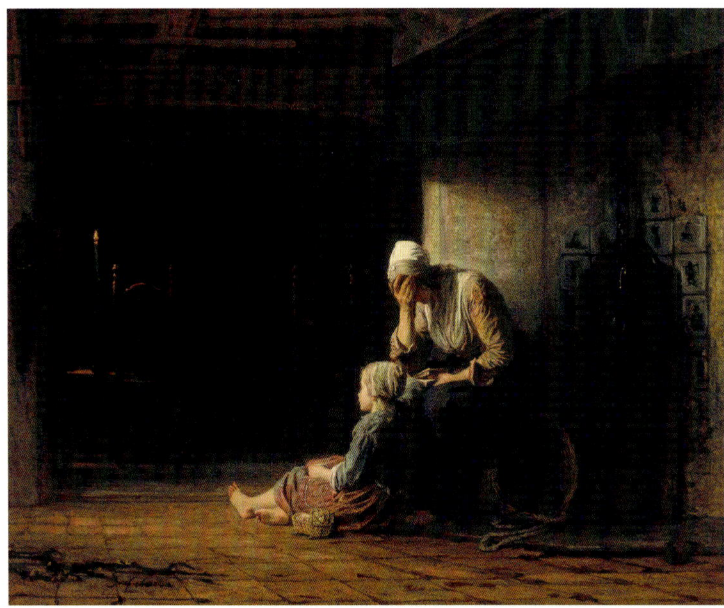

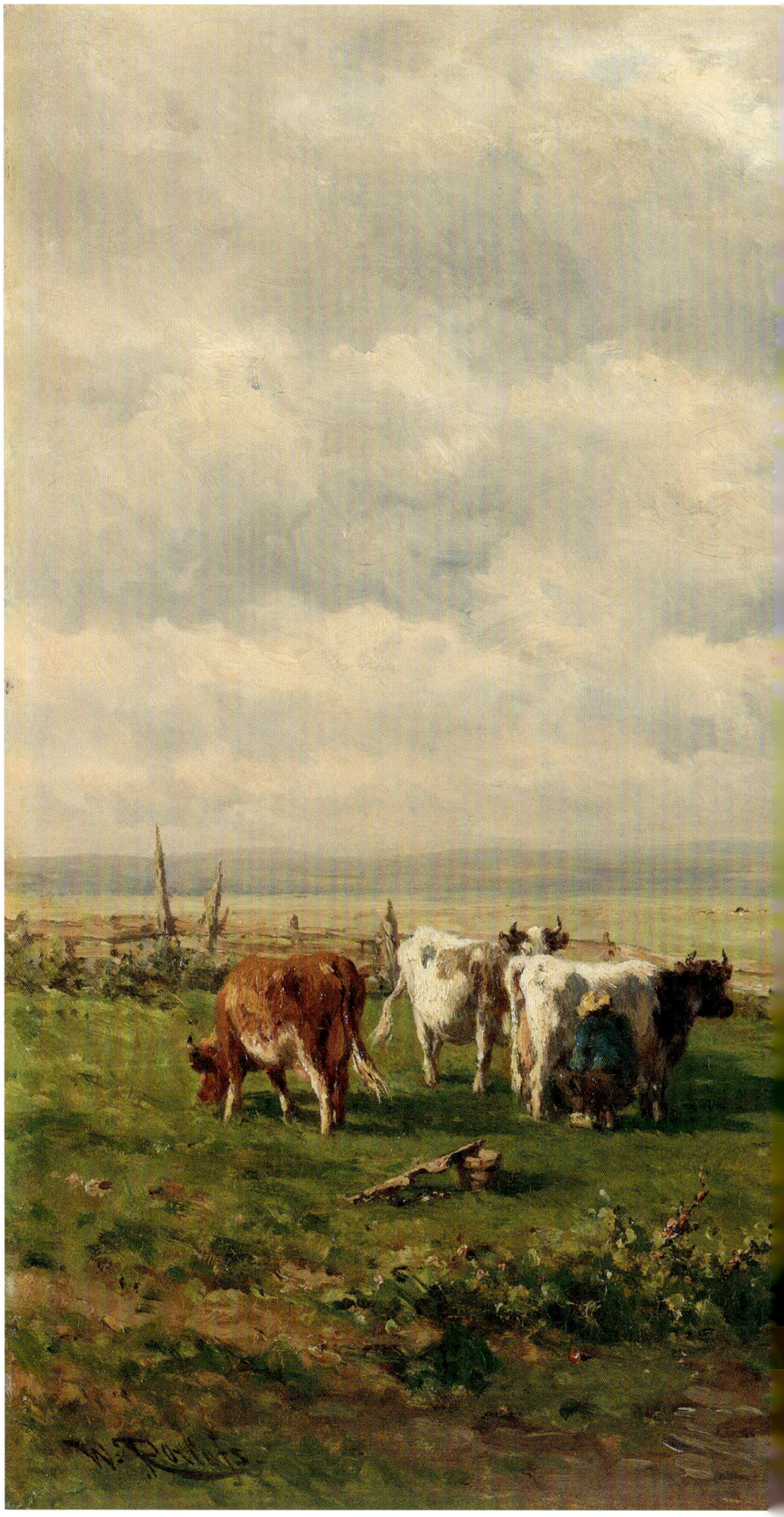

Although Hitchcock and Melchers exhibited these colorful works with Egmond subjects internationally – and not without success – none ended up in a Dutch public collection. Moreover, only a modest number of their works has been preserved in Dutch private collections and in European museums. As a result, the recognition of these artists in Europe, and certainly in the Netherlands, remains exceptionally limited. One of the rare occasions when their works were displayed in the Netherlands was during the *Dutch Utopia* show at Singer Laren in 2010 exploring the impact of Dutch art and culture on American art around 1900, the so-called "Holland Mania." In 2022, a modest number of works by Hitchcock and Melchers were presented in the *Kunstenaarsdorpen* (Artists' Villages) exhibition at the Zuiderzee Museum. Naturally, Stichting Historisch Egmond, Huys Egmont, and Museum van Egmond continue to keep alive the memory of these artists and the Egmond artists' colony. With this publication accompanying the exhibition *Longing for Egmond. From Source of Inspiration to Artists' Village* (2025), the Stedelijk Museum Alkmaar aims to document the history of George Hitchcock, Gari Melchers, and the Egmond artists' colony, bringing it back into the spotlight.

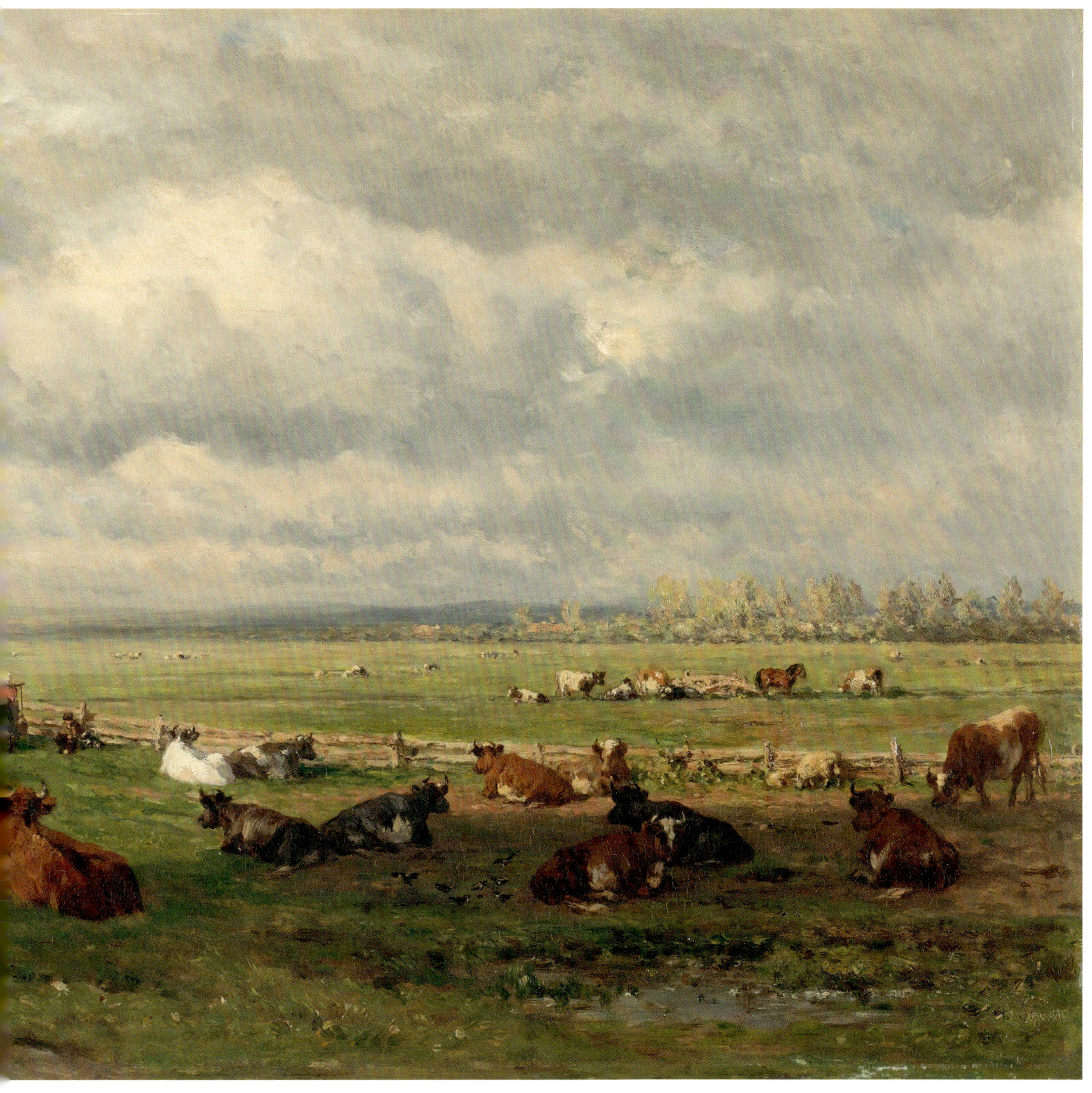

The Years of Training and Their Encounter

After having learned to draw and use paint, a painter can seldom develop further on their own

Algemeen Handelsblad (5 May 1888)[14]

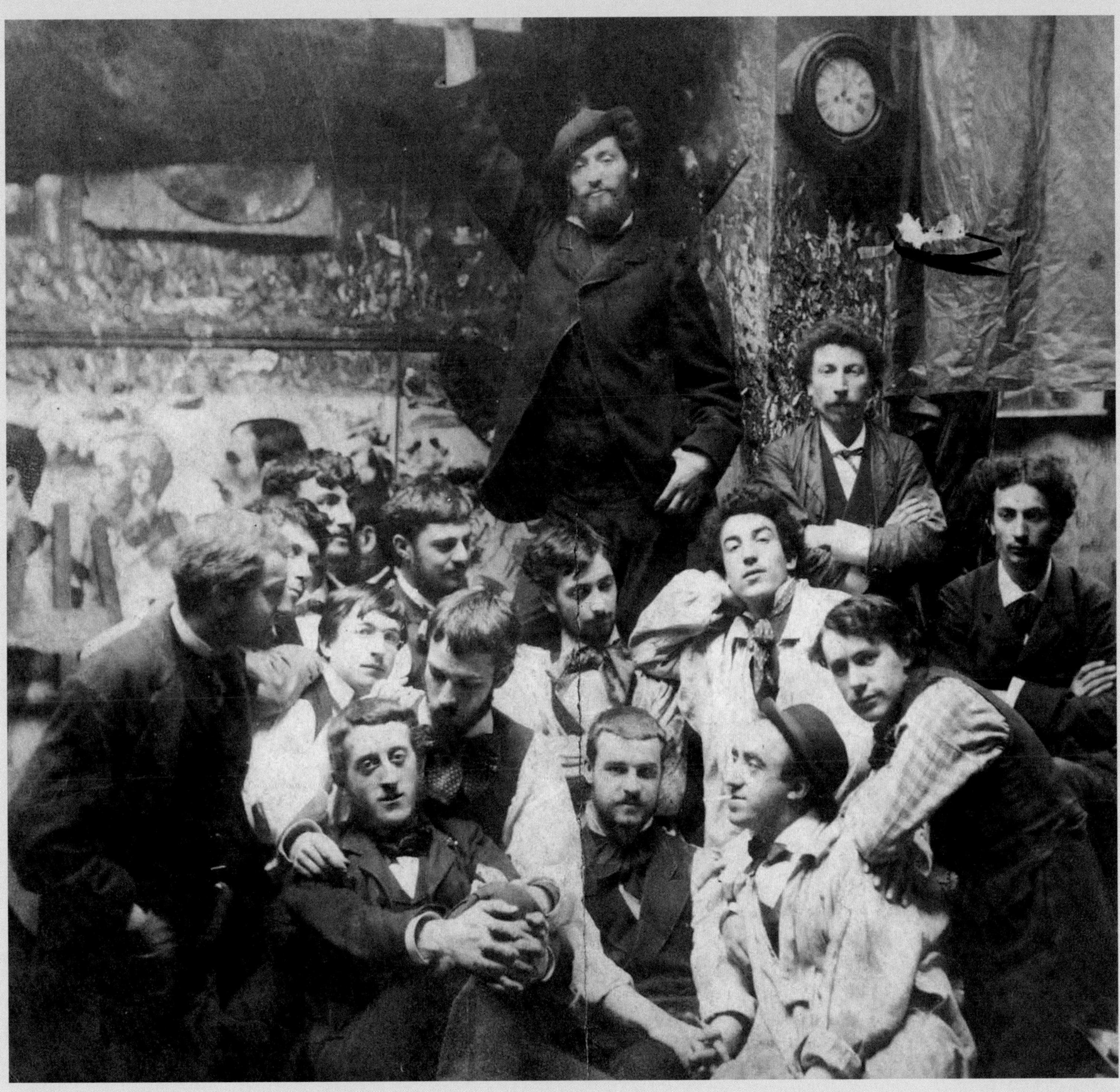

In the 1870s, American artists traveled to Europe in large numbers. This flow had started earlier in the nineteenth century, as art education in the United States was not yet generally well developed.[15] In addition, the opportunities to study the European Old Masters in museums and private collections in the United States were initially limited.[16] Museums now renowned for their fine collections of Old Masters, for instance The Museum of Fine Arts in Boston and The Metropolitan Museum in New York, were just beginning to open their doors to the public in the 1870s.

In Europe, Paris, in particular, was enormously appealing to artists.[17] In addition, the academies in London, Munich, and Düsseldorf were also popular. It is therefore not surprising that precisely these cities were chosen by Hitchcock and (the parents of) Melchers.

   6 Gari Melchers (front left) in the Académie Julian, Paris, ca. 1882. Photo Gari Melchers Home and Studio, University of Mary Washington, Fredericksburg

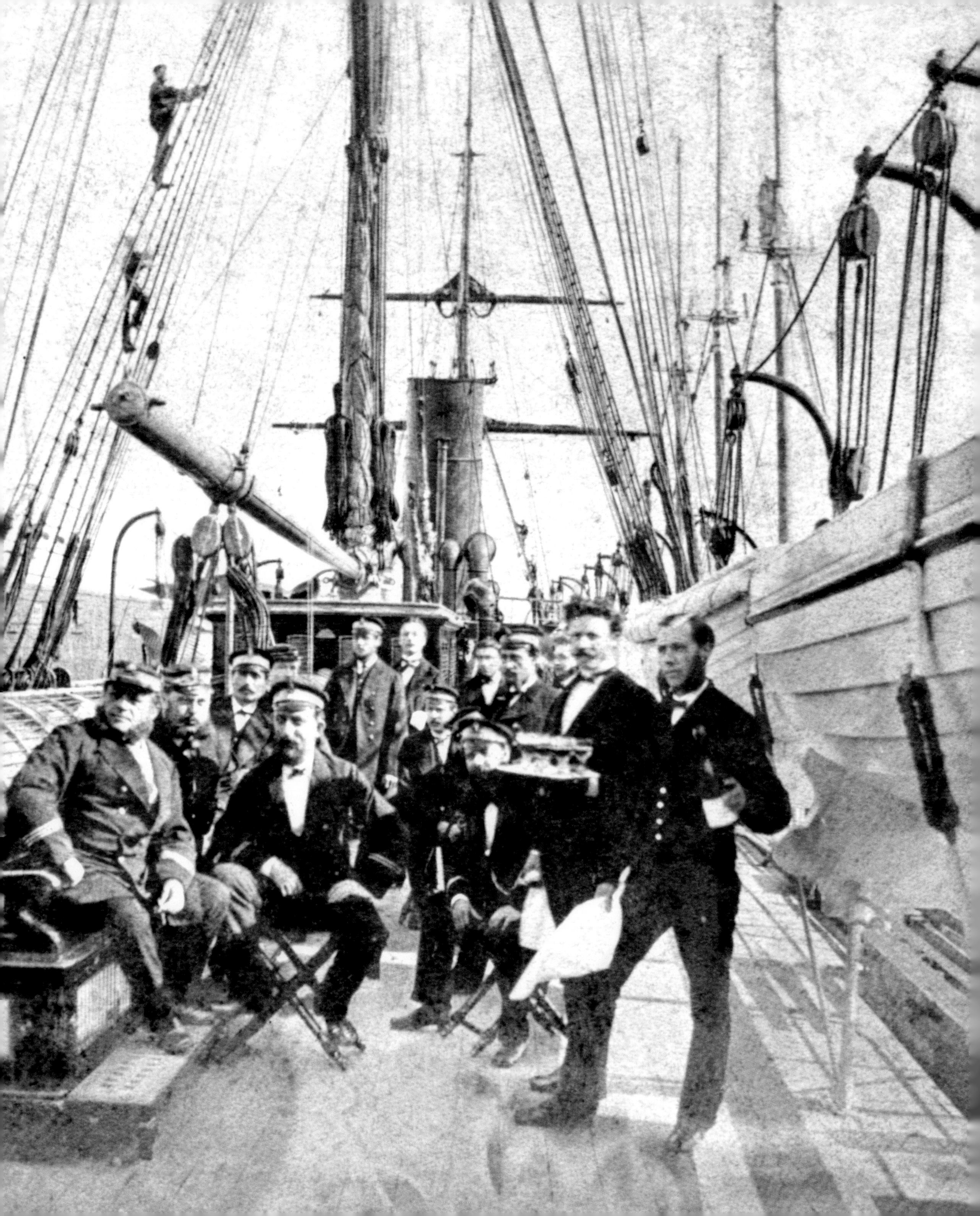

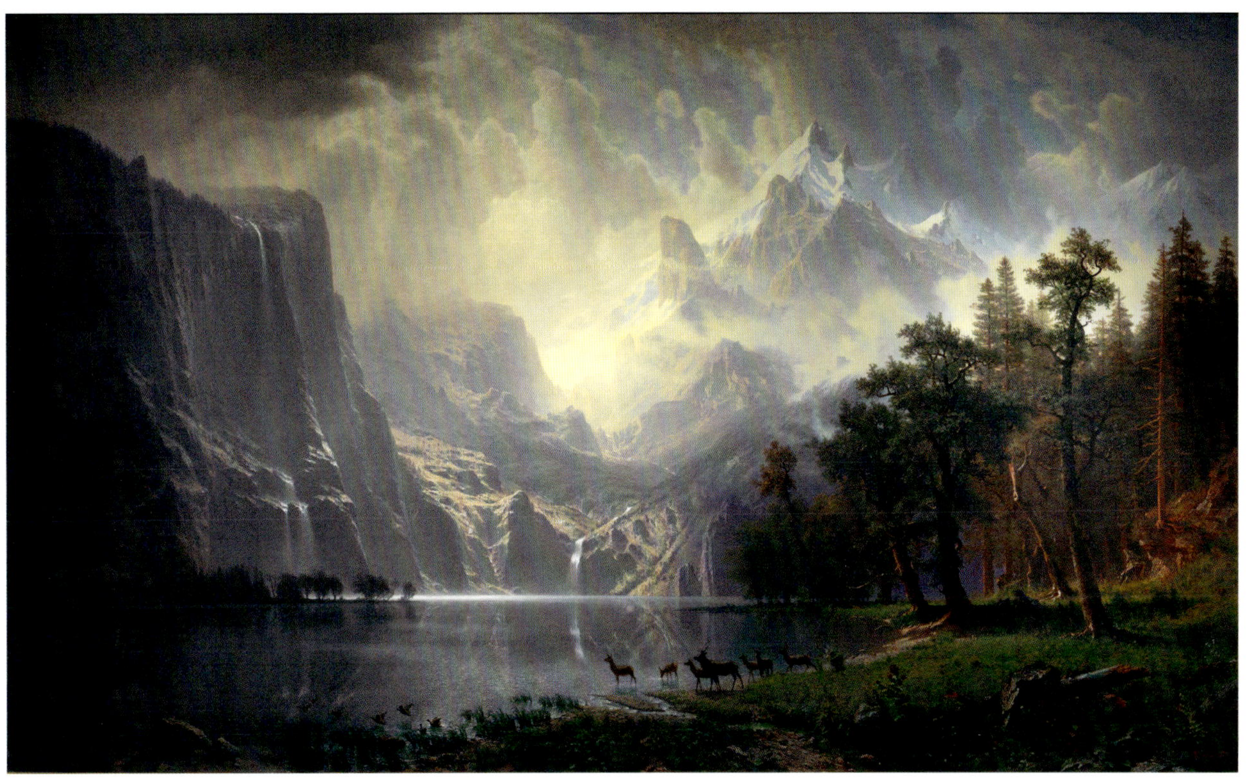

Melchers' Years in Düsseldorf: (1877-1880)

Independently of each other – it would be years before Hitchcock and Melchers would eventually meet – George Hitchcock and the ten-year-younger Gari Melchers decided to make the great journey across the ocean seeking to shape their careers as artists. Seventeen-year-old Gari Melchers was the first to leave for Europe.[18] In Gari's hometown of Detroit, his father, the sculptor Julius Theodore Melchers (1829-1909), had already introduced him to the fundamentals of drawing.[19] Originally from Germany, Julius Melchers himself had been trained in Paris, but chose to send his son to study in the German city of Düsseldorf. Presumably this was because several American artists, including Emanuel Leutze (1816-1868) and Alfred Bierstadt (1830-1902) were particularly successful in America after their training there [fig. 8].[20] Moreover, Melchers' grandfather lived in Dortmund, and Gari Melchers' parents considered Paris too decadent for their still-young son.[21] Additionally, the requirements for admission to the École des Beaux-Arts in Paris were particularly strict, especially for foreign students.[22]

Thus, in early August 1877, Melchers traveled by train from Detroit to New York in the company of his fellow townsman Julius Rolshoven (1858-1930). From there, they boarded the modern, four-year-old steamship *SS Pommerania* – which, incidentally, would sink a year later – setting sail to Hamburg [fig. 7].[23] After spending a fortnight at sea, the aspiring artists continued their journey to Düsseldorf to register at the city's renowned art academy. From 1 October 1877, until 1 July 1880 – the day he received his certificate – Melchers was enrolled at the Königlich-Preussische Kunstakademie zu Düsseldorf as a figure painter.[24]

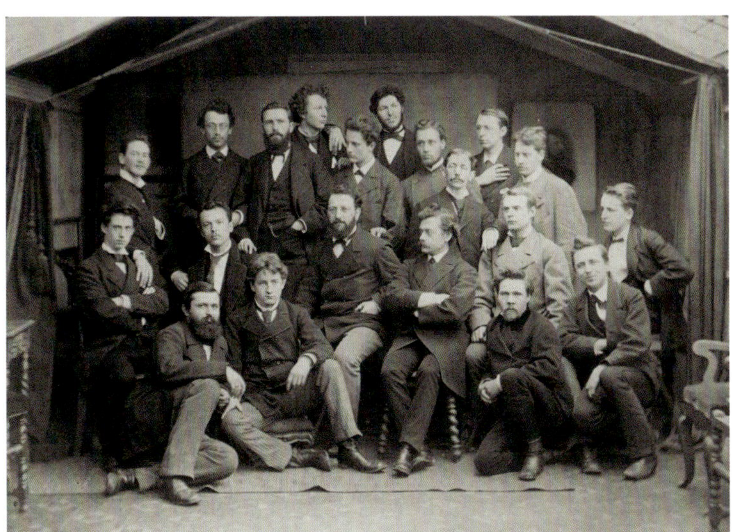

← **7** Scene on deck of the *SS Pommerania*, ca. 1873-1878. Photo Norway Heritage   **8** Alfred Bierstadt, *The Mountains of Sierra Nevada*, 1868, oil on canvas, 183 x 305 cm. Smithsonian American Art Museum, Washington   **9** Königlich-Preussische Kunstakademie in Düsseldorf, ca. 1877. Melchers is in the front row, second from left. Photo Gari Melchers Home and Studio, University of Mary Washington, Fredericksburg

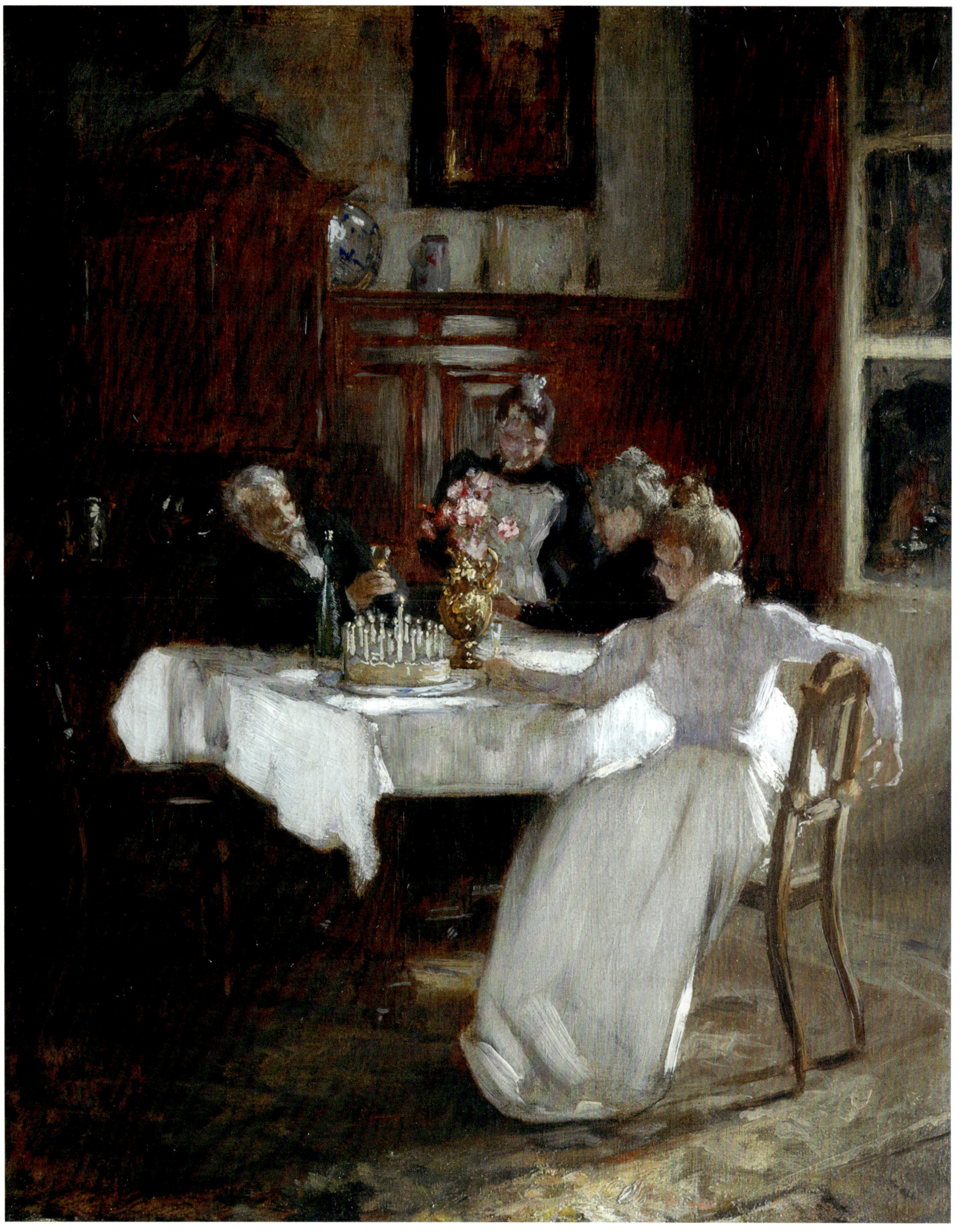

10 Hugo Crola, *The Birthday Party*, ca. 1898, oil on canvas, 59.1 x 48.1 cm. Simonis & Buunk Art Gallery, Ede

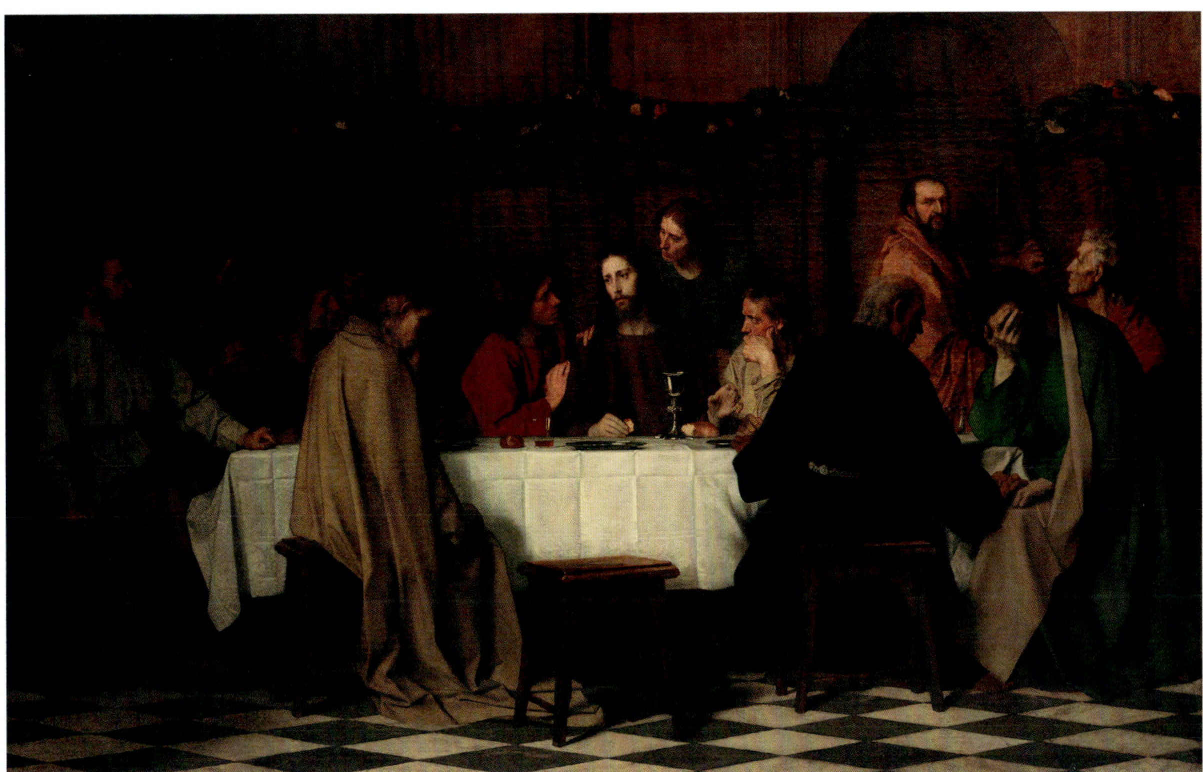

Talent: Läßt sich noch schwer beurteilen

Initially, Melchers attended the preparatory class under the direction of Hugo Crola (1841-1910) and the assistant teacher Heinrich Lauenstein (1835-1910) [fig. 10].[25] As Rolshoven remembered it, they made drawings there after the sixteenth-century artist Hans Holbein (1497/98-1543).[26] In 1877 and 1878, Melchers attended drawing classes and lessons in which students drew from plaster casts of ancient sculptures under the guidance of Peter Janssen (1844-1908) and Karl Müller (1818-1893), respectively.[27] Professor Janssen was particularly known for his thorough teaching, providing his students with a solid foundation in drawing and composition.[28]

As was customary at the time, Melchers was only allowed to pick up the paint brush after extensive drawing instruction. In 1879 and 1880, he took painting lessons from Julius Roeting (1822-1896) and the Russian painter Eduard von Gebhardt (1838-1925) in the brand-new academy building on the north side of the Altstadt [fig. 11].[29] At the building's formal opening, it was emphasized once again that the academy focused on "truth and beauty," concepts considered synonymous with "nature and idealism."[30]

During his years there, Melchers' conduct and commitment were described as "gut" (good) and "sehr gut" (very good), while his talent developed from "läßt sich noch schwer beurteilen" (difficult to assess) to "sehr begabt" (very gifted). Overall, his teachers rated his work and talent as notably good. The years in Düsseldorf must have been a special time for Melchers. In addition to Julius Rolshoven, his fellow students included the Hungarian Fritz Strobentz (1856-1929). There is a small portrait of Strobentz in one of the sketchbooks that Gebhardt advised his students to always carry with them in order to quickly record something. In 1878, they visited the Exposition Universelle in Paris together.[31] Cosmopolitan Paris, with its vibrant art scene, must have appealed to Melchers, for after receiving his certificate in the summer of 1880, the French capital became his next destination.

   11 Eduard von Gebhardt, *The Last Supper*, 1870, oil on canvas, 193 x 304.5 cm. Staatliche Museen zu Berlin, Nationalgalerie

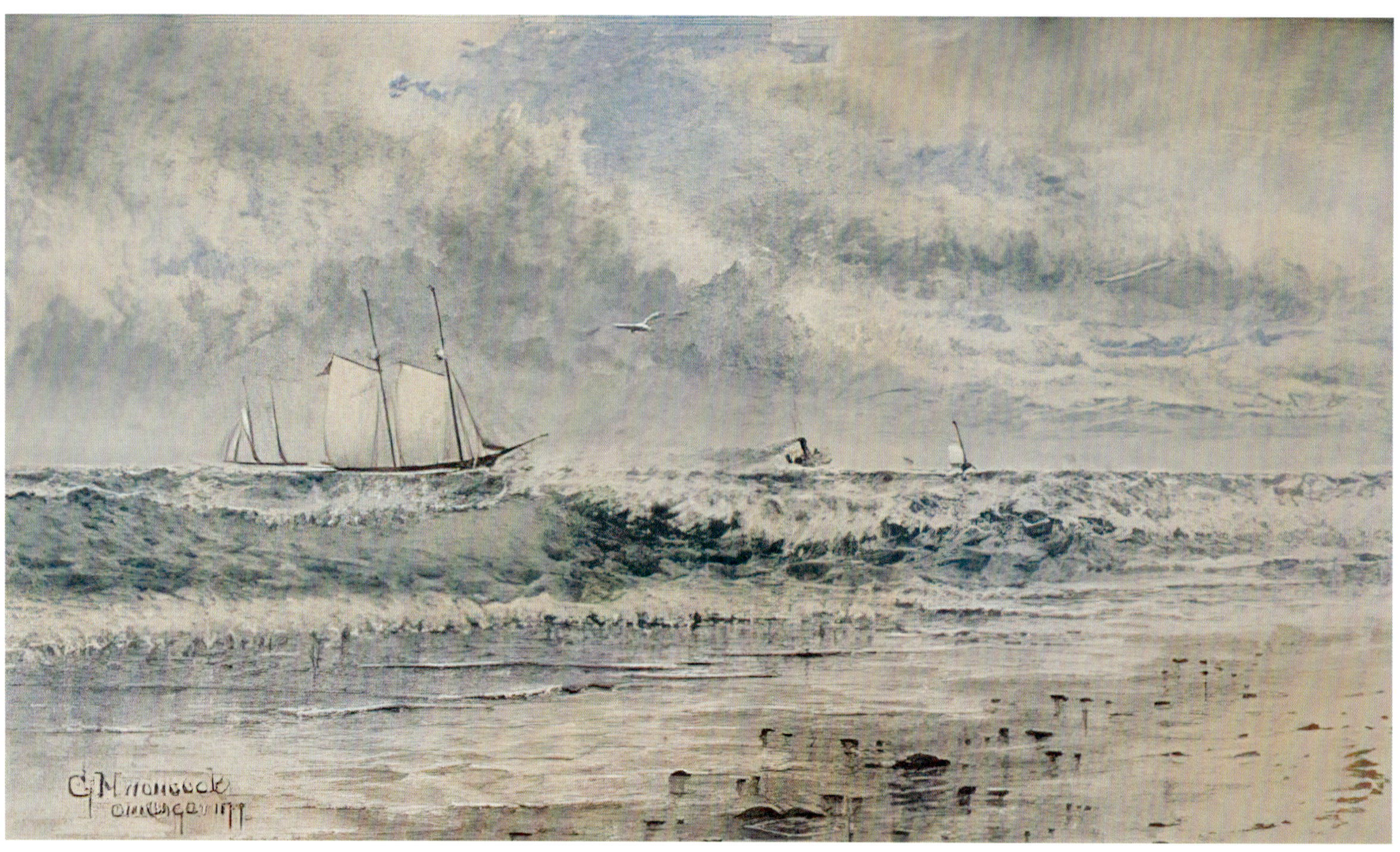

"If I succeed, I shall not return." Hitchcock's Art Education in London

Around the time Melchers boarded the *SS Pommerania*, the lawyer George Hitchcock decided to change course completely. As a scion of a prominent family, he had been educated in law at Brown and Harvard universities.[32] Upon joining the Rhode Island Bar Association in June 1875, he began practicing law in Providence.[33] However, after visiting a watercolor exhibition, Hitchcock, who had also been an amateur watercolorist, decided to follow his heart and pursue a career as an artist.[34] He left for Chicago, where he ran a small bric-a-brac shop and engaged in watercoloring [fig. 12].[35] In 1879, he too ventured to Europe for art training.[36] On 10 May 1879, he left New York for London aboard the steamship *SS Canada*.[37] According to a report in *The Brown Herald* from 2 November 1898, upon his departure, he said: "If I succeed, I shall not return."[38]

Hitchcock initially chose neither Paris nor Düsseldorf for his education, venturing to London instead. In preparation for admission to the South Kensington Art Schools, he spent months at the British Museum drawing ancient sculptures, and copied drawings by William Turner (1775-1851) at The National Gallery.[39] However, Hitchcock was not admitted to the academy, so he opted for Heatherley's Art School, an independent academy for both male and female artists on Newman Street in London.[40] From 1860, the academy was led by the somewhat eccentric Thomas Heatherley (1824-1913), who reportedly looked like a medieval necromancer. Heatherley deliberately avoided a fixed teaching method, encouraging his students to develop their own style.[41]

Thomas Heatherley was always present to provide his students with instruction and feedback. At the Art School, he amassed an impressive assortment of furniture, everyday objects, period costumes, and armor, which were ideal for painting history and genre pieces [fig. 13].[42] Hitchcock, somewhat disappointed by the casual attitude of his predominantly younger fellow students, did not attend classes at Heatherley's for long. However, he would adopt the practice of collecting all sorts of picturesque clothing and props.[43] Following in the steps of many American artists, he decided to try his luck in Paris as well.

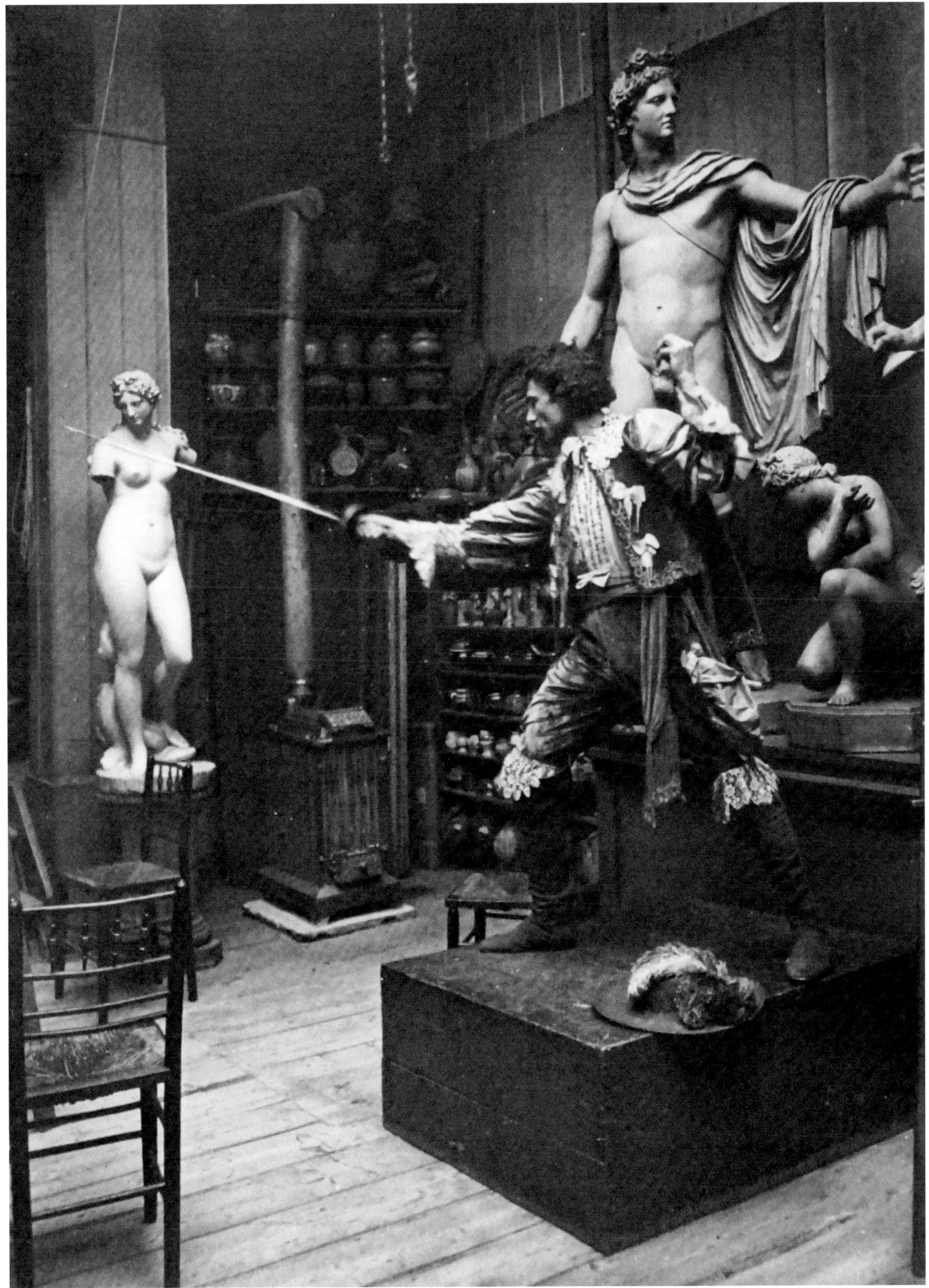

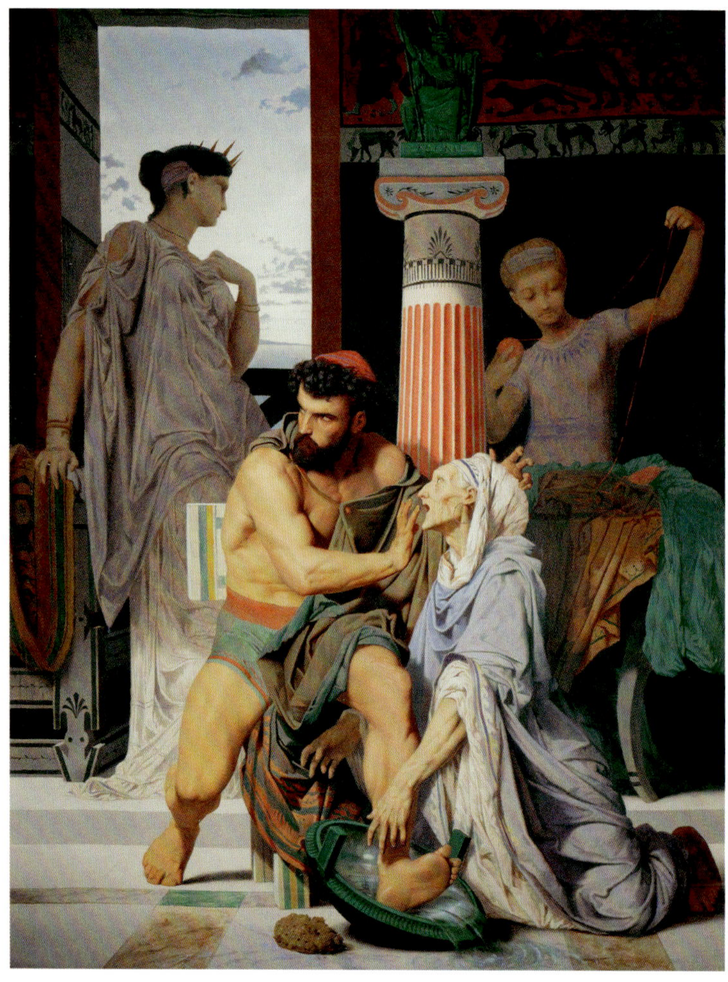

Hitchcock and Melchers Become Acquainted in Paris

In the last quarter of the nineteenth century, Paris exerted an enormous attraction on young artists from all over the world, including, as mentioned, from the United States. Around 1890, at least 1500 American artists were taking classes at the French academies.[44] The artistic climate was favorable: after all, the Louvre featured chefs d'oeuvres by European Old Masters. Additionally, contemporary art, ranging from conservative to highly progressive, was on display at the Musée du Luxembourg, the official Salons, other exhibitions, and in the many art galleries throughout the city. Life in Paris, although more expensive than in other European art centers, was still affordable.[45] There were plenty of accommodations available for young painters. In short, Paris was an enticing paradise for artists.[46]

Many international students attempted to study at the renowned École des Beaux-Arts. Classes at this prestigious institution were taught by practicing artists, and the curriculum included subjects such as art history, anatomy, perspective,

aesthetics, and archaeology. It provided young people with an understanding of the art of the past, its connection to the present, and opportunities for the future.[47] Moreover, it increased the chances of admission to the Salons. For foreigners, however, gaining admission to this prestigious institution was quite challenging; just securing the necessary letter of recommendation from the ambassador or consul could take months.[48] Melchers' letter arrived on 4 July 1881, after which he immediately took the entrance exams at the École des Beaux-Arts. He was admitted to the painting class on 9 August, but it is unclear whether he actually started, as he may have failed the language test.[49] In any case, Melchers attended afternoon drawing lessons with Aldolphe Yvon (1817-1893) at the École des Beaux Arts for two years.[50] This seasoned instructor assigned tasks that required drawing detailed and complex composition sketches.[51]

Like so many international artists, Melchers also pursued an alternative path. Many students worked in independent artists' studios, such as those of Thomas Couture (1815-1879) and Rodolphe Julian (1839-1907).[52] The latter founded the Académie Julian in 1869, with the aim of preparing students for the examinations of the École des Beaux-Arts and/or participation in the prestigious Prix de Rome.[53] Eventually, his academy consisted of several "studios" spread throughout the city – the men's studio on Rue Fontaine was likened to a barn – some of which, starting in 1880, were reserved for women artists.[54]

The Académie Julian admitted everyone, without any form entrance exam. Teaching there relied on experienced students, who were persuaded with some privileges to mentor newcomers.[55] There were classes in drawing, painting, and sculpture, but the main emphasis was on figure drawing.[56] The best drawings were judged at the end of the month in a competition, with prizes awarded.[57]

On Monday mornings, dozens of artists would choose a place to set up their easel in relation to the model, a spot they would then occupy for the rest of the week. The model arrived early each morning, and without further guidance the students worked diligently while awaiting the professors.[58] Renowned artists such as Gustave Boulanger (1824-1888), William Bouguereau (1825-1905), and Jules Lefèbvre (1836-1911) acted as "visiting professors," providing students with feedback and advice.[59] These gentlemen usually came to the academy twice a week to discuss and critique the students' most recent work.[60]

Boulanger and Lefèbvre worked as a team, collaborating as professors until Boulanger's death in 1888.[61] Gustave Boulanger was an academically trained artist who gained fame for his classical and orientalist subjects [fig. 14]. His colleague Lefèbvre primarily painted women, either in costume or nude [fig. 15].

14 Gustave Boulanger, *Odysseus Recognized by Eurycleia*, 1849, oil on canvas, 147 x 114 cm. École Nationale Supérieure des Beaux-Arts, Paris
→ **15** Jules Lefèbvre, *The Laughing Girl*, 1867, oil on canvas, 66 x 51 cm. Musée de Picardie, Amiens

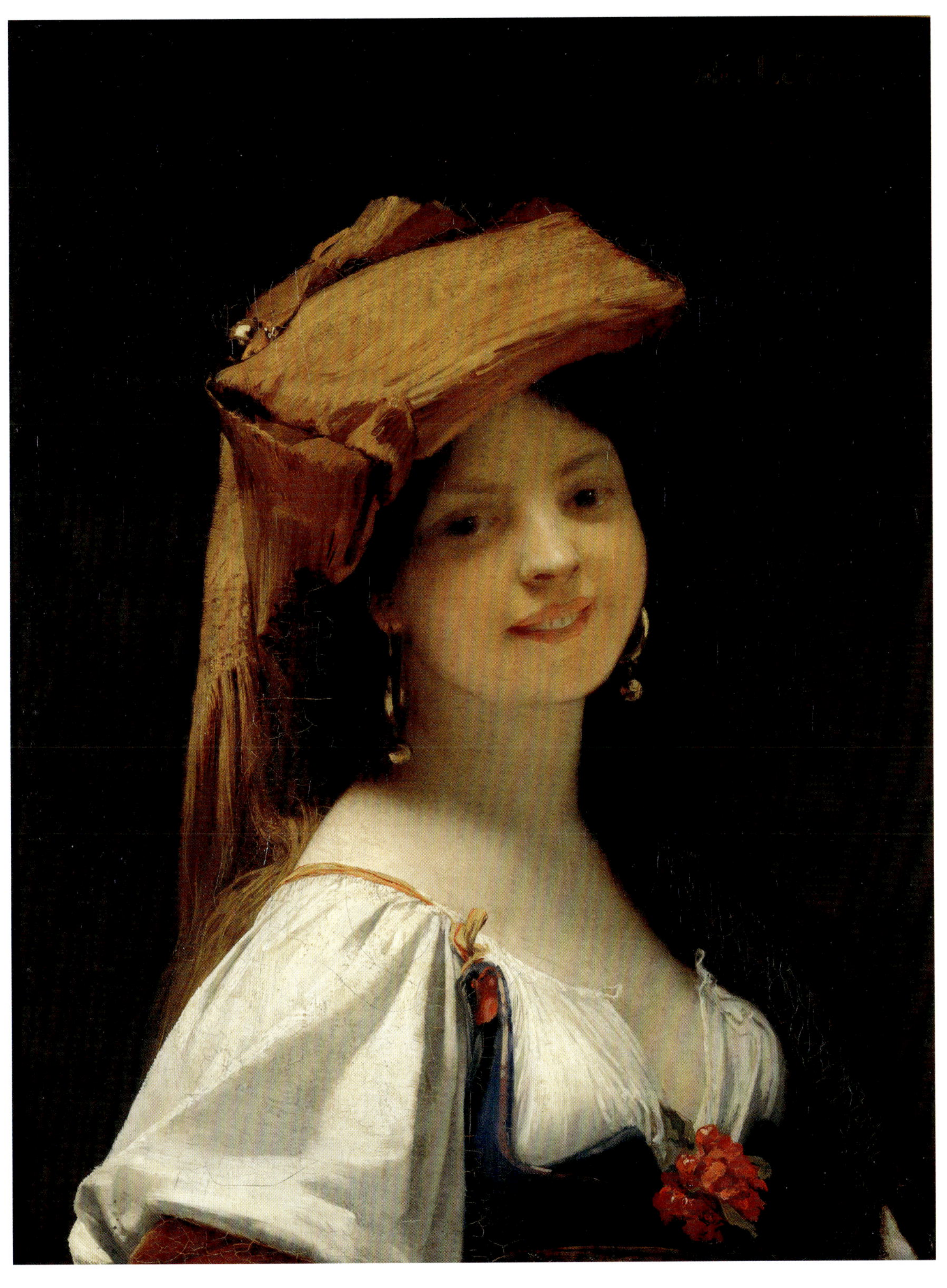

This barn [studio] has never been the birthplace of any special art movement; no new gospel has emerged from the Académie Julien

The atmosphere at the Académie Julian was significantly less competitive than at the École des Beaux-Arts. There was also no push for a uniform style: as one journalist wrote in 1903: "This barn [studio] has never been the birthplace of any special art movement; no new gospel has emerged from the Académie Julien."[62] The studios were said to be rather chaotic as well: "There is nobody there to keep order, the scholars are left entirely to themselves. There are a few Frenchmen who are always making a noise of some kind, singing, whistling, imitating cats, dogs, pigs or some thing else. [...] when the time comes for the model to rest most of the scholars go smoke right in the room and then we have to stay in that smoke the rest of the day."[63]

Among the numerous foreigners who enrolled at the Académie for 300 francs a year, there were many American and German artists, including George Hitchcock and Gari Melchers [fig. 16].[64] The extant archives reveal that they worked there for several years.[65] Hitchcock attended classes at the studio of Jules Joseph Lefèbvre and Gustave Boulanger in 1879 and again three years later, in 1882.[66] During his first full year, Hitchcock focused solely on perfecting his drawing skills: according to his biographer Robinson, he did not so much as touch a paintbrush.[67]

Melchers first enrolled as a student of Boulanger in 1880.[68] The academy's attendance lists suggests that he continued taking classes there until 1886.[69] It is likely that Melchers attended regularly, though not full-time, given the travels and activities he undertook during those years. In 1882, he must

have worked in the academy at the same time as Hitchcock. Their first meeting occurred after Hitchcock heard about a fight between Melchers and fellow students. Curious, Hitchcock introduced himself to Melchers.[70] This would mark the beginning of a long-lasting friendship, in which the three Egmonds would play an important role. However, before the three villages in the province of North Holland literally and figuratively came into the picture, both artists took their first tentative steps as independent, exhibiting artists.

Hitchcock's First Exhibitions

In the years between 1879 and 1882, during his time at the Académie Julian, Hitchcock explored all sorts of new avenues. In February 1880, he exhibited for the first time at the now highly successful American Water Color Society in New York. His watercolor *View of the Thames* was offered for sale for a modest 50 dollars.[71] We know that he traveled to The Hague in 1880, thus he probably did not visit the American city himself in that year.[72] His goal was to study with the marine painter Hendrik Willem Mesdag, who presumably did not really mentor him as a teacher.[73] Hitchcock's timing was not ideal, as in April 1880 Mesdag accepted the commission to produce a panorama, now known as *Panorama Mesdag*, a circular painting with a circumference of 114.5 meters.[74] Starting in June, Mesdag worked daily atop a dune with a large, round easel. On it, he captured his view in 360 degrees: the sea with the departing herring fleet, the beach, the dunes, and the old fishing

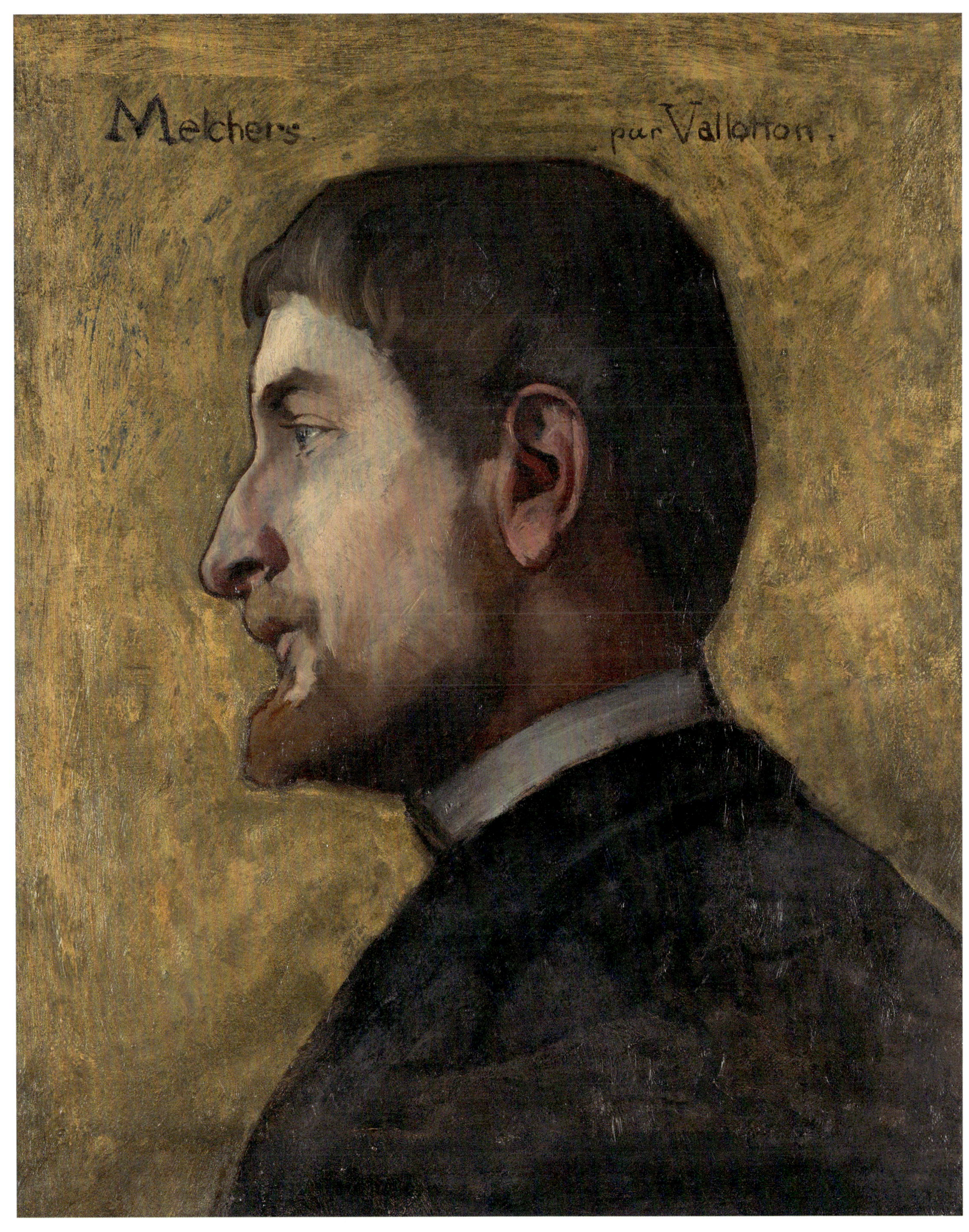

 16 Félix Vallotton, *Julius Gari Melchers*, ca. 1885–1886, oil on canvas, 44.9 x 37.5 cm. Telfair Museum, Savannah, Museum purchased with funds provided by the Gari Melchers Collectors' Society in honor of Courtney McNeil

village of Scheveningen.[75] Hitchcock probably received little more than some advice from Mesdag; the master recommended that everyone work from nature rather than models and to focus on drawing very loosely.[76] Students were allowed to look on while Mesdag worked: "in watching the methods of the Dutch painter [...] Mr. Hitchcock probably learnt more than he was aware of."[77] In an interview years later, Hitchcock recalled Mesdag telling him that he might become a good draughtsman, but he would never be able to paint.[78] Elsewhere, it is mentioned that Mesdag believed that Hitchcock would be better off concentrating on figure painting, as he would never become a good landscape painter.[79]

A few months later, in January 1881, it became clear that Hitchcock had nevertheless learned a great deal from Mesdag. At his second time at The American Water Color Society in New York, he displayed no fewer than seven watercolors, six of which depicted scenes from Scheveningen. His asking prices now ranged from 50 dollars for a study of a fisher girl to 225 dollars for a watercolor titled *From My Window (Scheveningen)* [fig. 17].[80] The exhibition's reviewer wrote: "Mr. Hitchcock is a new aspirant for attention in the picture called *From my Window*. It is well enough executed but indicates only talent. In *motif* it is too plainly a copy of the works of Mesdag, his master."[81]

Despite his lofty words, "If I succeed, I shall not return," Hitchcock traveled back to the United States via England in late November 1880, possibly to attend the exhibition himself.[82] However, just a few months later he was back in the Nether-lands, before continuing to travel to England.[83] There, on 6 July 1881, he married Henrietta Walker Richardson from Savannah, Georgia, in The Chapel of St Martin in the Fields in County Middlesex (part of London as of 1889) [fig. 18].[84] It is unclear when he returned to Paris to study again at the Académie Julian in 1882. By early 1883, he had listed London as his place of residence in the American Water Color Society catalog.[85] The fact that he still did not consider himself sufficiently skilled is evident from his choice – perhaps prompted by Melchers? – to enroll as a student at the academy in Düsseldorf in 1883. There, he was taught by the genre and landscape painter Hugo Crola (1841–1910), a professor specializing in landscape painting.[86] It is likely that Hitchcock refined his skills in oil painting there.[87] The conduct, diligence, and talent of the "landschaftsmaler" (landscape painter) Hitchcock were all rated as "sehr gut" (very good).

17 George Hitchcock, *From My Window*. Illustrated in the catalog of *The American Water Color Society* 1881 → **18** George and Henrietta Hitchcock in Rome, late 1880s. Photo, Gari Melchers Home and Studio, University of Mary Washington, Fredericksburg

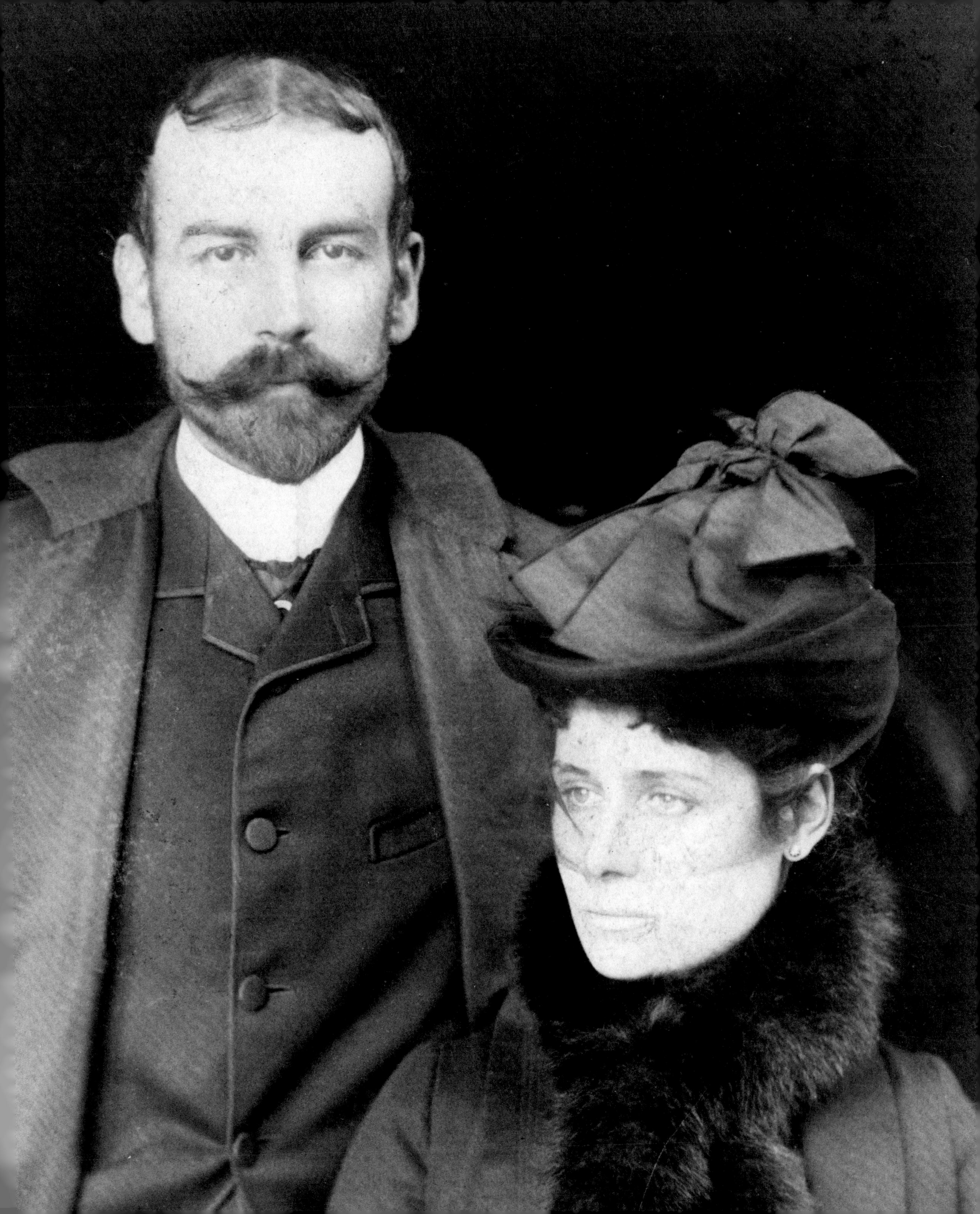

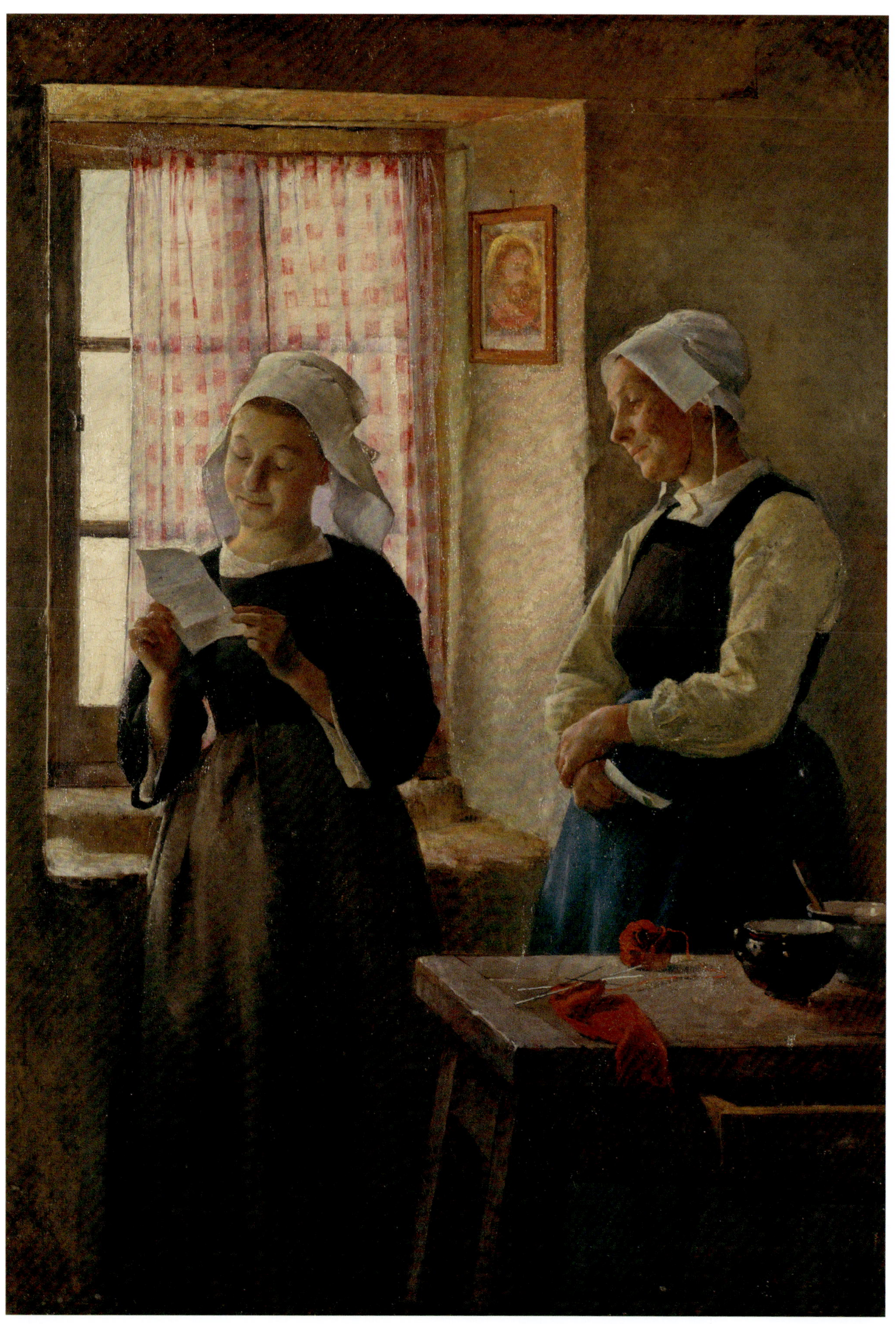

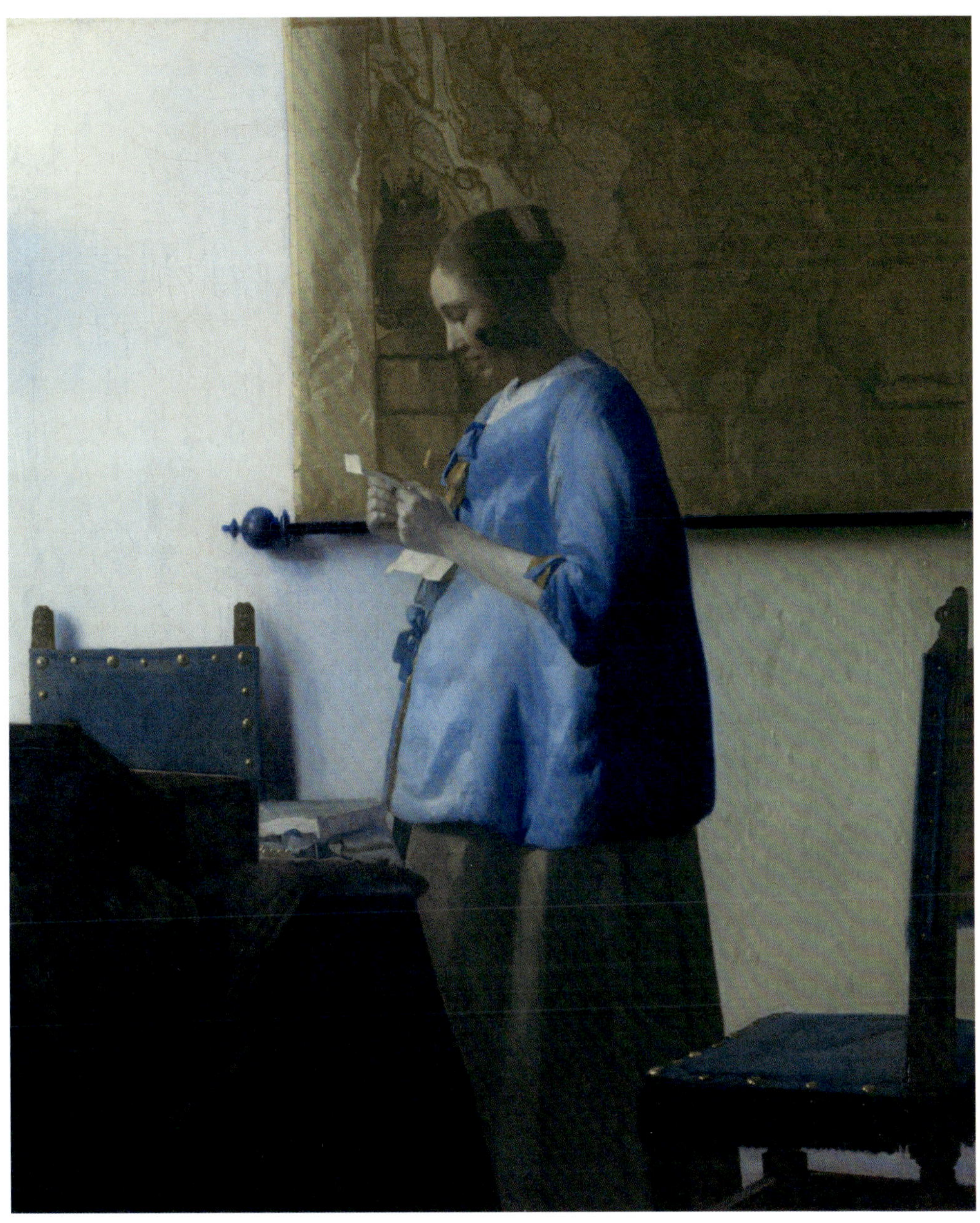

Melchers' First Exhibitions

The year 1882 was pivotal for Melchers' career, and not only because of his encounter with Hitchcock, with whom he formed a close friendship. It was also the year in which, for the first time, one of Melchers' entries was accepted by the jury of the Salon de la Société des Artistes Français. As of 1 May, his painting *The Letter* was on display at the Palais des Champs-Elysées, among no less than 5654 other entries [fig. 19].[88] The painting depicting two Breton ladies, one of whom reads a letter with a blissful smile, was also shown in Belgium a few months later at the request of the organizing committee of the Salon in Antwerp, which sought to impress with international entries.[89]

The kinship with paintings by Dutch Old Masters such as Vermeer is evident [fig. 20].

Shortly after the Paris Salon closed in June, Melchers embarked on a three-month journey through Italy in the company of two friends. He spent several weeks near Naples at the Benedictine Abbey at Casamari, then traveled to Atina before making his way to Paris via Rome and Florence. The impressions he gathered during this trip would later be reflected in his Salon submissions of 1883.[90] Melchers then returned to the United States, where his work was shown the following year in New York and in his hometown, Detroit. However, he ultimately decided to return to Europe.[91]

← **19** Gari Melchers, *The Letter*, 1882, oil on canvas, 94.6 x 67 cm. National Gallery of Art, Washington, Corcoran Collection (Edward C. and Mary Walker Collection)
20 Johannes Vermeer, *Woman Reading a Letter*, ca. 1662-1664, oil on canvas, 46.5 x 39 cm. Rijksmuseum, Amsterdam, on loan from the City of Amsterdam (A. van der Hoop Bequest)

Holland Mania

Ruysdael, Hobbema, and Vander Meer van Delft were the first and the greatest landscape-painters, and that the Dutch school of to-day is the first in landscape, is due directly to the beauty, the atmospheric beauty, of the country of their birth

George Hitchcock (1887)[92]

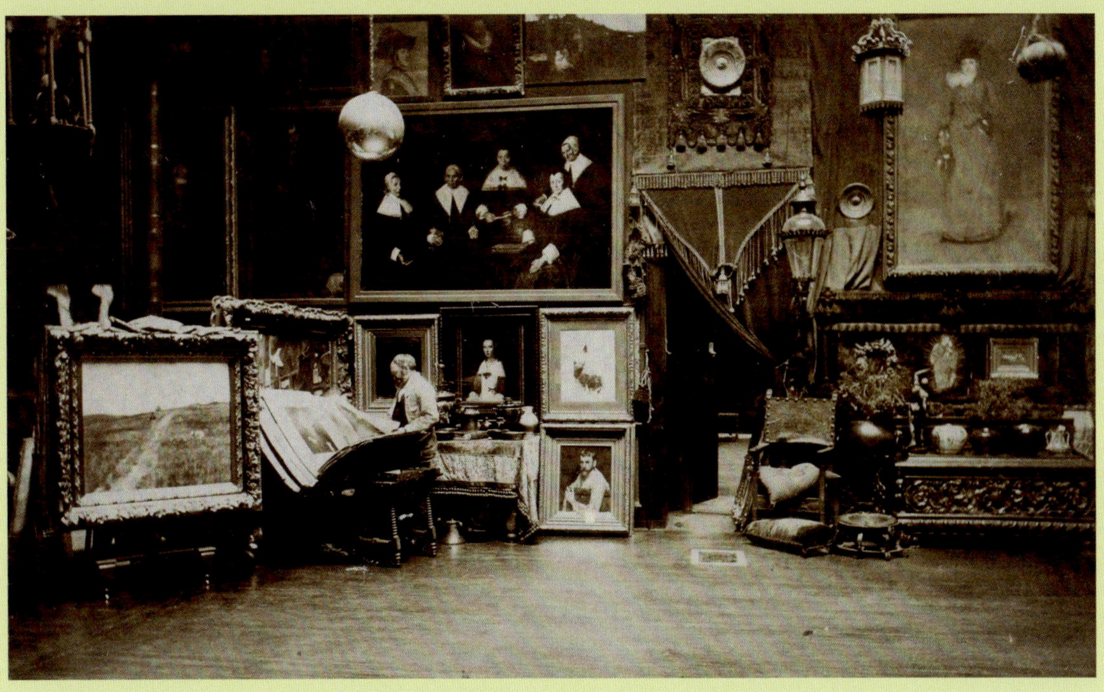

Initially, most American artists visited the Netherlands only briefly during the summer months.[93] From Europe's artistic training centers, it was more affordable for artists to travel within Europe after the academies closed than to return to the United States.[94] One of the main reasons for making such a journey to the Netherlands was to study – and sometimes copy – the works of the Dutch Old Masters, the seventeenth-century painters who enjoyed immense popularity in the United States [fig. 21]. Since the Declaration of Independence (1776), Americans had been searching for a national past and a distinct identity in the present. In the Netherlands of the seventeenth century, they recognized the origins of their own ideals and beliefs.[95] This sense of connection grew even stronger after the centenary of the Declaration of Independence in 1876, sparking an unprecedented awareness of the historical ties between the Netherlands and America. Attention was drawn to similarities in politics, economics, and culture,[96] which were emphasized in revisionist history books and popular travel guides.[97] The real-istic style of Dutch art – with its belief that even the imperfect contains beauty – and its interest in everyday middle-class life strongly resonated with American audiences: "Dutch art is of the people and for the people."[98]

However, the focus of American artists – as well as that of col-lectors and other enthusiasts – was not solely on studying the Old Masters. There was also significant interest in contemporary Dutch masters, particularly the internationally successful painters of The Hague School. The works of Willem Roelofs, the Maris brothers, Anton Mauve, Jozef Israëls, and Hendrik Willem Mesdag were perceived as a revival of seventeenth-century Dutch art due to their emphasis on polder landscapes and the daily life of farmers and fishermen. Consequently, paintings by Hague School masters were widely collected in America – Israëls even remarked that, according to Americans, he could not produce new work fast enough. For those with more modest means, reproductions of their works were also available for purchase.[99]

Such was the interest in Dutch art in the United States that hundreds of American artists began working in the Netherlands (annually). They were particularly drawn to the "authentic" Holland they found more often in remote countryside places than in the cities. Around 1890, several artists' colonies arose in the Netherlands, including in Volendam, Laren, and Katwijk.[100] The artists devoted themselves to capturing the Dutch people, preferably in traditional dress, and the unspoiled landscape; naturally, without traces of modernity, such as harbors, railways, telegraph poles, and factories.[101] According to Hitchcock, this was entirely possible. In 1889 he wrote: "That Holland has entirely escaped the commonplace utilitarian spirit of our own times is too much to expect, but to this wind-swept half sub-merged corner of the earth it has been last to come…"[102]

21 William Merritt Chase in his Tenth Street Studio, New York, with copies after Hals and other Old Masters, ca. 1895, albumen print, 14 x 17.8 cm. The William Merritt Chase Archives, The Parrish Art Museum, Water Mill, New York

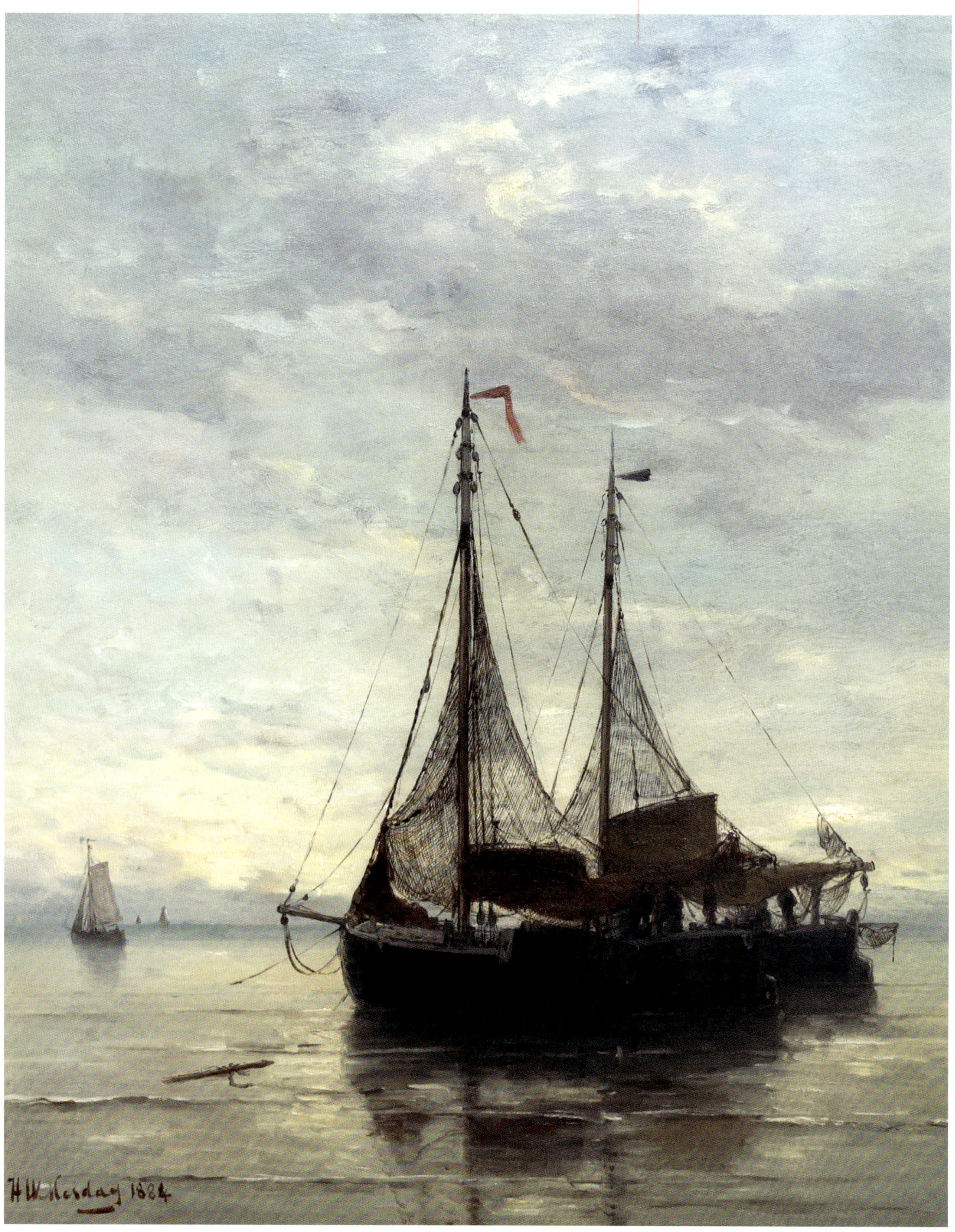
H W Mesdag 1884

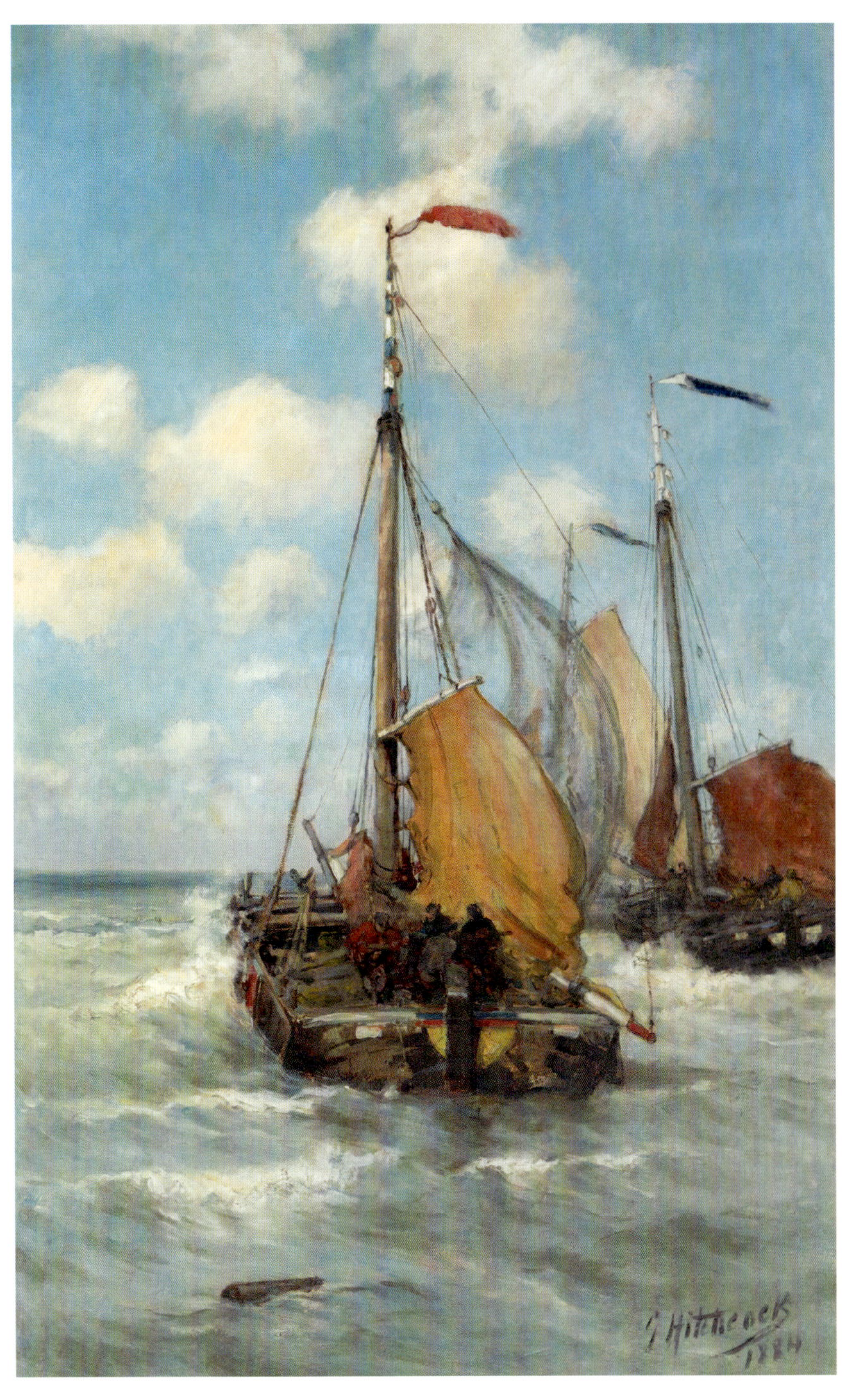

Hitchcock's and Melchers' First Visits
to the Netherlands

Both George Hitchcock and Gari Melchers followed in the footsteps of many of their compatriots when they independently decided to travel to the Netherlands. The first traces of the two artists in the country can be found in the museums. In September 1880, Hitchcock first signed the visitors' book at the Stedelijk Museum in Haarlem, now the Frans Hals Museum.[103] Nearly three years later, in June 1883, Melchers followed suit. He visited the museum in the company of the American painter and sculptor Henry Edward Bedford (1860-1932).[104] In the same month, Melchers, along with another American, Childe Hassam (1859-1935), viewed the Old Masters in Amsterdam's Trippenhuis before returning to the United States to attend his sister's wedding.[105]

Hitchcock and Melchers shared a deep admiration for the artists of The Hague School. As mentioned above, Hitchcock visited Mesdag in 1880, and thereafter, he painted in the style of this marine painter during his first years in the Netherlands [figs. 22, 23].

← **22** H. W. Mesdag, *Fishing Boats at Anchor*, 1884, oil on canvas, 70 x 57 cm. Hein A. M. Klaver art gallery, Baarn   **23** George Hitchcock, *Pinks at Egmond*, 1884, oil on canvas, 111 x 74 cm. Private collection

Melchers, on the other hand, was more drawn to the work of
Jozef Israëls, an artist widely known for his depiction of the
poverty-stricken, hard-working fishing population [figs. 24, 25].
Due to the pervasive stench in the fishermen's homes, Israëls
even created a "fisherman's corner" in his studio where he had
his models pose. Israëls also warned American artists that if they
wanted to develop their own national school, they should stop
imitating Dutch art.[106] Melchers, who had also purchased works
by Hague School masters such as Johannes Bosboom, Jozef
Israëls, and Anton Mauve for his private collection, seems to
have heeded this advice.[107] In Egmond, he changed his palette;
the distinctive browns, grays, and ochers of the Hague School
masters gave way to a much more colorful palette. Melchers
reportedly remarked later: "You Dutchmen all paint like Israëls."[108]

The First Stay in Egmond

The very first time the fishing village of Egmond aan Zee featured
in an exhibition was during the seventh annual exhibition of
The American Water Color Society, held in New York in the
early months of 1884. Hitchcock submitted a watercolor titled
Up from the Beach – Egmond aan Zee.[109] Most likely, it was
Hitchcock who discovered the coastal village in 1883 during
a trip in which judging from the titles of his other entries, he
also visited Zaandam. Reportedly, "chance" had brought him
to Egmond.[110]

Undoubtedly, Hitchcock and his wife Henrietta were a curios-
ity in the remote village, as was later somewhat romanticized

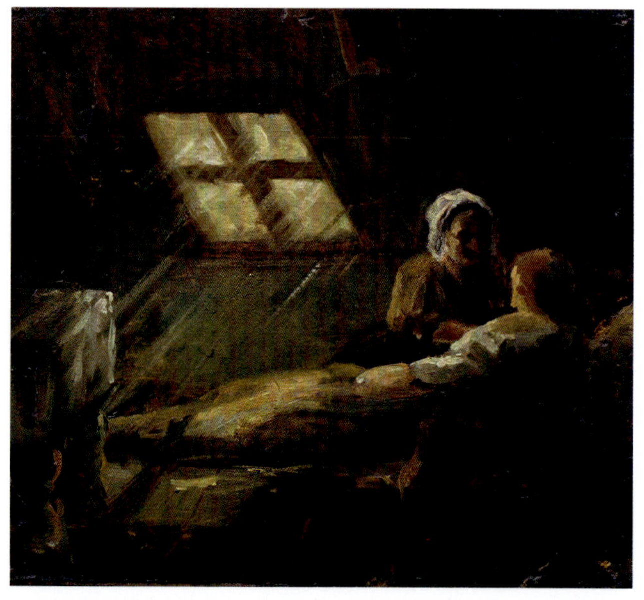

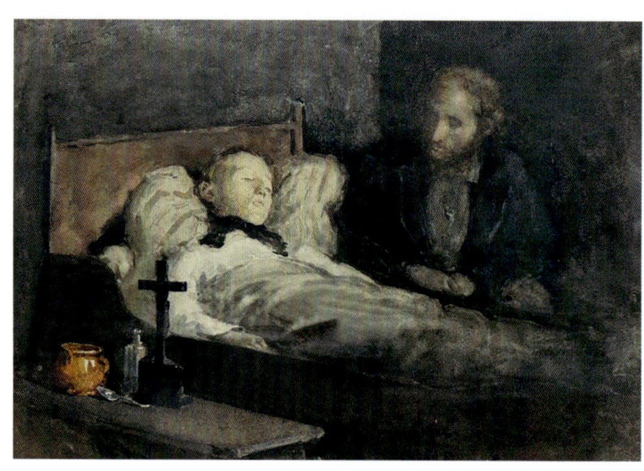

24 Jozef Israëls, *Sick Person in Attic Room* (study), oil on panel, 18.7 x 33.5 cm. Groninger Museum, Groningen **25** Gari Melchers, *The Sick Child*, 1884, watercolor,
30.5 x 40.6 cm. Gari Melchers Home and Studio, University of Mary Washington, Fredericksburg

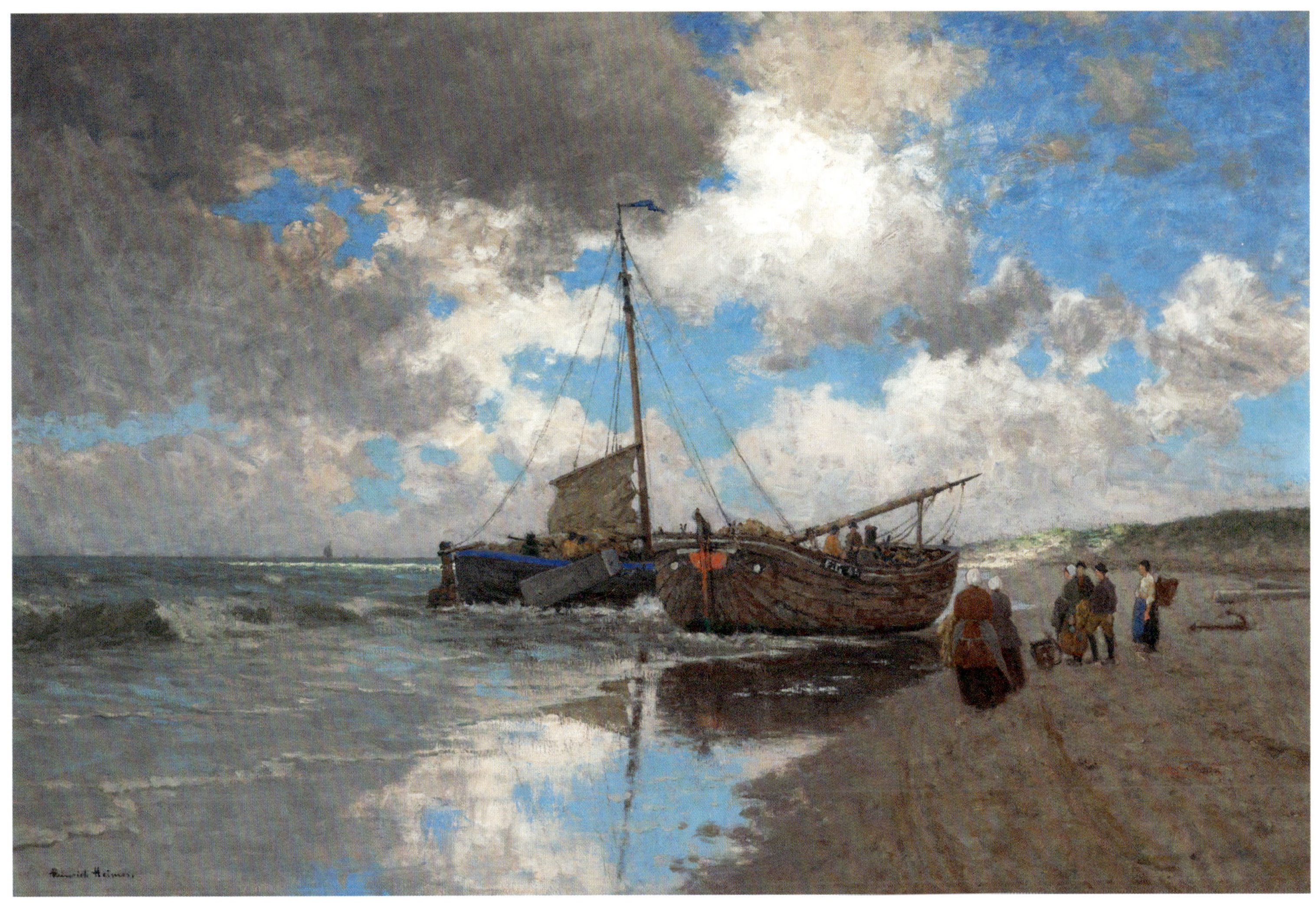

in the press: "On a fine summer's day, an English-speaking couple, a gentleman and a lady, arrived at Zeezicht Hotel. Their appearance and luggage immediately revealed them to be artists. The tall, slender, gentlemanly figure of the man made a pleasant impression and he clearly exuded the air of an artist. This couple settle into a few rooms overlooking the sea and immediately began carefully capturing the beach, the dunes, the streets, and alleys of the village. Daily, the gentleman and the lady would venture out, armed with all kinds of painting supplies, and spent entire days in or around the village, sketching or painting people, little streets, and houses, but mostly beach scenes [...]. He did not know Dutch, but soon he was able to make clear to the locals what he desired."[111]

In 1884, Melchers also traveled to Egmond. Originally he did not intend to go to the Netherlands: he was on his way to Italy when a cholera outbreak occurred. Not wanting to take unnecessary risks, he traveled north. "At Egmond I found friends, drawn, like myself, to the Dutch life and landscape," he later told a journalist.[112] In addition to Hitchcock the German artists Heinrich Wilhelm Petersen-Angeln (1850-1906), Heinrich Heimes (1855-1933), and Hans Hermann (1858-1942) were also working in Egmond that year, all students from the academy in Düsseldorf [fig. 26].[113] Heimes took classes with Hitchcock in 1883 under Hugo Crola in Düsseldorf, and they likely traveled together to the Dutch coastal village.[114] It is also possible that Walter MacEwen (1860-1943), an American artist trained at the academy in Munich and a student of Robert Fleury at the Académie Julian was in Egmond that year.[115] As of 1881, however, he spent most summers in Hattem in the province of Gelderland.[116]

   26 Heinrich Heimes, *After the Catch, Egmond aan Zee*, ca. 1883-1885, oil on canvas, 111.6 x 169.2 cm. Private collection

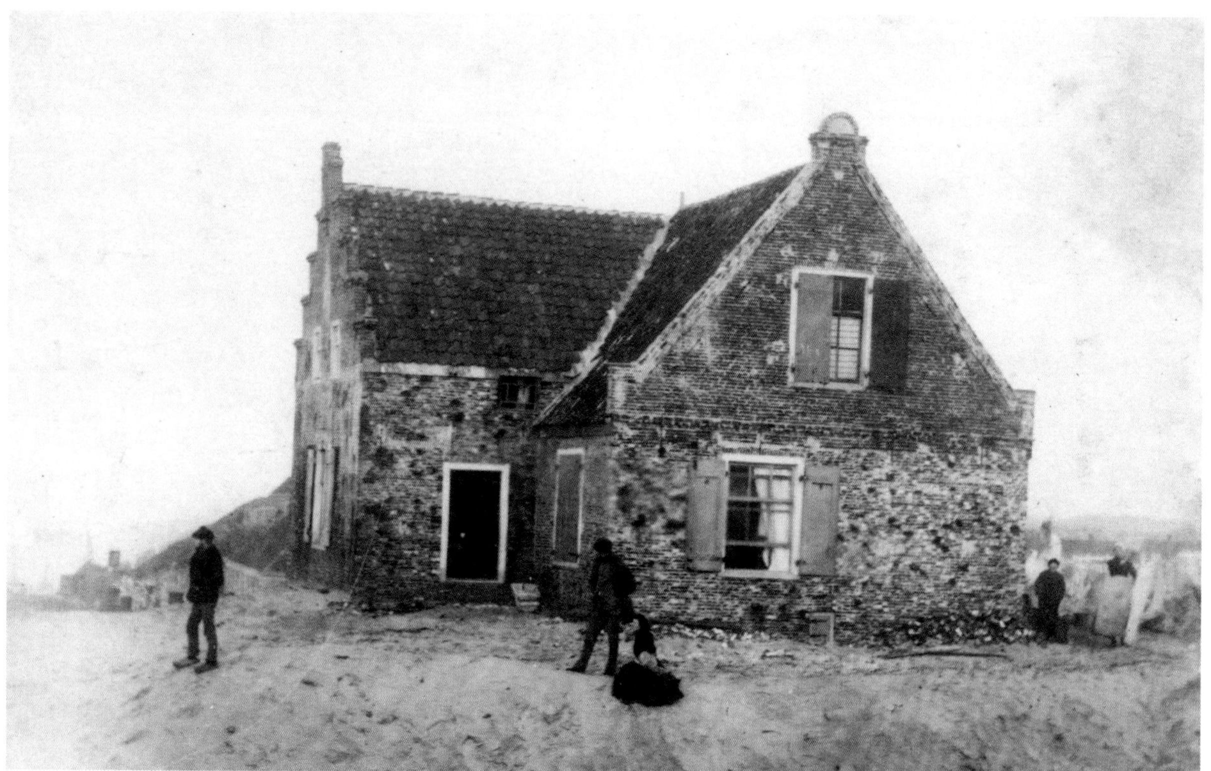

Reaching Egmond was no easy undertaking at the time. Since 18 December 1865, the nearby town of Alkmaar had been well connected by train, but from there, travelers had to rely on the omnibus. This horse-drawn vehicle was described by contemporary travelers as a "limb breaker," "stomach buster," and "headache causer," and was referred to as "the connection between lonely and desolate Egmond and the world."[117] The impoverished fishing village was scarcely visited by outsiders, and the Zeezicht Hotel was mainly used by traveling salesmen and the crews of stranded ships.[118] A later tourist wrote about Egmond: "that part of Holland was so primitive it might have been over a hundred years ago."[119]

It is therefore quite surprising that the Empress of Austria stayed in Egmond aan Zee in 1884. The 46-year-old Elisabeth had traveled "incognito" to Amsterdam in May of that year as Countess von Hohenembs to receive treatments for her joint pains from the innovative physician Johann Georg Mezger. From there, she made several excursions to the Zuiderzee villages of Marken, Edam, and Zaandam, and visited Zandvoort, Velsen, and Santpoort.[120] On Sunday, 1 June, she wanted to see the fair in Egmond. Upon arrival, she was allowed to use the room of the then absent Hitchcock in the Noordzeebad Inn and saw his work. A few days later, she sent two gentlemen from her entourage to Egmond to buy one of Hitchcock's seascape studies.[121]

Although the artists found much inspiration in the Netherlands, they hardly focused on the Dutch market for their income.

They only exhibited their work for sale in the Netherlands once. At the fall show of the Amsterdam artists' association Arti et Amicitiae in 1884, Hitchcock presented two paintings, *Egmond Pinks* and *Souvenir of Scheveningen*, which were priced 200 and 150 guilders, respectively. Melchers' *Grandfather* and *Looking at the Neighbor Woman* were both offered for 350 guilders. Compared to Mesdag's asking price of 4500 guilders for *Ready for Departure,* these were decidedly modest prices.[122] Unfortunately, it is not known if they actually sold their works.

The Artistic Crow's Nest on the Dune

In 1884, Hitchcock and Melchers decided to make Egmond their permanent residence. This decision must have been based on a number of factors. The main reasons for Hitchcock were doubtless the sea and the fishing life. Unlike in Scheveningen and Katwijk, as well as the villages along the Zuiderzee, where many artists were active, here he had the place – almost – entirely to himself. Furthermore, there was no harbor, and Hitchcock was drawn to the fishermen's pinks that were scattered here and there on the beach.[123] The coastline had not yet been spoiled by hotels and tourists. For Melchers, the daily life of the predominantly poor population also provided plenty of material for paintings. In addition, both gentlemen must have felt positive about the villagers' disposition towards them. The Egmonders were crucial to them, as not only did they have to be willing to pose as models, but

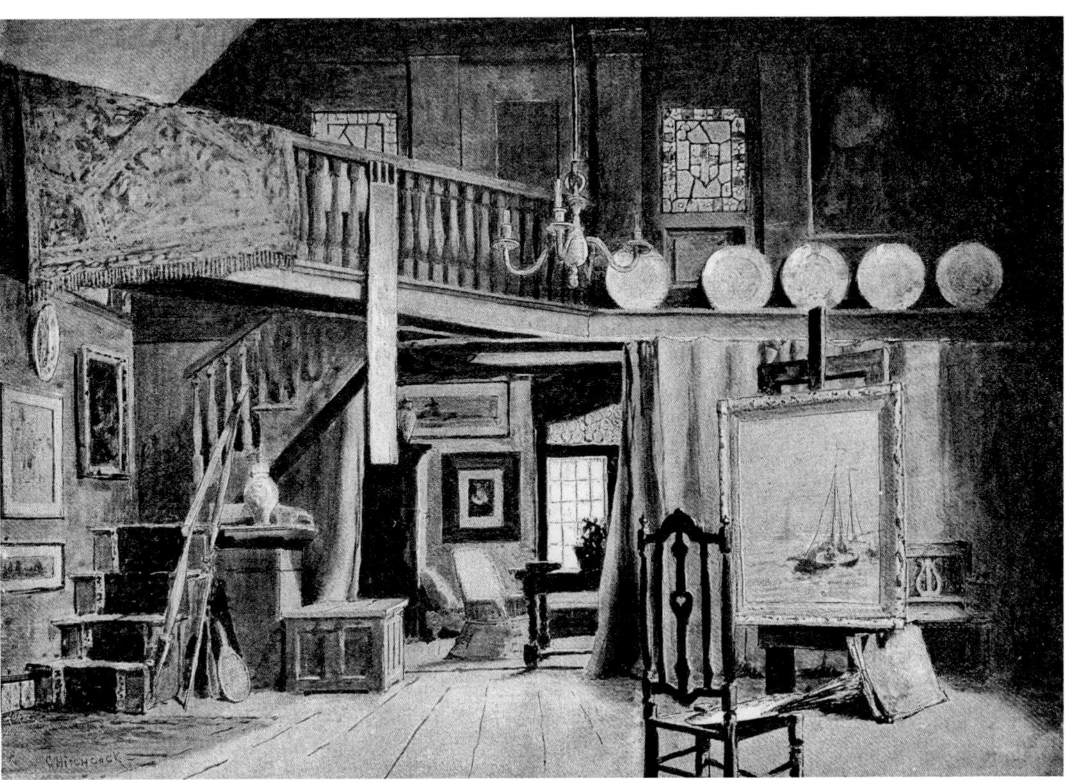

the artists were also completely dependent on them for various services, such as transportation, accommodation, and, not least, food and drink.[124] Melchers is known to have become fluent in Dutch fairly quickly, and Hitchcock likely mastered the language as well.[125]

In September, November, and December of 1884, Hitchcock, his wife Henrietta Hitchcock-Richardson, and Melchers visited various notaries regarding a leasehold agreement and several mortgages.[126] By the end of 1884, they had purchased sixteen aren (approximately 0.4 acres) of land on top of the Torensduin in Egmond aan Zee, where they built a house with an atelier. The house was a former fisherman's residence that had been moved from the lower part of the village to the highest dune.[127] It is said that Hitchcock furnished his "artistic crow's nest" as picturesquely as possible with all sorts of beautiful objects that he had collected in Egmond and elsewhere in the Netherlands, ranging from porcelain to old portraits.[128]

The artist's residence, clearly visible from the beach, was described twenty years later: "To the south and to the north, as far as the eye can see, the undulating line of the high, helmet grass covered dunes [...]. And to the south, high on the dune, one of the most beautiful things in Egmond, the white house, [of the] American painter Hitchcock, once his studio and now often serving as the studio of his friend Gari Melchers. On the seaward side, a pure white wall, with only white between the stones in the stepped gable, three windows usually closed with green shutters, on the north side a weathered gray wall under the brown-red roof with one window, usually hidden behind rough planks. And on the south side, protruding in the middle, yet another brown-red-roofed section of the house, also with white walls and green shutters. Always, in good weather or stormy skies, the eye is drawn to this beautiful "white house" [figs. 27, 28].[129]

To realize the artist's residence, Hitchcock, who is explicitly listed as a "marine painter" on all the deeds, borrowed 900 guilders (interest-free) from the "painter" Melchers, under the condition that the agreement could be terminated for various reasons, with a breach of friendship explicitly mentioned. Additionally, the deed stated that the house must always be accessible and available for Melchers to stay in.[130] It seems, therefore, that the white house was built as the permanent residence of George and Henrietta, while the younger, single Gari was less keen to commit himself. Nevertheless, on 19 December 1884, Hitchcock, his wife, and Melchers all recorded their names in the civil registry of Egmond aan Zee.[131]

  28 Interior of Hitchcock's atelier on the Torensduin in Egmond aan Zee 1890. Photo from *The Art Amateur* 1890

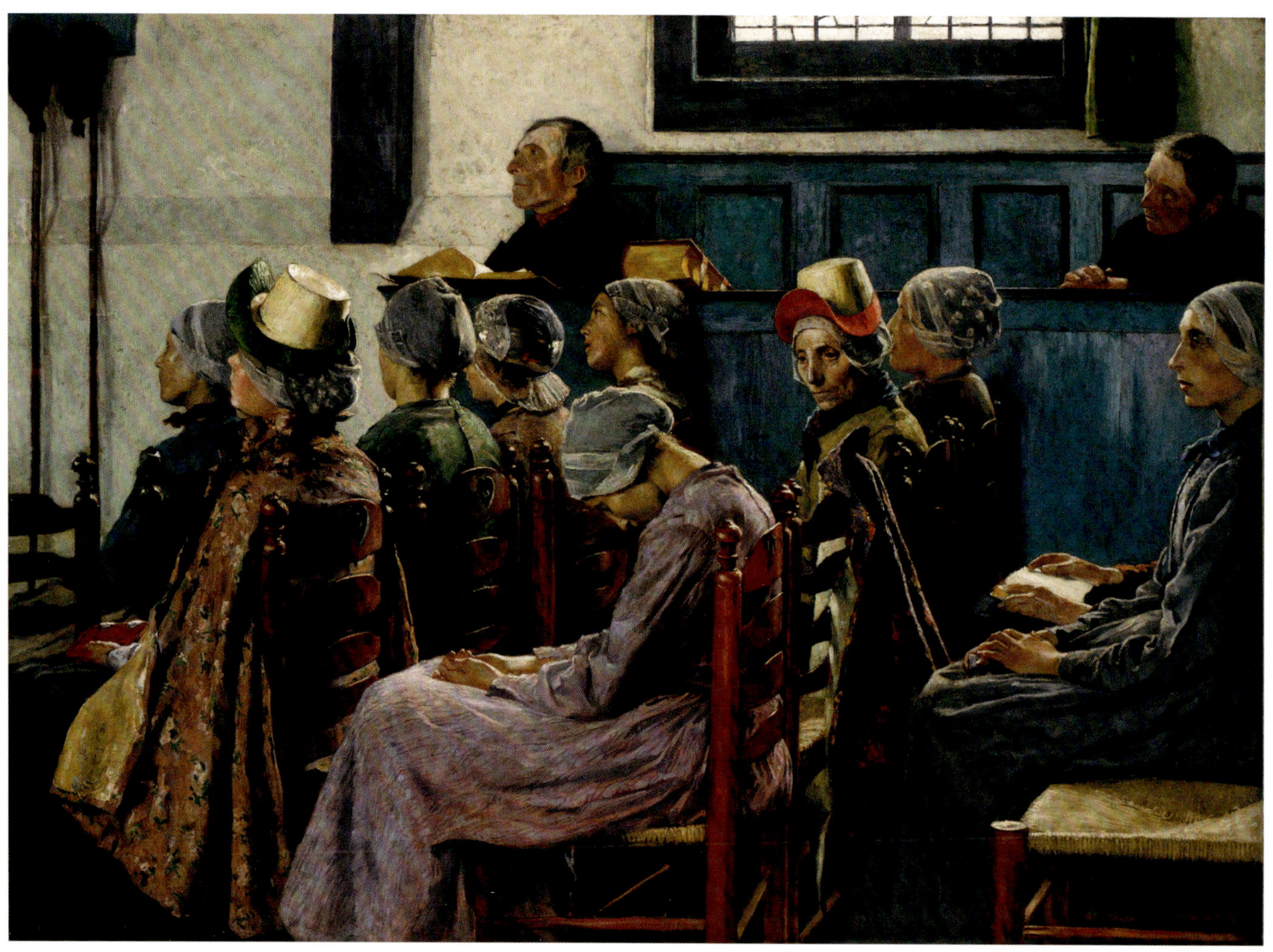

Twin-Artists from Holland

In the following year, both artists exhibited their work internationally, in Paris, New York, and London.[132] It was regularly highlighted in the press that they lived and worked together in Egmond during the summer and winter months.[133] In the British press, they were even referred to as "Dutch-American" "twin-artists."[134] In the American magazine *The Art Amateur*, Melchers was mistaken for a "Dutchman" by a reviewer because of where he lived![135] The same art critic was particularly complimentary about the watercolor *A Dutch Bachelor's Breakfast,* which Melchers had submitted to The American Water Color Society.[136] He called it a true masterpiece, noting that the technique was freely applied and the sheet "well balanced in composition and color."[137]

All the subjects painted by both artists were directly inspired by the lives of Egmond's fishing community by the sea: from ships departing and arriving, fisherwomen mending nets or waiting on the beach, to *The Sea Beggars,* a painting by Melchers of two Egmond fishermen at the winch.[138] For Hitchcock, the Netherlands and the sea were inextricably linked. He wrote, "Perhaps the most important element, pictorially, is the sea, for in a country mainly reclaimed from it, [...] whose riches are due to it [...] this must be so [...]. It was the sea as much as the Netherlanders which drove the Spaniards from the land."[139]

Meanwhile, Melchers had traveled to Paris immediately after the opening of the exhibition at Gladwell's Gallery in London – where he exhibited not only with Hitchcock, but also with Dutch colleagues such as Mesdag, Bernardus Johannes Blommers (1845-1914), and Pierre Jean Apol (1867-1947). In a letter to *The Dillettant,* he mentioned that while he had attended the opening in London, he had gone to Paris due to the English climate and the winter exhibition season.[140] There he "was reluctantly forced to tear [himself] away from [his] Paris studies and return to ...[Egmond], in order to finish [his] large Salon picture, 'La Prêche' (*The Sermon*)" [fig. 29].[141]

29 Gari Melchers, *The Sermon*, 1886, oil on canvas, 159.0 x 219.7 cm. Smithsonian American Art Museum, Bequest of Henry Ward Ranger through the National Academy of Design

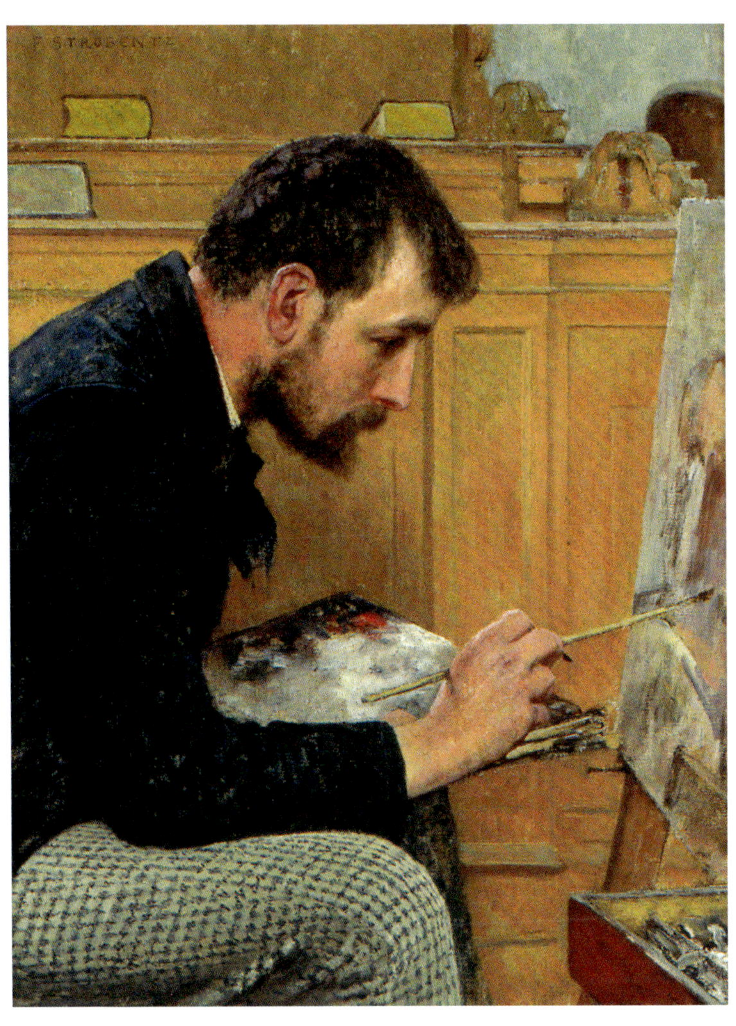

International Breakthroughs

At the Paris Salon, held at the Palais des Champs-Élysées, Melchers indeed exhibited *Le Prêche* (or *The Sermon*). This large painting depicts the interior of the Dutch Reformed Church in Egmond-Binnen, which, according to contemporaries, featured eleven "highly accurate portraits of Egmond locals" attentively listening to the preacher, who is not visible in the painting.[142] One of the congregants has dozed off, much to the dismay of her neighbor. It was this narrative element that greatly captured the imagination of viewers.[143]

During an interview, Melchers recounted that one Sunday morning, while on a walk, he heard singing coming from the small church. "Observing the scene before him, the painter was so deeply stirred by the absorption of the women that he himself heard nothing. He ached to get the scene on canvas. When the sermon was over he flung himself outside and made as rapidly as possible sketches of what he had gazed on. Hastening back to his studio, he made several color sketches with more detail. The first were almost wholly from the heart."[144]

Unlike his earlier work, Melchers now avoided the dark colors and shadows of Israëls.[145] He embraced naturalism, the popular style used by Jules Bastien-Lepage (1848-1884) and his followers to realistically depict rural scenes.[146] Additionally, he adopted a color scheme much more in line with that of the French Impressionists than with the artists of The Hague School. "I can *see* them in my church in certain lights. So why suppress them?" Melchers told the interviewer of *Cosmopolitan Magazine*. "We should thank Monet for the good he did in teaching us to view things with clear eyes."[147]

Featuring nearly life-size figures, the painting was well received and widely discussed in the international press. "There is no question of models being dressed up in a painter's studio with this or that costume – in this case, a North Holland outfit –placed in some picturesque light merely to be painted. Clearly, this artist sought out the figures he needed for his sermon scene on location, arranged them together in the small church, and, whether there or in his studio, captured it all on canvas with his sensitive brush, without concern for dramatic lighting and heavy browns."[148]

30 Fritz Strobentz, *Gari Melchers Painting in The Slotkapel*, ca. 1892, oil on canvas, 48.3 x 38.4 cm. Gari Melchers Home and Studio, University of Mary Washington, Fredericksburg

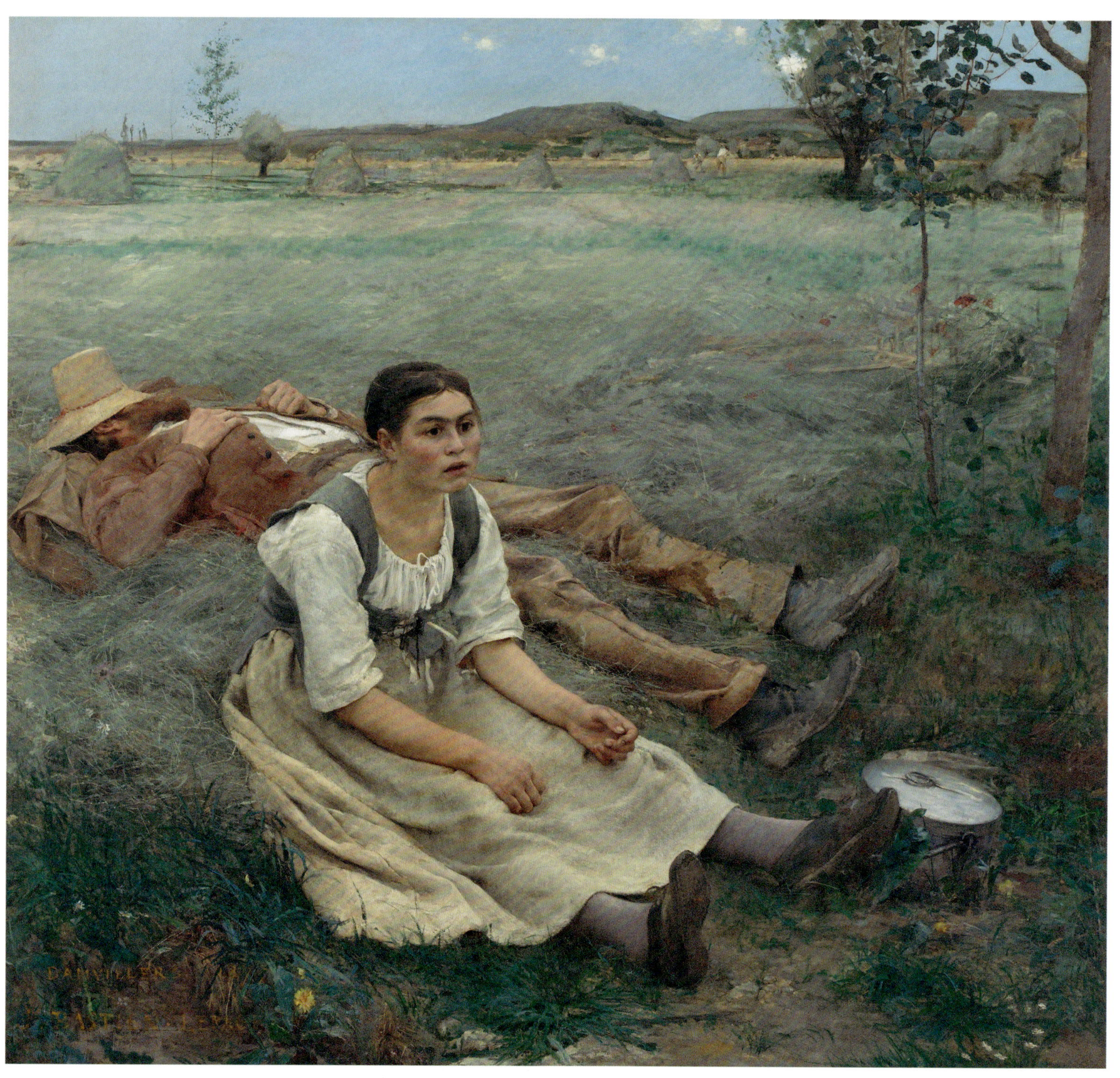

31 Jules Bastien-Lepage, *Haymaking*, 1877, oil on canvas, 180 x 195 cm. Musée d'Orsay, Paris

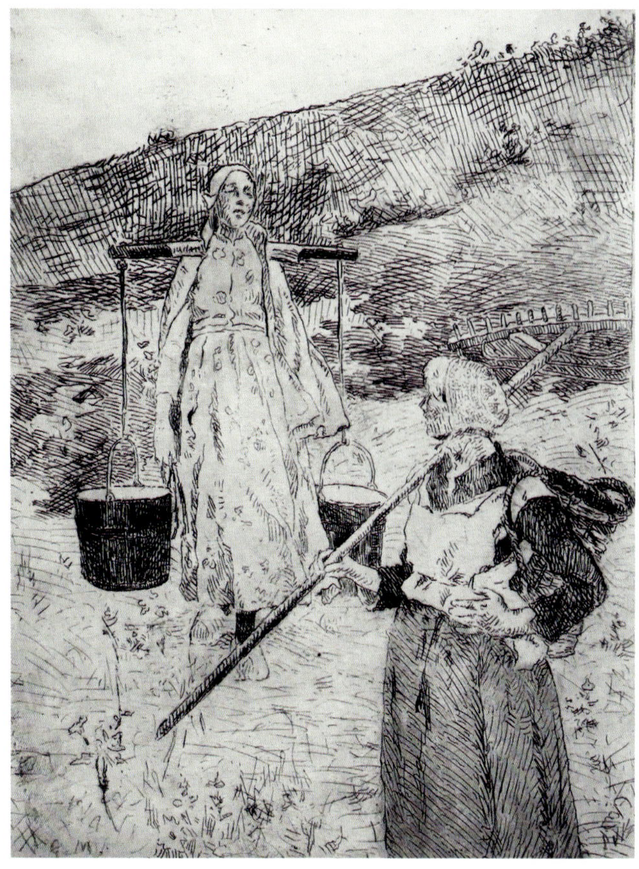

In Paris, Melchers received an honorable mention, after which he exhibited the painting in Amsterdam, where he won a prestigious gold medal.[149] It later traveled to Brussels (1887), Munich (1888), New York (1890), Chicago (1893), and Berlin (1895), firmly establishing his international reputation as a painter of hardworking and devout fishermen. However, success did not come without setbacks. In 1887, to Melchers' great disappointment, his painting *In Holland* was harshly criticized. The subject was dismissed as a "simple" study of two country women, unjustifiably – according to critics – painted on a life-size scale. "We had every right to expect something more significant and serious from a young man of his caliber," one critic remarked [fig. 32].[150] The painting, for which Egmond residents Maartje Wijker and Dieuwertje de Waard reportedly modelled, was also considered overly theatrical and too colorful.[151] Pundits pointed to the lilac cape and the light blue interior of the buckets, a color believed in Egmond folklore to repel flies.[152] In the following years, Melchers made several adjustments, most notably adding a windmill and houses in the background [fig. 33].

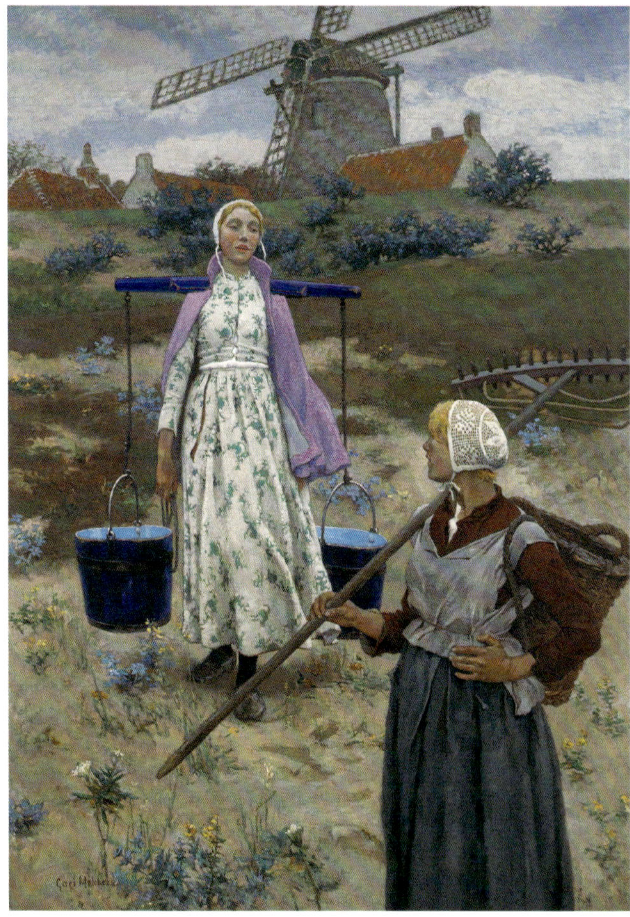

32 Gari Melchers, *In Holland*, 1887, etching, 19.7 x 14.9 cm. Gari Melchers Home and Studio, University of Mary Washington, Fredericksburg **33** Gari Melchers, *In Holland*, 1887-1890, oil on panel, 277 x 197.5 cm. Gari Melchers Home and Studio, University of Mary Washington, Fredericksburg

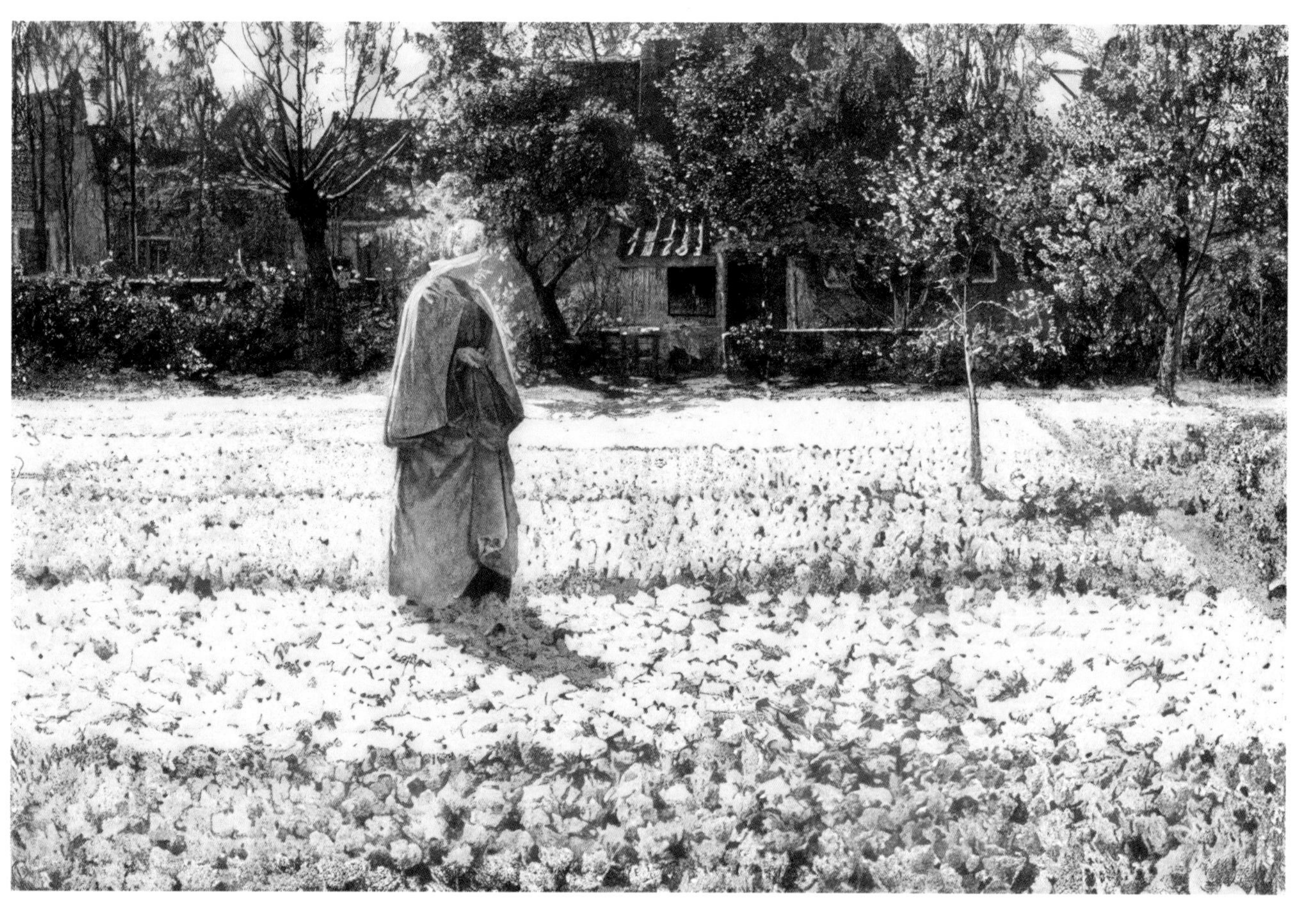

"The picturesque quality of Holland"

While Melchers fell short in the eyes of art lovers and critics with *In Holland*, Hitchcock's submission to the 1887 Paris Salon stood out all the more. Instead of a seascape in the style of Mesdag, he presented a quintessentially Dutch landscape with blooming tulips: *Culture des Tulipes* (Tulip Fields) [fig. 34]. The painting was widely admired: "Mr. Hitchcock [...] is one of the winners of this exhibition. From the very first day, his *Culture des Tulipes* was praised [...]. The remarkably bold choice of motif, the broad yet refined brushwork, the masterful execution and exquisite delicacy, the perfection of the landscape background, the spirit, grace, elegance, and the tasteful portrayal of the charming female figure have won over all the voices that matter."[153] Several renowned French artists, including Jean-Jacques Henner (1829-1905), Léon Bonnat (1833-1922), Jules-Joseph Lefebvre, and Jean-Léon Gérôme (1824-1904), expressed their admiration for this, until then, little-known artist.[154] The painting earned Hitchcock the nickname "The Tulip."[155]

In the fall, Hitchcock – now mistakenly referred to as *"Joris"* (Dutch for George) – also captivated the Brussels public with his painting of a "tastefully dressed woman, amid the floral tapestry of her garden."[156] Hitchcock and Melchers, who exhibited *The Sermon*, were not only both mistaken for Dutchmen on this occasion, but some even noticed a family resemblance between them![157]

34 George Hitchcock, *Tulip Fields*, 1887, oil on canvas, 109.2 x 167.6 cm. Private collection

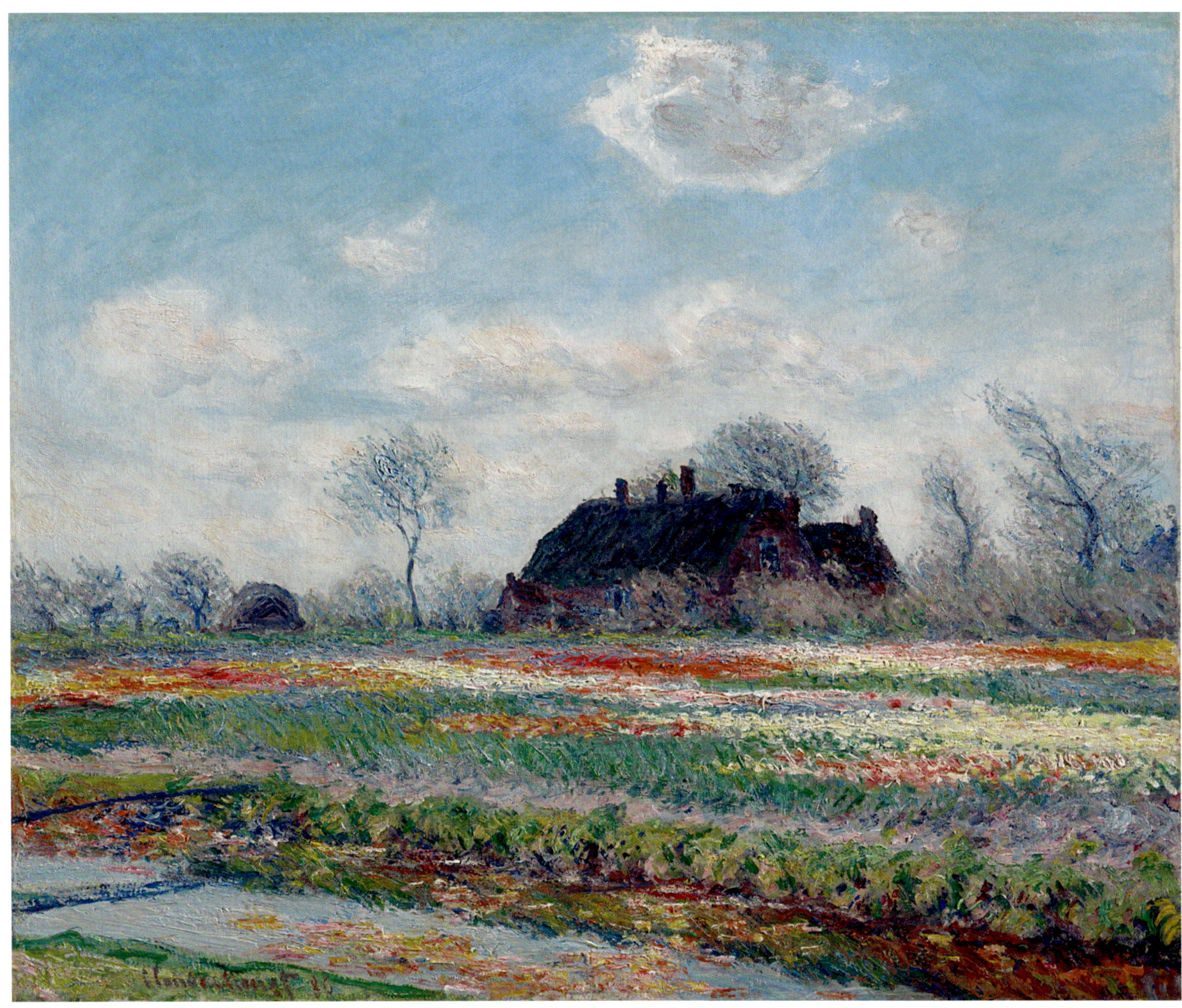

In the first of the three articles about "The Picturesque Quality of Holland" that Hitchcock published during this period in the brand-new American *Scribner's Magazine*, he presented a study for *Tulip Fields*. Without a shred of modesty, he wrote: "The colors of the large fields of hyacinths and tulips in the spring give a variety and opulence of primaries confusing to any but a skillful colorist and yet paintable by the exceedingly harmonious atmosphere. When grown in large fields in the open, this array of violent color is, perhaps, a little too strong; but when a smaller field of purple hyacinths or yellow tulips is enclosed in the heart of a small village, softened by subtle tree shadows, and tempered by the reds in the houses, it is more than agreeable."[158] The French Impressionist Claude Monet (1840-1926), who had captured the vibrant colors of the Dutch tulip fields a year earlier, expressed similar sentiments about them: "wonderfully beautiful, but enough to drive the poor painter mad. It's impossible with our poor palette" [fig. 35].[159] Monet showed his tulip fields in May 1886 at the Georges Petit Gallery in Paris, an exhibition that Hitchcock may have seen.[160]

   35 Claude Monet, *Tulip Fields at Sassenheim*, 1886, oil on canvas, 59.7 x 73 cm. Clark Art Institute, Williamstown, Massachusetts

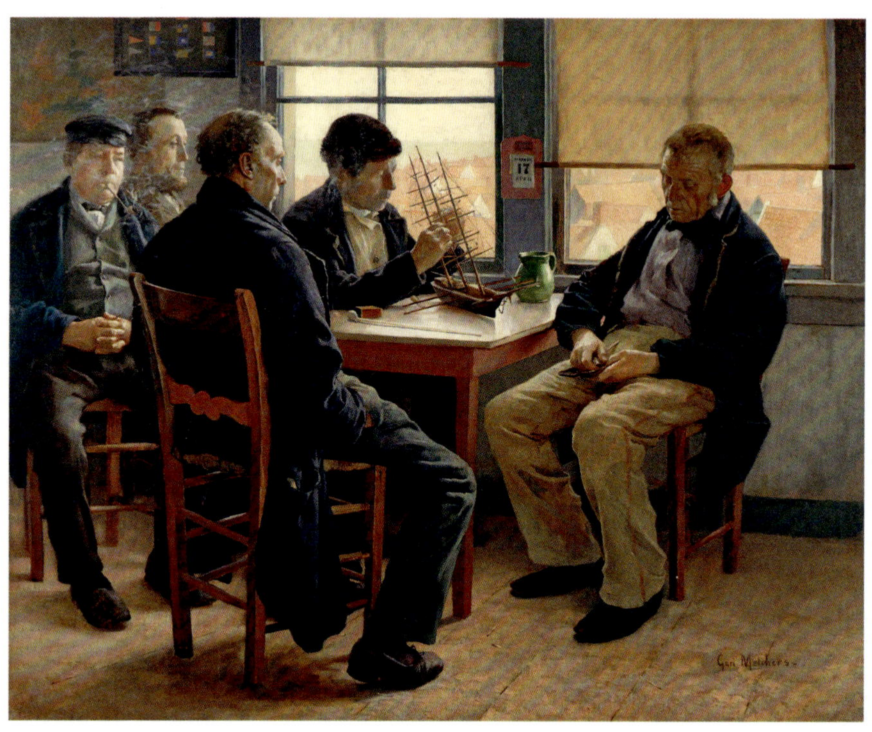

Conquering the Market: The Years 1888-1889

The international success of both artists heralded a new reality. Hitchcock and Melchers were now perceived as established artists whose activities were of interest. As a result, short bulletins about their goings-on suddenly appeared in the European-Paris edition of the *New York Herald*. For instance, on 25 February 1888, the newspaper reported that the Hitchcocks had returned to Paris after a trip to Rome and that Hitchcock planned to rent a studio there.[161] In March, *Galignani's Messenger* noted that the couple attended a reception hosted by the famous opera singer Emma Nevada. In May, detailed descriptions of Henrietta Hitchcock's outfit – along with those of other women present at the opening of the Salon – were published: "Mrs Hitchcock appeared in black silk, a light cover coat, and a black lace Directoire hat."[162]

Hitchcock and Melchers were also invited in April to a gathering of over a hundred American artists living in Paris who wished to participate in the 1889 Exposition Universelle in Paris. During this meeting, a committee was established to ensure that the selection for the American submission to the fair would not be made solely from Washington. Melchers joined the jury representing expatriate artists, alongside John Singer Sargent (1856-1925), among others. Hitchcock was appointed secretary and treasurer.[163]

Naturally, Hitchcock and Melchers submitted new works to the Salon in 1888, once again featuring paintings based on studies made in Egmond, with local residents as models. This time, it was Melchers who reaped success, while Hitchcock's entry received highly mixed reactions. Melchers exhibited *The Pilots*, which art critic André Michel described as the best painting he had created so far.[164] It depicts waiting, pipe-smoking pilots, one of whom is working on a model of a three-masted schooner [fig. 36]. The lower-lying Egmond is visible through the window.[165] Melchers' *The Pilots* was hailed as the best foreign painting of the Salon and earned him multiple awards in Paris and later in Munich. Following these successes, Melchers received a congratulatory letter from Hendrik Willem Mesdag.[166]

In 1888, Hitchcock once again surprised the public by changing his choice of subject matter – this time presenting a religious theme in a contemporary setting.[167] The addition of modern elements in this genre had been introduced in 1884 by the German artist Fritz von Uhde (1848-1911) and subsequently adopted by Hitchcock, as well as Melchers.[168] At the 1886 exhibition of the London Royal Academy, Hitchcock had made a modest first attempt in this genre with *Alma Mater*, depicting a modern-day Virgin Mary with a copper serving tray behind her head that functions as a halo [fig. 37].[169] For the Paris Salon,

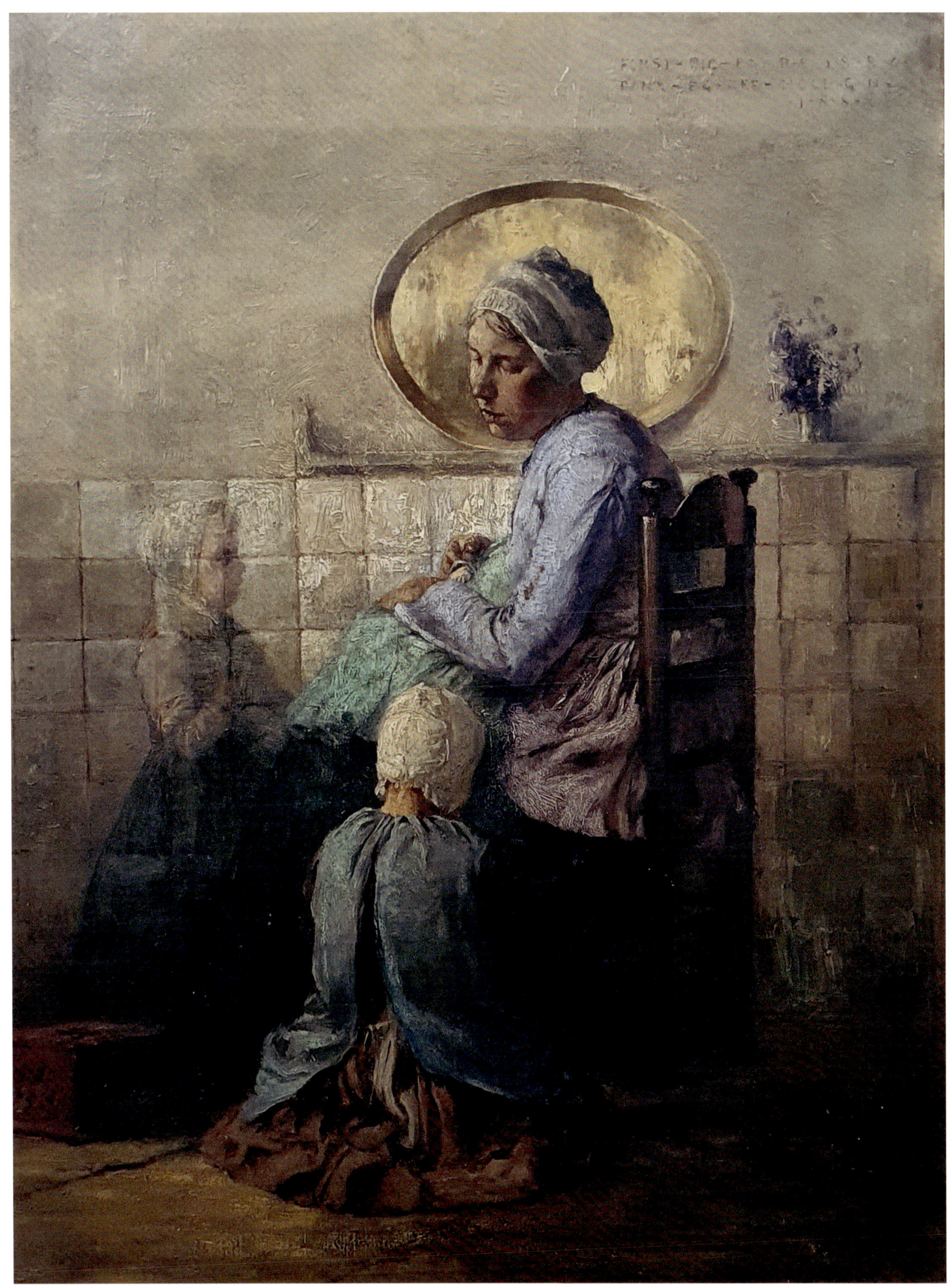

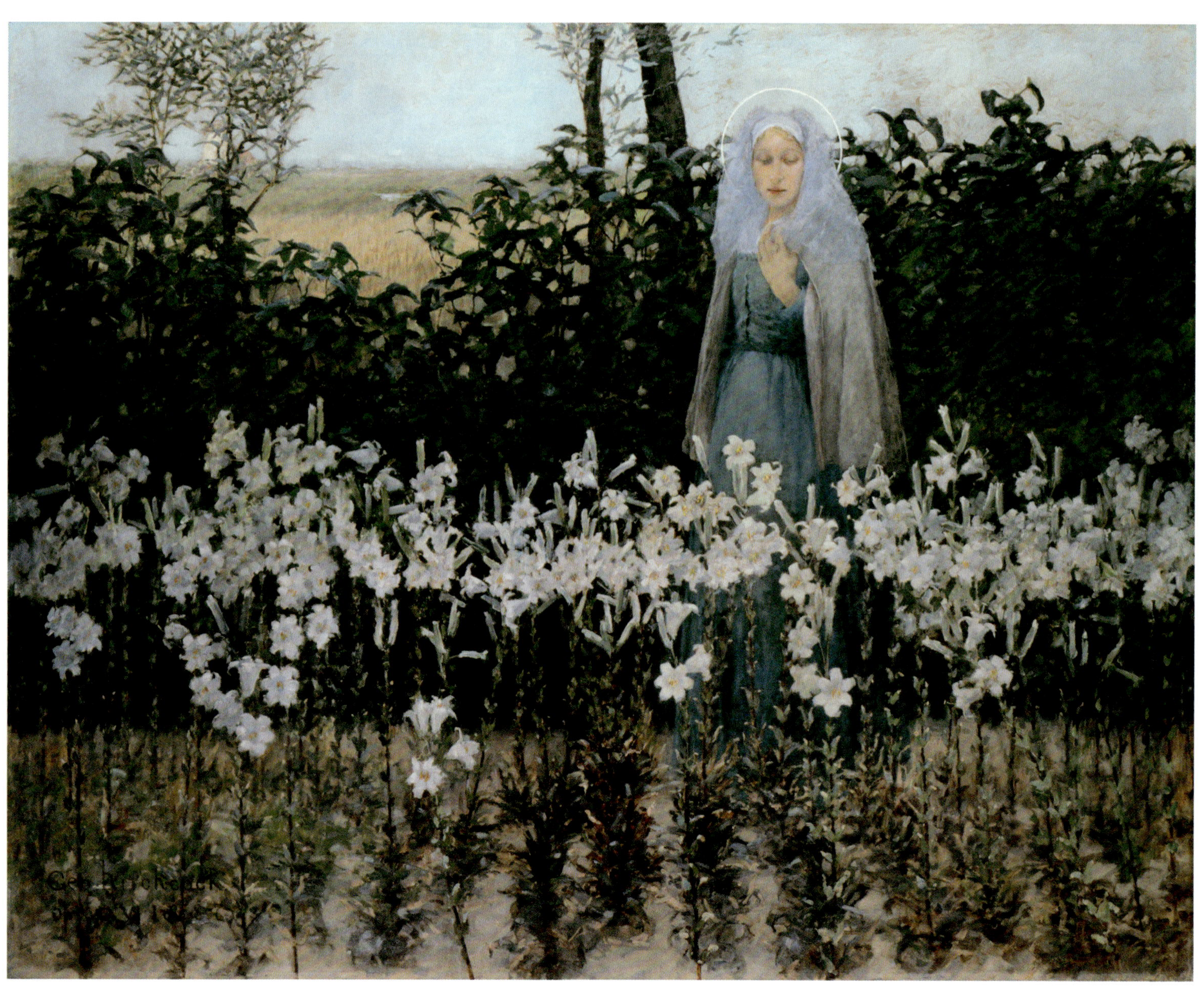

38 George Hitchcock, *The Annunciation*, 1887, oil on canvas, 158.8 x 204.5 cm. Art Institute of Chicago, Potter Palmer Collection

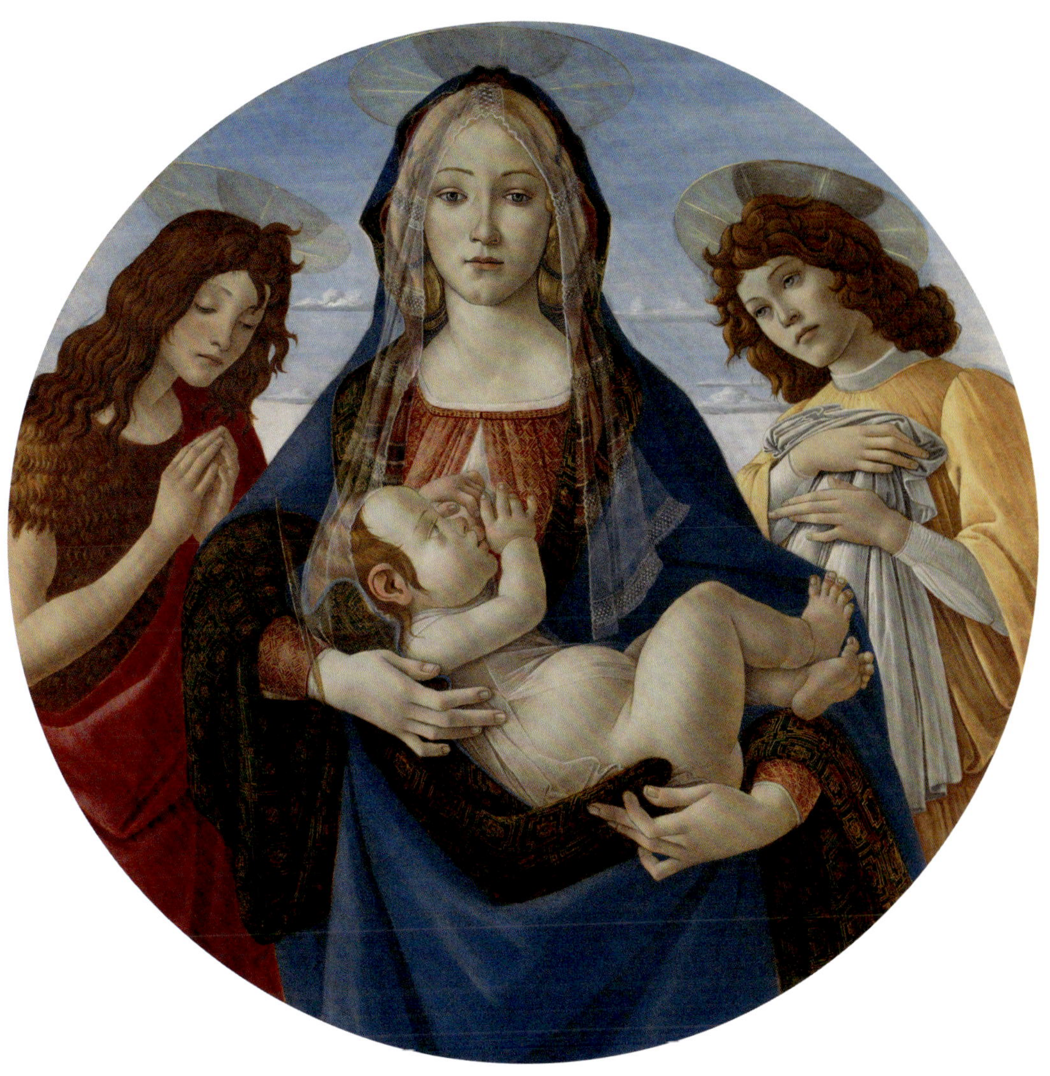

Hitchcock presented an unusual, contemporary interpretation of *The Annunciation*, the biblical story in which Mary learns that she is expecting the Son of God [fig. 38].[170] He painted the Virgin Mary with typically Dutch features standing in an enclosed garden among lilies. Interestingly, in Hitchcock's homeland, these flowers are called Annunciation lilies.[171] The elements in the painting – an enclosed garden and a white lily – are common in art history, symbolizing not only virginity but also the messenger, the Archangel Gabriel. However, Hitchcock's application of these elements was unprecedented. He depicted the religious theme in a realistic, commonplace setting: a realistically rendered Dutch farm girl standing in a flower-filled garden. One critic mockingly wrote that it was fortunate Hitchcock had explained the subject of his painting himself, as otherwise, no one would have recognized it.[172] However, some art experts, such as the influential Paul Leroi from *L'Art* magazine, lambasted the exhibition's organizers for placing the painting in a poorly visible spot: "It is a glaring injustice, and it saddens me."[173]

Later that year, it became clear what had inspired Hitchcock: he published an article in *Scribner's Magazine* about the Italian Renaissance painter Sandro Botticelli (ca. 1445–1510).[174] In it, Hitchcock expressed his admiration for Botticelli, who had revitalized Christian art by incorporating truth – through realism, contemporary clothing, and live models – into the pious sentiment evoked by his artistic predecessors. As an example, Hitchcock referenced Botticelli's *Virgin and Child*, which he had studied extensively in London, describing her as "pure realism" [fig. 39]. According to Hitchcock, this type of idealized woman could still be found on the streets of Florence, possessing "the same pearly skin, golden hair and deep grey eyes."[175] Moreover, he noted that Botticelli placed his Madonnas in natural settings with beautiful lighting, further enhancing their lifelike quality.[176]

  39 Workshop of Sandro Botticelli, *The Virgin and Child, with Saint John and an Angel*, ca. 1490, egg tempera on wood, 84.5 x 84.5 cm. National Gallery, London

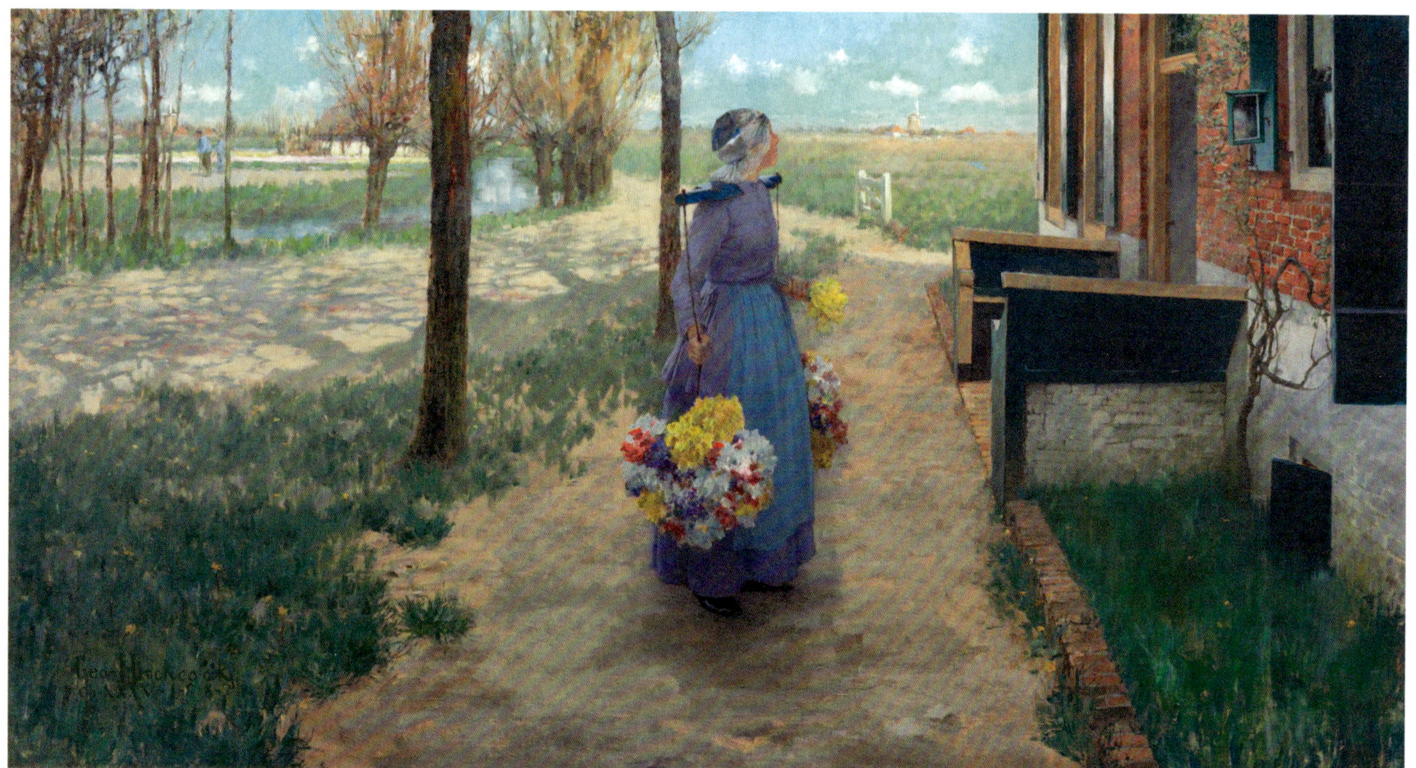

In the fall of 1888, Hitchcock also exhibited the *Flower Seller* in his former hometown of Chicago, a city that had by then gained a reputation as the best market for paintings in the United States [fig. 40].[177] Hitchcock himself described what had drawn him to the scene: "A fresh complexioned girl, with [a] large ball of many-colored flowers, composed of separate bunches of tulips or hyacinths hanging at the ends of a milk-bucket yoke, is often seen in the spring turning a honest penny in a beautiful way by selling the useless blossoms when the bulb has reached its maturity."[178]

The painting now known as *Flower Girl in Holland* was created at the centuries-old Hoeve Overslot farm on Slotweg in Egmond aan den Hoef [fig. 41]. It was purchased by the business magnate Potter Palmer and his wife Bertha Palmer, who built an extensive collection of contemporary art. Hitchcock had known the couple since his time as an artist in Chicago, and their friendship would last a lifetime.[179] That same year, in 1888, the Palmers donated Hitchcock's painting to the Art Institute of Chicago, marking the first time his work entered a museum – an achievement that elevated his status as an artist. Two years later, the Palmers would also add *The Annunciation* to their vast collection.[180] Hitchcock later created several variations of the successful subject – a young woman carrying a yoke with buckets full of colorful flowers – possibly upon request [fig. 42].

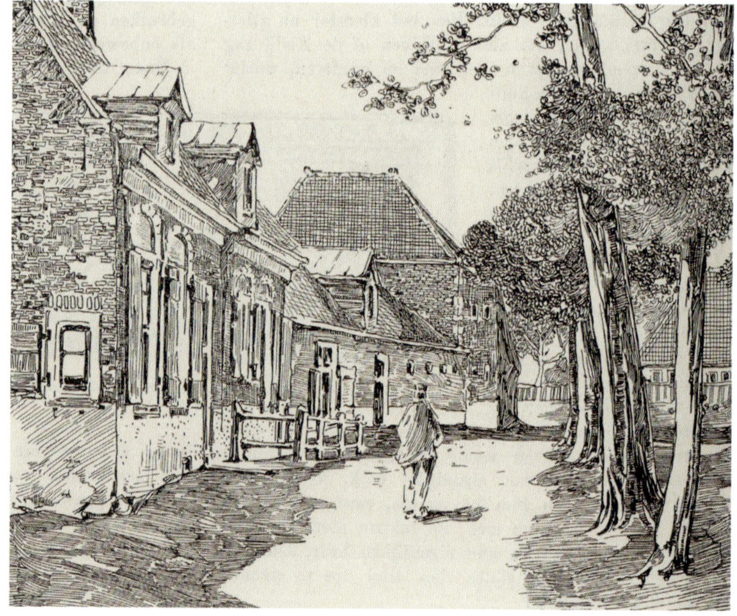

40 George Hitchcock, *Flower Girl in Holland*, 1887, oil on canvas, 79.1 x 147.3 cm. Art Institute of Chicago, Potter Palmer Collection
41 Jaap Veldheer, *Street in Egmond aan den Hoef, near Hoeve Overslot*, ca. 1899, reproduction from *Eigen Haard, 1899*

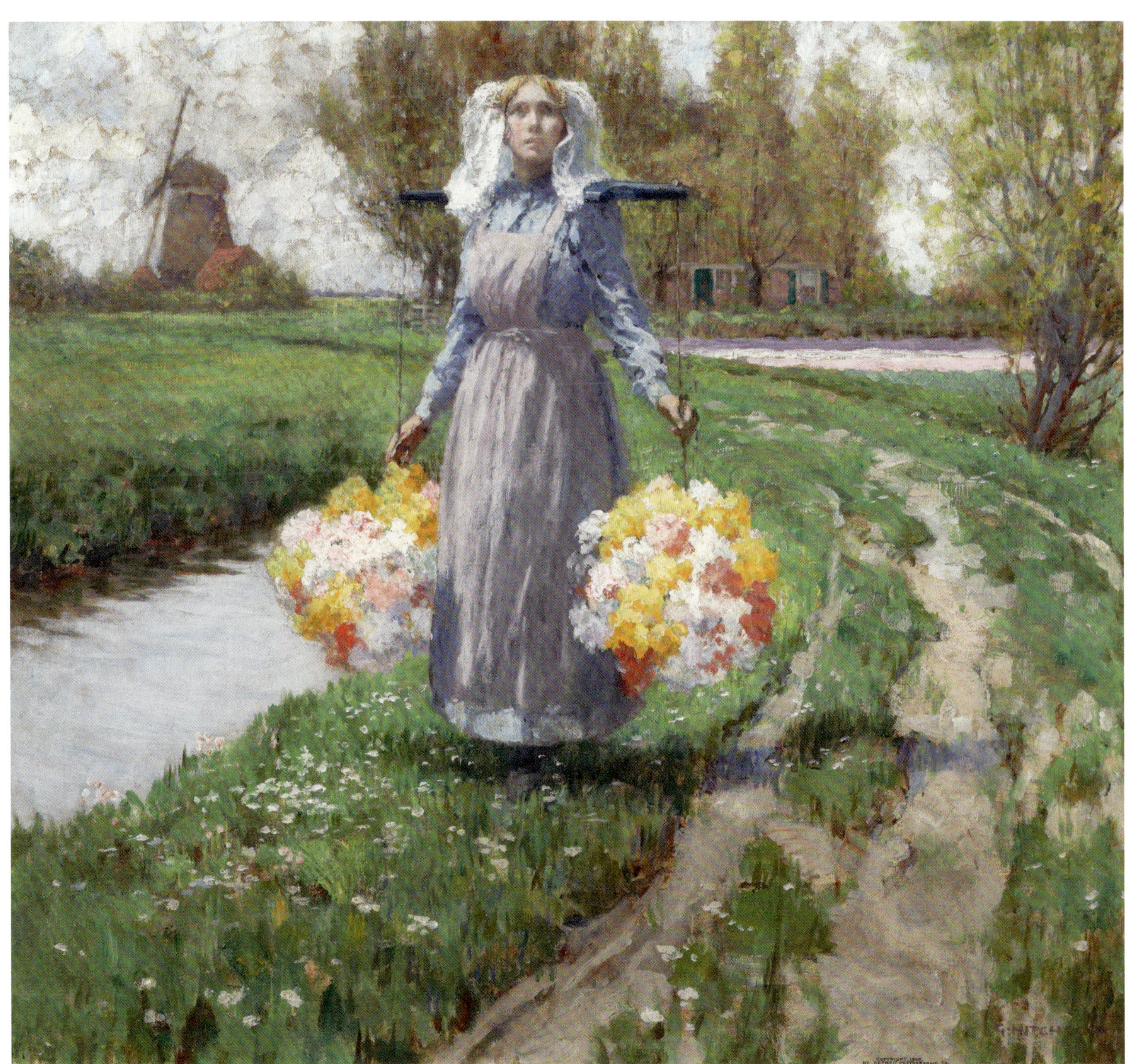

57   **42** George Hitchcock, *Flower Girl*, oil on canvas, 72.7 x 80 cm. Private collection

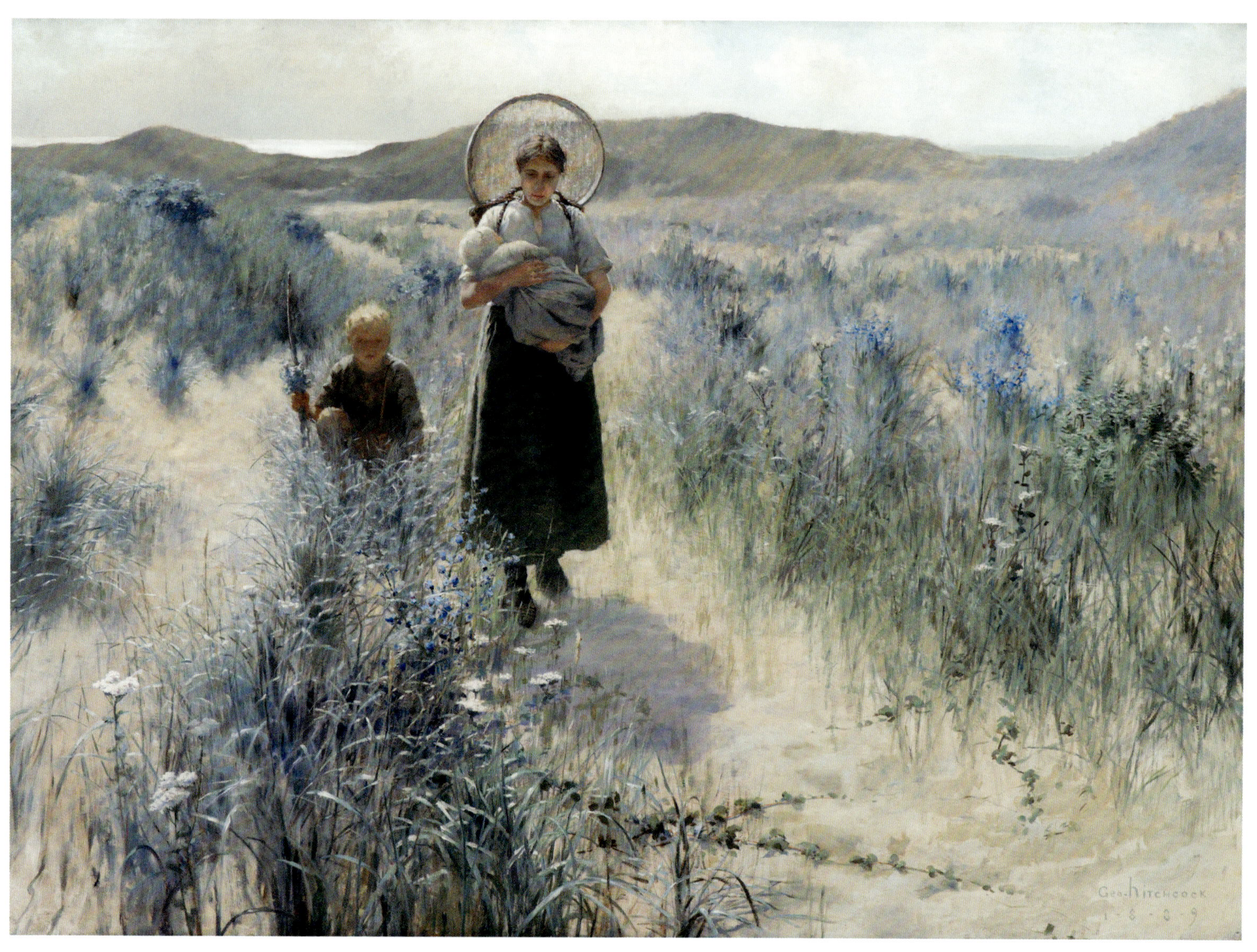

43 George Hitchcock, *Maternity*, 1889, oil on canvas, 179 x 251.3 cm. Aberdeen Archives, Gallery & Museums

The Salon and the 1889 Exposition Universelle

Both the annual Salon des Artistes Français and the 1889 Exposition Universelle began in May 1889. Of the two artists, only Hitchcock submitted a painting to the annual Salon, which opened on 1 May at the Palais des Champs-Élysées. His *Dutch Country Women*, depicting two Dutch girls making tulip bouquets for the market, sold within three weeks for 10,000 francs, roughly 4750 guilders at the time [fig. 44].[181]

Almost simultaneously, on 6 May, the Exposition Universelle in Paris opened to commemorate the French Revolution. The fair covered nearly a square kilometer and attracted over 32 million international visitors in just six months. The entrance to this showcase of the latest advancements in technology, science, and art was the Eiffel Tower, which was completed in that year.

In the realm of the visual arts, an overview of a century of French painting was displayed, alongside contemporary French and foreign art. This naturally included the section dedicated to American artists, curated by committees in Washington and Paris. The secretary of the Paris admissions committee, George Hitchcock, who was referred to by one critic as "a late comer in art," submitted his previous successes for the world audience: *Tulip Fields* and *The Annunciation* [see figs. 34 and 38]. In addition, he presented a new painting: *Maternity* [fig. 43].[182] In a pearly white dune landscape, Hitchcock painted a mother with a baby, accompanied by a blond boy. As in *The Annunciation*, Hitchcock referenced Mary through a contemporary Dutch model. The sieve the woman carries on her

back frames her head like a halo.[183] A cross formed by dewberry at her feet seems to subtly foreshadow the crucifixion.[184] The blond boy beside her alludes to John the Baptist.

The painting was praised by the press: "*Maternity* is the finest conception and the best executed work that Mr Hitchcock has yet achieved." *The Annunciation* was lauded once again; the American journalist Theodore Child even regarded it as one of the most refined and original paintings in the entire American section.[185] For his contribution, Hitchcock was awarded a silver medal, which allowed him to be admitted to the Salon *hors concours*, meaning he would no longer be subject to jury evaluation and could no longer compete for medals in France.[186]

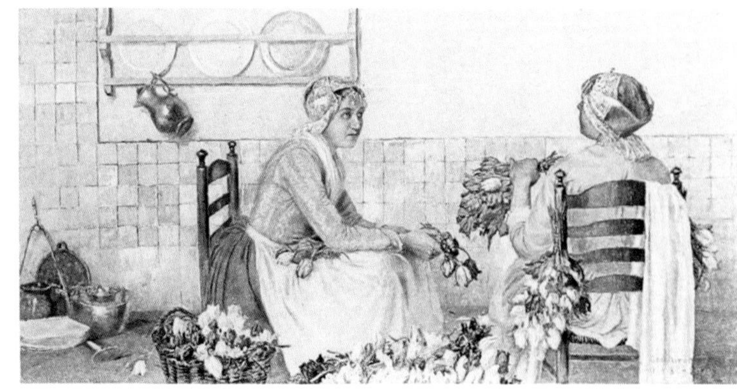

    44 George Hitchcock, *Dutch Country Women*. From G. Lafenestre, The Salon of 1889, Paris 1889

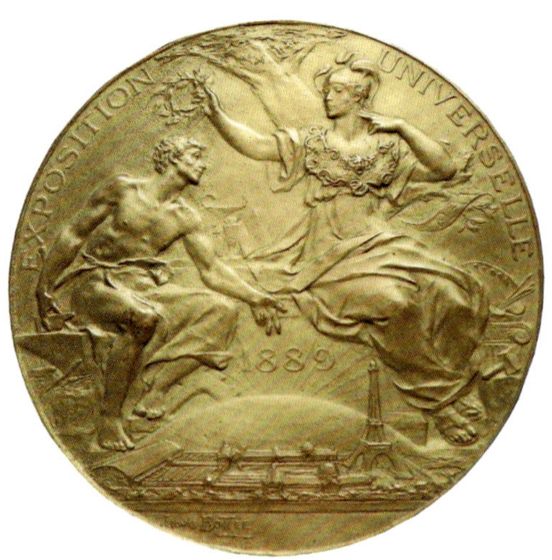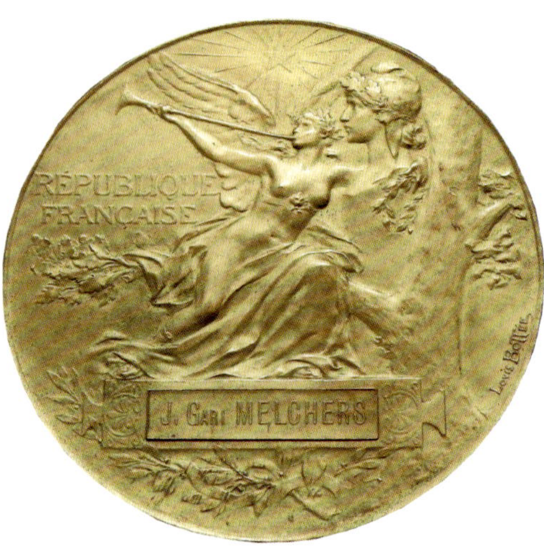

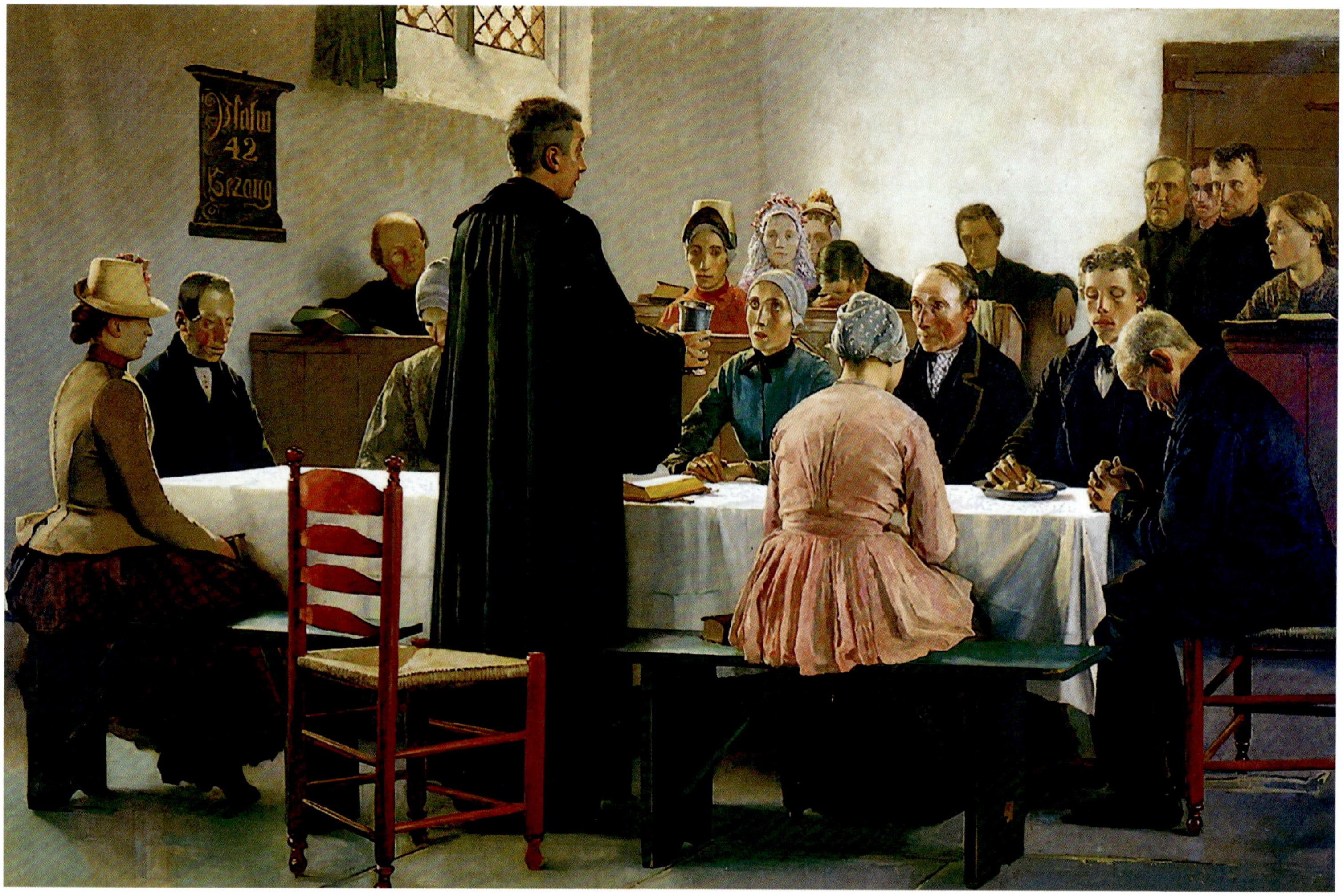

45 Melchers gold medal from the 1889 Exposition Universelle. Gari Melchers Home and Studio, University of Mary Washington, Fredericksburg
46 Gari Melchers, *The Communion*, 1888, oil on canvas, 220 x 341 cm. Herbert F. Johnson Museum of Art, Cornell University

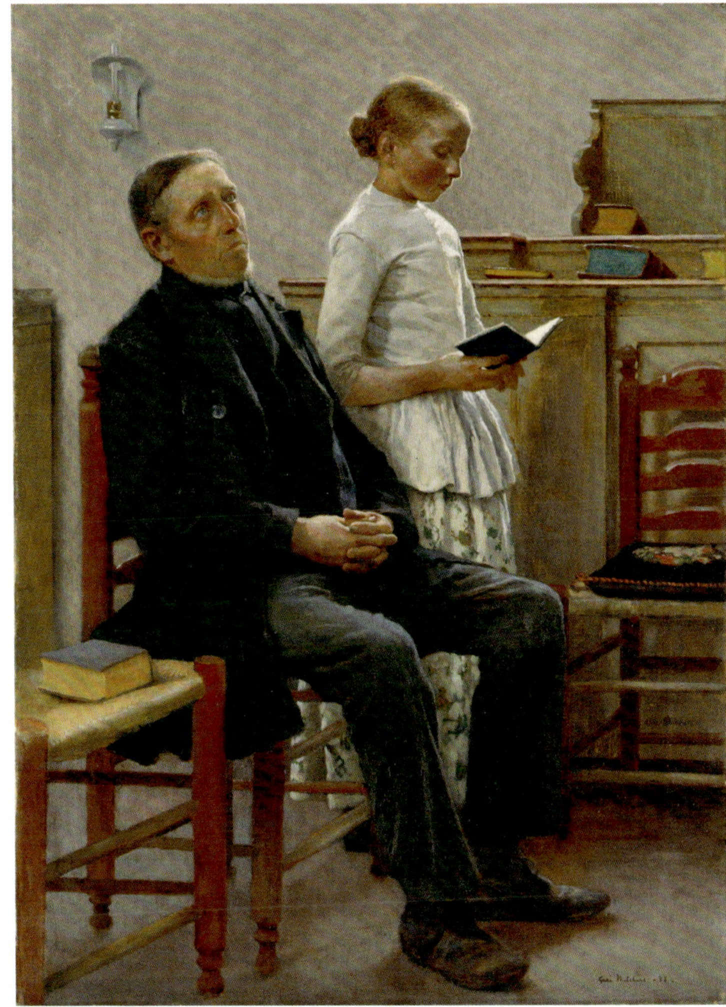

Gari Melchers was also represented with the paintings that had earned him successes in previous years. In addition to *The Sermon* and *The Pilots*, he exhibited a newly created painting, *The Communion* [see figs. 29, 36 and 46]. According to the aforementioned Theodore Child, the roughly twenty life-size Dutch peasants – "cheesy-faced people" – gathered to celebrate communion, were "remarkably ugly."[187] Nevertheless, he praised Melchers for his strong, unconventional composition and realism: "He paints figures round and solid, with a tendency toward the complete illusion of materiality [...] he is marvelously skillful."[188] Once again, Melchers had chosen the church in Egmond-Binnen as the setting for his scene, and he worked on-site. One of his biographers wrote: "For several weeks the interior of the edifice was placed at Mr. Melchers' disposal, and he had no difficulty in persuading the pious peasants to pose for him."[189] By December, the several-meters-long canvas, on which he had worked throughout the summer, was brought to Paris for completion.[190] Melchers, who at the age of 28 had already won several medals, was now awarded the Grand Prix, along with his fellow countryman John Singer Sargent [fig. 45].

In less than five years, George Hitchcock and Gari Melchers had firmly established their names within the international art world. The press was largely enthusiastic about the works on display, they won awards, and managed to sell their pieces featuring Egmond scenes. Melchers, who was called "our strongest American artist" by the influential American art advisor Sara Tyson Hallowell, also received portrait commissions and worked

in June on a portrait of the collector Potter Palmer.[191] Both artists also participated in the annual exhibition in Chicago that year. There, Melchers won the 500 dollar prize with *Vespers* [fig. 47]. By now a well-known and respected artist, Hitchcock began to focus on something new. Since 1888, he had been mentoring students in Egmond, which would prove to be highly lucrative. However, his growing fame also had its drawbacks, as the artist would soon discover.

    47 Gari Melchers, *Vespers*, 1888, oil on canvas, 96.5 x 71.1 cm. Detroit Institute of Arts, Gift of The Witenagemote Club

"For Art's Sake": The Art Summer School

Mr. George Hitchcock has arranged to leave Paris on Tuesday for his Dutch Studio at Egmond-aan-Zee. He will take with him a select class of pupils, which he has generously volunteered to instruct during the summer for Art's sake

The New York Herald (12 May 1888)[192]

The First "Art Class" in Egmond

From 1884 onwards, Hitchcock and Melchers primarily spent
the summer months in Egmond, while they mainly worked in
their Paris studios during winter – Hitchcock also sometimes in
London.[193] Other artists regularly joined them during the summer months, many of whom were part of their circle of friends
from Düsseldorf. For example, in 1887, Hans Hermann once
again worked in Egmond [fig. 48]. However, starting in 1888,
new visitors began arriving in Egmond as Hitchcock, now a
celebrated artist, offered to teach "for Art's sake" during the
summer months.[194]

Thanks to reports on the comings and goings of high society
in the European edition of *The New York Herald*, we know who
were among Hitchcock's first guests. The newly married American artist couple Robert van Vorst Sewell (1860-1924) and
Amanda Sewell-Brewster (1859-1926) traveled to Egmond in
1888 to spend the summer there, as stated in the newspaper,
"under [the] artistic counsel" of Hitchcock. However, Robert
Sewell quickly issued a correction, clarifying that the guidance
did not apply to him, but rather his wife![195] Be that as it may,
Sewell-Brewster in fact was not a fledgling artist; after studying
in New York and Paris at the Académie Julian, she had already
exhibited three times at the Paris Salon.

Agnes O'Halloran (1862-1960), a young American from
Saint Paul, Minnesota, left for Egmond on 2 July to join Hitchcock's "art class."[196] She was somewhat less experienced but
copied works in the Louvre. She may have arrived just in time

for the celebration of Eagle Day, the commemoration of the
signing of the Declaration of Independence on 4 July 1776.
According to reports in *The New York Herald*, Melchers, Hitch-
cock, and the Sewells celebrated the holiday exuberantly in
Egmond, with the entire village taking part.[197] Later that year,
Miss Ida M. Clark also joined George Hitchcock's art class.[198]

Most of the guests who would later participate in Hitchcock's
art classes typically arrived around May (after the festive opening of the Salon, of course) and left the village by the end of
September. While the number of participants was modest in
the first year, it would steadily increase during the 1890s (see
the Appendix on pp. 126-130).[199] In 1899, an article appeared
in the magazine *Eigen Haard* about the three Egmonds, stating:
"The village seems to have gained a certain fame among
American painters. During the summer, a whole colony settles

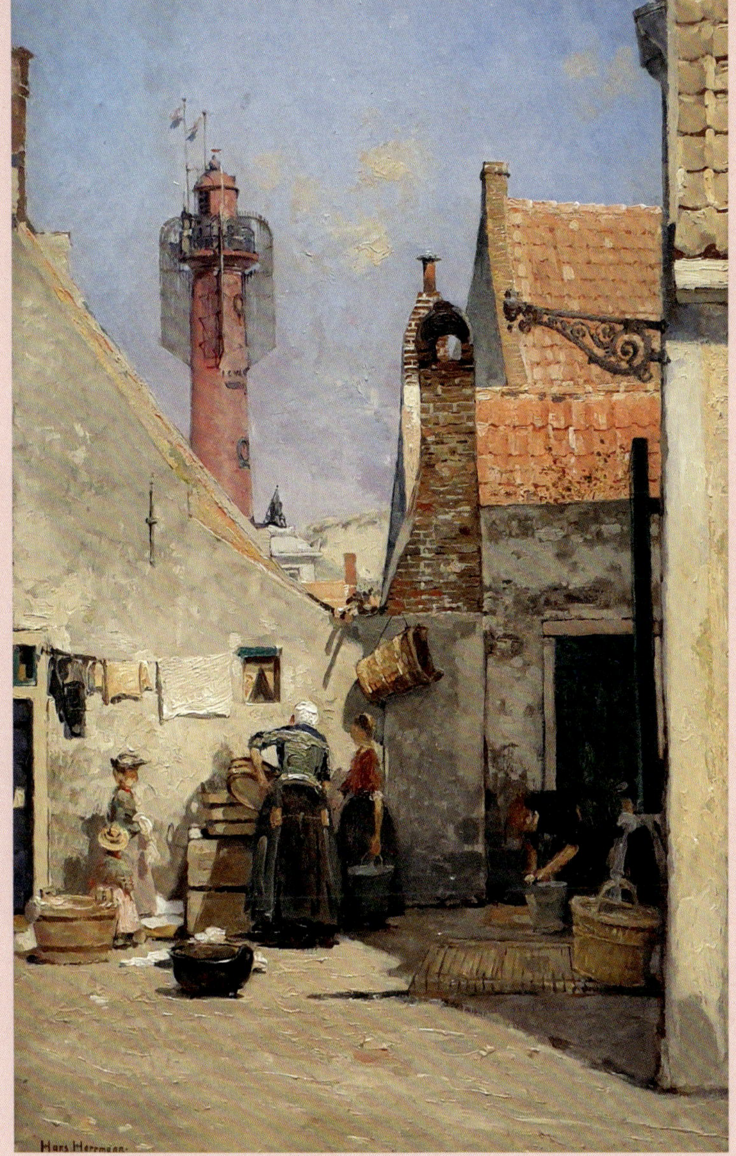

 48 Hans Hermann, *Egmond aan Zee*, 1887, oil on canvas, 62 x 45.5 cm, Museum van Egmond

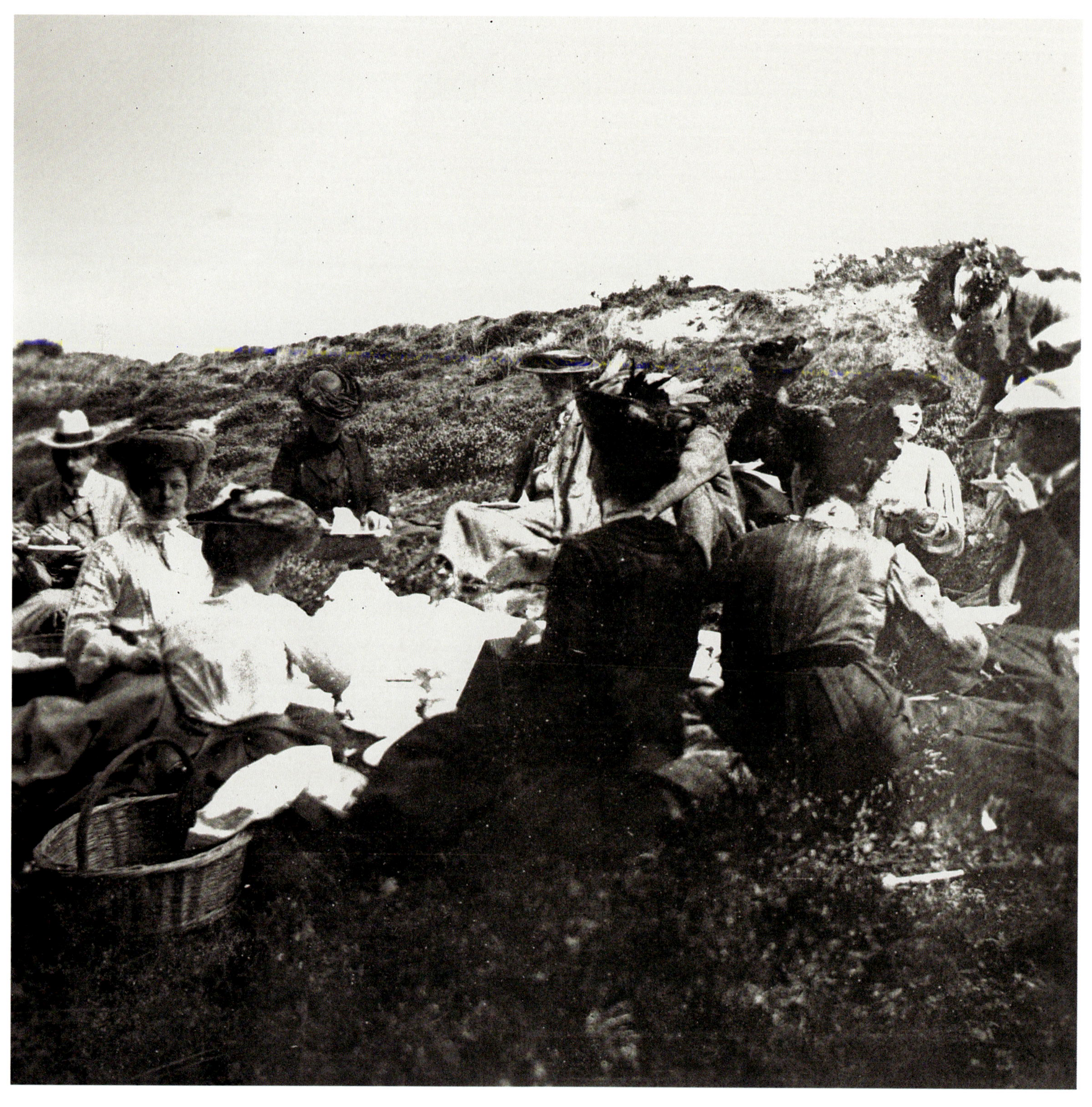

[...] it's a most amusing sight to see such a group of both American men and women [...] under their white sunshades [...] diligently at work

here, and it's a most amusing sight to see such a group of both American men and women, as the female artists are well represented – under their white sunshades like a collection of giant mushrooms, diligently at work. That they all tend to paint nearly the same subject and that originality is somewhat lost in the process seems to be of little concern to them" [fig. 49].[200]

The Scandal: Hitchcock's Affair with Agnes O'Halloran

Just after the very first year in 1888, there were likely no art classes in 1889. Following the openings of the Salon and the Exposition Universelle, Hitchcock reportedly did not feel "fit" to travel. The artist was exhausted from the responsibilities he had assumed regarding the American jury for the Exposition Universelle.[201] However, in late June 1889, shortly after the opening of the fair, Hitchcock suddenly made international news. This time, not because of his artistic contributions or activities for the American committee, but because of a scandal. Hitchcock, "the heartless villain," had run off with the twelve-year-younger Agnes O'Halloran, one of the first students in his art class in Egmond. [202] Since their initial meeting in Paris, Hitchcock had taken her under his wing; he had arranged for his wife Henrietta (who was the same age as Agnes) to act as her chaperone and for the young lady to stay with them.[203] He had also personally ensured that one of her paintings would be displayed in the American gallery at the Exposition Universelle.[204] Hitchcock's "disappearance" was minutely described in the press, complete with quotes from notes to his wife Henrietta Hitchcock: "I know that I have ruined your life; I have my own […]."[205] The Canadian newspaper *The Toronto Daily Mail* gave a particularly detailed account of the situation. Another newspaper reported that Hitchcock had written to a friend, stating it was a matter of life and death.[206] While he fled to the island of Jersey with O'Halloran, Henrietta Hitchcock traveled to friends in London before continuing on to George's brother, Charles Hitchcock, in America. What happened after that remained outside the public eye, except for the reaction of O'Halloran's father, who tried to mitigate the damage. News then followed of the Hitchcock couple's reconciliation.[207] Around 11 July, George and Henrietta left London for Egmond to spend the summer there.[208]

Melchers, who had left for Brussels just before the scandal broke, missed all the commotion in Paris.[209] In the fall of 1889, he stayed in Volendam, the fishing village on the Zuiderzee (now the IJsselmeer), where many international artists gathered. Melchers was there with several German painters to seek inspiration, but the endless rain left little opportunity for outdoor painting.[210]

← **49** George Hitchcock (left) and Gari Melchers (right) sketching in the dune with various pupils, ca. 1902-1905. Photo Gari Melchers Home and Studio, University of Mary Washington, Fredericksburg

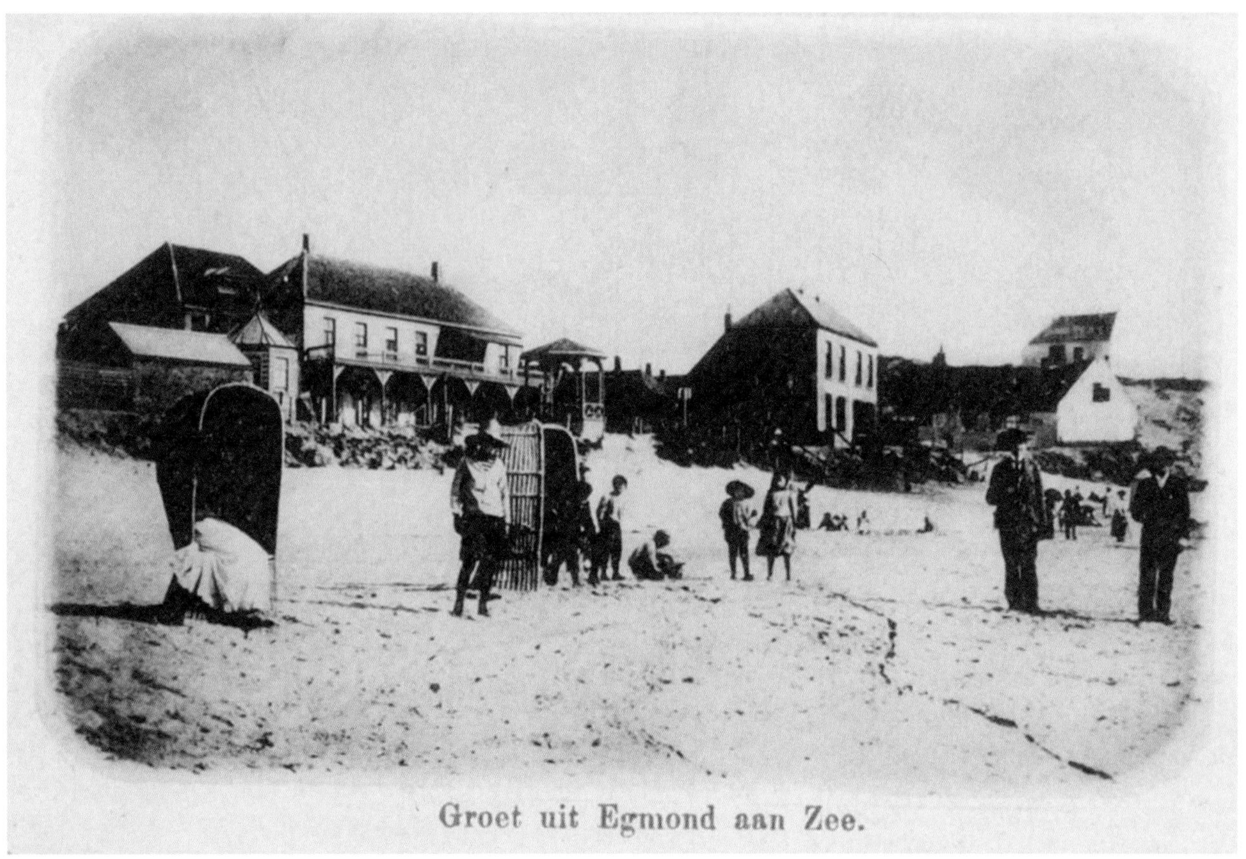

Egmond: From Source of Inspiration to Artists' Colony

Thanks in part to publications like *Sketching Rambles in Holland* (1885) by the "explorer" George H. Boughton and Hitchcock's three articles in *Scribner's Magazine* on "The Picturesque Quality of Holland" (published in 1887, 1889, and 1891), artists' interest in the Netherlands grew even further.[211] Along with Katwijk and Laren, Volendam became one of the most popular artists' colonies in the country.[212] Artists were drawn to the traditional and authentic nature of the (fishing) villages with their regional character and local costumes.[213] The pre-industrial era that still seemed intact there, and life close to nature, attracted artists. Furthermore, collectors, who usually lived in cities, were eager to purchase their work.[214] The paintings mostly depicted the idyllic side of rural life. The physically demanding labor of farmers and fishermen, the impoverished existence, and the sometimes anxious waiting for the fleet's return were rarely captured by foreign artists.[215]

As in other small artists' communities that had formed across Europe, in the Netherlands the artists would often stay for weeks, often in hotels and inns. Initially, there were barely any facilities for them in the rural villages, let alone artists' associations or exhibition opportunities. Gaining inspiration and enjoying the freedom were the primary focuses. However, within these communities, the artists did follow a certain routine: they all woke up early, worked outdoors during the day, drawing inspiration from nature, and often spent the evenings together playing cards and other games, billiards, dancing, singing, and so forth.[216] While the colonies did not always share stylistic similarities, the subjects of their works often overlapped, and the outcomes of a day's hard work were usually discussed collectively.

In accommodating the increasing flow of artists – and later tourists – the Egmonds gradually changed. Whereas previously, an omnibus would arrive only twice a day, by 1905, one could take the steam tram from Alkmaar, passing through Egmond aan den Hoef, all the way to Egmond aan Zee no less than thirteen times a day.[217] The influx grew so large that in 1895, a Tourist Association (VVV) was established in Egmond aan Zee. Despite the improvements in transportation and accommodation, one of the regular guests who stayed in Egmond remarked, "That part of Holland was so primitive it might have been over a hundred years ago."[218]

The very first artists to arrive in Egmond took up residence at Zeezicht Hotel, Welgelegen Hotel owned by Peter de Graaf, or stayed elsewhere in the village, such as at the Het Slot van den Hoef Inn, run by the Bult family. As often happened in other artists' colonies, decorations were added to the interiors of the guesthouses [fig. 51].[219] However, it would not become as lively or extravagant as the popular Volendam Spaander Hotel in Egmond.[220]

The ferry operator Kraakman capitalized on the demand for good accommodations and around 1900 built a house with chambrettes for painters and artists' studios with northern light near the Mallegat (now Julianaweg) in Egmond aan den Hoef. Later, he also opened an antique shop and rented out costumes and objects to provide artists with "authentic" Dutch props.[221] As the number of artists and visitors grew, more hotels and guesthouses were built in Egmond [fig. 50].[222] For example, in 1901, Florence Upton (1873-1922) stayed at Pension Winkel, run by the local cobbler.[223] Additionally, shops like Dorpzicht run by the widow H. J. Belleman opened, offering not only pastries, bread, and sweets but also beach hats, writing supplies, home-cooked meals, and rental cribs.[224] In Egmond aan den Hoef, the bookseller N. Schild decided to deal in "artists' supplies."[225]

Due to the presence of Hitchcock and Melchers in Egmond and the success they achieved with their "typically" Egmond scenes, ever more artists began to visit the three villages of Egmond. Friends and acquaintances from Düsseldorf, Paris, and London arrived to find inspiration there. Among them was Heinrich Wilhelm Petersen-Angeln, who visited Egmond not only in 1884 but also in the 1890s.[226] In 1893, for instance, he was there simultaneously with Hermann and Heimes, who also returned from time to time [fig. 52].[227] Another example is James Jebusa Shannon (1862-1923). Known for his society portraits, this painter was impressed by Hitchcock's work after seeing an exhibition in London. He reached out to the artist because he was enthusiastic about the colors Hitchcock had used to paint the countryside. For the first time, Shannon saw the Netherlands not as "a country with a slight yellow fog."[228] This meeting led to a years-long friendship with the Hitchcocks and later with Melchers. From 1892 to 1905, Shannon spent nearly every summer with his family in Egmond. He painted George Hitchcock working in his garden in Egmond aan den Hoef and, years later, his own wife and daughter on the dune [figs. 53 and 54].[229]

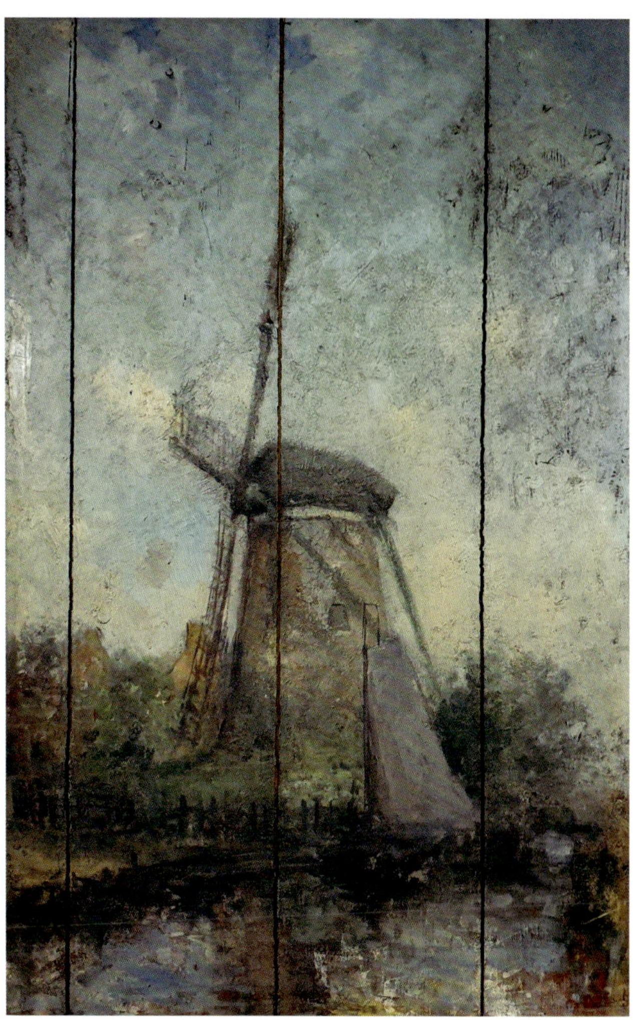

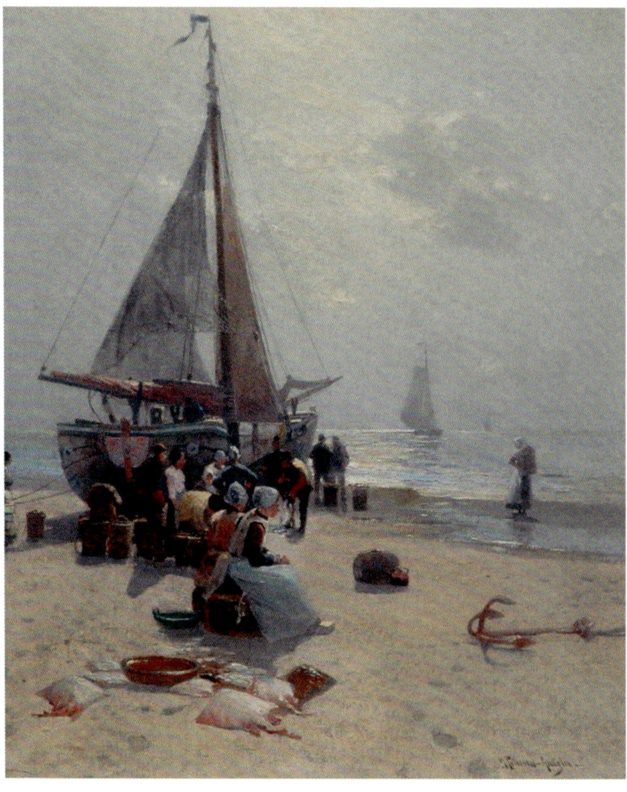

 51 Max Clarenbach, *Mill (De Hoop?)*, oil on panel, from the Zeezicht Hotel, 115 x 83 cm. Museum van Egmond   **52** Heinrich Wilhelm Petersen-Angeln, *Before the Fish Auction, Egmond*, ca. 1893-1895, oil on canvas 112 x 90.4 cm. Private collection, previously Simonis & Buunk art gallery, Ede

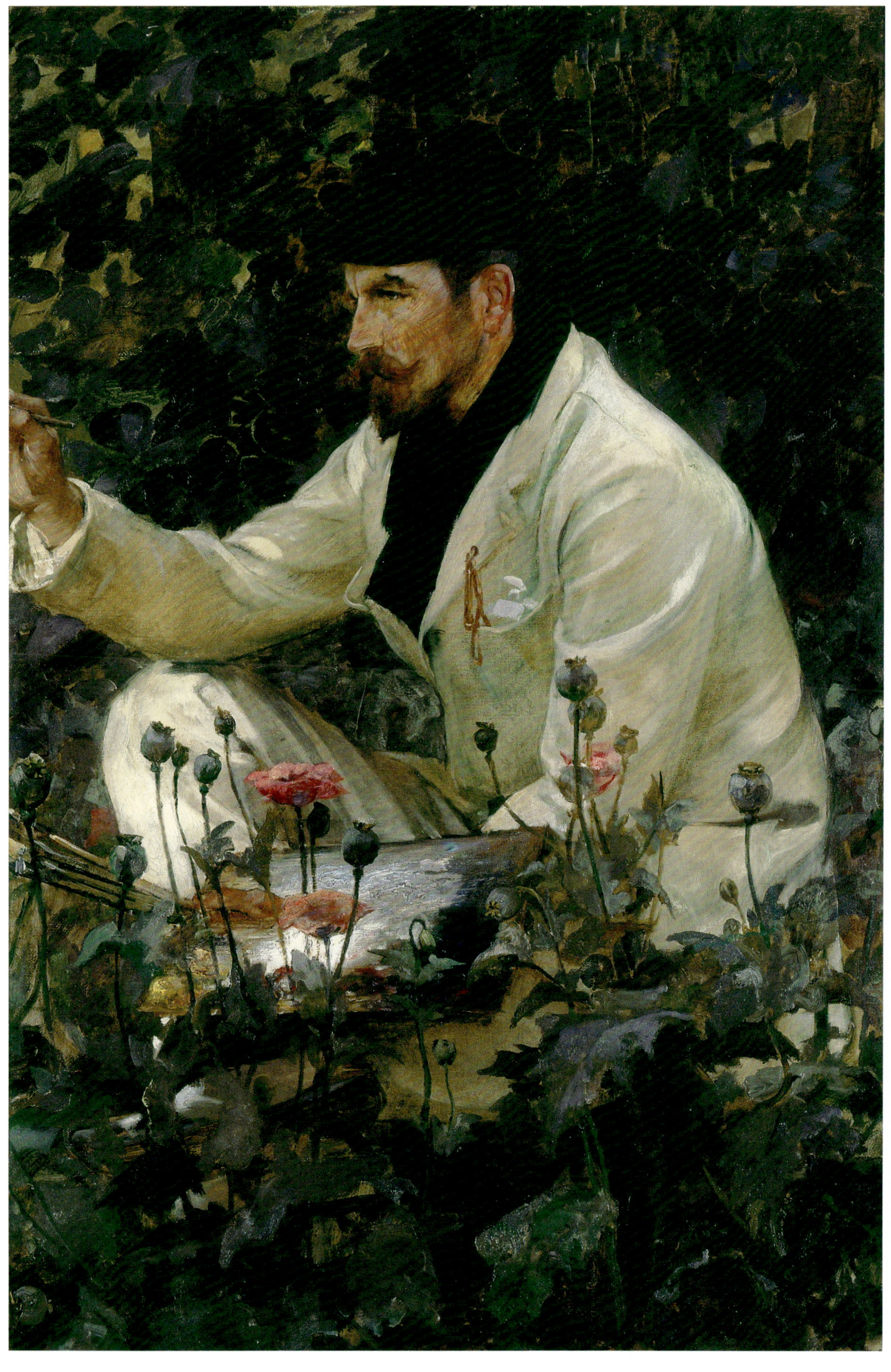

53 James Jebusa Shannon, *George Hitchcock,* ca. 1892, oil on canvas, 129.9 x 89.4 cm. Telfair Museum, Savannah, Georgia

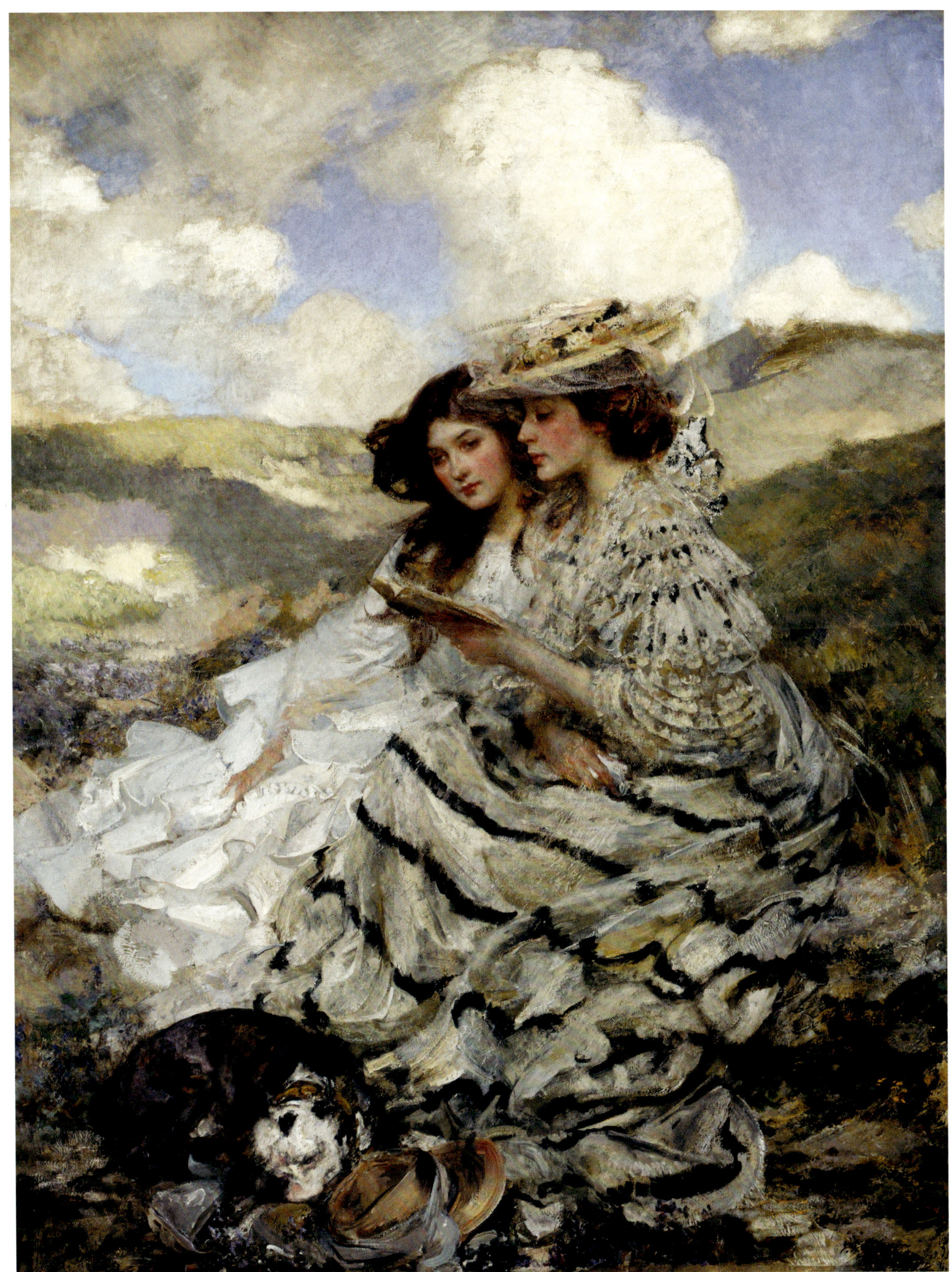

  54 James Jebusa Shannon, *On the Dune (Lady Shannon and Kitty)*, ca. 1905, oil on canvas, 186.4 x 143 cm. Smithsonian American Art Museum, Gift of John Gellatly

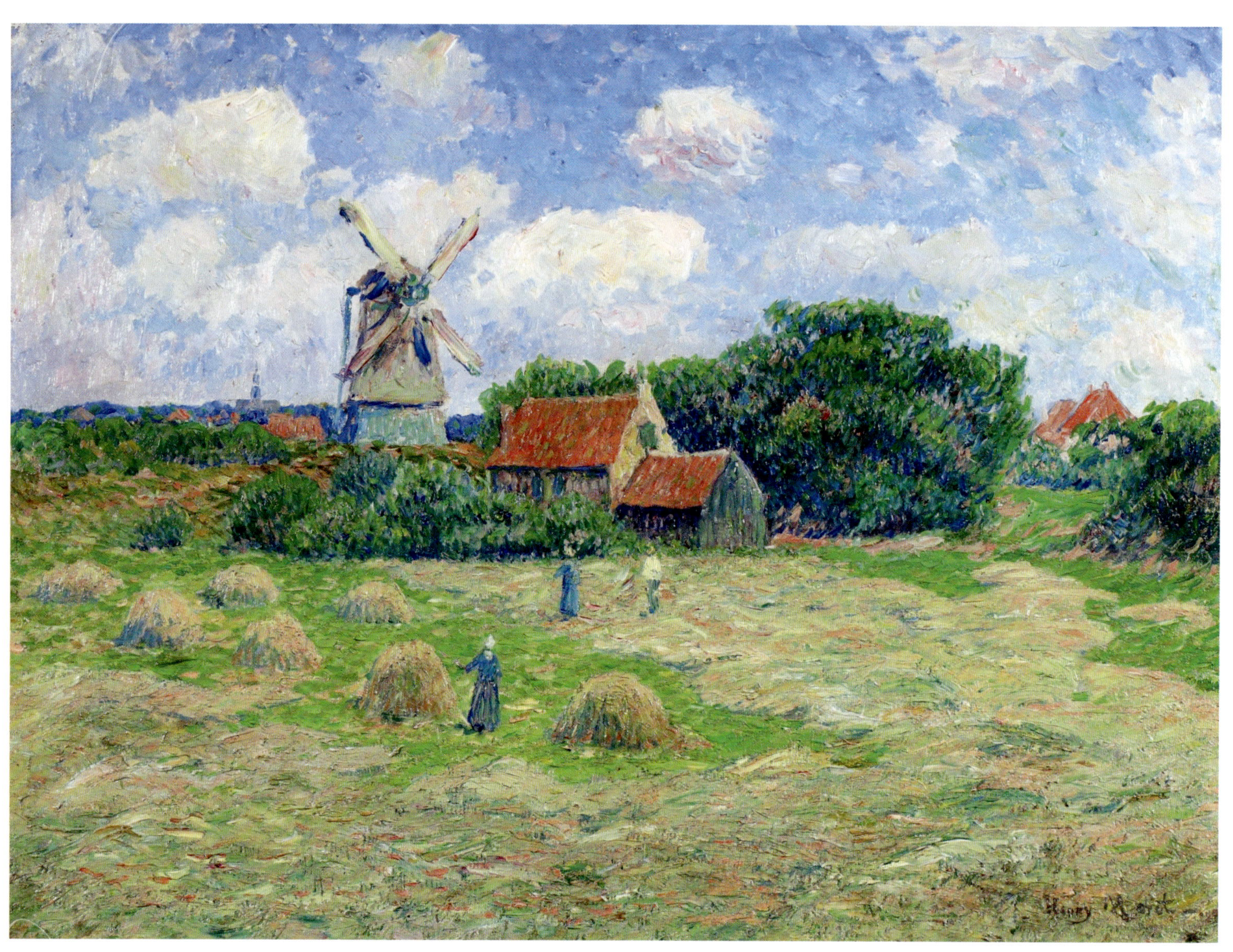

55 Henry Moret, *The Harvest in Egmond aan Zee*, 1900, oil on canvas, 55.9 x 73.7 cm, Leighton Fine Art, Marlow

In addition to old friends, other artists also settled in Egmond. The American cattle painter William Henry Howe (1846-1929) was there around 1888-1889 [fig. 57].[230] The Frenchman Henry Moret (1856-1913) traveled through the Netherlands at the urging of the Paris art dealer Paul Durand-Ruel, and stayed in Egmond in 1900, among other places [fig. 55]. A comparison of his Impressionist painting *The Harvest in Egmond aan Zee* with the work of Petersen-Angeln, Shannon, Hitchcock, and Melchers clearly shows that there was no stylistic kinship or communal ambition. The artists who worked in Egmond were not consciously united into a cohesive movement. The only binding factor was the geographical location that they shared for several weeks each year. In Egmond, no "school" emerged, like The Hague School (around 1870) or the Bergen School (after 1914), the latter developing a stone's throw from Egmond during the First World War. [231] However, there was another type of "school" in Egmond: one with a teacher and students. Hitchcock's art classes attracted ever more artists in the 1890s. Quite logically, within this "school" there was greater unity in subject choice and style. While Petersen-Angeln does not appear to have been a student of Hitchcock, the landscapes he created after 1893 were clearly inspired by him [fig. 56].

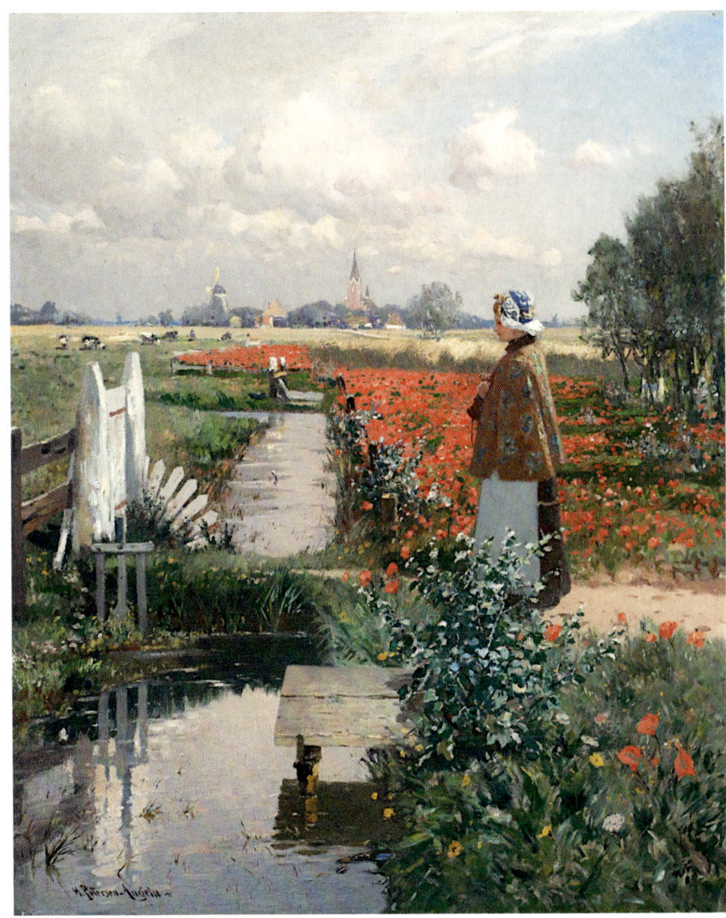

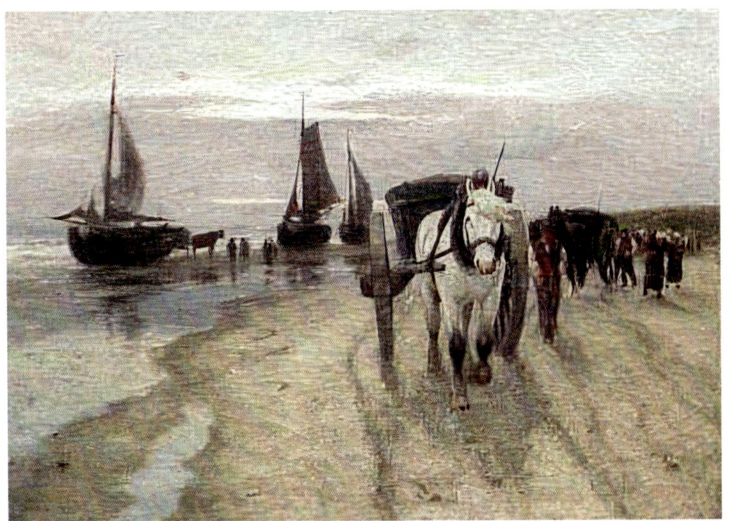

 56 Heinrich Petersen-Angeln, *Poppy Field with a Girl Knitting by a Canal*, 1898-99, oil on canvas, 112.5 x 96.5 cm, Kunstpalast, Düsseldorf, Bequest Dr Franz Schoenfeld 1911 **57** William Henry Howe, *On the Beach – Egmond Holland*, oil on canvas, 61 X 81.3 cm. Private collection

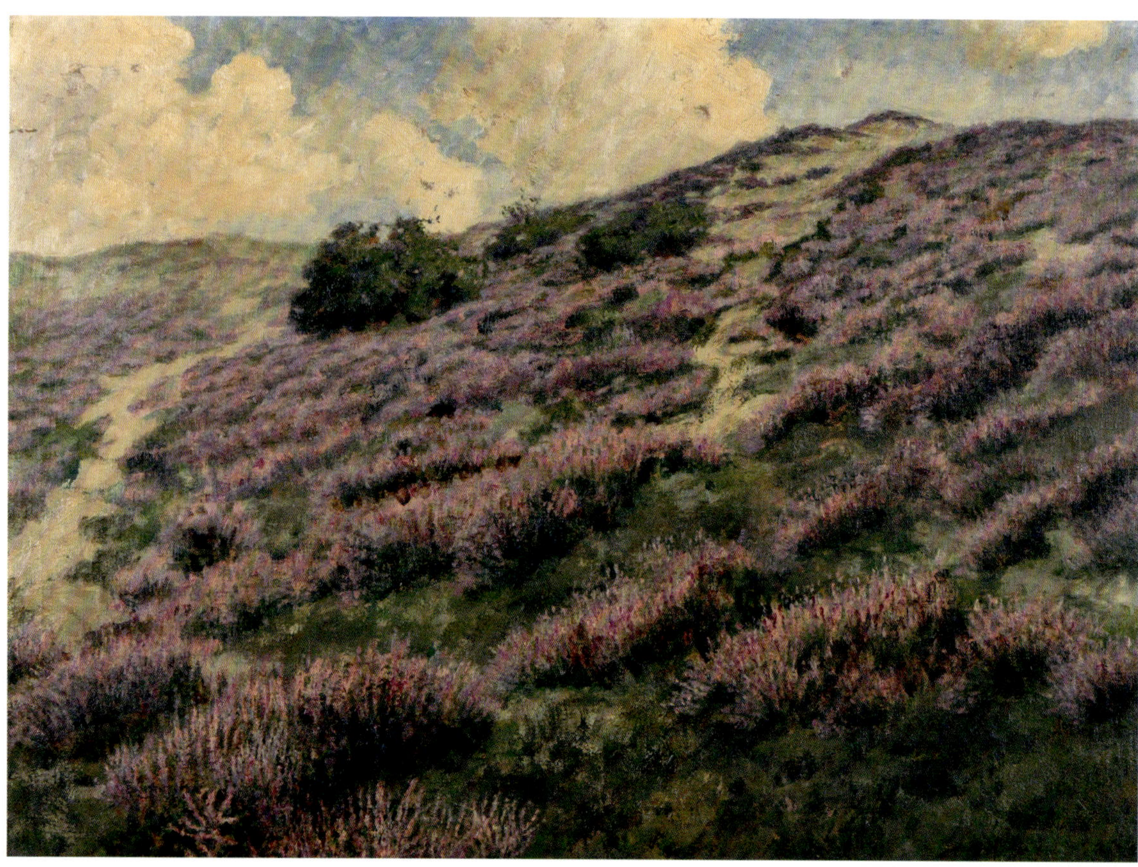

Lesson with the "great man"

In the last quarter of the nineteenth century, art classes, or summer courses, were increasingly organized within the artists' colonies. Around the turn of the century, Summer Art Schools were widely advertised in art magazines in both the United States and Europe.[232] For example, William Merritt Chase organized courses along the coast between Scheveningen and Zandvoort starting in 1896.[233] His advertisements read: "In addition to working from the landscape and model out of doors, one of the features of the trip will be the study of the old Dutch Masters."[234] Similar courses were also offered by others, such as Robert Henri (1865–1929) and Alexander Robinson (1867–1940), who taught in Volendam.[235]

Thanks to the preserved letters and diaries of Corinne Lawton Mackall (1880–1955) (a student of Hitchcock and later the wife of Melchers) and her mother, we know how Hitchcock ran his art classes in Egmond around 1902. The six students who were staying there at the time mostly worked independently. A considerable amount of initiative and effort was expected from them, but they were usually not beginners in the field. Florence Upton, for example, was already known as an illustrator of children's books and was chipping away at her career as an artist [fig. 59]. Anna Woodward (1868–1935) and Letta

Crapo Smith (1862–1921) both studied at the Académie Julian [figs. 58 and 60]. Carl Gordon Cutler (1873–1945) and Marion Eliza Crocker (1868–1951) had also taken classes at the School of the Museum of Fine Arts in Boston.[236] Most students came for a single visit, but others, including Upton, returned regularly to the Egmonds.[237] Interestingly, Egmond or Hitchcock attracted relatively many female artists.[238]

Corinne Lawton Mackall woke up early to sketch outdoors, usually returning by around eleven o'clock for lunch. Afterward, she worked until five or six in the afternoon.[239] Hitchcock often had his students work outdoors (even in the rain), preferably on large formats.[240] The artists got around the villages and surrounding areas by bike. On other days, Lawton Mackall worked in her studio from a model, with Hitchcock stopping by to offer advice and critique.[241] Sometimes he was particularly complimentary: "Remarkable, quite incredible talent," "Wonderful progress!" "Can he think I believe him?" Lawton Mackall wrote in her diary.[242]

Almost weekly, Hitchcock worked with his students in a sketching class, as Lawton Mackall noted: "Prepare for a lesson with the 'great man.' This was most pleasant. We went to a spot beyond the windmill and I did a sketch that was principally foreground, blue flowers, mill etc."[243] The sketches were made using

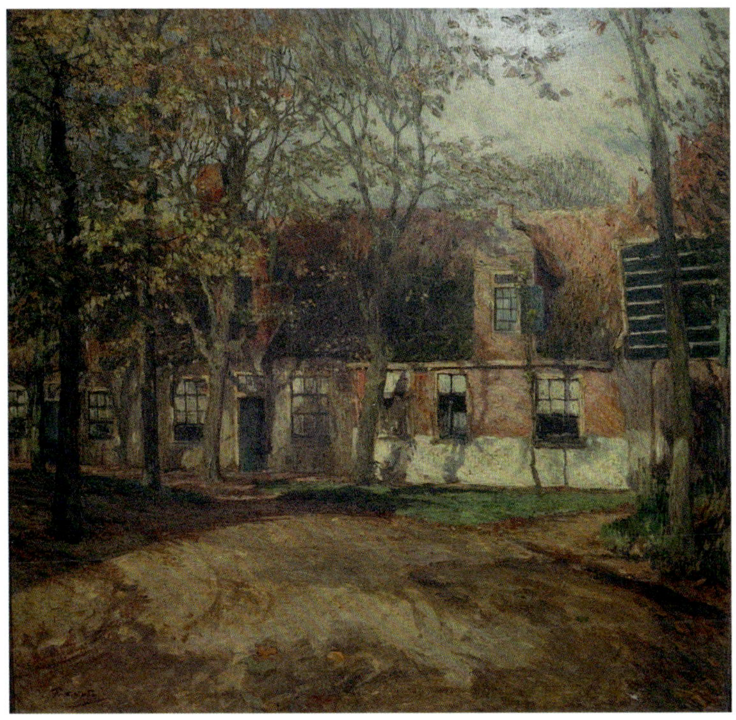

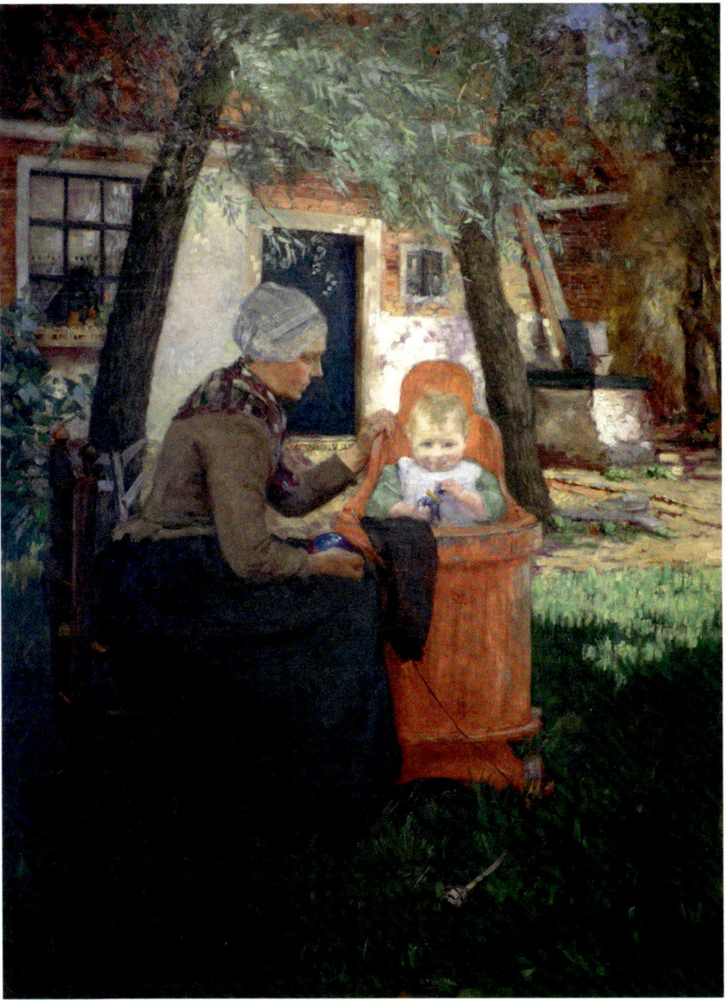

various techniques, probably both in pencil, watercolor and oil paint.[244] Working in color was a valuable addition to the lessons at the Académie Julian, where the focus was primarily on drawing. According to Alice Worthington Ball (1869-1929), sometimes the wind was so strong that the canvas had to be secured, and the artist's supplies flew around in the air.[245] To wrap up the week, the students were invited to tea at the Hitchcocks' house, where the works, techniques, and progress were once again discussed.[246]

Hitchcock, "the great man," was quite the character. He is described as an exceptionally tall – almost 6 feet 6 inches – and handsome man with regular features, black hair, a mustache, and a goatee.[247] In addition to his nickname "The Tulip," he was also dubbed "Gorgeous."[248] Hitchcock was a charmer and was sometimes called a rascal. He was always dressed in the latest fashion, walked with "the most tremendous swagger," and exuded self-assurance.[249] The ten-year-younger Gari Melchers was also described as a handsome young man, with "cool grey eyes and a fine forehead."[250] He had an optimistic and cheerful demeanor with a contagious laugh, earning him the nickname "Mad Melchie" in the Egmonds.[251] Apparently, Melchers was indifferent to comfort; especially when working, he was content with the basics.[252] Moreover, he cared little about his appearance: "his clothes were a joke," Kitty Shannon remembered.[253] Melchers was also known as an unassuming man, earning him the moniker "Modest Melchers."[254]

Melchers did not play a prominent role in the summer courses. While he would occasionally offer some words of encouragement or advice, and sometimes join the sketching lessons, his studio was off limits [see fig. 49].[255] The notable exception to this was Corinne Lawton Mackall, whom he met aboard a ship.[256] After Melchers recommended she take Hitchcock's summer course, he began giving her a few lessons, likely quite charmed by her.[257] They married a year later.[258]

 59 Florence K. Upton, *In North-Holland/ Houses on Slotweg, Egmond aan de Hoef*, 140 x 145 cm. Private collection   **60** Letta Crapo Smith, *Dirkje's First Birthday*, 1902, oil on canvas, 143.5 x 106.4 cm. Flint Institute of Arts, Gift of Mrs. Jay C. Thompson

The Success Consolidated

George Hitchcock and Gari Melchers established themselves at Egmond [...]. The soft, hazy landscape [...] offers infinitive possibilities for the artist, not to mention the quaintly picturesque inhabitants, their red-tiled cottages and the gorgeous effects to be found in the hyacinth and tulip fields

American Art News (18 February 1905)[259]

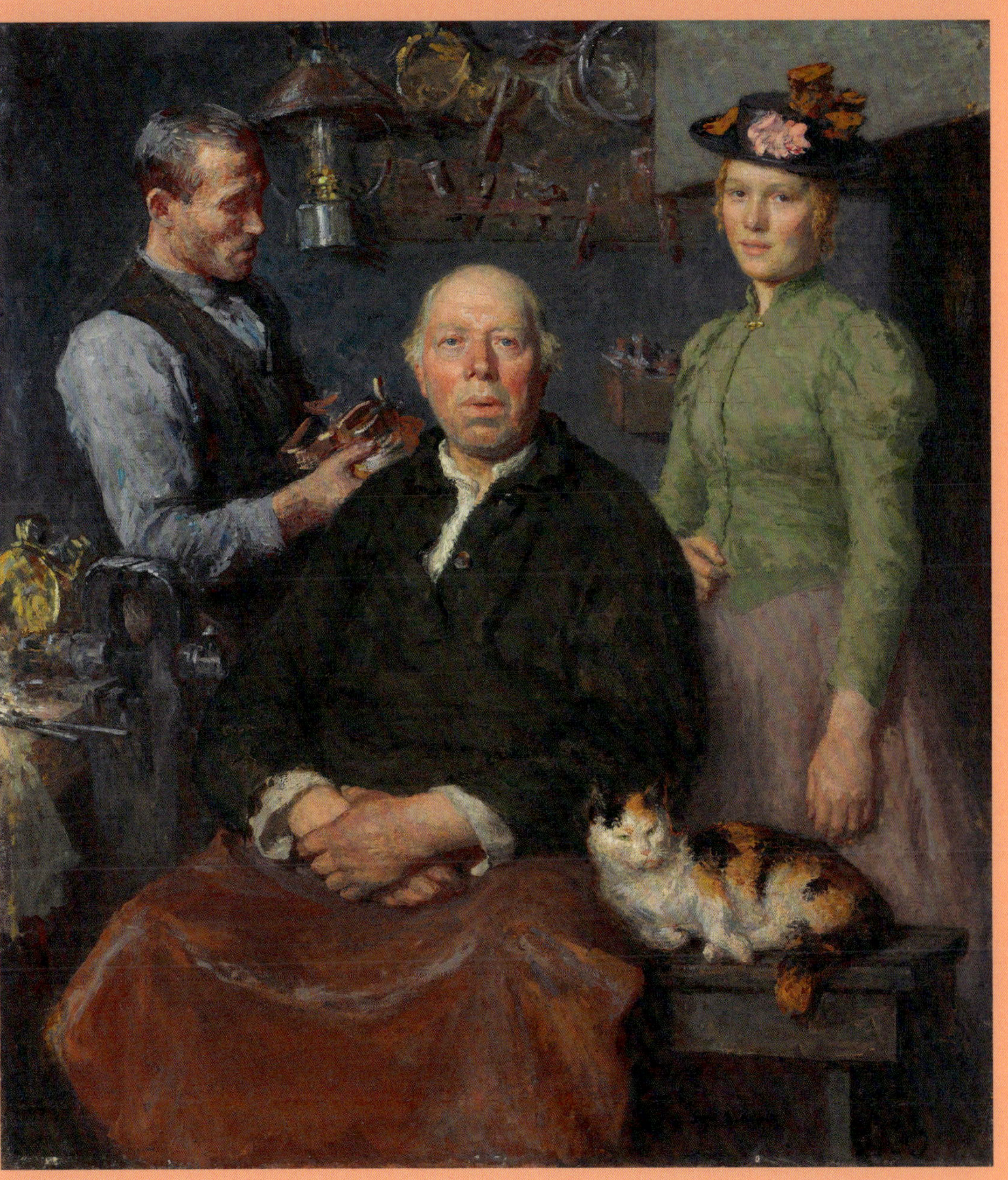

Around 1890, the three Egmonds and their residents gained international fame thanks to the paintings of George Hitchcock and Gari Melchers. Both were regular exhibitors in the United States, France, the Netherlands, Germany, and Belgium. Their careers flourished, especially that of Melchers. By the time he was 30, Melchers claimed to have won nearly every medal he could in Europe.[260]

Melchers showcased his work wherever possible, exhibiting, among other places, in Paris at the art gallery of Paul Durand-Ruel, a major promoter of the French Impressionists.[261] In Chicago, Melchers won yet another award, this time not a medal, but a 250 dollar cash prize.[262] He also remained actively involved in supporting American émigré artists. Together with Walter MacEwen and his old hometown colleague Julius Rolshoven, he served on a committee representing American artists living in Paris for the 1891 International Berlin Exhibition.[263] On this occasion, he was also awarded a Grand Diploma of Honor and had the opportunity to meet Emperor Wilhelm II personally.[264]

Hitchcock, too, achieved success, even though his 1890 Salon submission, *Une Pastorale* (A Pastoral Scene), fell short of art critic Paul Leroi's expectations.[265] Unlike Melchers – "known all over the world, except in England" – Hitchcock exhibited his work in England during the 1890s.[266] In February 1890, he presented pastel drawings in London under the title *Atmospheric Notes*, an exhibition that travelled to New York in November of

  61 Gari Melchers, *The Smithy*, oil on canvas, 146.1 x 130.8 cm. Private collection

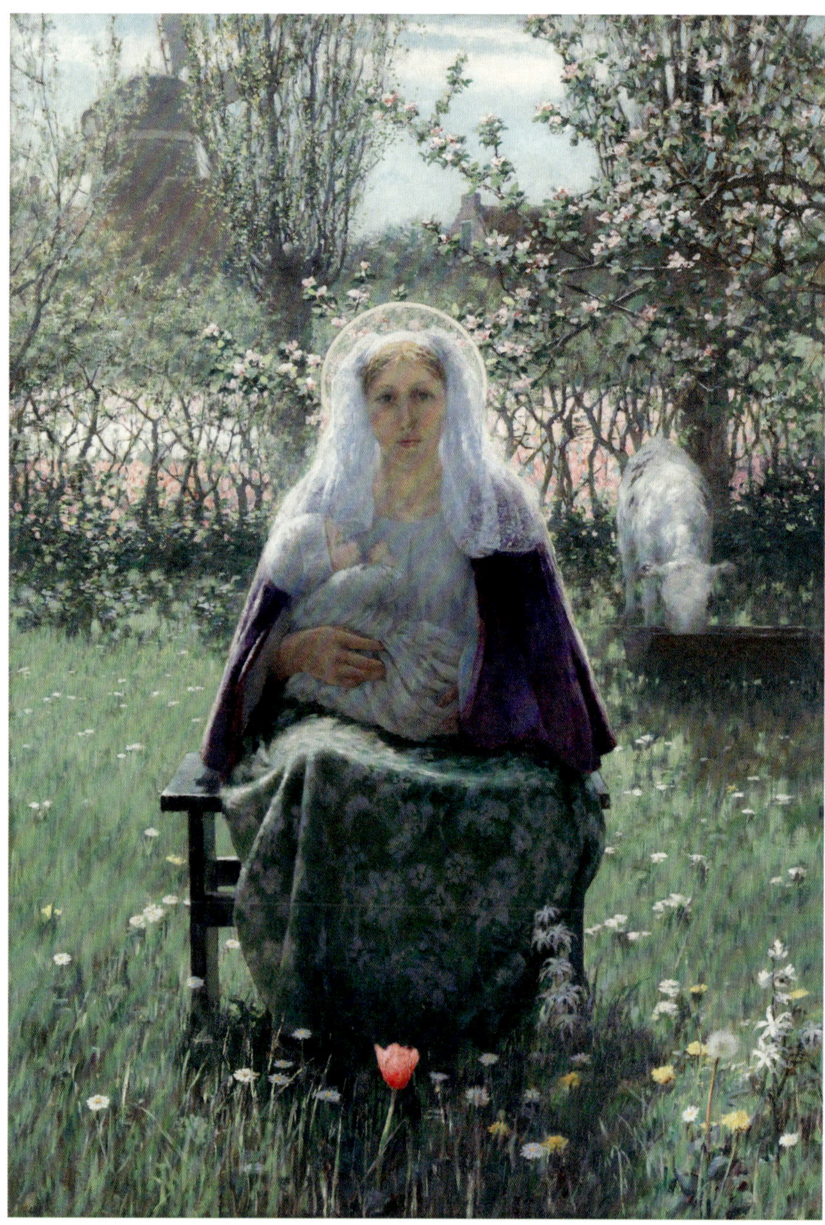

that year and was well received. He was praised as an artist with a deep appreciation for the beauty of nature.[267] Additionally, in December 1890, he exhibited paintings at the English branch of the renowned Goupil Galleries[268]

One of these works, described by a journalist as an *unfinished* painting, titled *The Manger*, once again featured a Madonna with Child in an enclosed garden.[269] The completed painting is most likely *The Blessed Mother*, in which Hitchcock not only changed the title but also altered some elements in the background [fig. 62].[270] The artist painted a serene Dutch mother and child on a sunny spring day.[271] Visible in the background are a field of tulips in bloom and a windmill. In this multivalent painting, Hitchcock also referenced biblical stories: behind the young woman's head, a halo glows, the young

bullock at the manger alludes to the birth of Jesus (the ox and the crib), the blooming apple tree symbolizes the lost Eden, and the prominent red tulip represents the cup of sorrow. Hitchcock seems to have also intentionally included Drooping Star of Bethlehem flowers in the right foreground.[272]

Two years later, Hitchcock canceled a show at the same art gallery upon learning that an exhibition by the highly successful James McNeill Whistler (1834-1903) was scheduled just before his own [fig. 63].[273] According to correspondence between Whistler and his wife Beatrix, Hitchcock was furious. Hitchcock is reported to have told the writer Oscar Wilde, "My things won't stand a chance after a Whistler exhibition."[274] Nevertheless, his work was certainly appreciated. Its poor

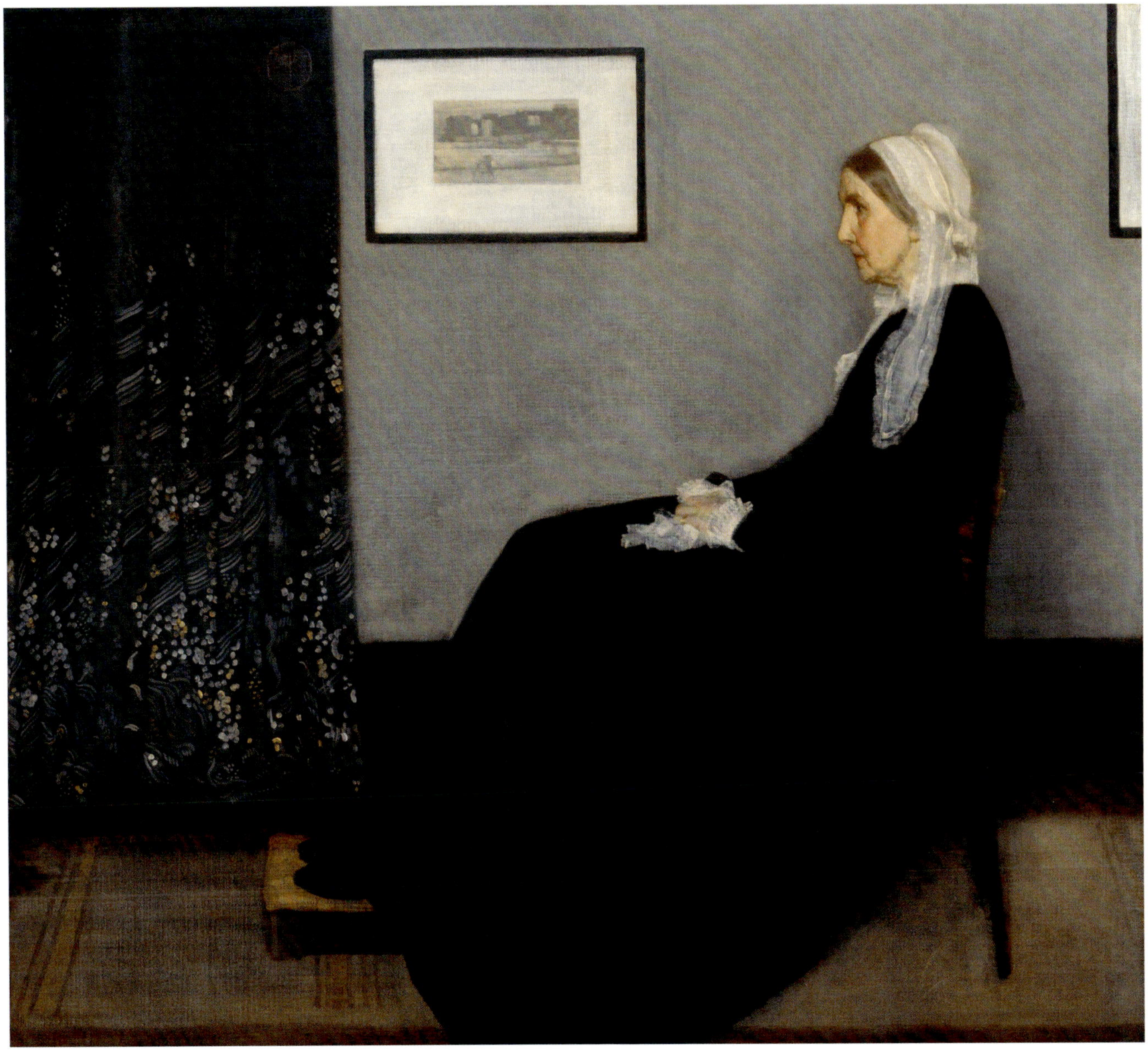

placement high up on the wall notwithstanding, *Maternity*, sold
for an impressive 5000 dollars in 1891 [see fig. 43].[275] The
other painting, *The Scarecrow* – a farm girl in the middle of
a wheat field – was singled out as "the most beautiful canvas
in the galleries" [fig. 64].[276]

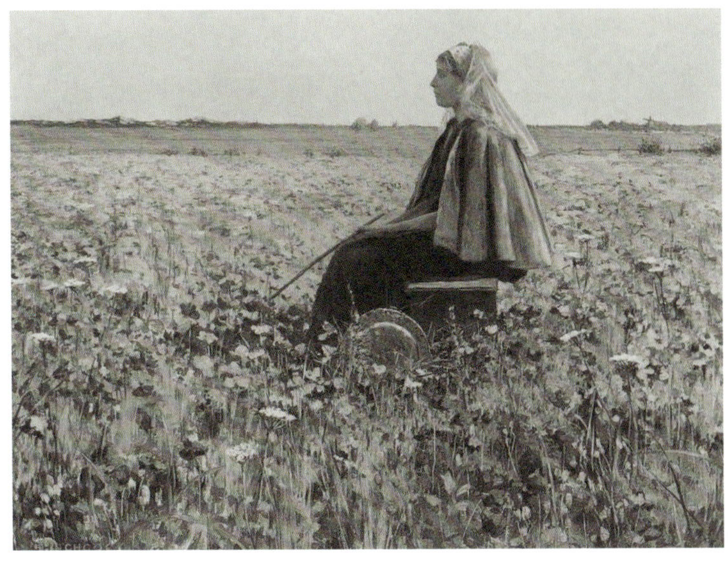

63 James Mc Neill Whistler, *Arrangement in Gray and Black: Portrait of the Artist's Mother*, 1871, oil on canvas, 144.3 x 162.5 cm. Musée d'Orsay, Paris
64 George Hitchcock, *The Scarecrow*, ca. 1892, dimensions and present whereabouts unknown

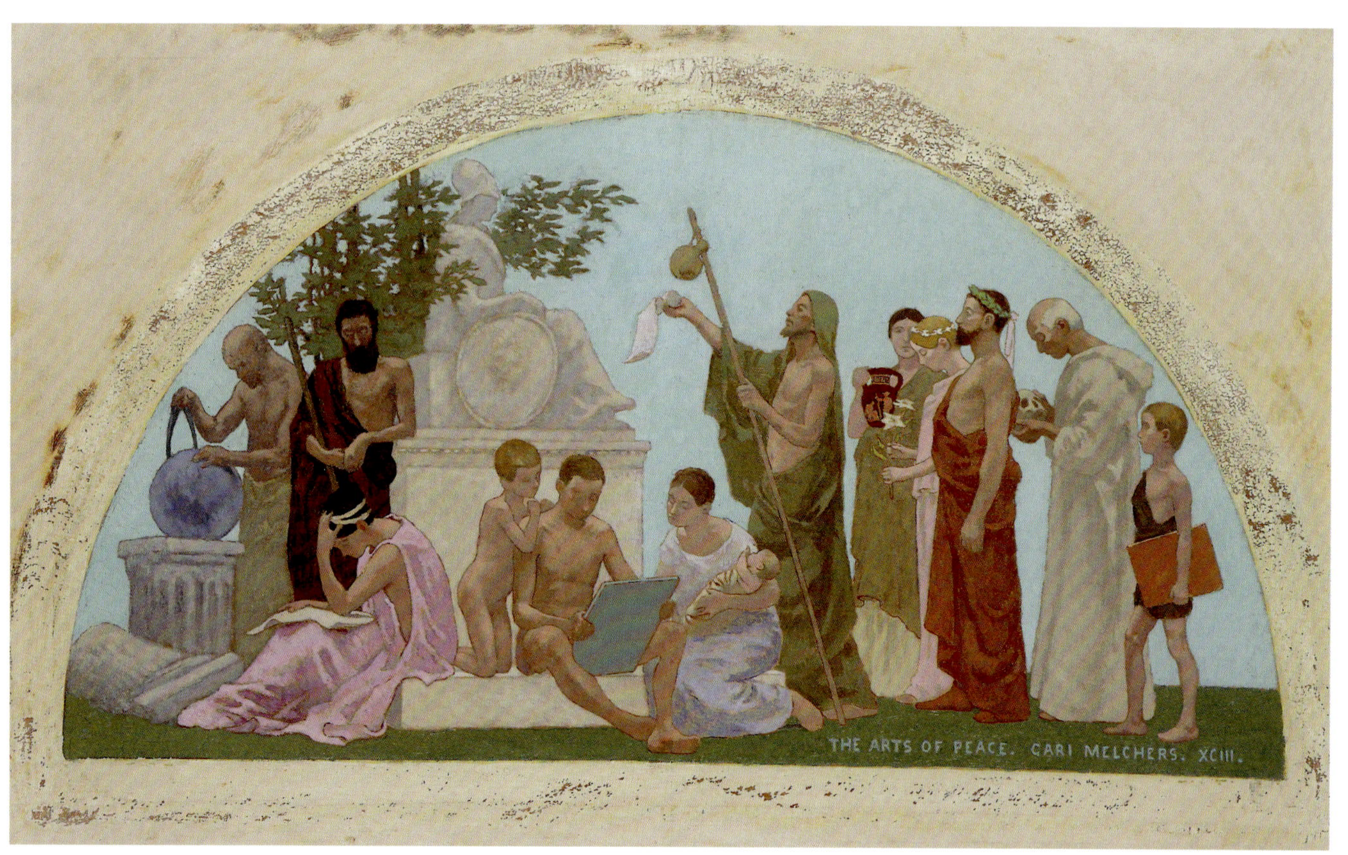

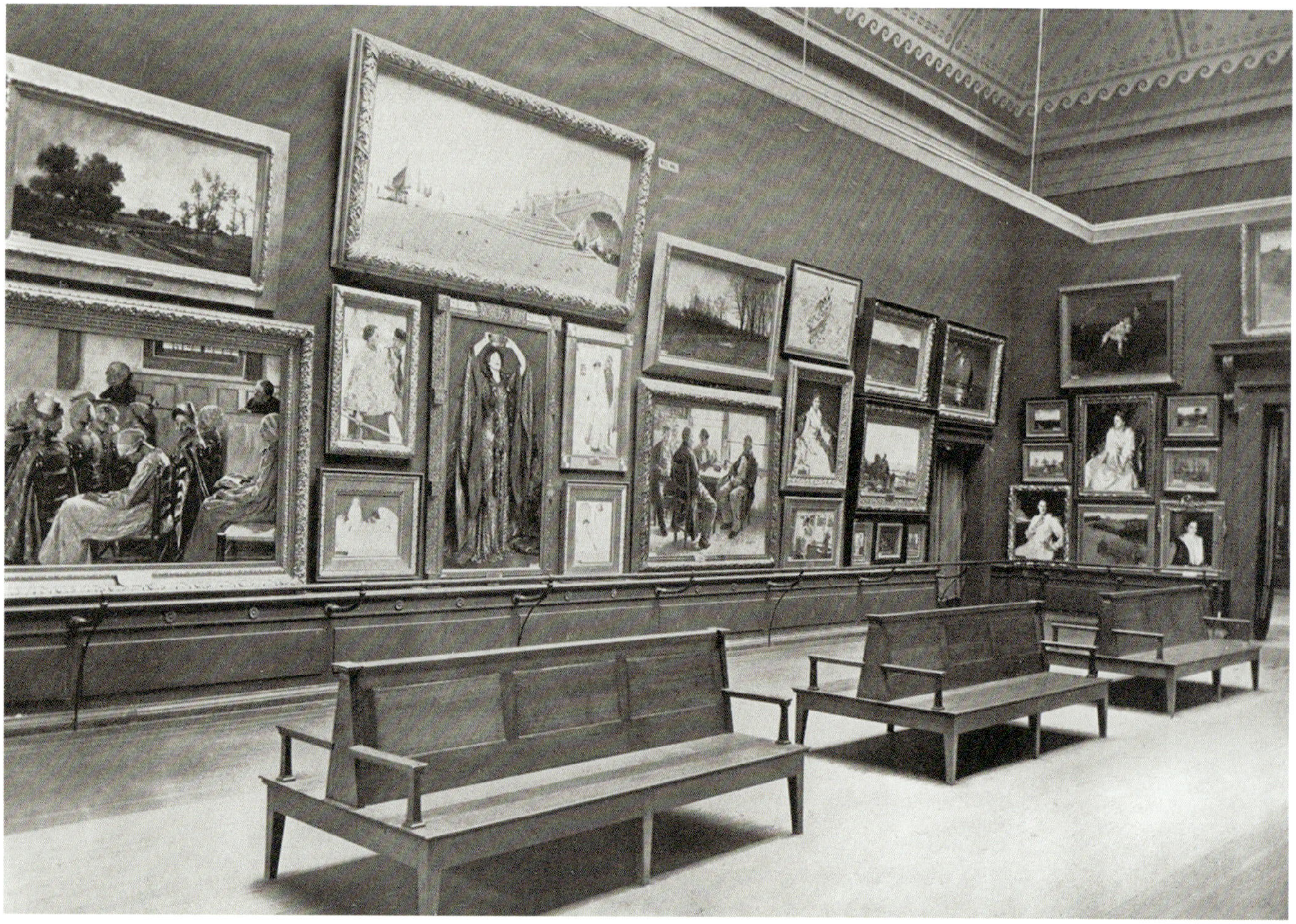

65 Gari Melchers, Design for *The Arts of Peace*, 1893, oil on canvas, 38.5 x 73.6 cm. Minneapolis Institute of Art, Gift of Lucile and Stanley Slocum
66 One of the exhibition galleries at The World's Columbian Exposition, Chicago 1893, with various works by Gari Melchers

The World's Fair in the "White City" of Chicago

The artists' established reputation led to a special request: according to *The American Register for Paris and the Continent*, Hitchcock and Melchers were asked to provide decorations for one of the exhibition pavilions at The World's Columbian Exposition in Chicago.[277] Melchers indeed painted two enormous murals for the pavilion dedicated to industry and the fine arts: *The Arts of War* and *The Arts of Peace*. Contrary to his usual style, he executed the decorations in the manner of his 36-year-older friend Pierre-Cécile Puvis de Chavanne (1824-1898), that is as fairly flat and delicate in tone [fig. 65].[278] The subjects of both murals – in *The Arts of Peace*, homage is paid to the gathering of knowledge – bear no direct relation to Melchers' realism or the Egmonds. Other decorations were painted by Walter MacEwen, but to date, Hitchcock is not known to have contributed.[279] Both Melchers and MacEwen, however, were among the fifteen artists who created decorations for the new Library of Congress two years later in 1895.[280]

The World's Columbian Exposition in Chicago was held in 1893 to mark the 400th anniversary of Columbus' "discovery" of America. Due to the extensive use of white stucco in the construction of the classical buildings across the vast exhibition grounds, the area earned the nickname "The White City." The organizers aimed to showcase America's development since the "discovery" of the continent. In the field of the arts, juries were established in various cities, including New York, Boston, Philadelphia, and Chicago, as well as in Paris, Rome, and Munich. They ultimately selected 1024 paintings and 160 sculptures by 521 artists. Melchers, who was also a member of this jury, was therefore not eligible for awards. He exhibited seven paintings in Chicago, including a *Portrait of Mrs. H.* (Henrietta Hitchcock). The high quality of this work subsequently landed him many more portrait commissions.[281] Additionally, Melchers showcased works such as *The Sermon*, which by then was part of the Potter Palmer collection, *The Communion*, *The Pilots*, and *Skaters* [see figs. 29, 46, 36, 66 and 67].[282]

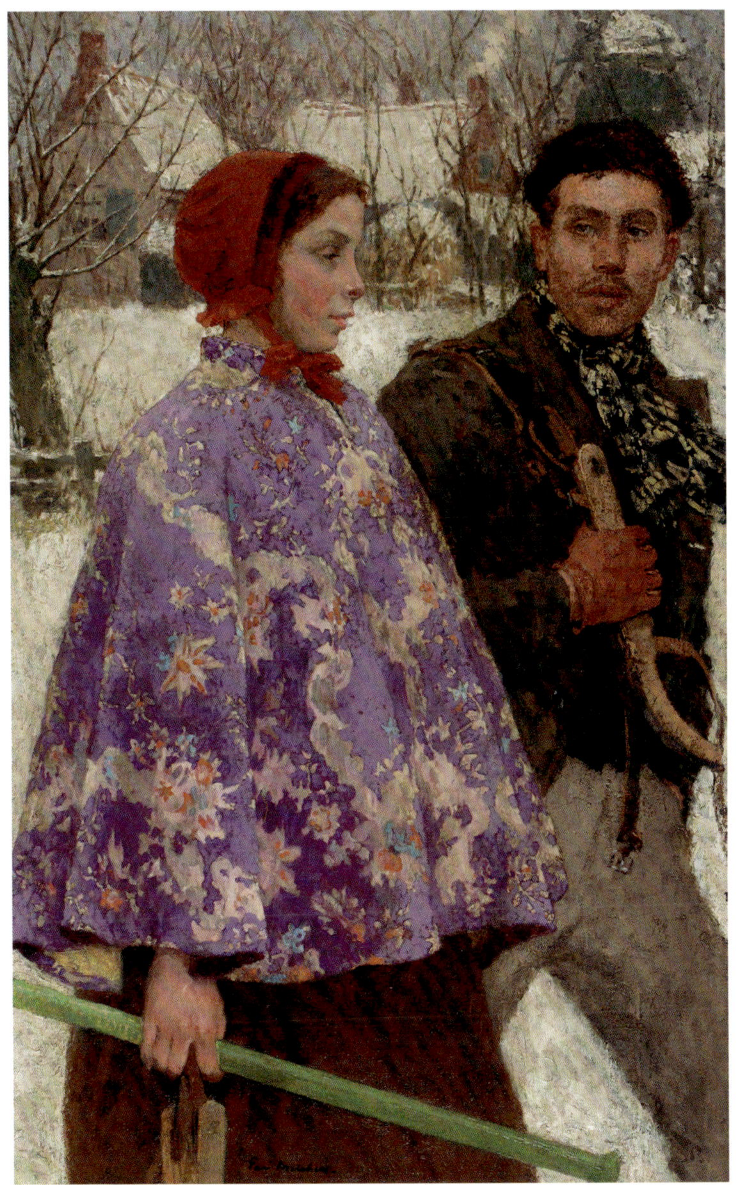

After a long absence, Hitchcock set foot again on American soil, submitting two of his masterpieces: *Tulip Fields* and *The Scarecrow*, winning yet another prize [see figs. 34 and 64].[283] Just like the previous year at The Royal Academy in London, the latter painting was particularly well-received: "In 'The Scarecrow' […] Mr. Hitchcock indulges his love of the quaint costumes, glowing fields, and elusive atmosphere of Holland. The poppies are nearly ready to harvest, and the seeds are to be guarded from the birds – a task which could not be performed in a manner more picturesque, or more inviting to the eye of the artist."[284]

   67 Gari Melchers, *Skaters*, ca. 1892, oil on canvas, 110 x 70 cm. Pennsylvania Academy of the Fine Arts, Philadelphia, Joseph E. Temple Fund

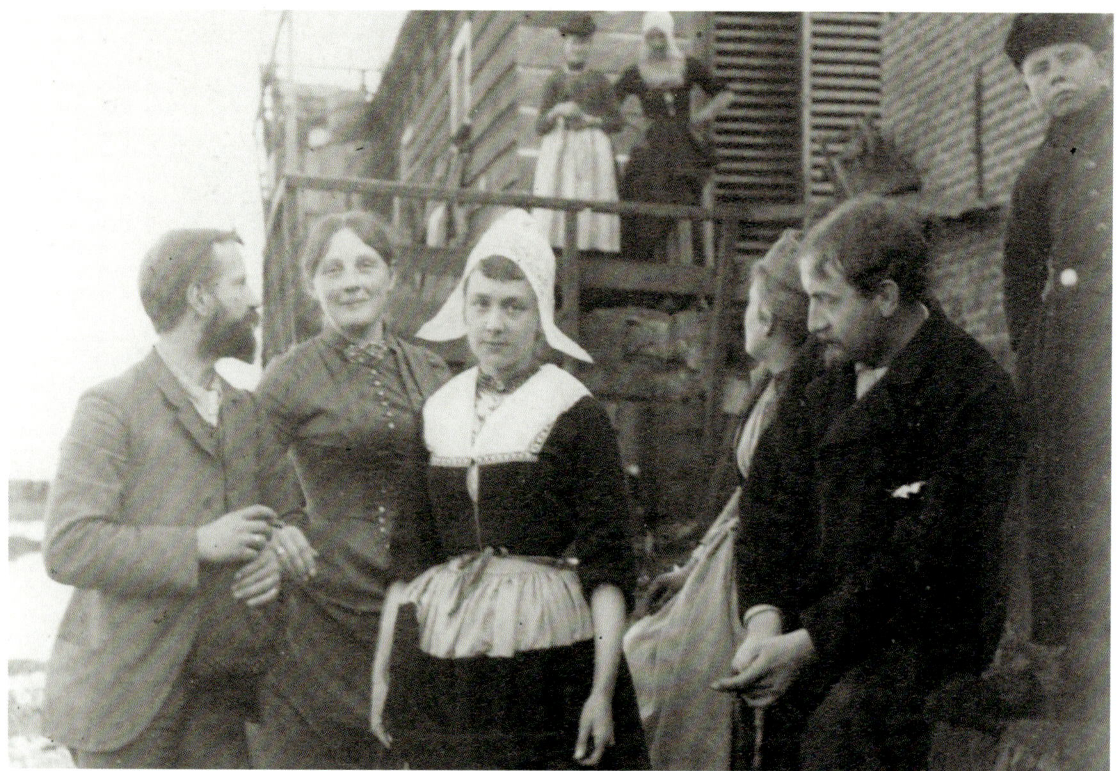

Following the exhibition in London, the girl in the faded red cape standing in a wheat field colored red by a multitude of poppies in *The Scarecrow*, was described as a "Zeeland farm girl."[285] This characterization is unsurprising, given the distinctive elements of her attire – the long veil cap and the cone-shaped ear irons – both of which were typical of Zeeland's traditional dress rather than that of Egmond.[286] Hitchcock and Melchers did not limit themselves to the clothing and objects from the three Egmonds for inspiration. In the late 1880s and 1890s, they explored different regions of the Netherlands, sometimes together, sometimes separately, accompanied by students or friends like Shannon [fig. 68].[287] Along the way, they bought various costumes and headgear, later dressing their models in these outfits. This clothing was stored in an old wooden chest.[288] The shoulder cape worn by Melchers' model for *Skaters* was likely purchased during one of their trips. With its beautiful decorative pattern, the cape appeared in multiple works by both Melchers and Hitchcock – quite understandably as they shared a studio on the dunes for years and often used the same models.[289] These excursions also included visits to museums and art galleries, as well as long hours spent browsing around bric-à-brac shops in search of trinkets and Delftware pottery.[290] The "Zeeland farm girl" in *The Scarecrow* could therefore have been based on studies Hitchcock made in Zeeland, but it could just as well have been painted in Egmond, with a model posing in Zeeland clothing.

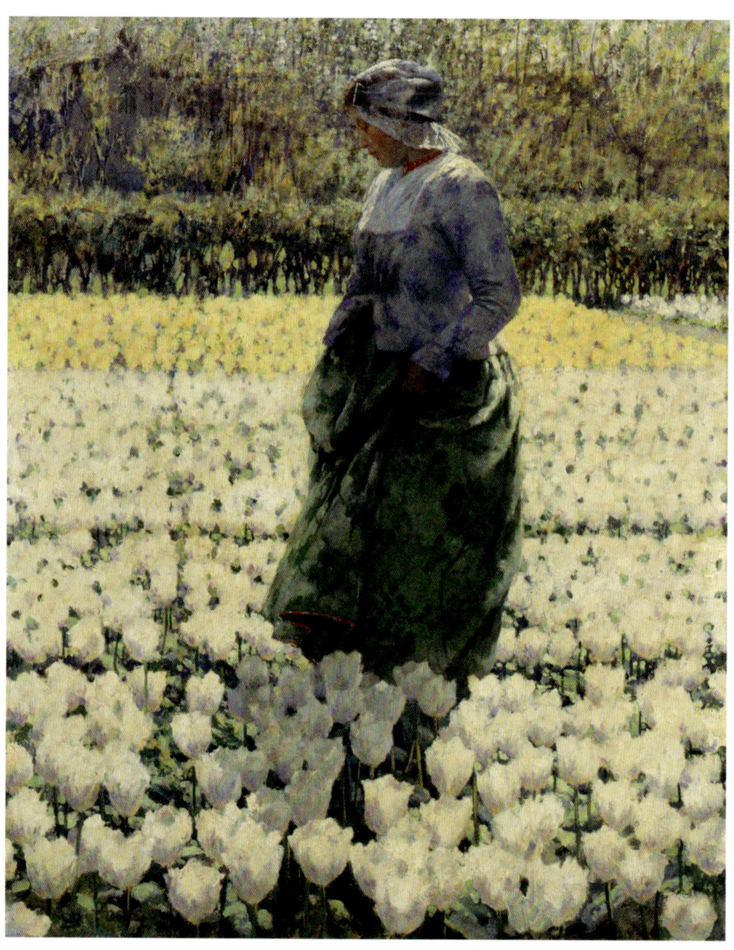

68 George Hitchcock and Gari Melchers in Volendam. Photo Gari Melchers Home and Studio, University of Mary Washington, Fredericksburg
69 George Hitchcock, *Among the Tulips*, ca. 1895, oil on canvas, 111.5 x 89.5 cm. Albertinum, Dresden

"Only that which has character is truly beautiful"

The models for Hitchcock's and Melchers' paintings were typically drawn from the local population of the Egmond villages. In the third article he published in *Scribner's Magazine* about picturesque Holland, Hitchcock devoted considerable attention to the models and their clothing.[291] Unsurprisingly, he was particularly captivated by young Dutch girls with pearl-like complexions, blonde hair, and blue eyes – especially when depicted wearing lace caps against a scenic backdrop, such as a bulb field or a dune landscape [fig. 69].[292] He also thought the clothing of North Sea fishermen was very quaint.[293] They generally sported a simple red shirt under a well-worn black smock with shorter sleeves, paired with either red baize breeches or black trousers. However, it was mainly Melchers who portrayed fishermen in his paintings [figs. 70 and 71]. Unlike Hitchcock, Melchers believed that beauty was not found solely in comely young women but also in distinctive faces. As he put it, "Only that which has character is truly beautiful."[294] Although Hitchcock wrote that the most striking subjects could still be found in the rural, somewhat isolated communities of fishermen and farmers, neither he nor Melchers often depicted their subjects engaged in physically demanding labor, such as harvesting or haymaking.

Many villagers served as models for the artists, and some of their names have even come down to us.[295] Several women posed for Melchers' masterpiece *The Sermon* [see fig. 29]. The painting vividly captures traditional daily Egmond attire, including a West Frisian headcovering, a *hul* or lace bonnet with or without the *hullehoedje*, a straw hat with a fabric-covered brim. A few women wear an *oorijzermuts*, a cap with a pleated back.[296] Melchers' seems to have been unaware that bonnets were mandatory on Sundays, and so his sitters shown wearing daily headgear would not have posed for him on the day of rest.[297] The Bult family, owners of Het Slot van den Hoef Inn, where Melchers stayed for many years, frequently posed for him. For *The Wedding*, painted in the Slot Chapel, Maartje Bult stood for the bride and the contractor Jac Schuit for the groom [fig. 75].[298] Additionally, Chris Schuit, the Veenhuizen family, and the real-life Reverend Claassen were asked by Melchers to pose as witnesses and other attendees of the staged wedding. Hitchcock often used his maid, Dirkje, as a model. Kitty Shannon recalled: "Dereke [sic] […] was very beautiful. Gorgeous painted her often. She looked just like a Madonna from an early Italian painting."[299]

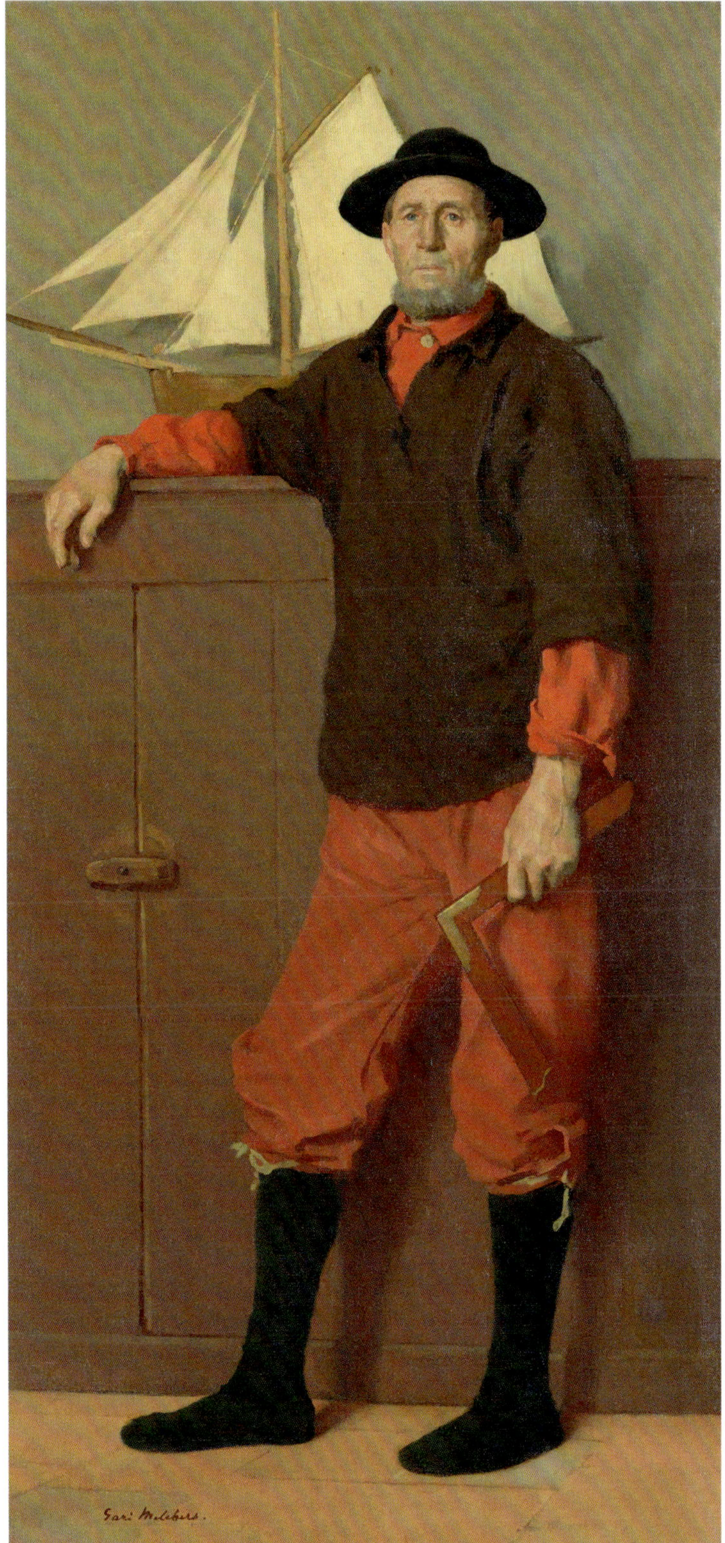

  70 Gari Melchers, *Dutch Shipwright*, ca. 1895, oil on canvas, 205 x 100 cm. Albertinum, Dresden

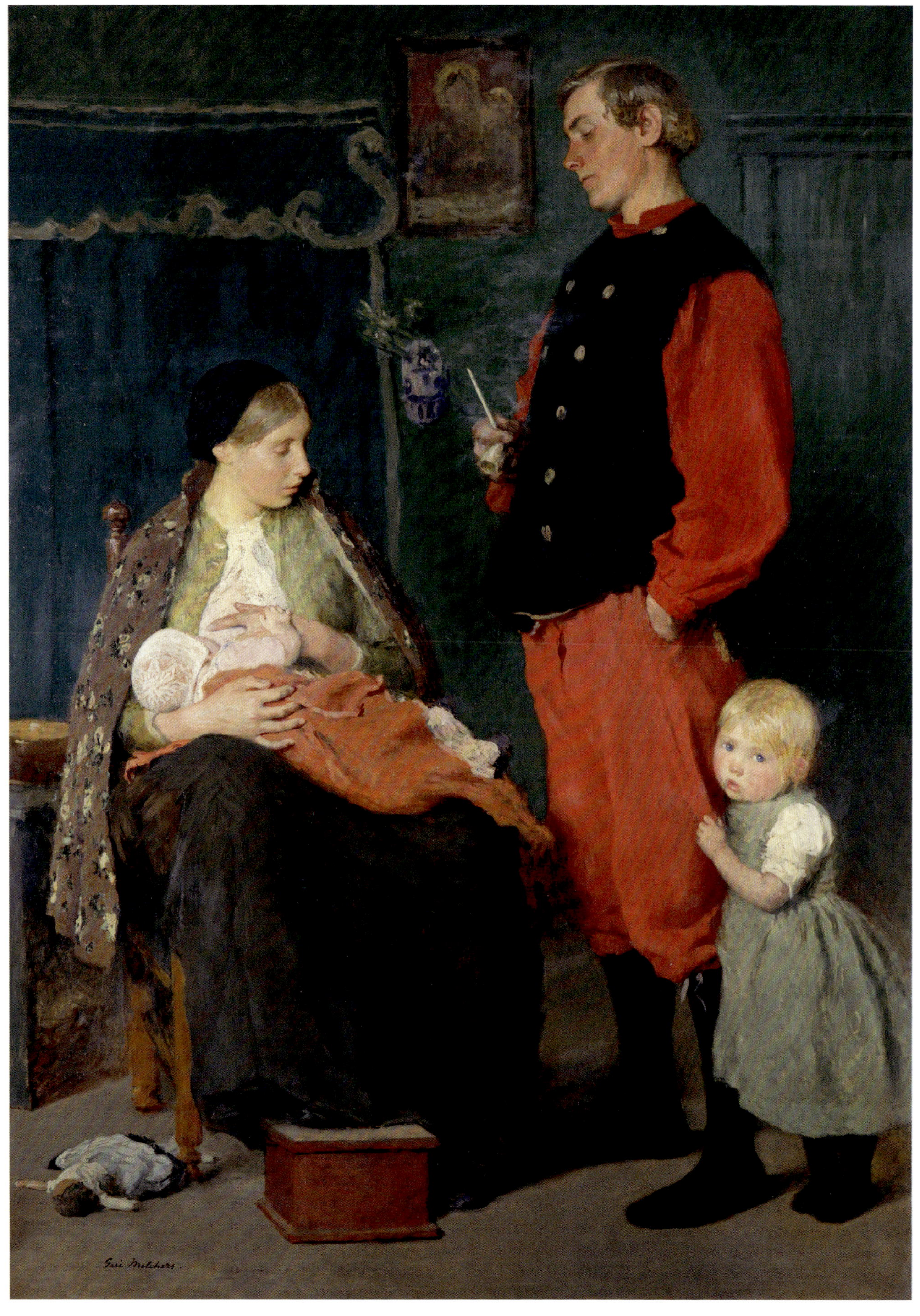

71 Gari Melchers, *The Family*, ca. 1895–96, oil on canvas, 190 x 135.5 cm. Staatliche Museen zu Berlin, Nationalgalerie

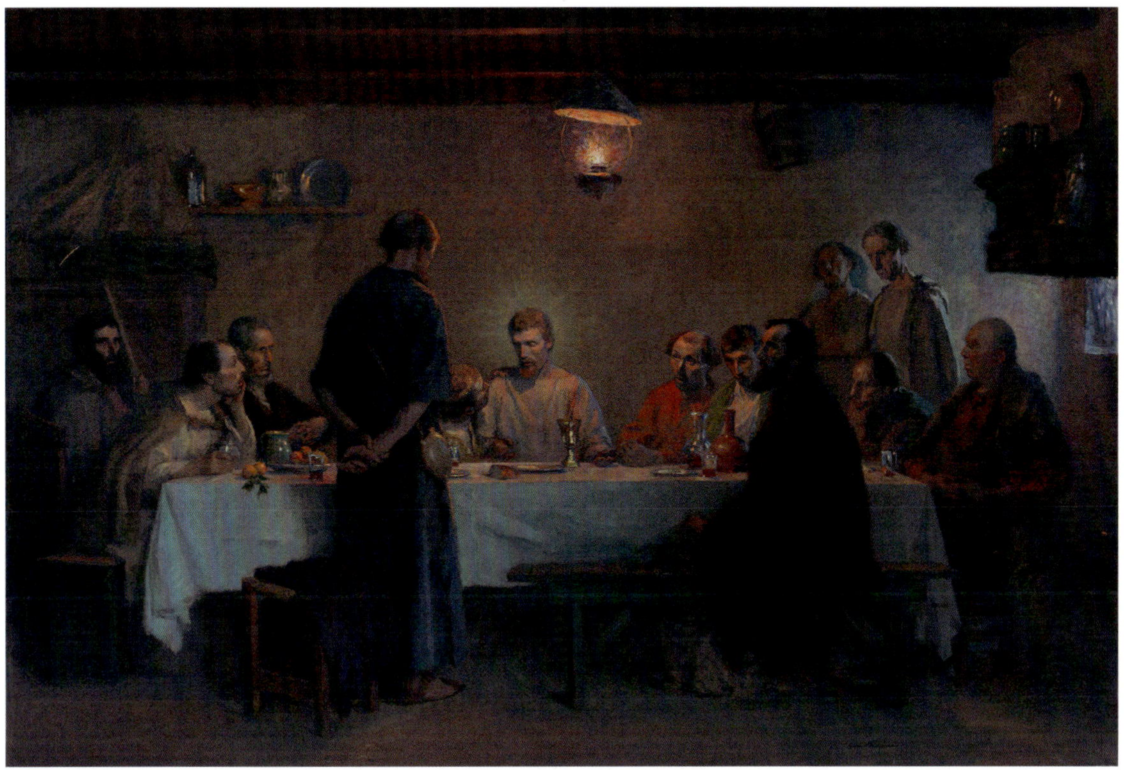

For *The Last Supper*, Melchers reportedly faced some difficulties finding models for his *tableau vivant* painting sessions in his studio at Torensduin [fig. 72].[300] Jacob Stam, whom he wanted to have pose as Judas, refused to "betray the Lord" for seven *stuivers*. However, he was willing to model as Peter, earning him the eponymous nickname. Jan Visser, in the guise of Jesus, became known as *Onze Heer* (Our Lord).[301] Allegedly, Melchers had initially offered the role to the poacher Albert Wijker which, however, he declined, believing himself unworthy of the part.[302] Another challenge for Melchers and Hitchcock was working around their models' daily routines. As Corinne Melchers wrote to her mother: "Well last week G's models all went off fishing so he had to stop the big picture."[303]

The seven *stuivers* (35 cents) reportedly offered for posing were likely a welcome supplement to the villagers' income. Around after a long day of hard work, while a skilled laborer, such as a cigar maker, made eight to nine guilders for a 60-hour workweek.[304] Children, it is said, were rewarded with a chocolate bar for posing.[305]

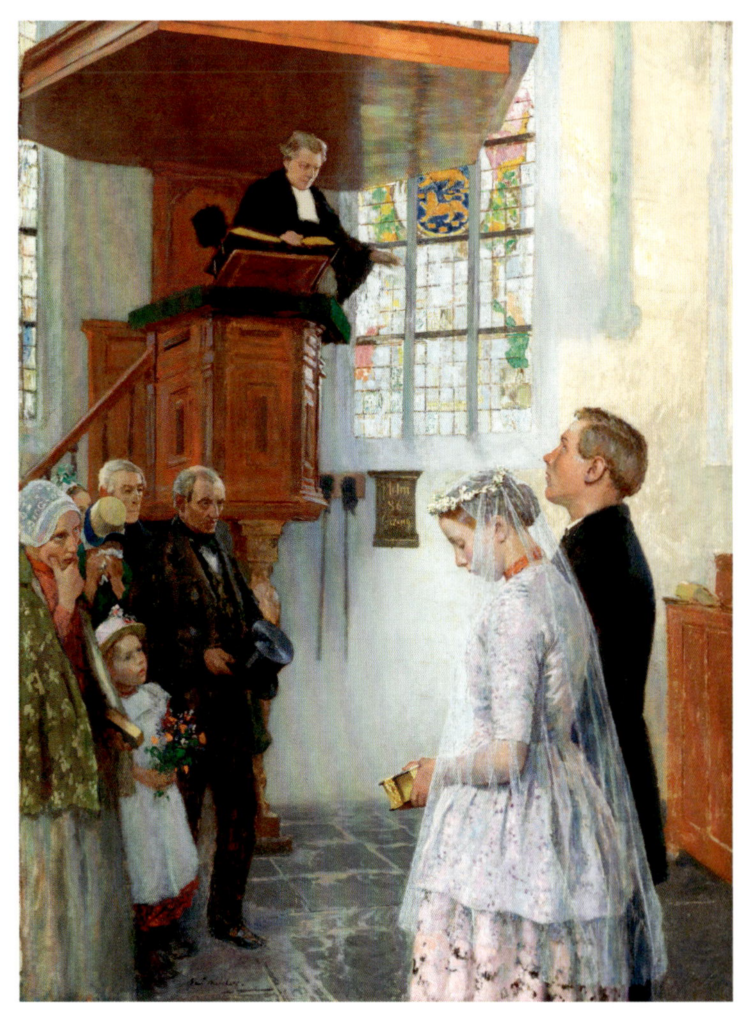

72 Gari Melchers, *The Last Supper*, ca. 1900, oil on canvas, 248.9 x 353.1 cm. Virginia Museum of Fine Arts, Richmond, Bequest of Mrs. Corinne Lawton Melchers
73 Gari Melchers, *The Wedding*, ca. 1900, oil on canvas, 114.3 x 86.4 cm. Detroit Institute of Arts, Gift of Edward Chandler Walker

[...] he spends a couple of afternoons a week, driving in his cart and alighting for two or three hours to make a charming little thing – and really they are charming

Schuijlenburg

The sum of 4000 guilders that Hitchcock paid in May 1893 for the seventeenth-century Schuijlenburg Estate at 292 Herenweg in Egmond aan den Hoef, along with its accompanying land (over one hectare [2.47 acres]), must have seemed staggering to most local residents [fig. 74].[306] In a letter to an old classmate, Hitchcock wrote: "Last year [...] I left the studio at Egmond Zee & purchased an old, old house a mile or so back from the sea, amid fine old trees with a large pack & some land. [...] The house is small but I have built on a large studio & have stabling for six horses with only two good ones in it."[307] In addition to these two carriage horses, Hitchcock owned a stagecoach, which he used – sometimes accompanied by friends – to travel throughout Holland.[308] He also entered his horses in harness races, likely at the urging of Shannon, who had begun training one of them.[309]

Schuijlenburg became an important gathering place for Hitchcock's students. On Sunday afternoons, they, along with their chaperones, were regularly invited for tea. Lawton Mackall's mother wrote to her family: "The H's [...] have a dream of an old house - & fine carriage. They like style. They are very kind, but in the past have put up with poverty & discomforts for art's sake."[310] That period of poverty was by then far behind Hitchcock. Following a visit to Schuijlenburg, Petersen-Angeln wrote that he and his wife had been treated to a seven- or eight-course dinner, all served on fine English porcelain. According to Petersen-Angeln, Hitchcock was even referred to in the Egmond area as "the knight of the castle."[311]

Dutch bulb fields proved to be a highly profitable subject for Hitchcock. In 1904, Corinne Melchers wrote to her mother: "George is furiously busy painting them [...]. He calculated for Gari's benefit the other day and announced that, making two sketches a day as he could do, at the end of a year his income would be 180,000 dollars and that is too much for any man, more than his share! So the consequence is that he spends a couple of afternoons a week, driving in his cart and alighting for two or three hours to make a charming little thing – and really they are charming" [fig. 75].[312] By his own account, Hitchcock produced 800 paintings of Dutch bulb fields, selling 299 of them.[313]

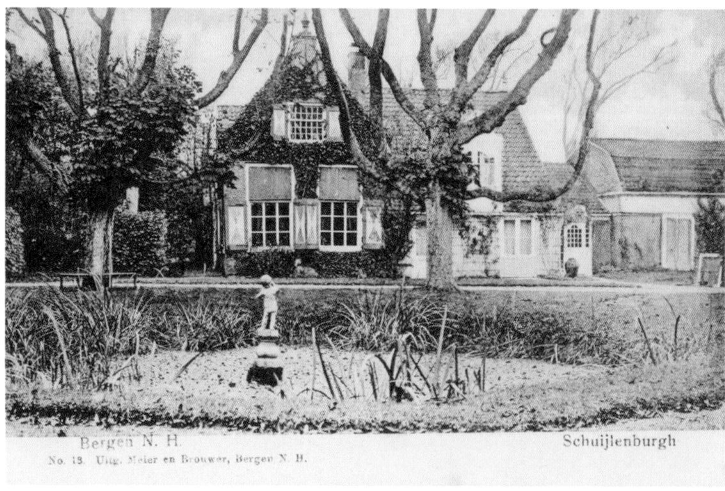

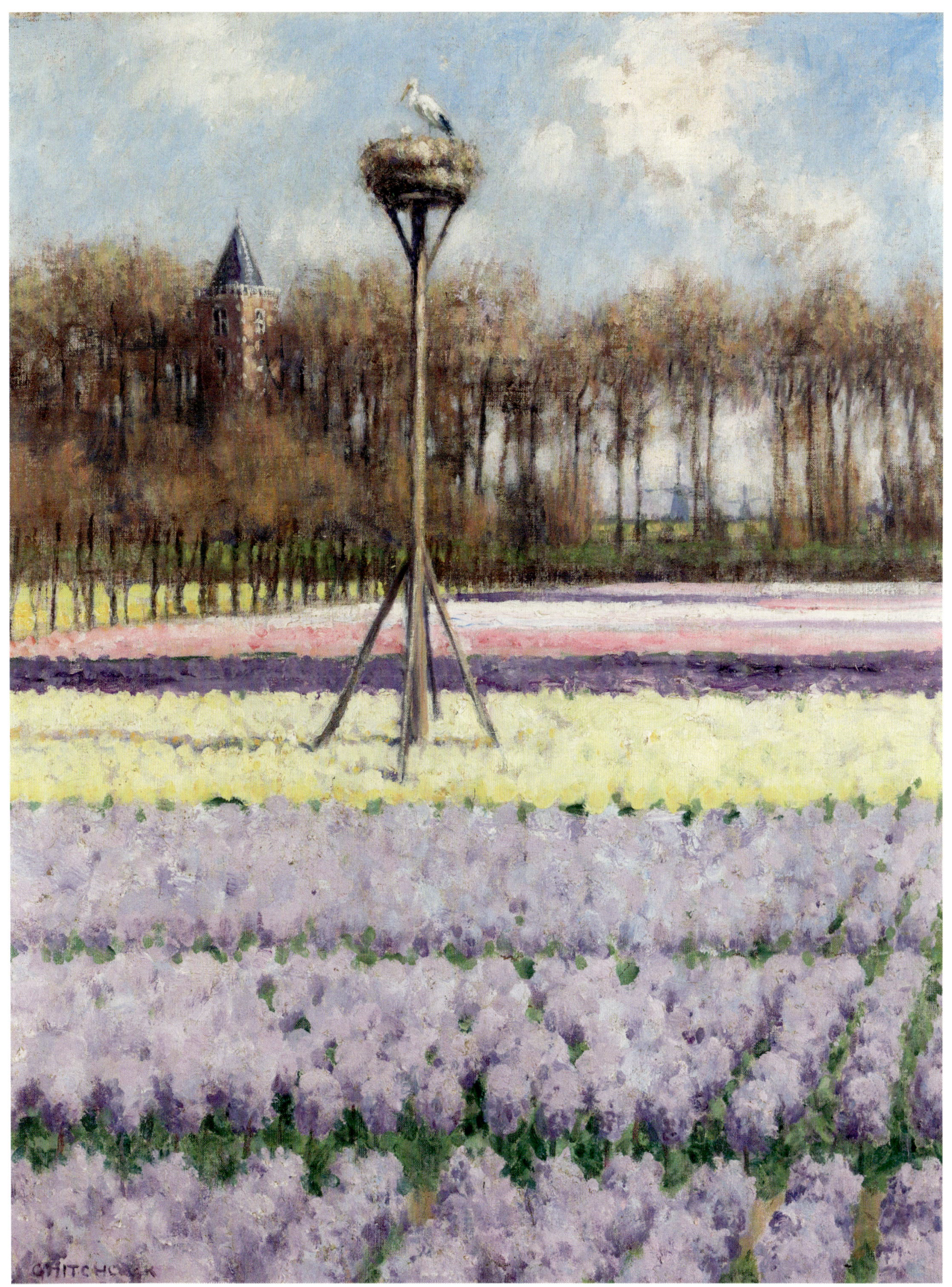

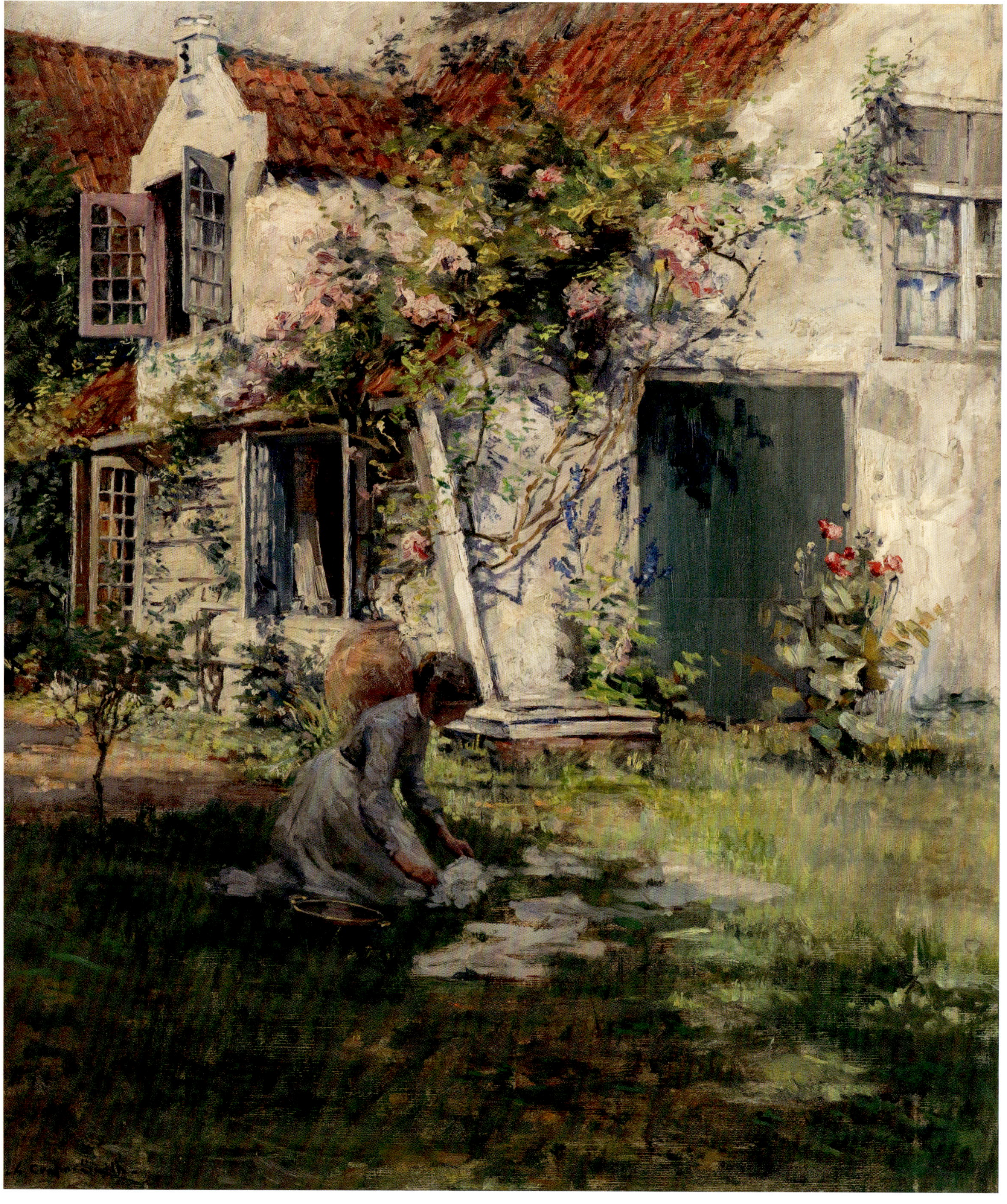

76 Letta Crapo-Smith, *Home of Madame H.,* 1909, oil on canvas, 62.5 x 54.6 cm. Thomas H. and Diane DeMell Jacobsen Ph.D. Foundation, Florida

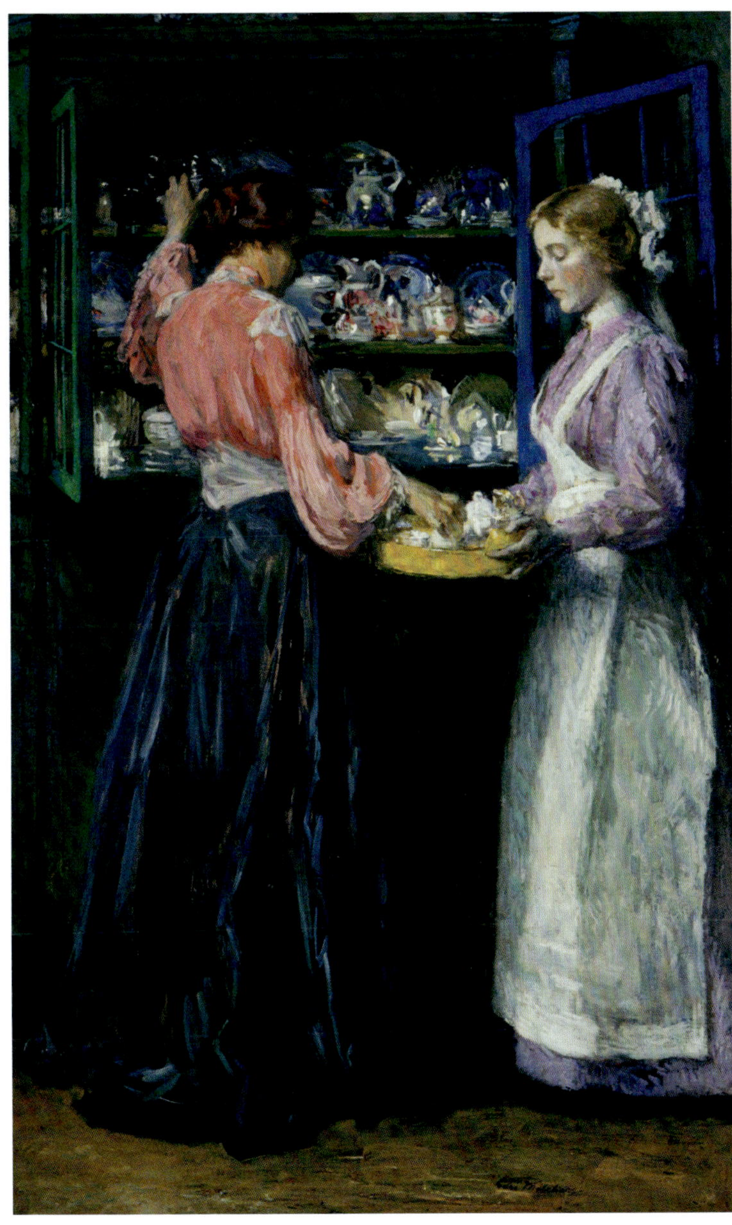

Dubbed 'Miggles' for unknown reasons, Henrietta Hitchcock had trained several fishergirls as housemaids, including the aforementioned Dirkje.[314] In addition, Hitchcock employed a cook named Mensie, a coachman, and people who maintained the garden. Mensie's younger sister, Kierie Blok, was also trained as a housemaid and was probably painted by Letta Crapo-Smith while bleaching laundry in the garden of Schuijlenburg [fig. 76].[315] For *The China Closet* [figs. 77 and 78], Melchers – who of course also spent time with his friends at Schuijlenburg – painted Henrietta Hitchcock and her housemaid Kierie Blok based on a photograph.[316] Later, he would also begin using Hitchcock's studio at Schuijlenburg.

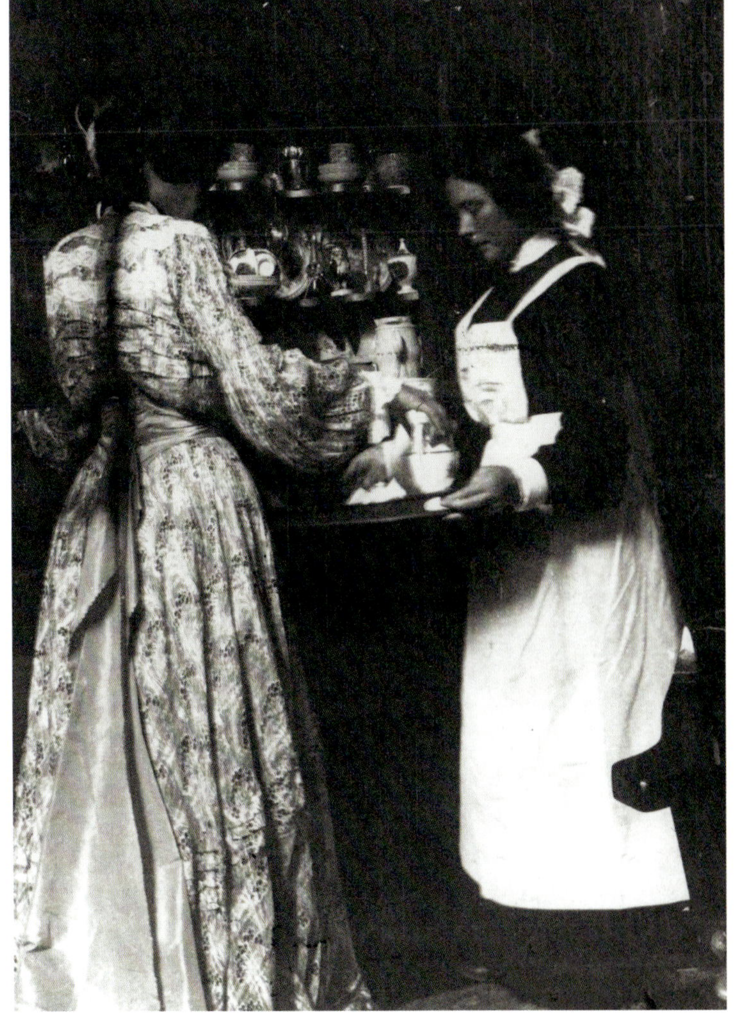

 77 Gari Melchers, *The China Closet*, ca. 1904, oil on canvas, 127 x 76.2 cm. Gari Melchers Home and Studio, University of Mary Washington, Fredericksburg
78 Photo for *The China Closet*. Gari Melchers Home and Studio, University of Mary Washington, Fredericksburg

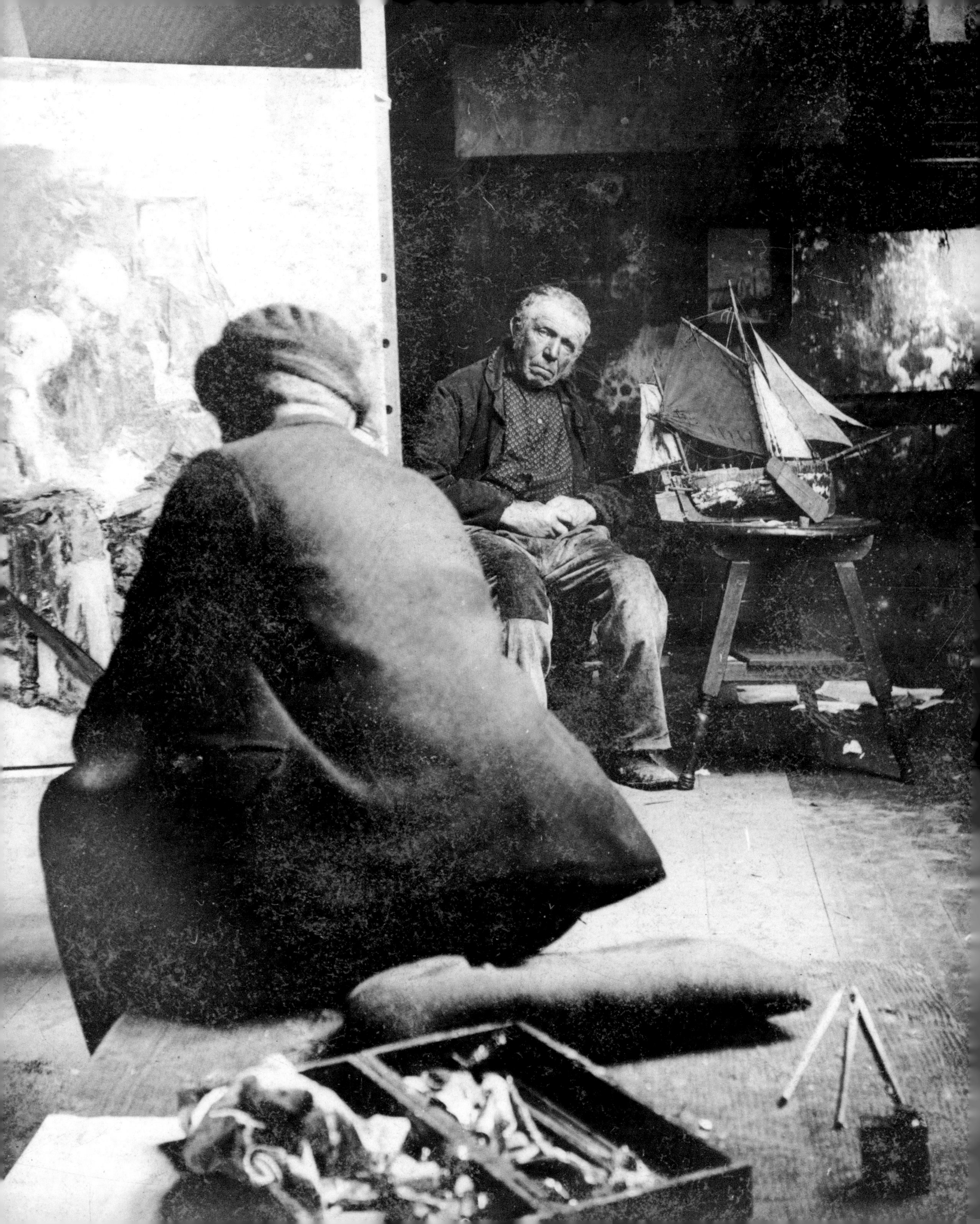

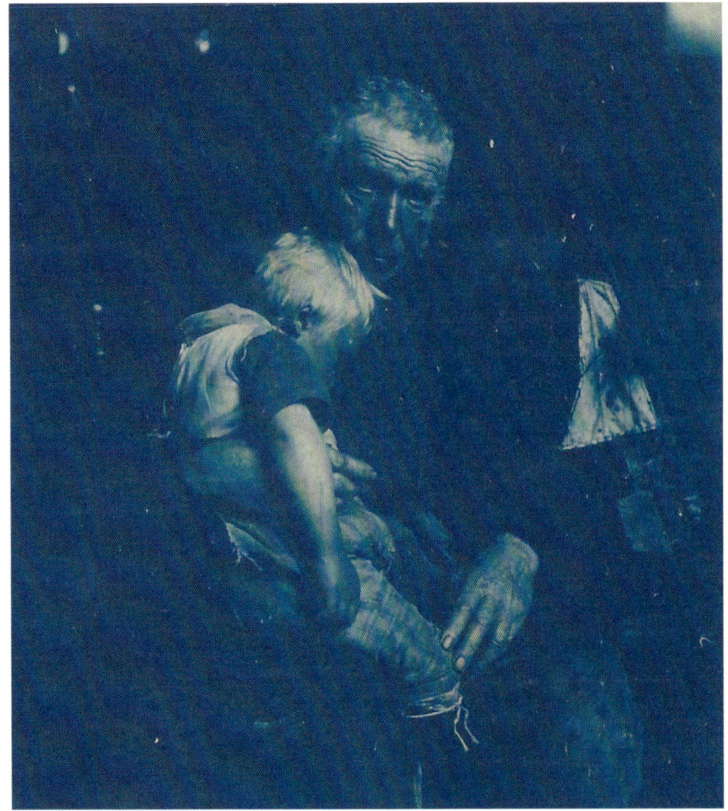

"A dozen lines on the back of an envelope"

Partly due to the purchase of Schuijlenburg and, of course, because of his art classes, Hitchcock spent more time in the Egmonds during the summer than Melchers, although he did occasionally summer in Spain or Italy.[317] Melchers, on the other hand, had access to several studios in various large cities and was much less frequently in Egmond, but he did visit to find inspiration for his paintings.[318]

The composition for *Old and Young* was created in the Egmond aan Zee studio [figs. 79 and 80]. Incidentally, Melchers used not only a live model but also one or perhaps several photographs for reference. This was likely because it was difficult for the young child to sit still for long periods [fig. 81]. Unlike some of his contemporaries, who used photography to incorporate unusual cropping into their compositions, it seems that Melchers primarily used photographs as an aide-memoire.[319] In addition to the studio in Egmond, Melchers also had one at 3 Rue Viète, later at 47 Rue Laugier and 20 Rue Galvani in Paris [fig. 82]. In one studio photograph, *The Choirmaster* can be seen on the easel to the left. This painting was executed in the Slotkapel in Egmond aan den Hoef and shown at the 1891 Salon [fig. 83].

 ← **79** Gari Melchers painting *Old and Young*. Photo Gari Melchers Home and Studio, University of Mary Washington, Fredericksburg **80** Gari Melchers, *Old and Young*, oil on canvas, ca. 1890, 110.2 x 85 cm. Private collection **81** Cyanotype. Gari Melchers Home and Studio, University of Mary Washington, Fredericksburg

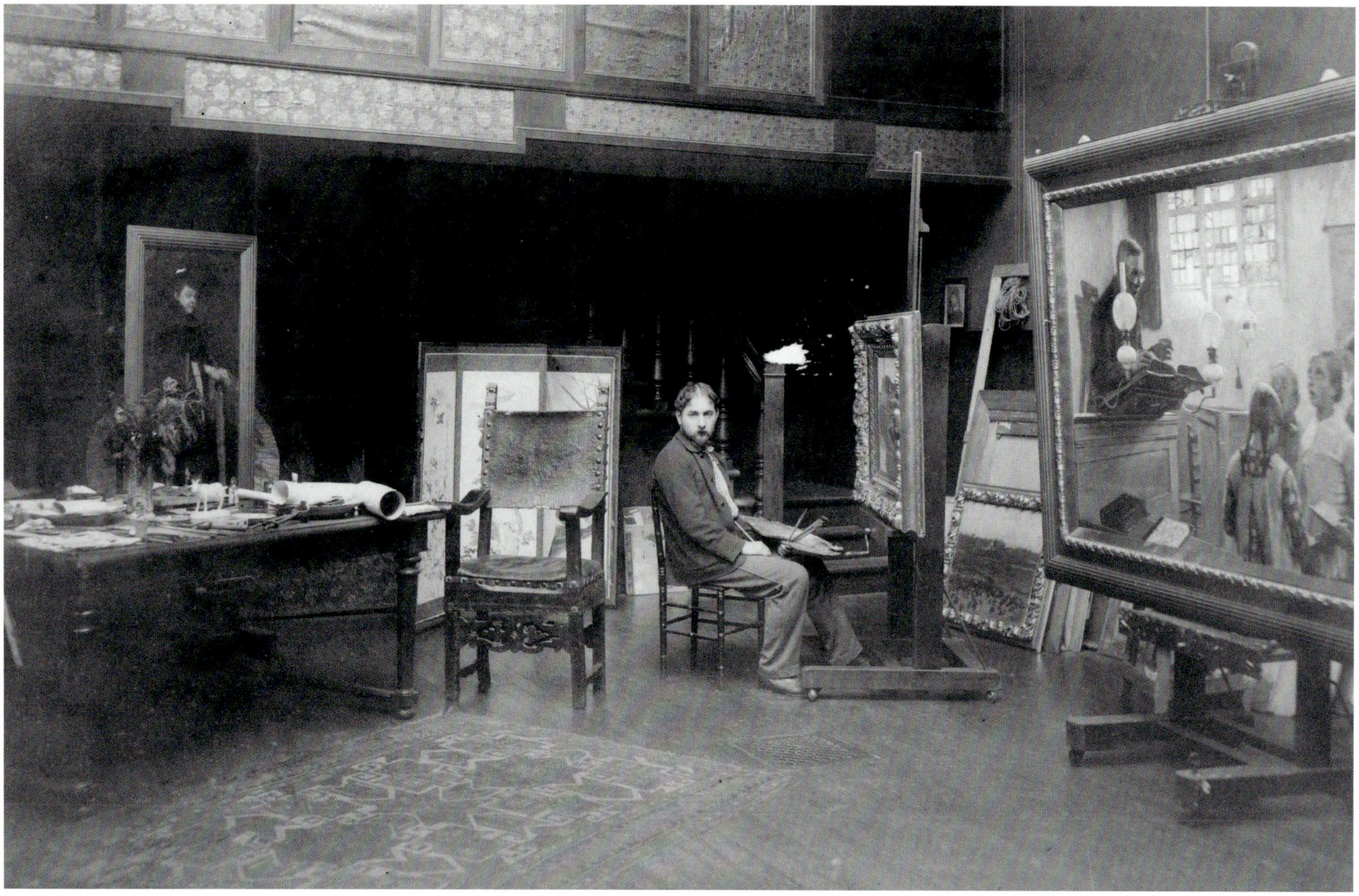

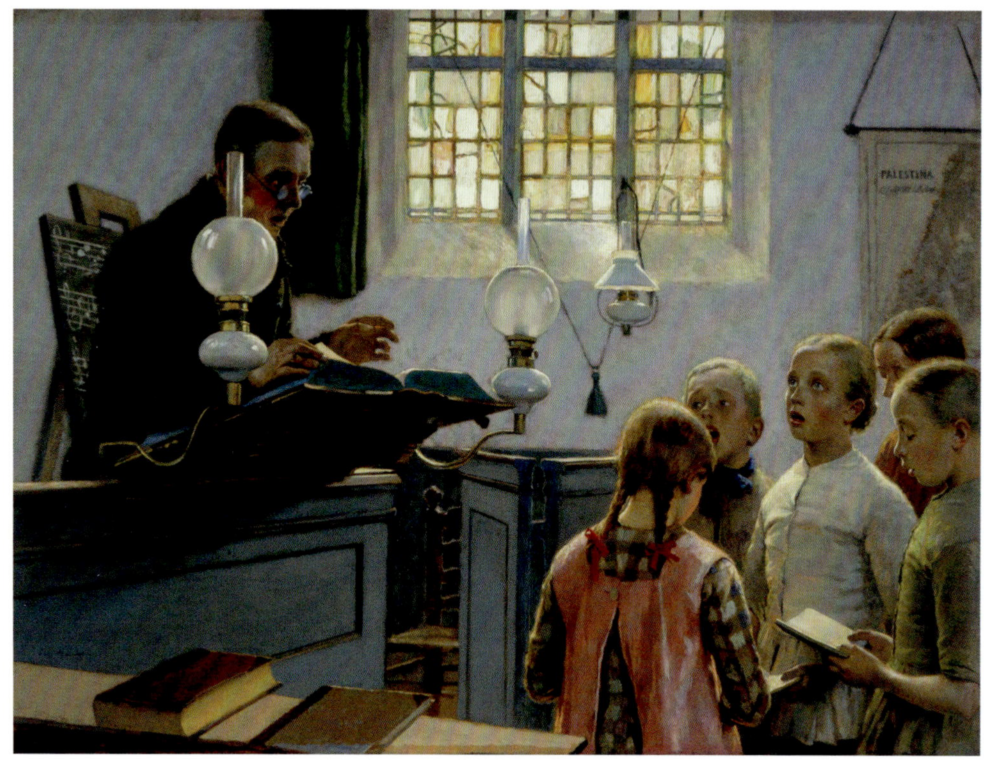

82 Gari Melchers in his Paris atelier on Rue Viète, ca. 1891. Photo Gari Melchers Home and Studio, University of Mary Washington, Fredericksburg
83 Gari Melchers, *The Choirmaster*, 1888–1891, oil on canvas, 124.5 x 172.5 cm. Gari Melchers Home and Studio, University of Mary Washington, Fredericksburg

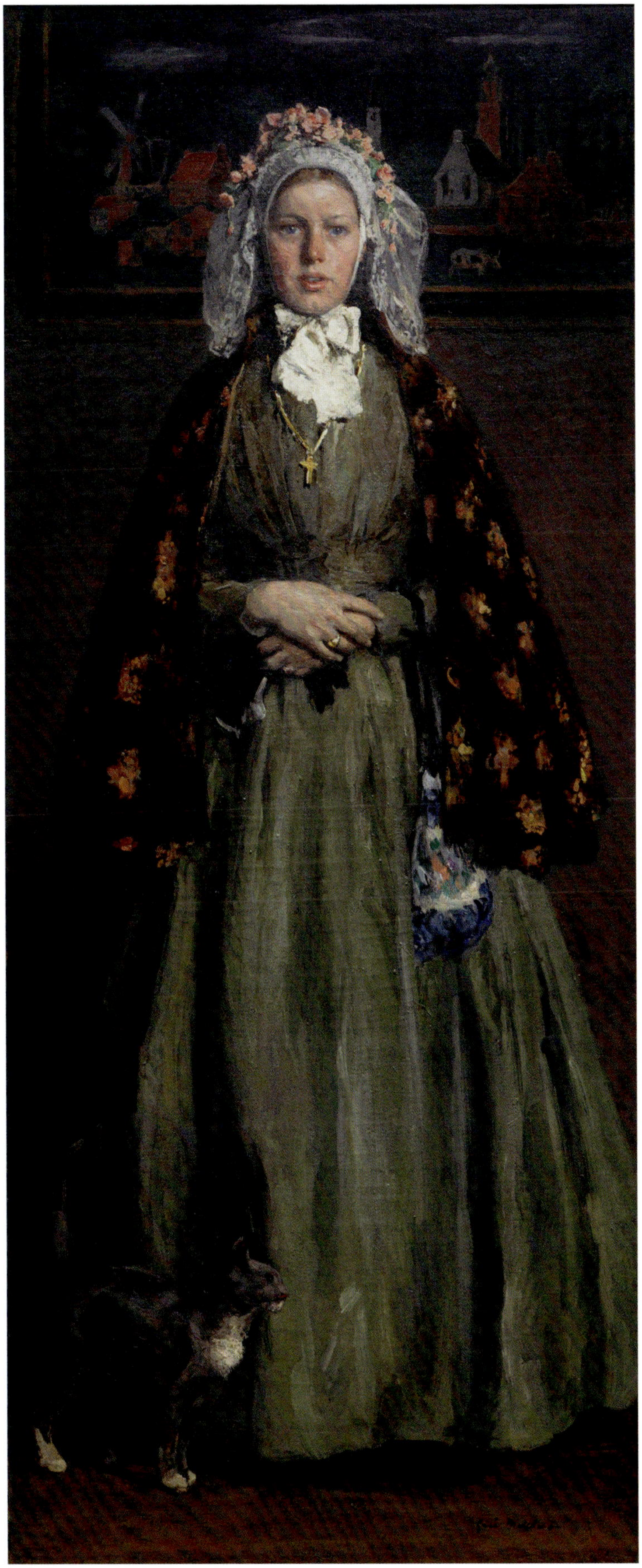

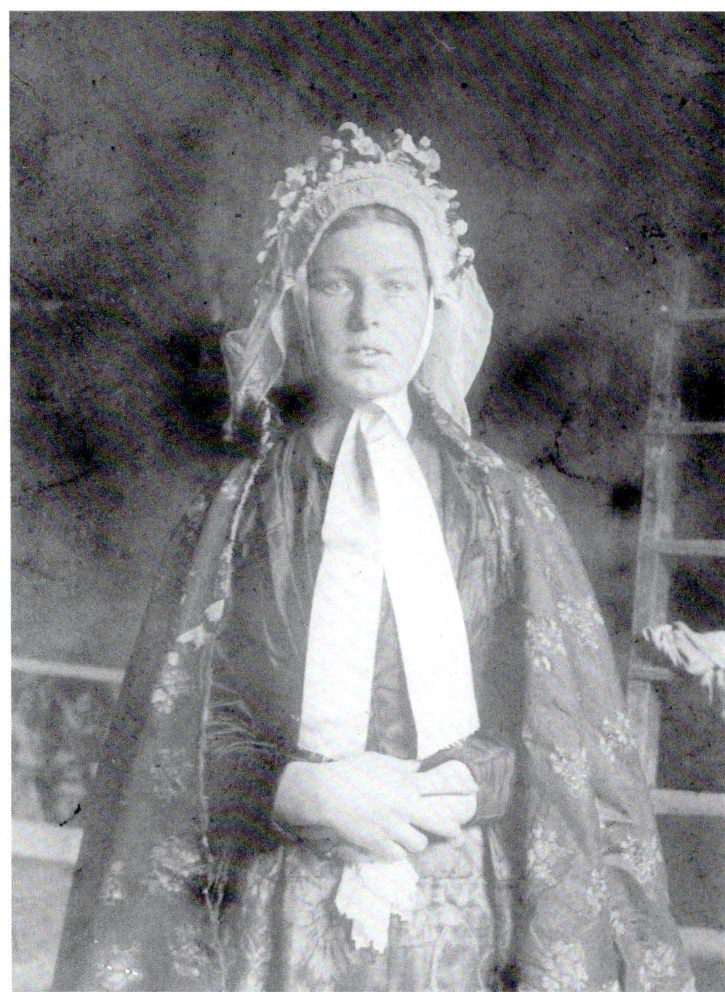

As many artists did – and still do – Melchers captured a scene that moved him in a quick sketch.[320] Years later, even the smallest scribble could serve as the starting point for a painting. In Melchers' own words, "a dozen lines on the back of an envelope" could be of immeasurable value.[321] In 1903, Melchers wanted to begin a new painting based on a small sketch he had made years earlier. When none of the Egmond girls he had invited looked Dutch enough to pose, Corinne, wearing one of the quaint gowns from the dress collection, was called upon to evoke the desired effect. In the end, she posed with a white cap tied under her chin [figs. 84 and 85].[322]

 84 Gari Melchers, *The Girl of Brabant*, 1904, oil on canvas, 185.4 x 78.7 cm. Annmary Brown Memorial, Brown University **85** Gari Melchers, Corinne Melchers posing for The Girl of Brabant. Photo Gari Melchers Home and Studio, University of Mary Washington, Fredericksburg

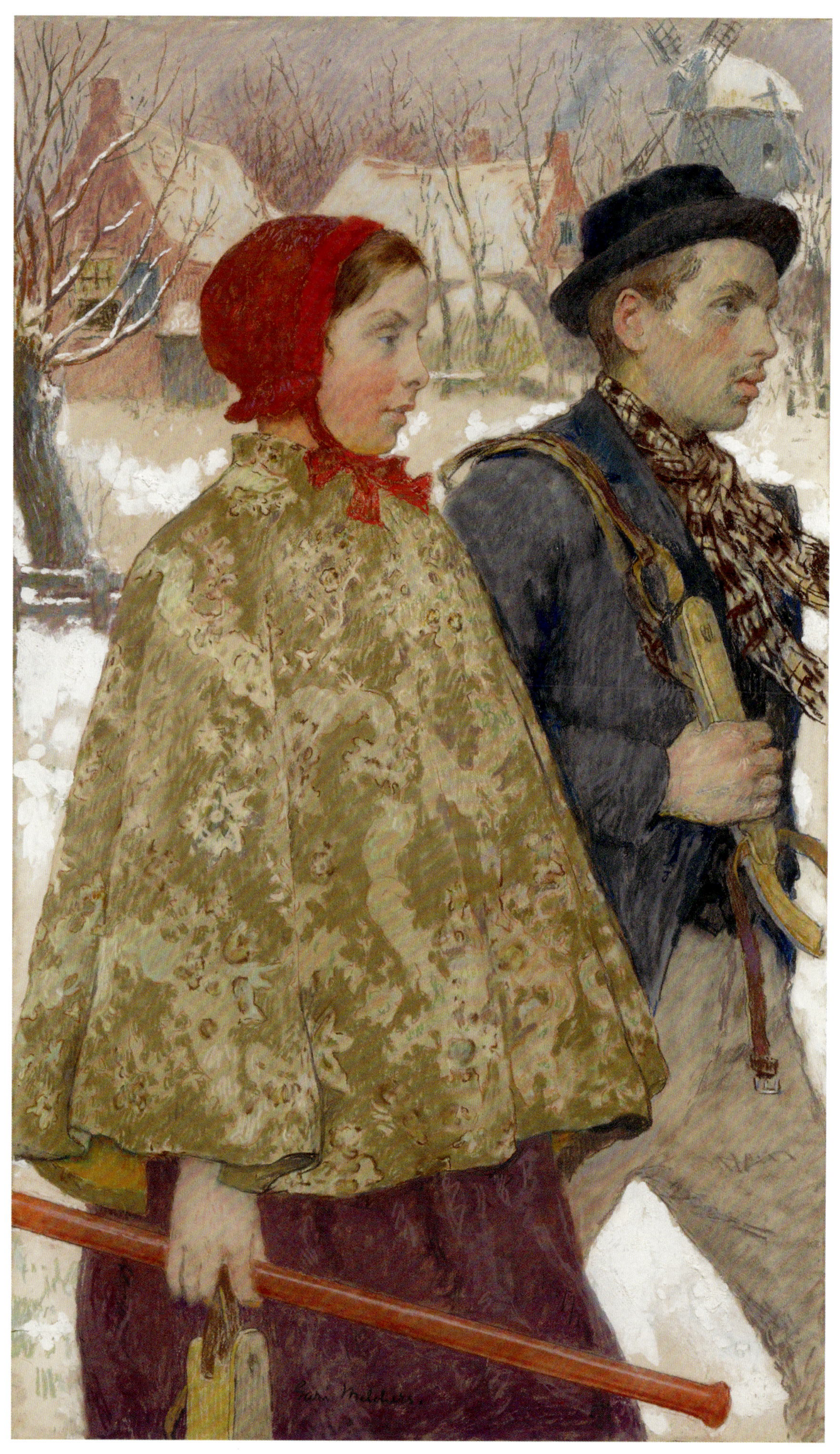

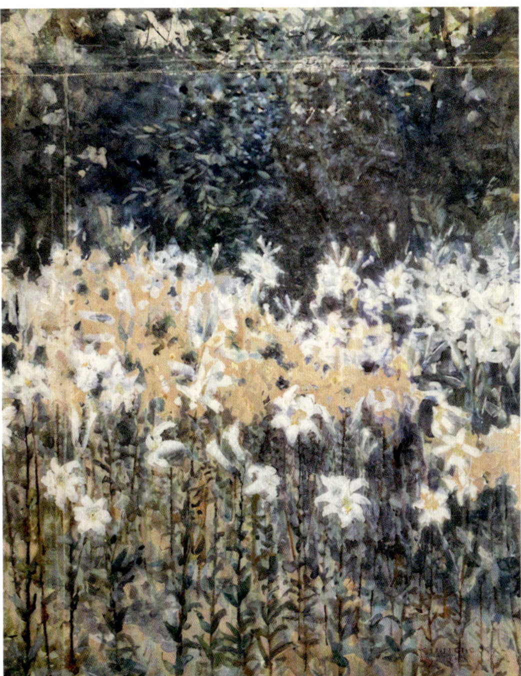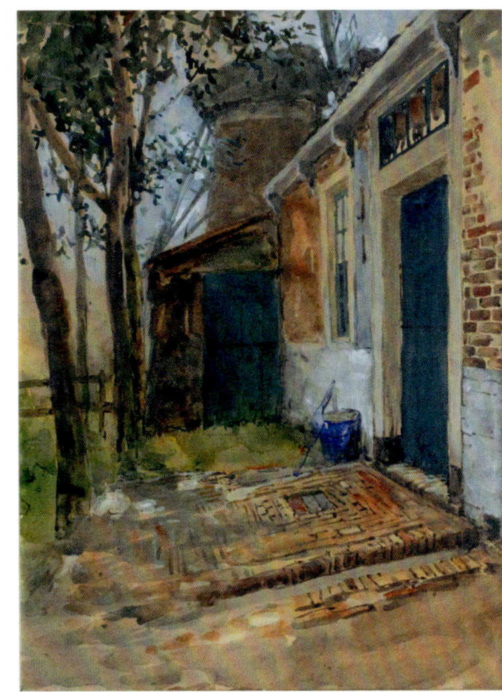

For each painting, Melchers created various studies in chalk, watercolor, and/or gouache. He also experimented with color and poses for the sake of composition.[323] In the preserved preliminary studies and variations for *Skaters*, it is clear that the color scheme underwent significant changes [figs. 86 and 89]. The posture of the male model also varied; in the final version, he does not face forward but looks toward the girl [see fig. 67]. In that painting, it is also evident that Melchers alternated thick layers of paint with very thin ones.

Over the years, Melchers' brushstrokes became looser, and he sometimes used his thumb or palette knife to achieve a particular effect.[324] Just before his marriage to Corinne, he wrote that an artist occasionally needed the perspective of an independent person: "It takes two to paint a picture, one to paint it and the other fellow to hit him over the head with a club when it's time to stop, and in the future, you will have to be the other fellow."[325]

Hitchcock, too, undoubtedly relied on quick sketches, preliminary studies in pencil, chalk, pastel, and watercolor [figs. 87 and 88]. For example, he exhibited several pastels – as mentioned above – under the title *Atmospheric Notes* in London and New York. Unfortunately, much less of this type of work has been preserved compared to Melchers, whose house in Falmouth, along with his studio and artistic legacy, was bequeathed to the State of Virginia by Corinne Melchers.

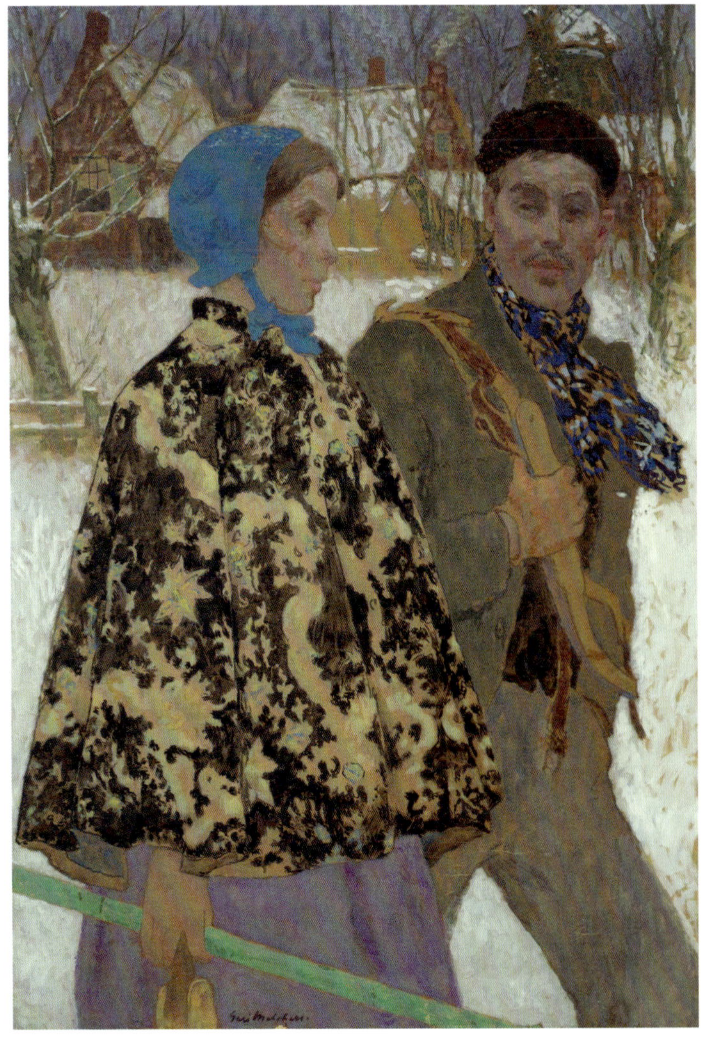

← **86** Gari Melchers, *Winter*, pastel and gouache on paper and canvas, 109.2 x 66 cm. Private collection **87** George Hitchcock, *Lilies*, study for *The Annunciation*, 1887, watercolor, 41.5 x 32 cm. Private collection **88** George Hitchcock, *Blue Door*, watercolor and gouache on papier, 32.7 x 24.4 cm. Telfair Museums, Savannah, Gift of Gari Melchers **89** Gari Melchers, *Skaters*, tempera on brown paper on canvas, 109.2 x 76.2 cm. Gari Melchers Home and Studio, University of Mary Washington, Fredericksburg

Sacred art seems most to appeal to me.
'The Annunciation', 'The Flight into Egypt',
'The Madonna' […] 'Hagar & Ishmael, St George

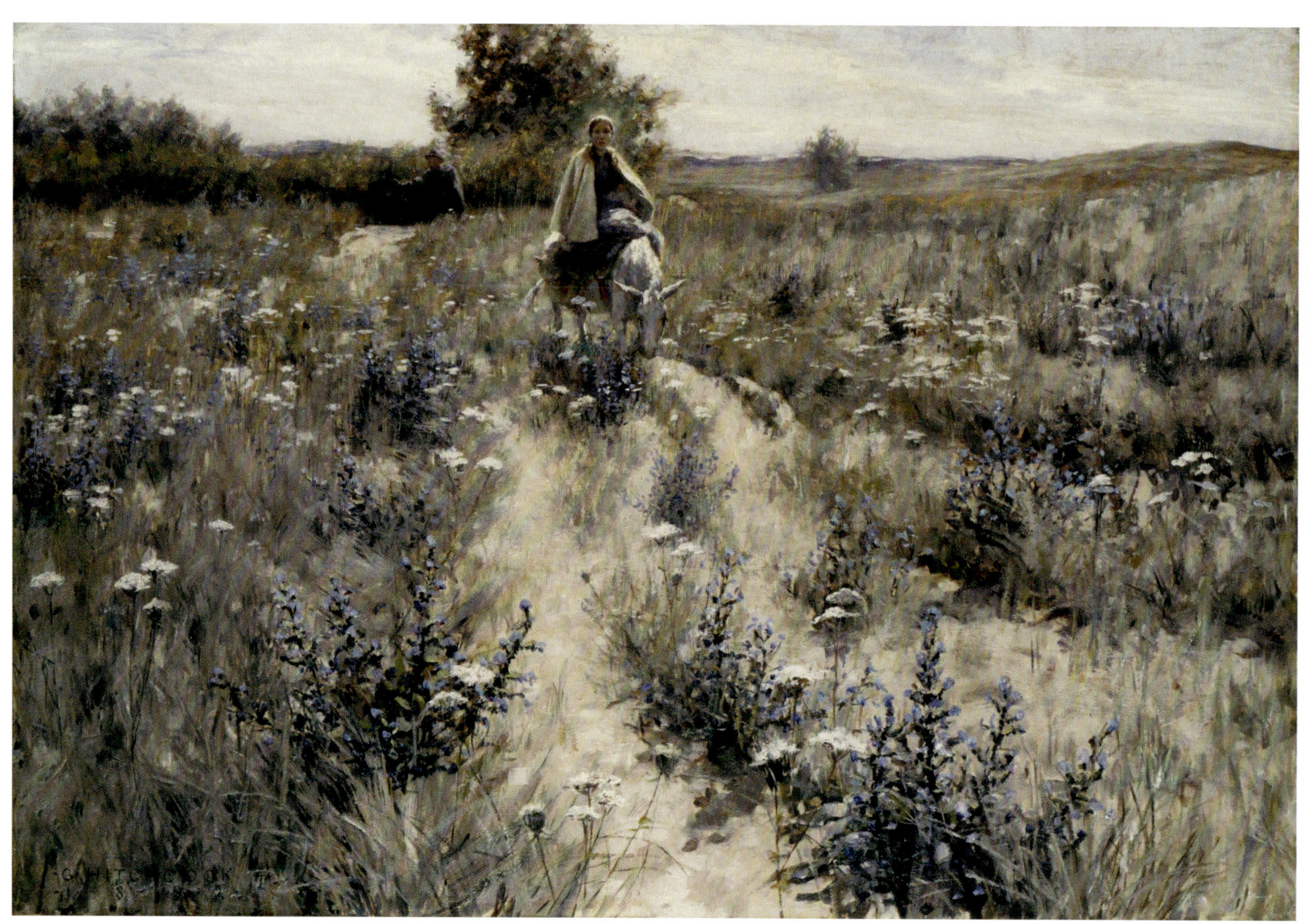

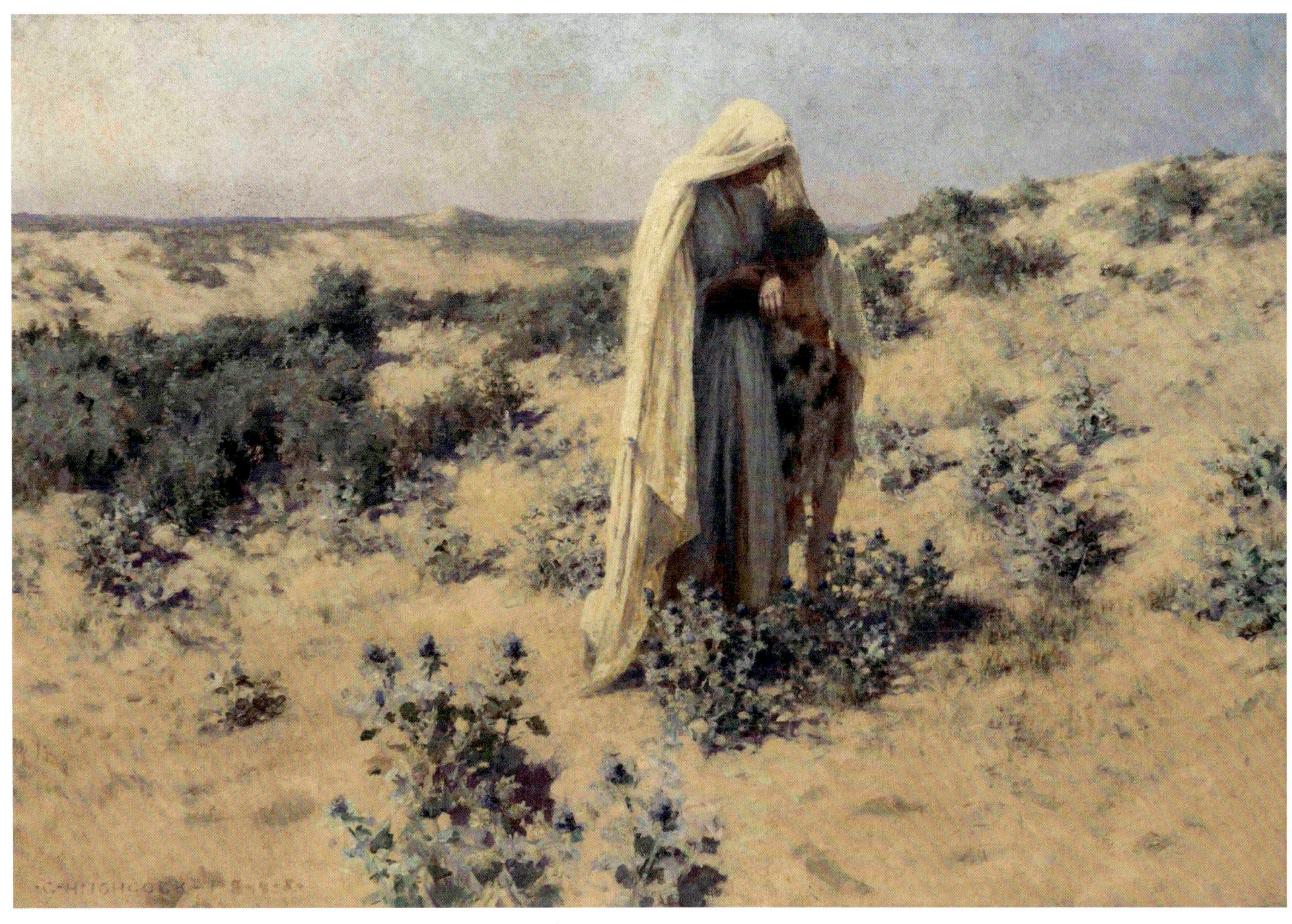

"All of my honors": The Religious Themes

While Hitchcock's paintings of Dutch girls with tulips and hyacinths brought him a considerable income, he wrote to a friend around 1895 that his true fascination lay with religious works: "What do I Paint? Well chiefly holy pictures, sacred art seems most to appeal to me. 'The Annunciation', 'The Flight into Egypt', 'The Madonna' (several times) 'Hagar & Ishmael', St George & landscapes of course, Tulips, Pop[p]ies, but only two large ones & many small ones, work in oil, watercolor & pastels: all of my honors but one have been given for the holy pictures."[326]

As was the case with *Maternity*, Hitchcock set the biblical stories *The Flight into Egypt* and *Hagar and Ishmael* in the Egmond dune landscape [figs. 43, 90 and 91]. There, he found the characteristic meteorological atmosphere of the Netherlands, with its mysterious light and beautiful pearlescent tones: "The shadows are never the crude, purple, cut-out spots of a southern sun [..] the brightness is always diffused [...] the tonality is always fine," he wrote.[327]

In *The Flight into Egypt*, Hitchcock did not paint a traditional halo around Mary's head but instead used a light source behind her. In the far background, Joseph follows the donkey through the overgrown dune field in Egmond, covered with flowering snakeweed and wild carrots.[328] Similarly, the biblical female figure Hagar – who was a servant of Abraham and Sarah and gave birth to Abraham's son Ishmael, but was banished after Sarah herself miraculously gave birth to a child – walks with Ishmael through the typical Egmond dune landscape, but this time closer to the shoreline.[329]

    91 George Hitchcock, *Hagar and Ishmael*, 1898, oil on canvas, 111.8 x 162.6 cm. Private collection

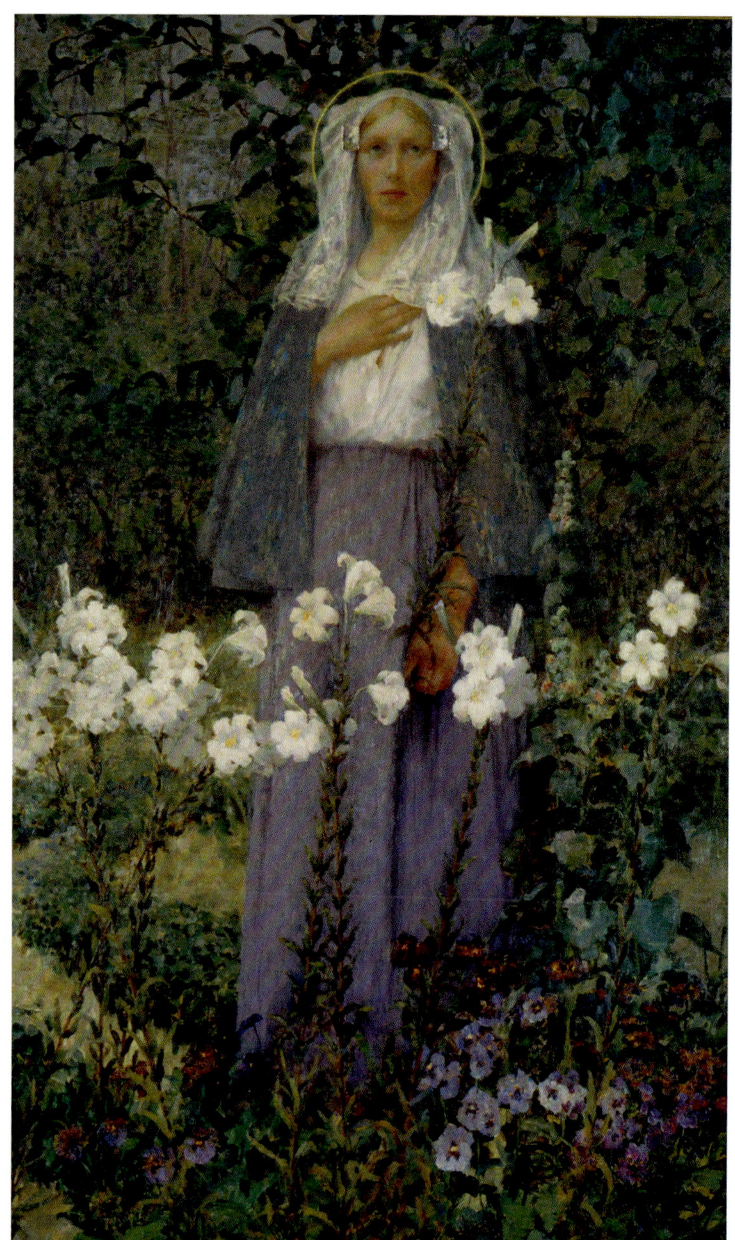

Hitchcock created multiple versions of some biblical subjects. For example, he presented a different version of *The Flight into Egypt* at the international exhibition in Dresden in 1897, in which Mary is positioned closer to the viewer.[330] In the version he showed in Berlin in 1902, the donkey stands directly in front of us.[331] In 1900, Hitchcock won a bronze medal at the Paris Exposition Universelle for *Magnificat*, a vertical variant of *The Annunciation* from 1887 [see figs. 38 and 92]. In 1894, he created a third version titled *Mary in the House of Elizabeth*.[332] Hitchcock did not only paint "images of saints." Like Melchers, he had a keen eye for the religious practices and sacraments – such as baptism, communion, and marriage – of the people of Egmond, as is evident in *Vespers* [see fig. 93]. In one of his articles about "picturesque Holland," he wrote: "Though not an obtrusively religious people the Dutch are only second to the English in their strict observance of Sunday, and an almost mediaeval effect is produced by their solemn Sunday afternoon walk in all the finery."[333] The painting that he submitted to the international exhibition in Munich in 1900 depicts that Sunday afternoon stroll: a young woman with her prayer book in hand making her way to the church through a beautiful autumn land- scape to attend vespers.[334] She wears a North Brabant *poffer* on her head: a horseshoe-shaped (fake) flower wreath over a finely laced or embroidered cap. However, the scene was most likely painted in Egmond aan den Hoef, near the small bridge close to the house De Eenhoorn.[335] In the background is a typical North Holland polder mill.

92 George Hitchcock, *Magnificat (Annunciation)*, 1894, oil on canvas, 160 x 96.5 cm. Gari Melchers Home and Studio, University of Mary Washington, Fredericksburg → 93 George Hitchcock, *Vespers*, ca. 1895–1900, oil on canvas, 112.7 x 90.8 cm. The Metropolitan Museum of Art, New York, Gift of Edward Drummond Libbey, 1917

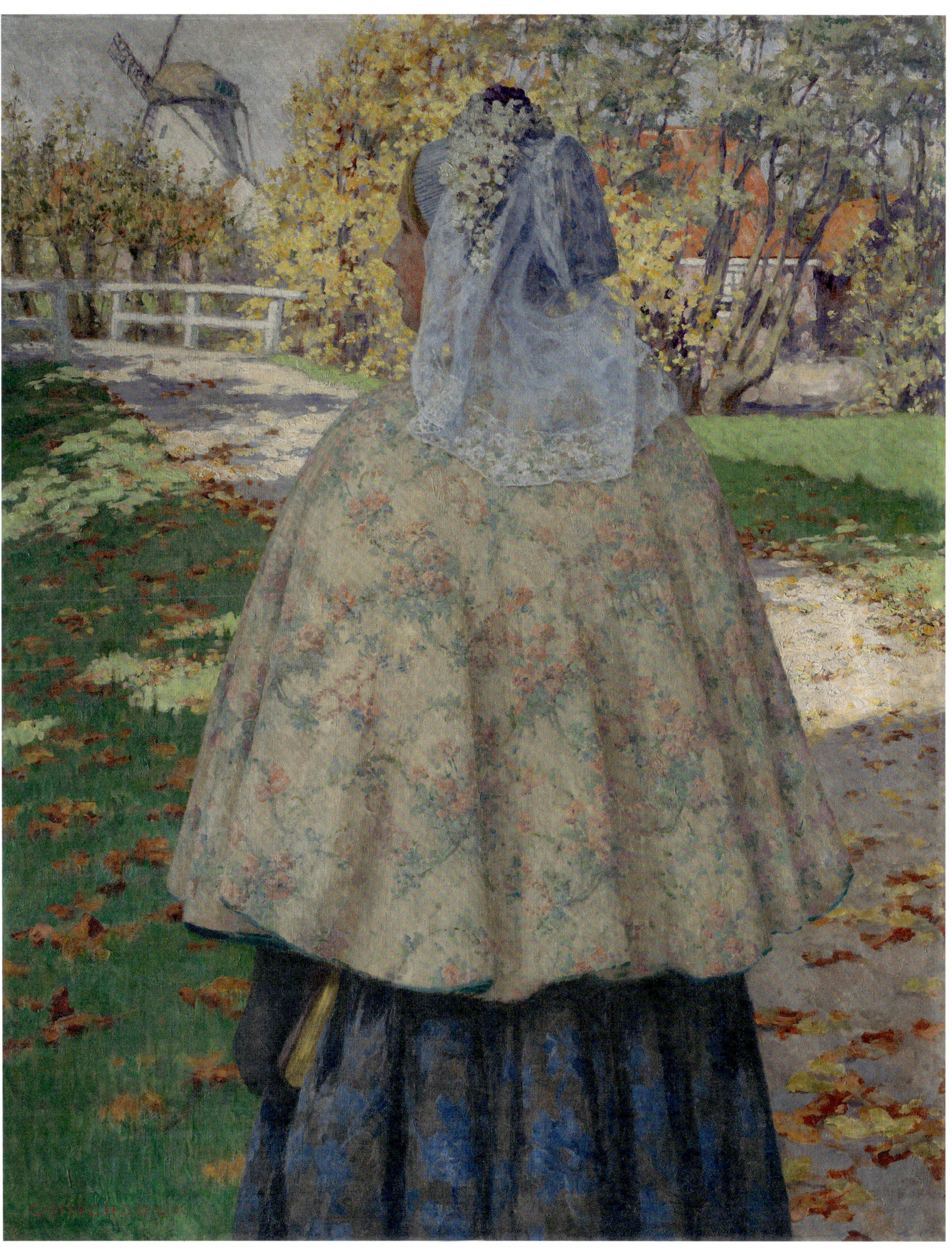

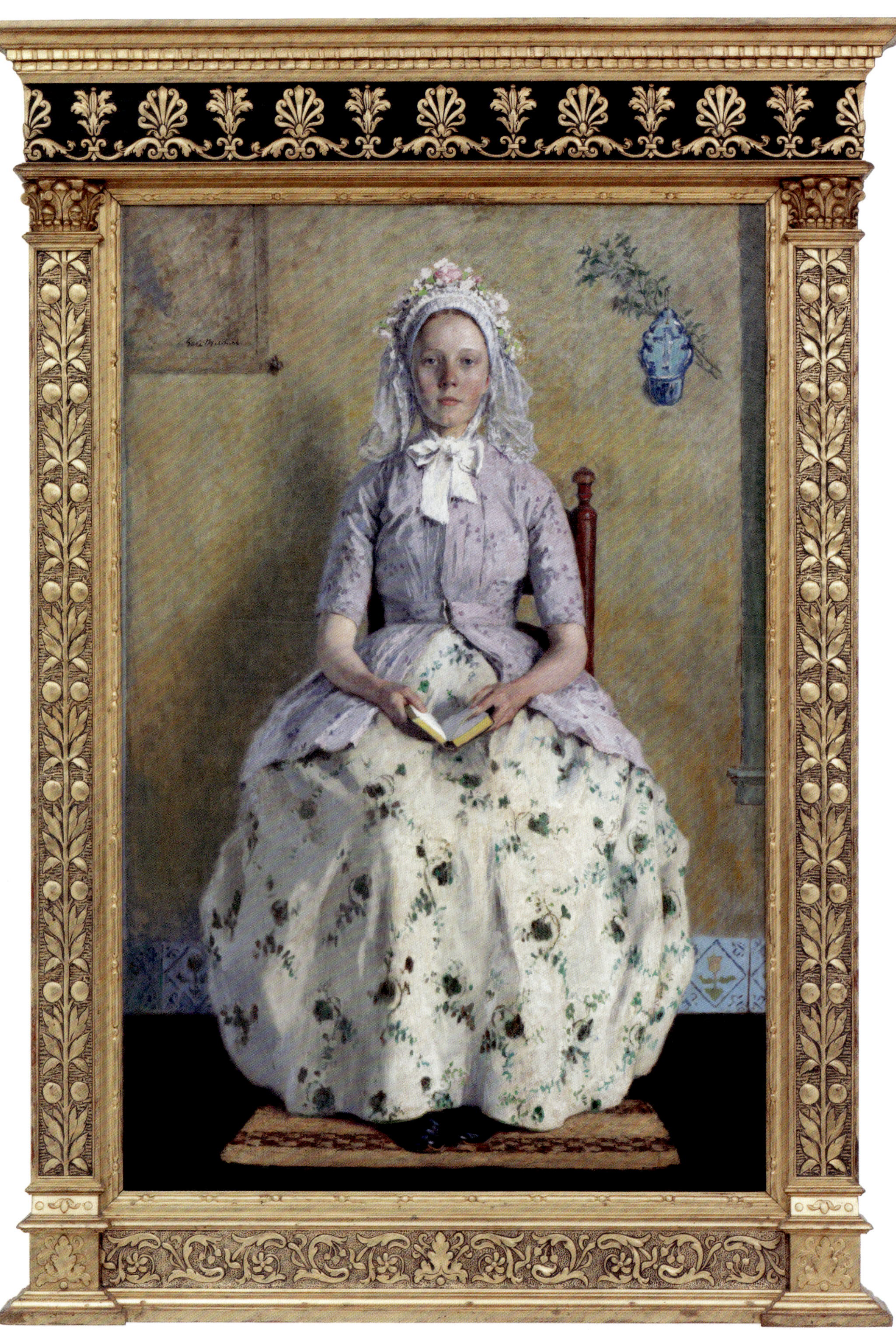

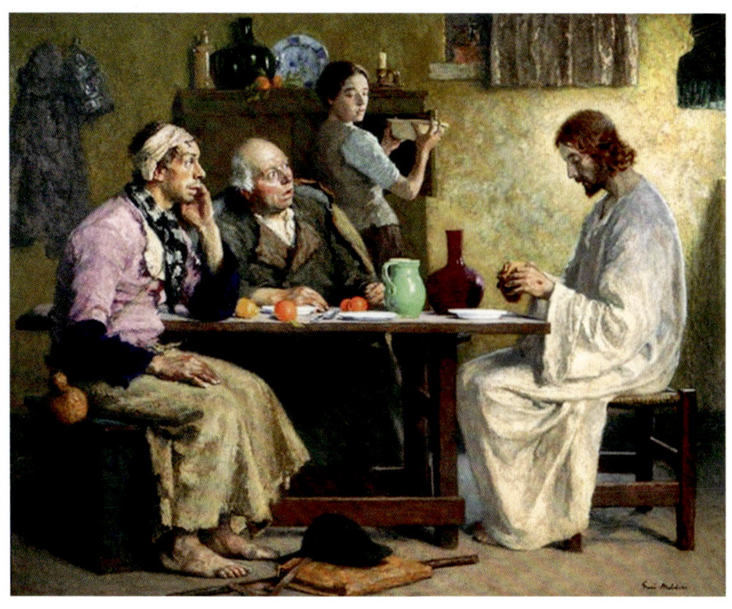

During the same period, Gari Melchers also painted a model wearing the Brabant *poffer* from the collection of clothing and accessories that the artists had gathered. The sixteen-year-old girl Pietje (Petronella van der Burgh), who frequently posed for Melchers, was the model for *The Communicant* [fig. 94].[336] Unlike today, where the age for this Roman Catholic sacrament is seven, at that time it was twelve. Thus the painting with the slightly older model was still faithful to tradition. In the monumental canvas, Melchers depicted the communicant frontally, as a crowned Madonna from fifteenth- or sixteenth-century art. The inspiration from religious Italian art of the past is further emphasized by the monumental frame that Melchers placed around the painting.[337] It was first exhibited in Chicago and later in Dresden, which is noteworthy because Melchers almost always debuted his latest work in Paris.[338]

In the 1890s and around the turn of the century, Melchers also painted several biblical scenes, such as *The Communion* and *The Last Supper* [see figs. 46 and 72]. *The Supper at Emmaus* fits into this series of works in which he combined historical and contemporary realities. Christ – risen from the dead – is depicted in an ancient robe, while the disciples – who at first did not recognize him – are dressed as contemporary Egmond villagers [see fig. 95].

The Emmaus painting was, as usual, first displayed at the Salon in 1898 and later at the Grosse Berliner Kunstausstellung in 1900. There, Melchers showcased as many as 39 works in his own dedicated gallery![339] While the painting found little favor in Paris, the German art aficionados were more enthusiastic.[340] In September, it was purchased by Baroness Margaretha von Ende Krupp.[341]

A Dutch reporter covering the exhibition wrote that Melchers was one of the most admired "Dutch" painters due to his striking and vivid portrayal of his subjects. He even called *The Supper at Emmaus* sublime: "Over the almost ethereal figure of Christ [lies] a veil of tender mystery… that makes him different from an ordinary man, while in the two table companions, a vague sense of the holiness of the Savior awakens. The entire expression on the faces of these two simple souls is so striking and so full of truth that one can almost follow their train of thought."[342]

← **94** Gari Melchers, *The Communicant*, ca. 1900, oil on canvas, 160.7 x 109.2 cm. Detroit Institute of Arts, Bequest of Mr. and Mrs. Charles M. Swift, 69.527
95 Gari Melchers, *The Supper at Emmaus*, 1898, oil on canvas. Dimensions and present whereabouts unknown

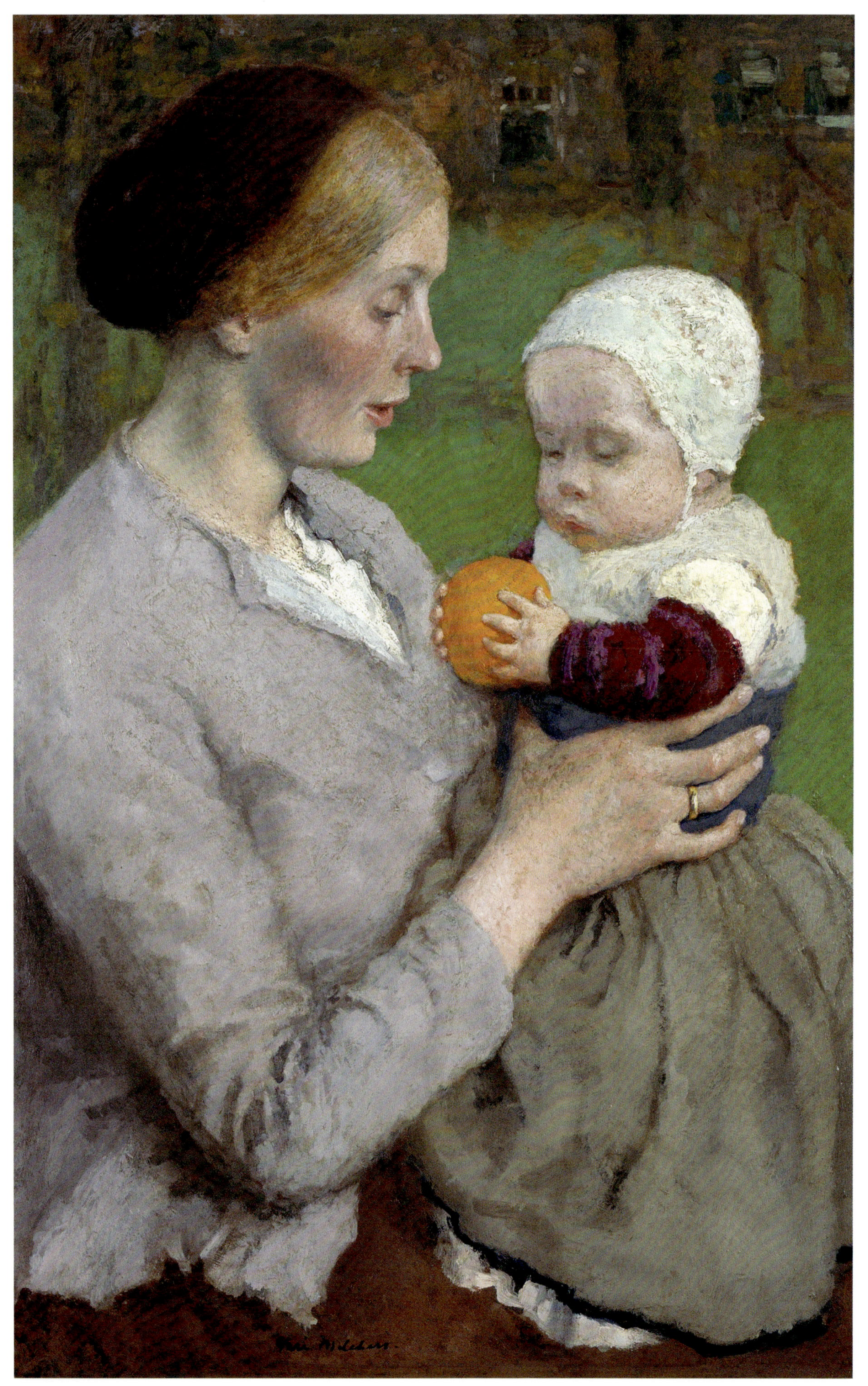

As of 1892, Melchers frequently portrayed a mother with child. In some of these works, there is a clear connection to – particularly Italian – Madonna and Child depictions. For instance, in one of his early paintings with this theme, the baby holds an orange in its hands, a symbol of the knowledge of good and evil, likely a reference to Christ as the Savior [fig. 96].[343] In other pictures, the religious undertone is absent, and the focus is primarily on the loving bond between mother and child. The painting *Maternity*, which Melchers exhibited at the Salon in 1895, was purchased for the collection of Musée du Luxembourg, the Paris museum for contemporary art [fig. 97].[344]

At the end of the nineteenth century, the theme of mother and child was hugely popular and painted by many, including the American artist Mary Cassatt (1844–1926), whom Melchers greatly admired.[345] For Melchers, "The tenderness of the mother, the wonder of the baby, and the intimacy of their love – that is the most beautiful thing in life."[346] Adaline Piper, a regular participant in Hitchcock's art classes, offered a more grounded perspective: "There is no sentimental prettiness about these babies: they are round eyed and ugly, the mothers full off character, but of the stolid, enduring peasant type that accepts all and gives all."[347]

 ← **96** Gari Melchers, *Mother and Child with Orange*, ca. 1892, oil on canvas, 73.7 x 49 cm. Gari Melchers Home and Studio, University of Mary Washington, Fredericksburg **97** Gari Melchers, *Maternity*, ca. 1895, oil on canvas, 69 x 46.5 cm. Musée d'Orsay, Paris

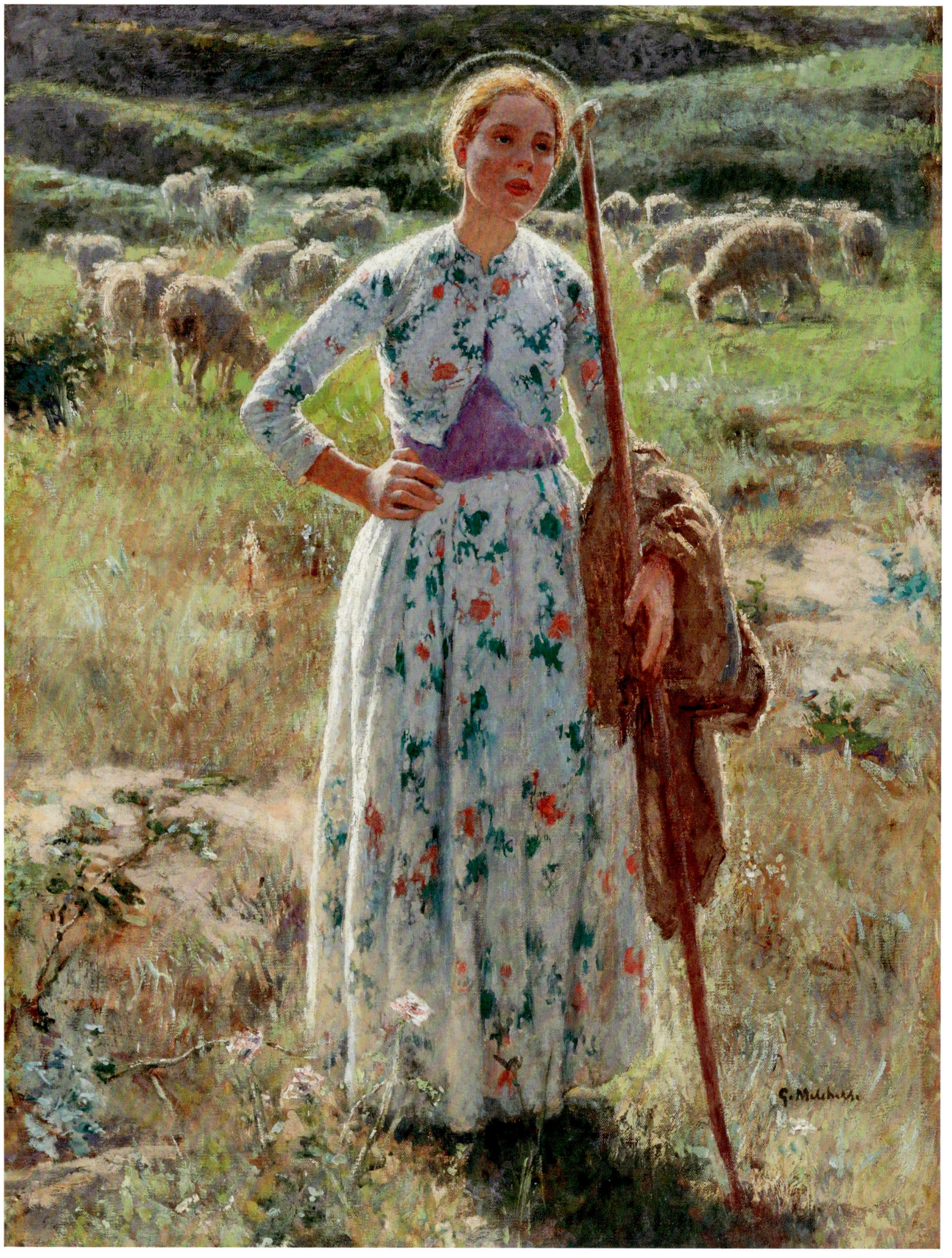

98 Gari Melchers, *Joan of Arc*, ca. 1895–1900, oil on canvas, 76.2 x 58.4 cm. Indianapolis Museum of Art at Newfields, Gift of Mrs. Albert J. Beveridge

Epic Folklore, Myths, and Fairy Tales

In addition to painting biblical stories and the church-going traditions of the residents of Egmond, starting in the late 1890s Melchers and Hitchcock also depicted other narratives. Hitchcock began placing figures drawn from epic folklore or Greek and Roman mythology amid blooming fields of tulips, hyacinths, or cornflowers. In 1897, he submitted a painting titled *Joan of Arc* to the international exhibition at the Glaspalast in Munich, and the same year, he showcased *Saint George* at the Royal Academy.[348] The latter was described as: "a fairy-tale forest shrouded in blue-green mist; the knight, approaching from behind the trees, on horseback; in the foreground, the maiden on the moss."[349] The painting was praised for its fairy-tale atmosphere and because Hitchcock avoided expressing the "unreal" too sharply.

A year later, Hitchcock exhibited another knight on horseback: *Defeated* [fig. 99].[350] The contrast between the beautiful blooming tulips and the despondent, exhausted knight dragging his tattered banner along the ground resonated with the audience, particularly the color scheme.[351] In the following years, Hitchcock displayed more works with narrative themes from history or mythology at the Salon. He painted *Saint Genevieve*, the patron saint of Paris who tends her sheep (1899), *The Last Moments of Sappho* – the Greek poetess from the island of Lesbos (1901), and *The Return of Proserpina*, the goddess who had to spend several months each year in the underworld, with the arrival of spring marking her return (1907). In 1906, Hitchcock also exhibited *The Birth of Venus* at the Knoedler gallery in New York.[352] When he became a member of The New York National Academy of Design in 1909, *Saint Genevieve* was even cited as one of his most admired paintings.[353] Unfortunately, most of the locations of such works, once considered "bold ventures," remain unknown.[354]

During these years, Melchers also painted similar themes, including *Joan of Arc* (ca. 1895-1900), *Saint Geneviève* (ca. 1901-1902), and *Saint Gudula* (ca. 1897) [fig. 98]. Additionally, he even submitted a fairy tale at the Berlin exhibition of 1902: *Little Red Riding Hood* [fig. 100]. Featuring a young girl in a bright orange dress, this painting was appreciated for its color effects and execution.[355]

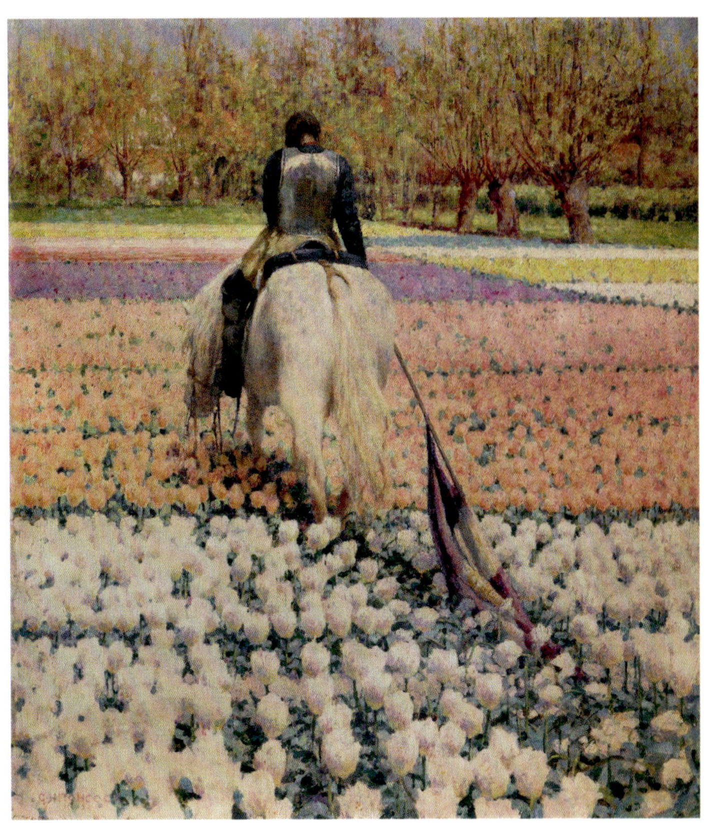

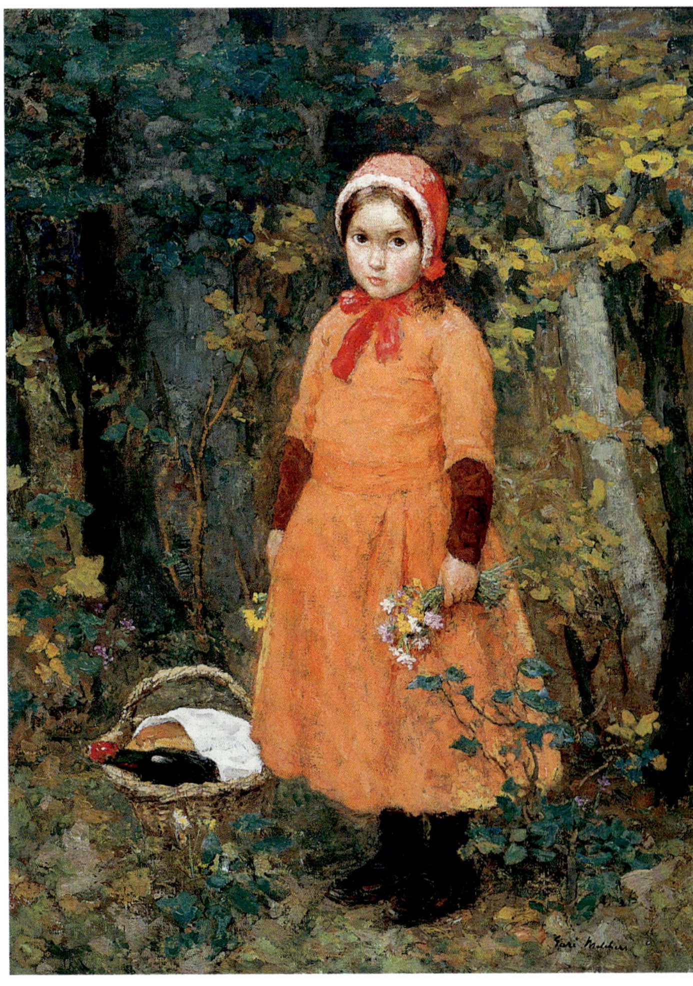

99 George Hitchcock, *Defeated*, ca. 1898, oil on canvas, 100 x 90.5 cm. Musée d'Orsay, Paris   **100** Gari Melchers, *Little Red Riding Hood*, 1897, oil on canvas, 132.5 x 94.4 cm. The Maier Museum of Art at Randolph College, Lynchburg, VA, Purchase made possible by the Fine Arts Fund, 1938

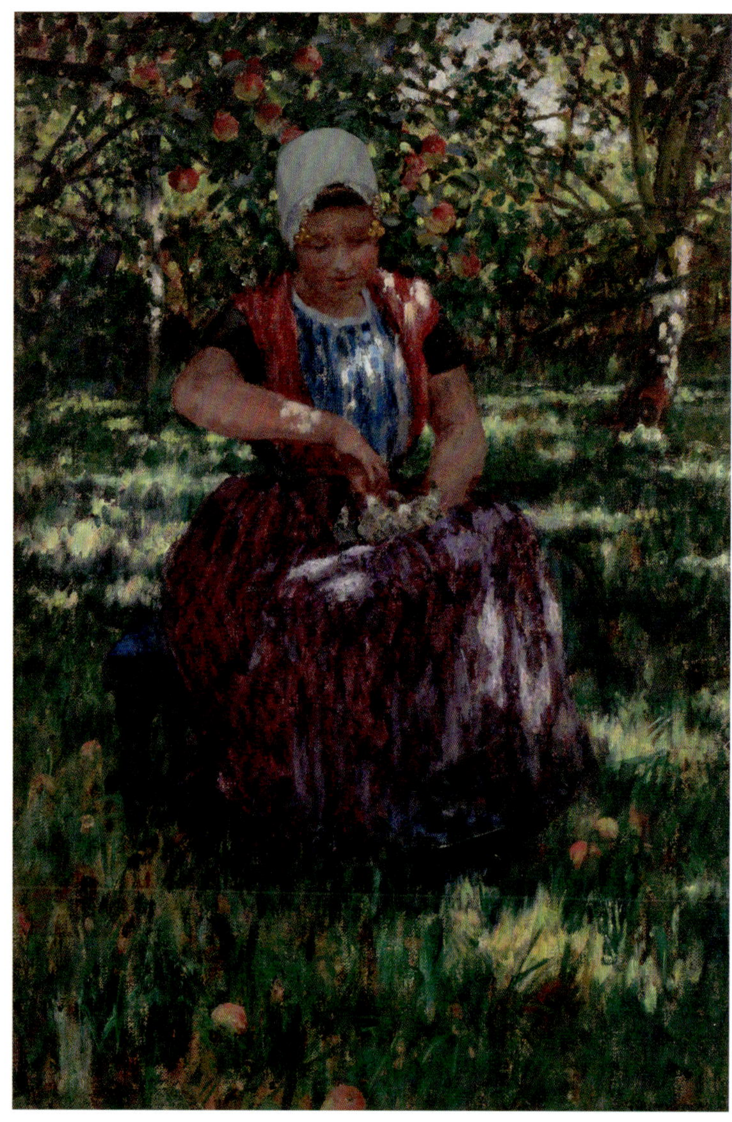

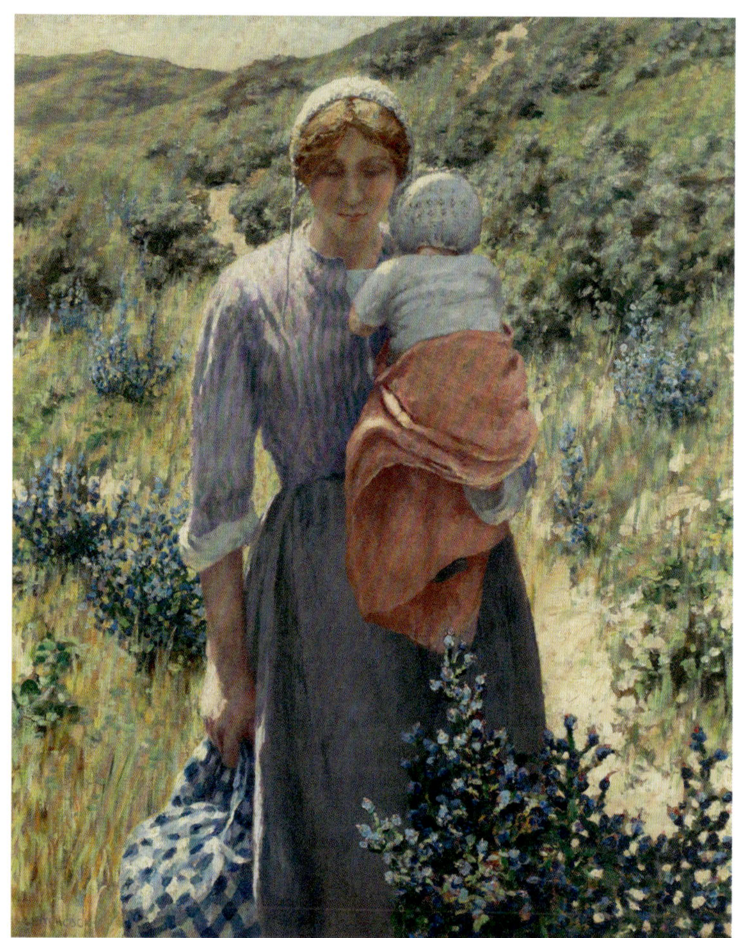

Alongside biblical and historical stories, the artists continued to portray scenes "taken from life," with subjects like *The Spring*, *The Smoker*, or *The Embroiderer*. Known as "the painter of sunlight," Hitchcock also painted *In the Orchard* and *The Wayfarers* [figs. 101 and 102]. Melchers produced several renderings of shepherdesses, including *The Goat Herd*, again partly based on photographs [fig. 103]. Such paintings were likely made as a counterbalance to the much larger Salon works, for market reasons.

One of Melchers' typical Salon pieces was initially exhibited in Paris as *La Poupée* (The Doll). The painting was later retitled *The Sisters* [fig. 104]. In the following years, this substantial canvas was often displayed alongside *The Family*, which depicted the same fair-haired, blue-eyed girl [see fig. 71].[356] In one of the surviving studies, the same girl – wearing a sagging

stocking and clogs – is seen holding hands with a boy, probably her brother [fig. 106]. In this loosely painted study, the girl is dressed much more simply than in the Salon piece, in which she wears an elegantly decorated skirt and a striped bodice. Her older "sister," whom Melchers portrayed during the summer months in *The Butterfly*, is now shown in a bright orange dress instead of the lilac one, which, incidentally, is the same one worn by *Little Red Riding Hood* [figs. 100 and 105]. The artist, who nailed a plaque above the door of his Torensduin studio, which read "Waar en Klaar" (True and Clear), worked very realistically, yet still shaped the reality to his own vision.[357] Moreover, Melchers sometimes introduced a symbolic layer to these lifelike depictions. The group in *The Family* subtly references the Holy Family, with a painting of the Holy Family hanging on the wall behind them – and the mother with the baby at her breast in the same painting appears to be rendered as a crowned Madonna [see fig. 71]. *The Sisters* has even been interpreted as a reference to innocence in the Garden of Eden.[358] Additionally, Melchers may have derived the subject of *The Sisters* from the Dutch artist Albert Neuhuys (1844-1914) [fig. 107].

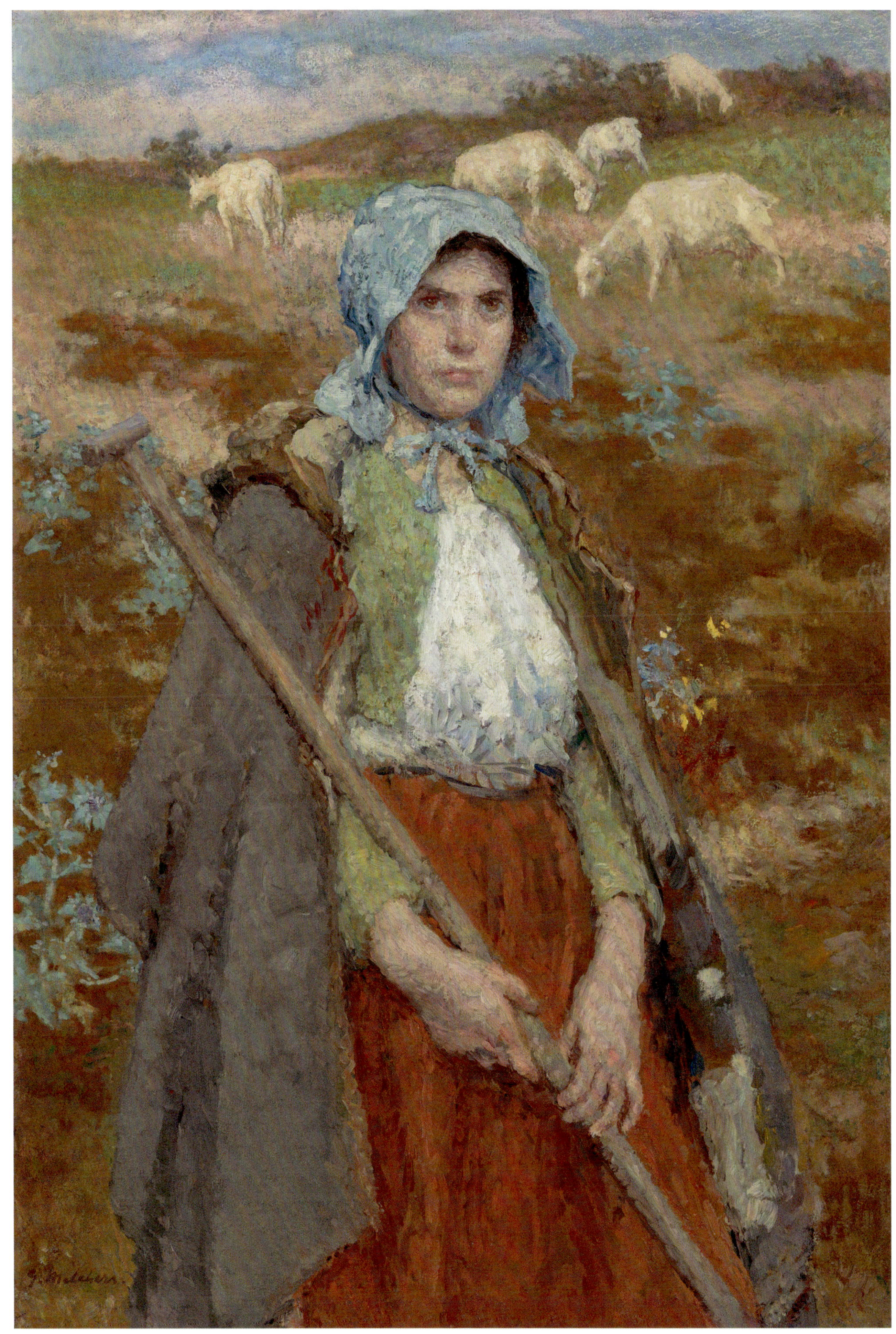

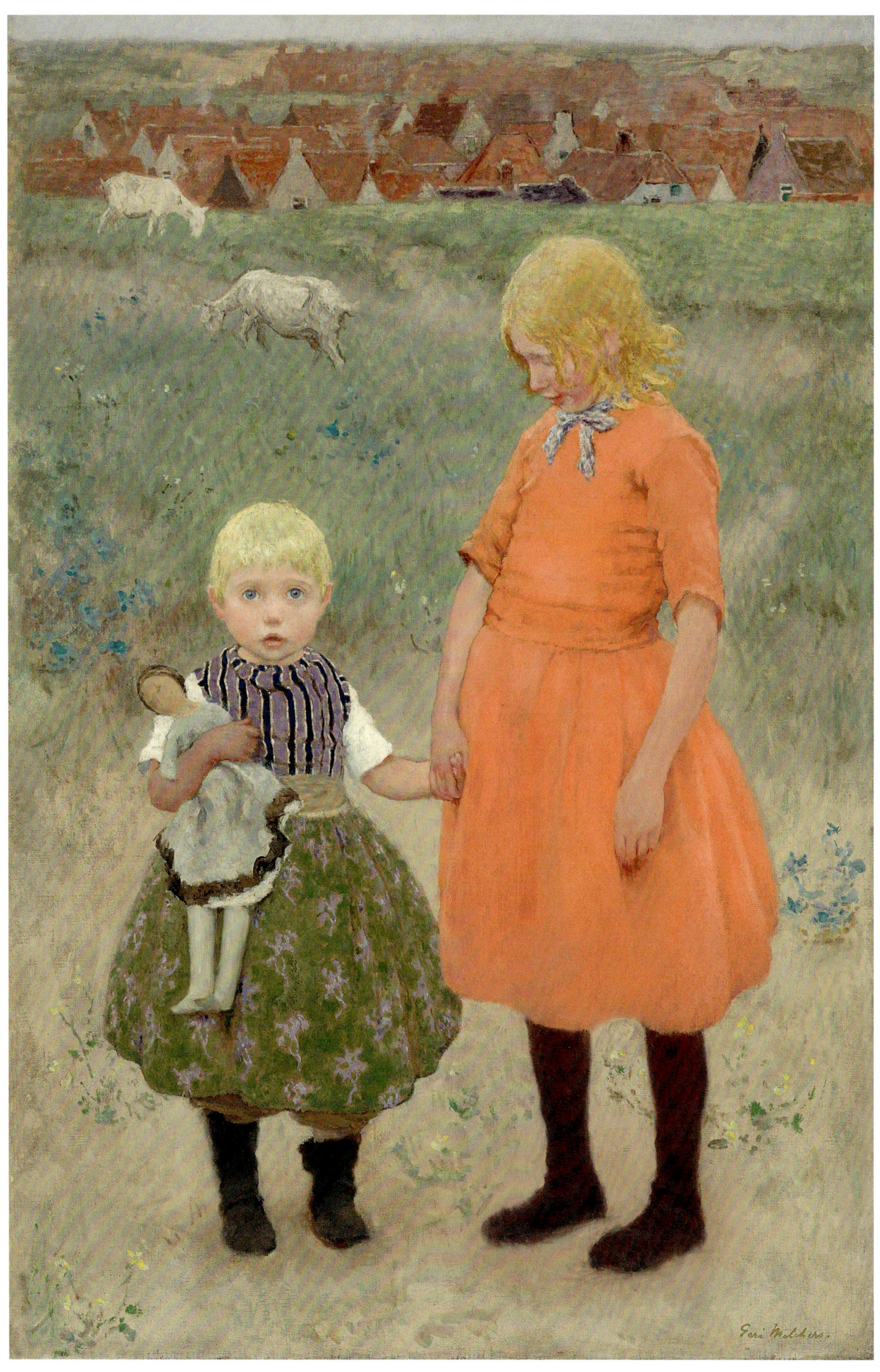

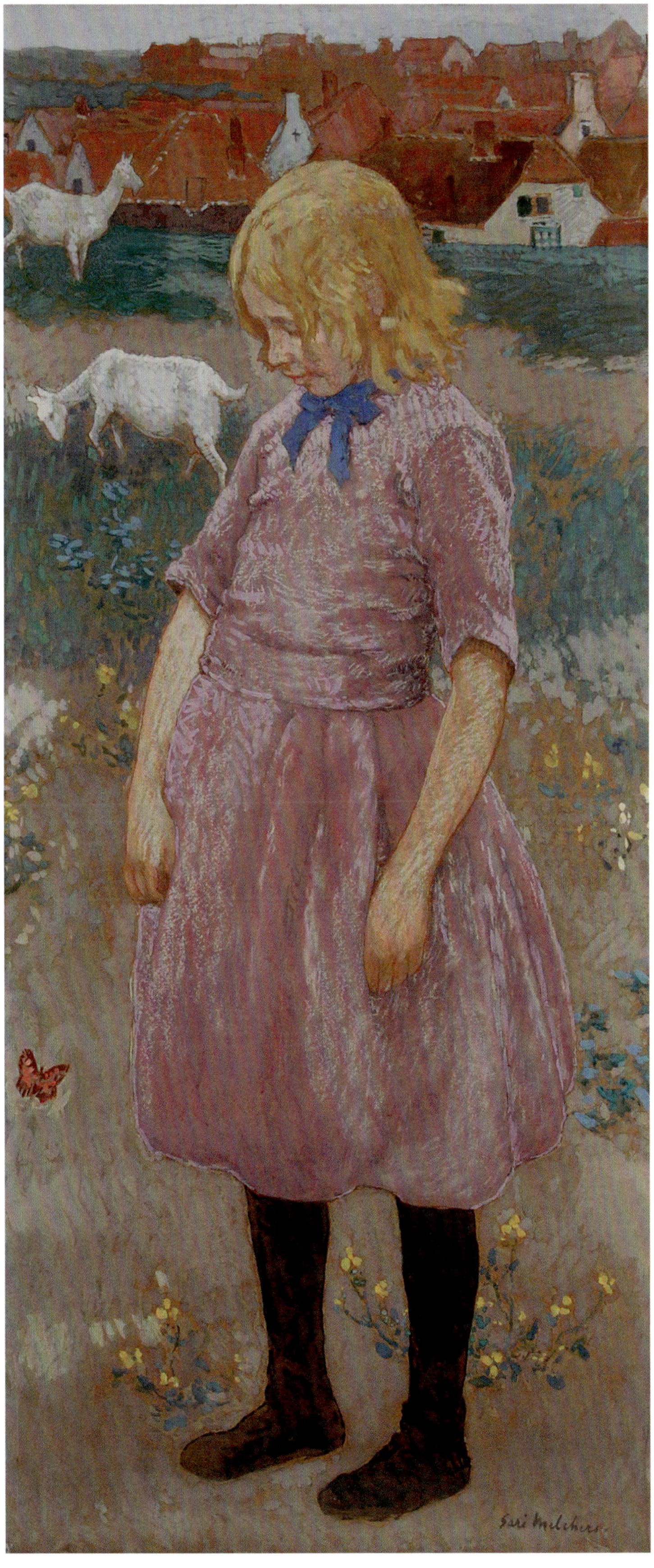

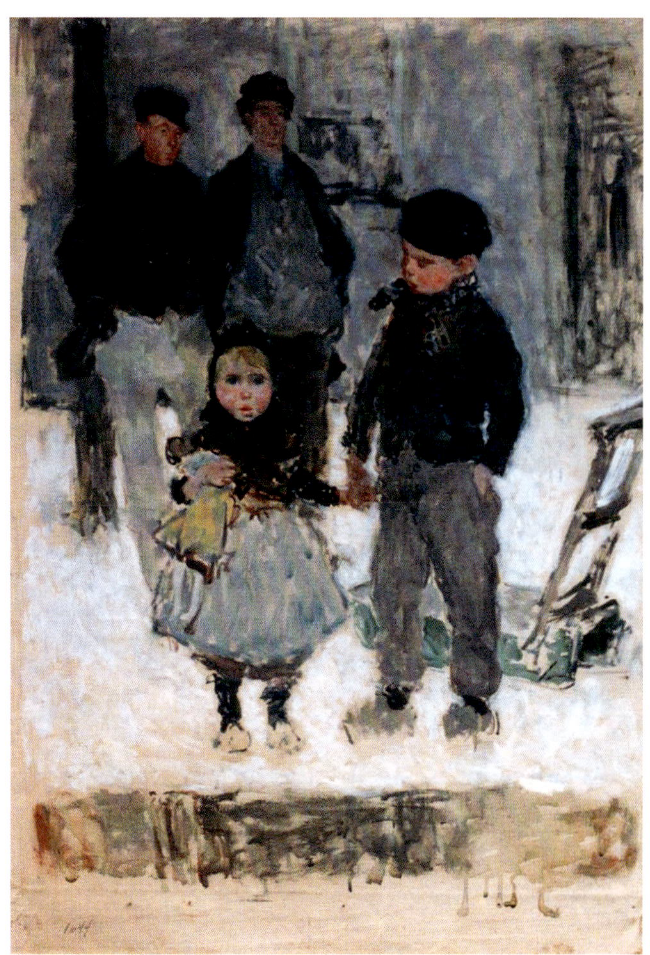

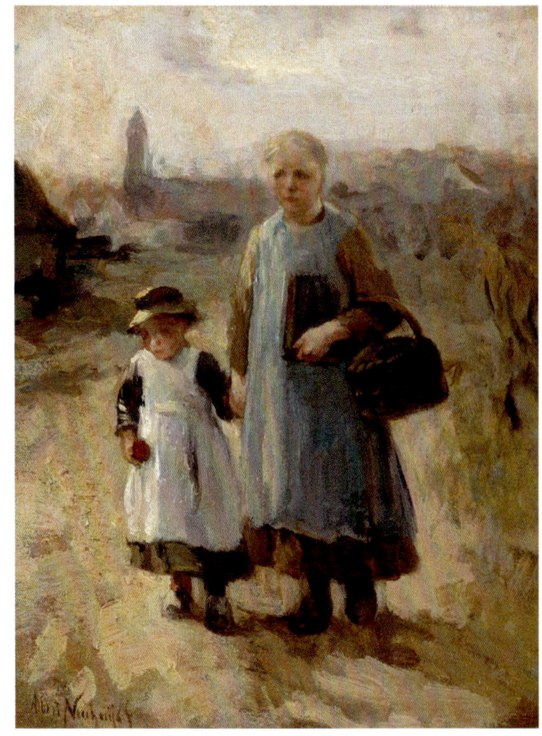

← **104** Gari Melchers, *The Sisters*, ca. 1895, oil on canvas, 184.2 x 133.7 cm. National Gallery of Art, Washington, Gift of C. H. Reisinger **105** Gari Melchers, *The Butterfly*, gouache on canvas, 132 x 59.7 cm. Gari Melchers Home and Studio, University of Mary Washington, Fredericksburg **106** Gari Melchers, *Dutch Children with Sleigh*, ca. 1895, oil on canvas, 88.9 x 66 cm. Gari Melchers Home and Studio, University of Mary Washington, Fredericksburg **107** Albert Neuhuys, *Going to School*, 1888–1889, oil on panel, 37 x 26 cm. Kunstmuseum Den Haag, Acquired from Mr. E. H. Crone with support of the Rembrandt Association

The Final Years in Egmond

[...] there are great changes at Egmond aan Zee [...]. The inhabitants there are foolish enough to believe they can make a Scheveningen out of the place so they are raising their board prices enormously – the consequence is no one is there. Only two of George's class are here this summer

Corinne Melchers (1905)[359]

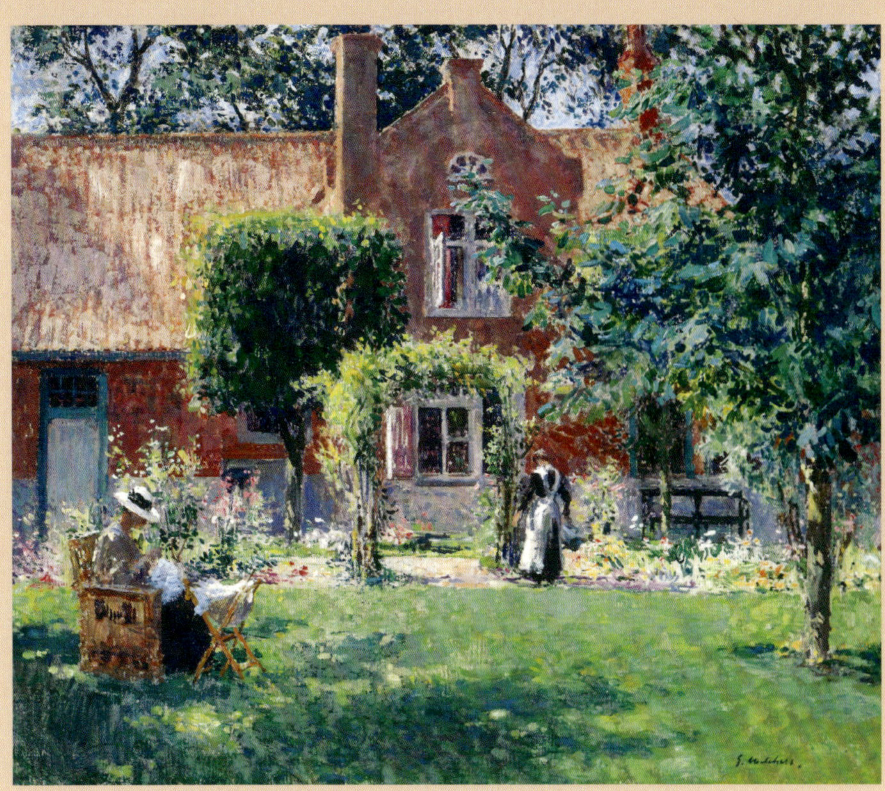

Married Life

Around the turn of the century, developments in Egmond followed rapidly. The fishing pinks hauled onto the beach and the activity surrounding them had become a thing of the past.[360] The number of (bathing) guests had quintupled in just over five years, from about 100 guests in 1896, to 500 in 1902. Accordingly, the number of hotels and guesthouses had also mushroomed. Although people still depended on the omnibus, great efforts were being made to lay the track for the steam streetcar, which would greatly improve accessibility.[361]

On 27 December 1902, Gari Melchers proposed to Corinne Lawson Mackall, who was twenty years his junior. A romance had blossomed during the months she attended Hitchcock's art class, leading to their marriage on 14 April 1903 on the British island of Jersey, in the parish church of Saint Brelade.[362] Before the wedding, Melchers had gone house hunting in Egmond. During this time, he usually stayed at Het Slot van den Hoef pension, run by the Bult family.[363] He wrote to his fiancé: "If I get the little house I will at once act out to buy old furniture and old china, galore – so that it may be presentable for the lady of my heart. [...] I will at the same time get a maid, the sister of one of Mrs H's maids who is already in her service."[364] Melchers initially rented a house in Egmond-Binnen, but later purchased the property at 8 Schoolstraat in Egmond aan den Hoef.[365] Behind the house lay a vast garden, and in the right wing, where a stable once stood, he created a studio [figs. 108 and 109].[366]

For many, it was a relief that Melchers finally settled in a more permanent residence. Indeed, as a bachelor, he had a habit of coming and going as he pleased, often leaving suddenly without any notice.[367] "No one, in those bachelor days, ever knew where to find him [...] his friends were amused or annoyed according to their several temperaments, and dealers on the hunt for pictures were driven to distraction."[368] Despite having a fixed address in Egmond, Melchers regularly traveled to Paris in his role as representative of American artists in Europe, while Corinne remained in Egmond, in part to learn Dutch.[369] On the rare occasion she did accompany him, she would immerse herself in Paris' high society. The couple's social life included spending the days around New Year's Eve 1903-1904 with musicians, for instance Mrs. Nevada and the pianist Barthelemy, art lovers like "miss" Hallowel, the Potter Palmers, and artists such as Walter MacEwen, with whom Melchers often served in juries and similar committees.[370]

In 1904, Henrietta and Corinne stayed behind in Paris while Gari embarked on a journey through Spain by automobile – a rare luxury at the time – with the wealthy collectors Charles and James Deering. Henrietta was to assist Corinne in ordering gowns from the city's dressmaking ateliers and together would enjoy Paris from Gari's apartment on Rue Galvani.[371] Meanwhile, Hitchcock was staying in London, where he spent several months almost annually and frequently socialized with the Shannons. His career continued to flourish – he was the only

108 Gari Melchers, *The Unpretentious Garden*, ca. 1903-1914, oil on canvas, 85.5 x 103 cm. Telfair Museums, Savannah, acquisition with funds provided by the Button Gwinnett Autograph Fund 1916

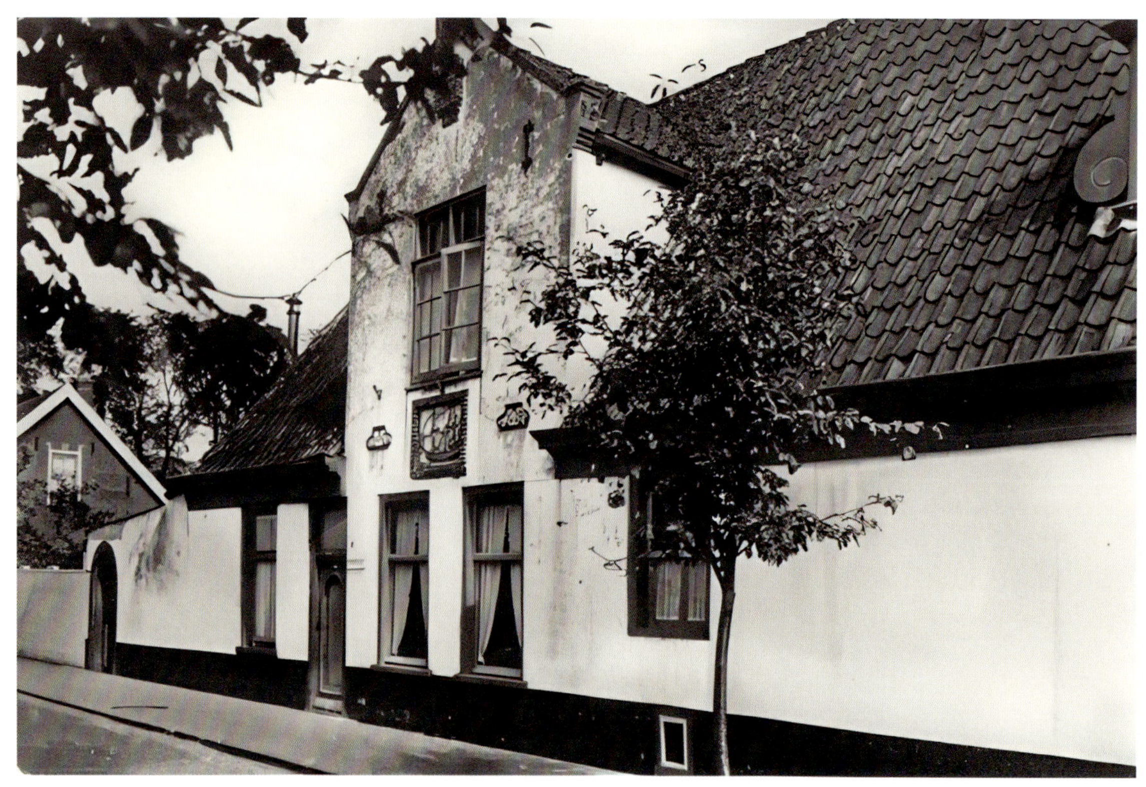

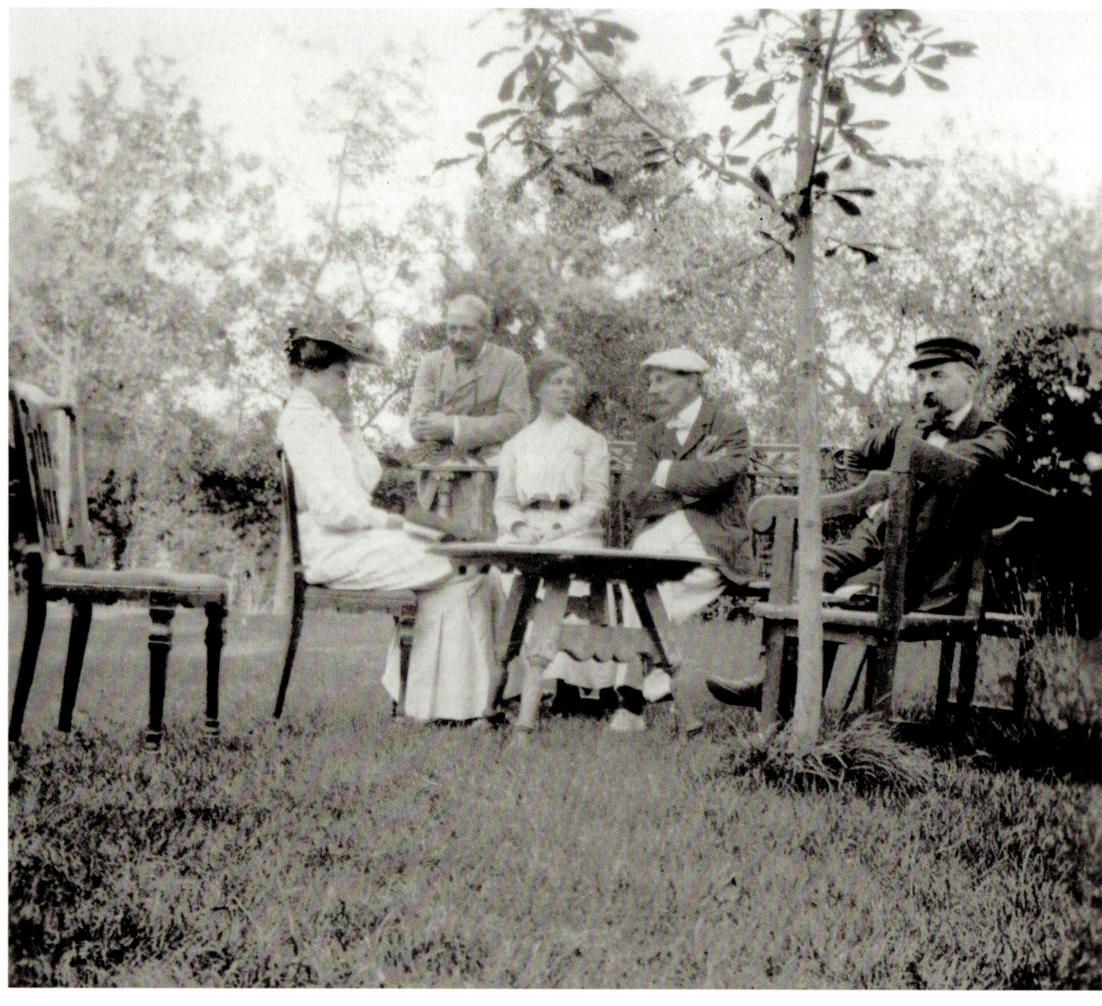

109 The house at 8 Schoolstraat, Egmond aan den Hoef. Photo Stichting Historisch Egmond   **110** From left to right, Henrietta Hitchcock, unknown, Corinne Melchers, George Hitchcock, Gari Melchers. Gari Melchers Home and Studio, University of Mary Washington, Fredericksburg

American artist to be appointed an Officer in the Order of Franz Joseph I by Emperor Franz Joseph I in recognition of his submission to the Vienna Exhibition.[372] Additionally, two of his works were published as postcards.[373]

Hitchcock's personal life, on the other hand, was anything but smooth sailing. In the summer of 1903, thirteen students attended his art class, including Florence Upton, Adaline Piper, and Cecil Jay (1880-1954). The latter had already studied at the Royal Academy of Art in England and at the academy of Hubert von Herkomer (1849-1914) in Bushey, Hertfordshire. A romance developed between Hitchcock and Jay, who was 30 years his junior, likely deepening in London during the winter of 1904. By the following summer, this affair led to George and Henrietta's divorce on grounds of adultery.[374] According to Corinne Melchers, the Hitchcocks' marriage had already been troubled for the past three to four years: Henrietta Hitchcock "knew that his best friends wouldn't trust him."[375] As part of the divorce settlement, Henrietta was granted ownership of Schuijlenburg and awarded an annual alimony of 2400 guilders.[376] In her new will, she named Corinne Melchers as her sole heir, though their maid, Kierie Blok, was to receive an annual allowance.[377] On 7 August, George Hitchcock officially deregistered as a resident of Egmond and married Cecil Jay just two days later in England.[378]

Art Classes Before and after Egmond

Hitchcock's departure marked the end of the Egmond Art Summer School. The divorce, combined with the sharply rising cost of accommodation in the Egmond villages, led to only four artists showing up for the classes in 1905. According to Corinne Melchers, they were divided between the guesthouses of Maartje Bult and Kraakman.[379] However, the studio at Schuijlenburg, which had long been *the* center for Hitchcock's art classes, did not remain vacant: Melchers arranged for Henrietta Walker Richardson to rent the studio.[380] The burgeoning tourism had also affected the studio at Torensduin. On 13 August 1906, Corinne Melchers wrote to her mother: "Gari is very busy – no he has not started any new pictures, but on the contrary, is working hard to finish all those begun at Egmond Zee for, can you believe it? They are going to tear down his house! The land having been sold to some building company."[381]

Having lived and worked in the Egmond villages for over two decades, starting in the winter of 1904-1905 Hitchcock no longer derived subjects from the typical North Holland coastal landscape and its inhabitants. In the following years, a clear shift in his oeuvre became evident. The foundation of his work – depictions of biblical and mythical stories – remained unchanged, but the landscape that served as the backdrop and the clothing of the main figures evolved. Take his *Calypso*,

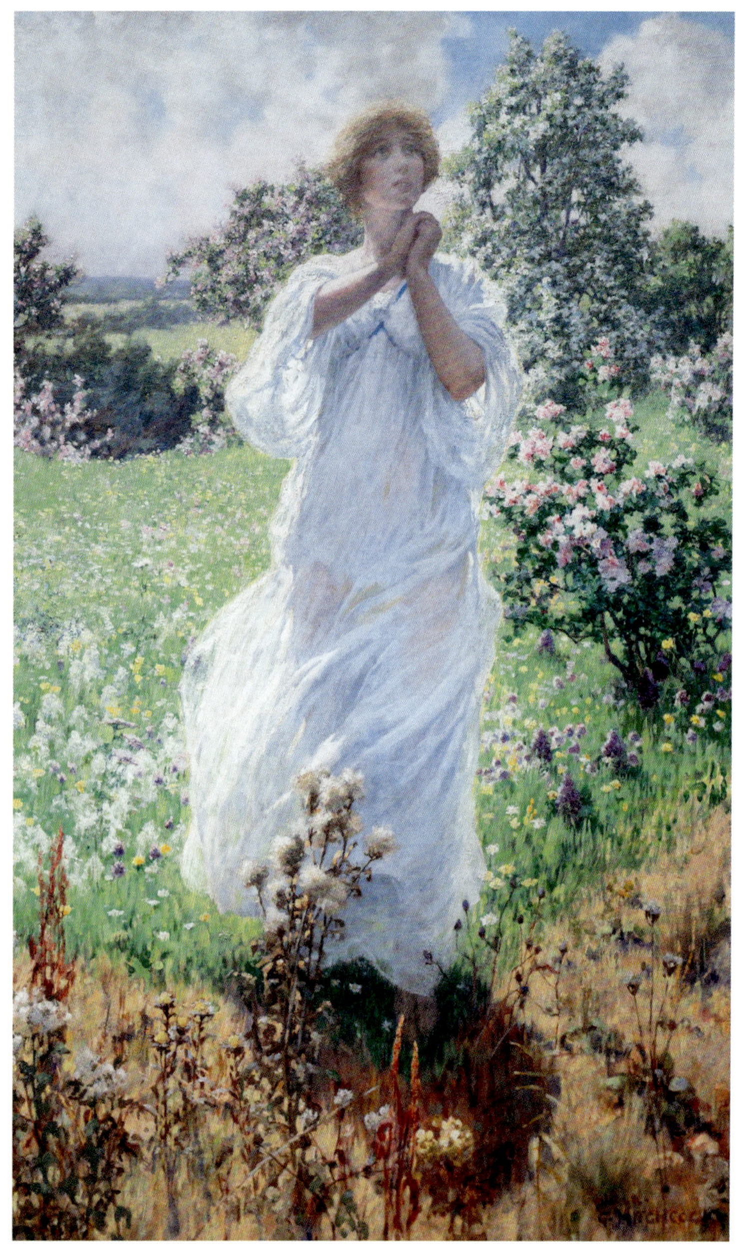

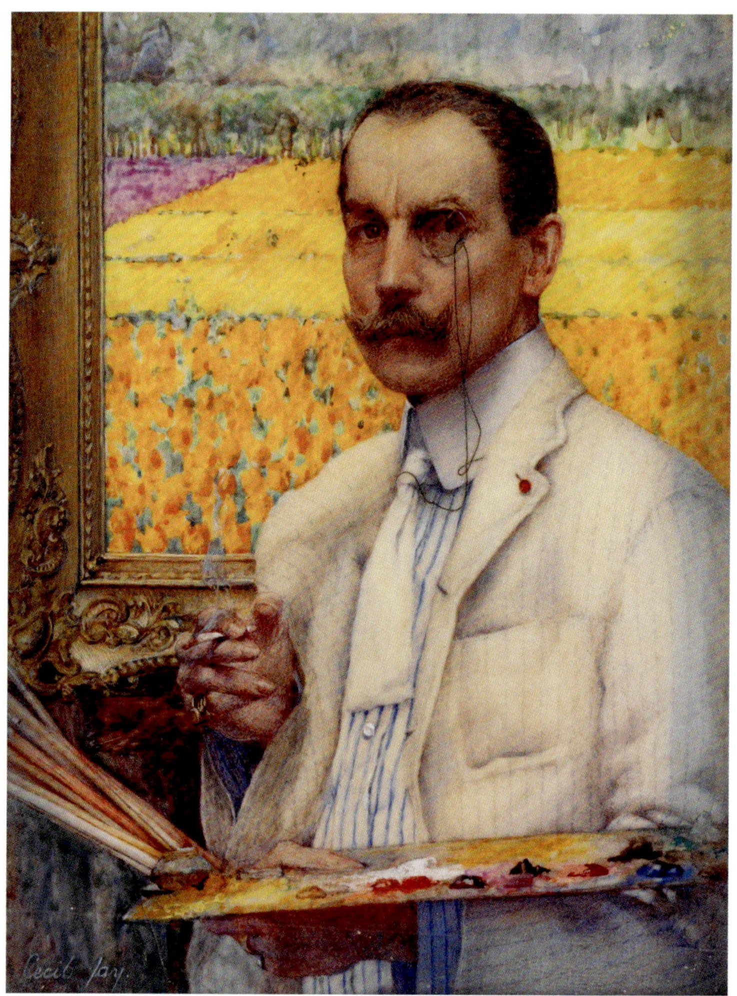

portraying the daughter of Atlas, on the mythical island of Ogygia, to which she had been exiled for not siding with the gods [fig. 113]. Both the rocky outcrop and the white, wind-blown, translucent garment no longer bear any relation to Egmond. The painting was shown from late April 1905 onward at the sixth international exhibition in Venice, in a hall for American artists curated by Gari Melchers.[382] One reviewer of the Venice exhibition was impressed: "a refined and lovely picture entitled 'Calypso,' representing a beautiful woman on a hillside, where the violets bloom and seem to scent the air."[383] The painting that Hitchcock showed at the 1907 Paris Salon is also illustrative of the new sources of inspiration. The 1907

Annunciation differs greatly from earlier "Egmond" paintings of the same subject [see figs. 38, 94 and 111].[384] Incidentally, Cecil Jay, or the new Mrs. Hitchcock, exhibited a portrait of Hitchcock with one of his successful pictures of flowering tulip fields in the background at that same Salon [fig. 112].[385]

Hitchcock's departure from Egmond, however, did not mean that he turned his back on the Netherlands. On the contrary, Hitchcock and Cecil Jay regularly stayed in the country, including in Zeeland. In 1908, *La fleur de février; Zeelana* [sic] (The Flower of February; Zeeland) was displayed at the Salon. The catalog accompanying the exhibition listed a different address: instead of "Egmond-sur-Hoef (Hollande)," it was 59 Rue de Provence, Paris.

As usual, the Hitchcocks visited England and in addition, they now traveled with some regularity to the United States. There, the newlywed Mrs. Hitchcock gave art history classes in Baltimore and New York.[386] She divided the lectures into three sections: American art, French art, and "Modern Athens."[387]

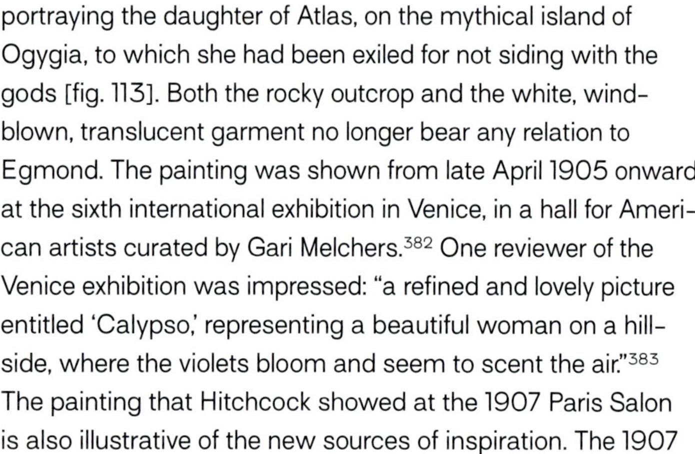

111 George Hitchcock, *The Annunciation*, 1906, oil on canvas, 198,1 x 137,2 cm. Lightner Museum, Florida, Gift of David E. Gonzales   **112** Cecil Jay, *Portrait of George Hitchcock*, 1907, watercolor on ivory, 15.2 x 11.4 cm. Rhode Island School of Design, Providence, Gift of Mr. O.V. Calder   → **113** George Hitchcock, *Calypso*, 1905, oil on canvas, 111.8 x 88.9 cm. Indianapolis Museum of Art at Newfields, acquisition with funds provided by Mrs. John M. Judah, Newton Booth Tarkington, Clarence Wulsin, Stoughton Fletcher, an Anonymous Donor, and the John Herron Fund

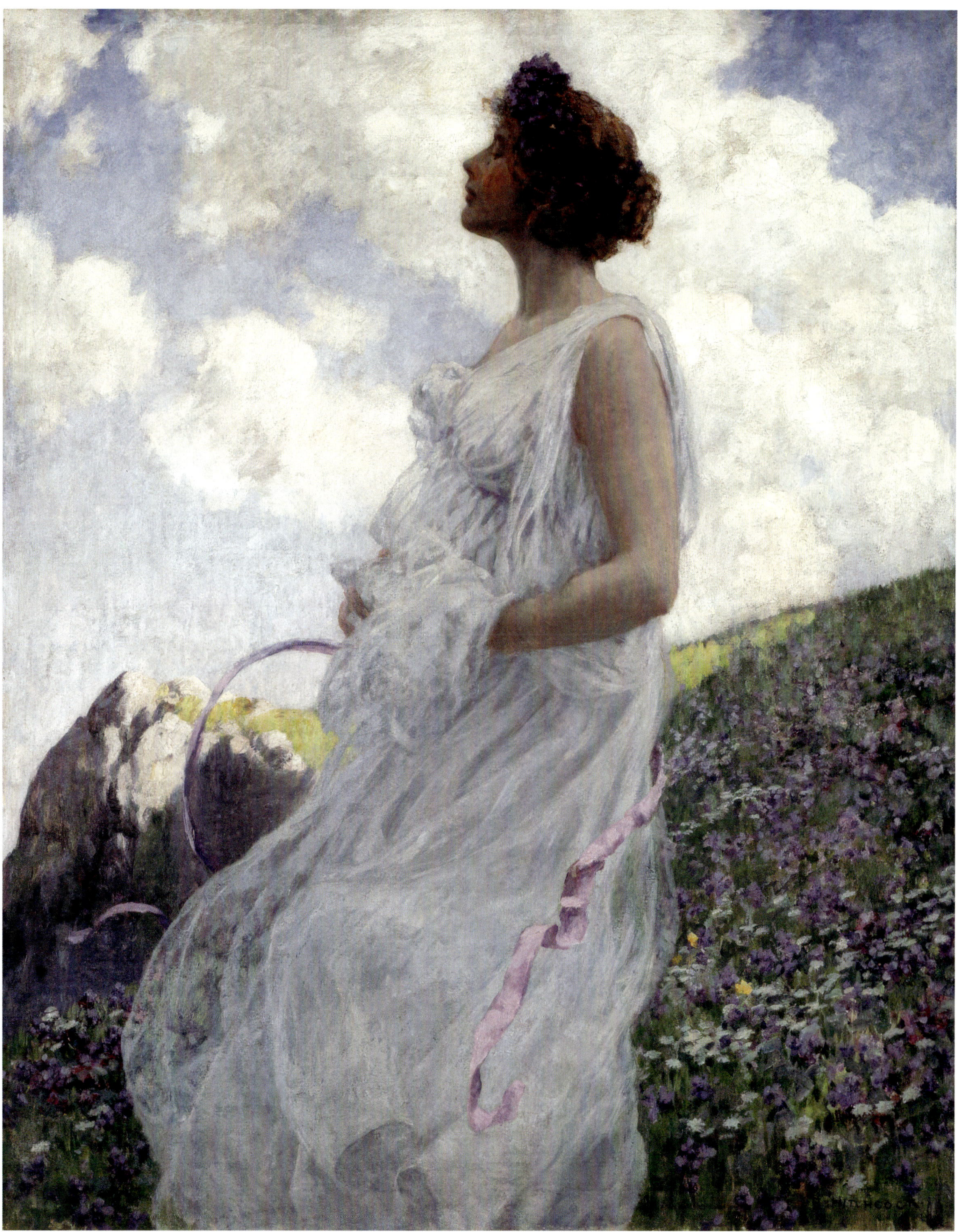

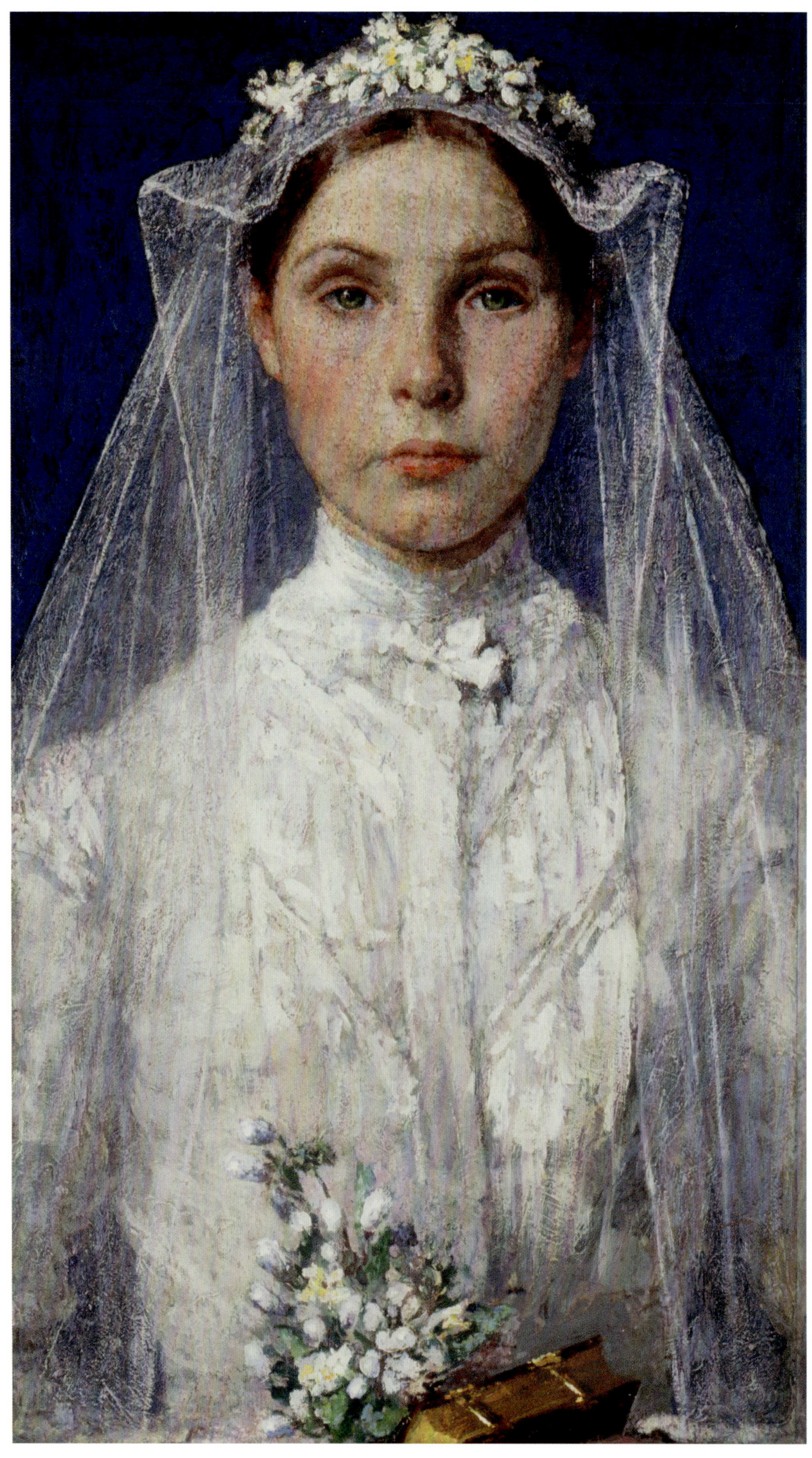

114 Gari Melchers, *The Bride*, 1903, oil on panel, 54 x 30.8 cm. Gari Melchers Home and Studio, University of Mary Washington, Fredericksburg

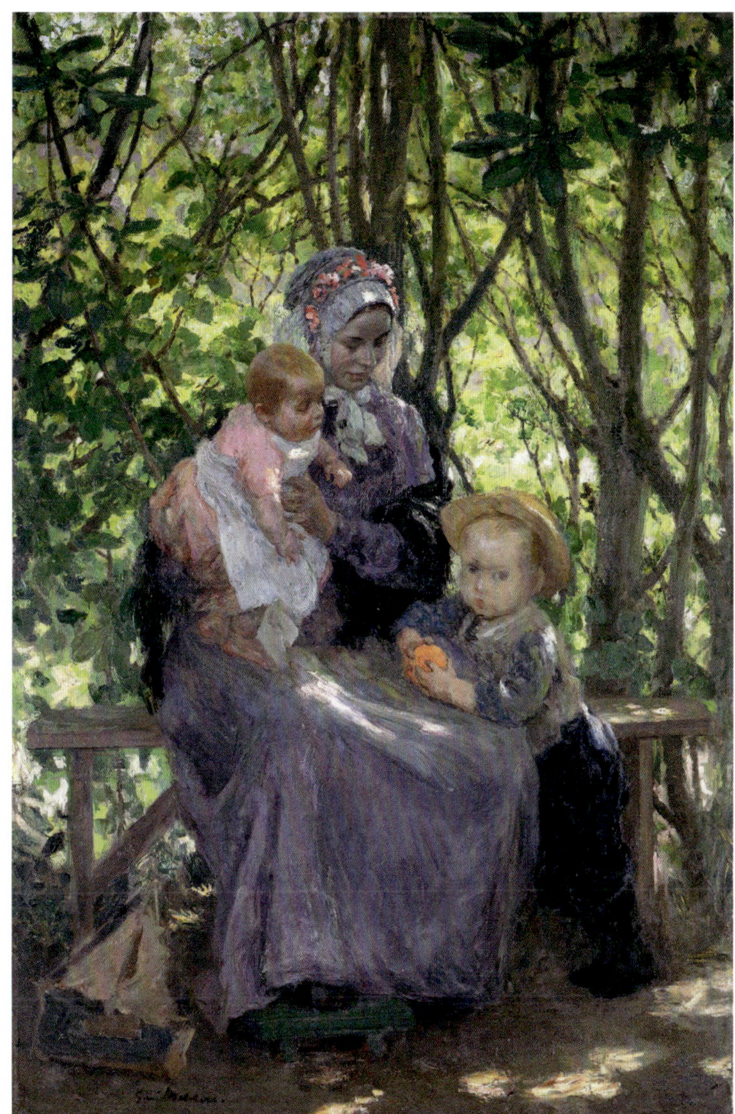

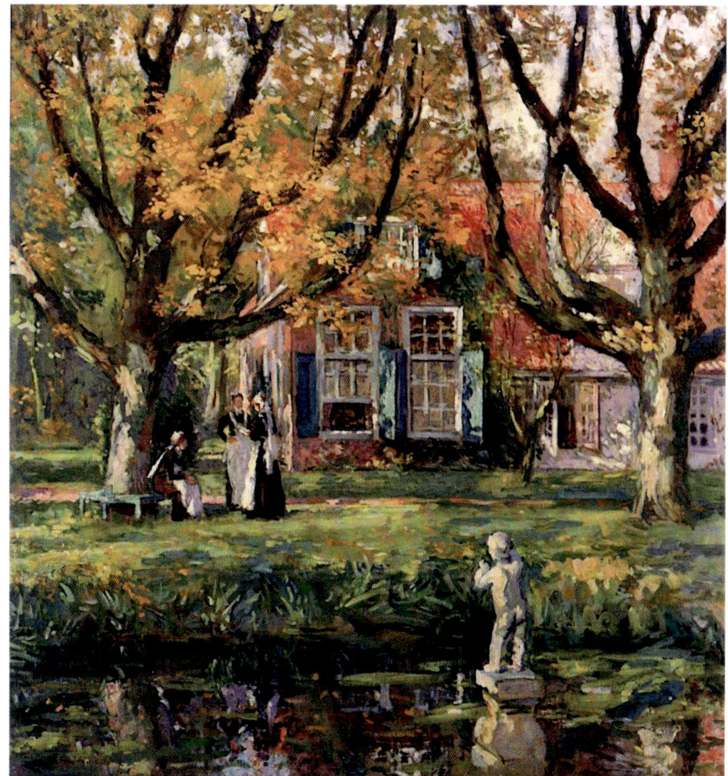

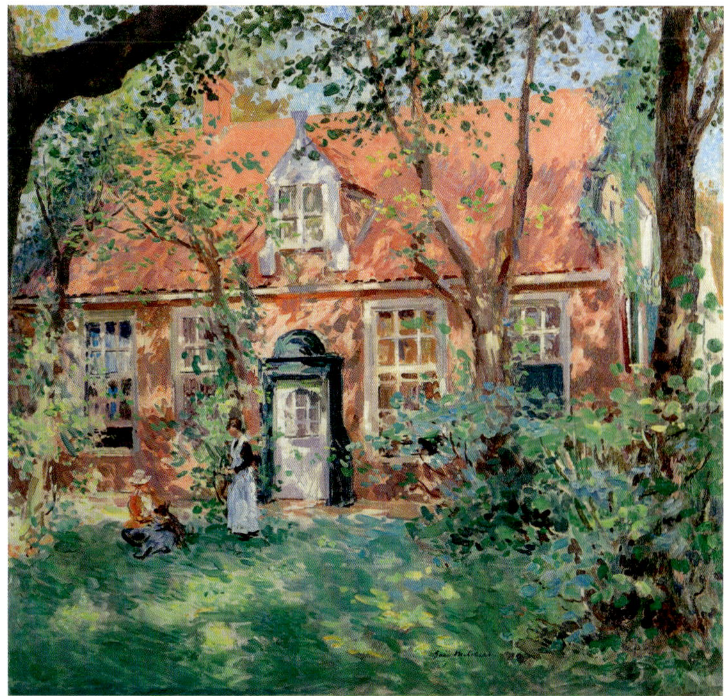

Melchers' Oeuvre after the Turn of the Century

Not only Hitchcock, but Melchers, too, changed course in terms of subject matter and style after the turn of the century. This was due to a combination of factors: his new social status, the rapidly changing character of Egmond, and the innovative movements in the arts that followed each other in rapid succession from 1870 onward. Initially, Impressionism was considered extremely radical because of its spontaneously painted, somewhat sketchily rendered "impressions" of modern life and its particular focus on painting light effects outdoors. However, as the style grew increasingly popular, such works were widely collected in the United States as well by 1900.

In the early years of the twentieth century, Melchers still elaborated on familiar themes in his realistic style, as in *The Bride*, a painting for which Anna Dekker, a young lady from Egmond, posed [fig. 114]. At the same time, his painting style increasingly moved in the direction of French Impressionism, as seen in the loose brushwork of the works he made outdoors, such as *The Grove,* and the depictions of the garden of his house on Schoolstraat and that of Schuijlenburg [see figs. 108, 116 and 117]. Melchers painted these studies of sunlight and reflections for relaxation, as a break from the larger genre scenes.[388]

 115 Gari Melchers, *The Grove*, ca. 1908, oil on canvas, 167 x 111 cm. Musée d'Orsay, Paris **116** Gari Melchers, *My Garden (Schuijlenburg)*, ca. 1903, oil on canvas, 104.1 x 101.6 cm. The Butler Institute of American Art, Youngstown, Ohio **117** Gari Melchers, *House under the Trees*, ca. 1908, oil on canvas, 95.3 x 106.7 cm. Private collection

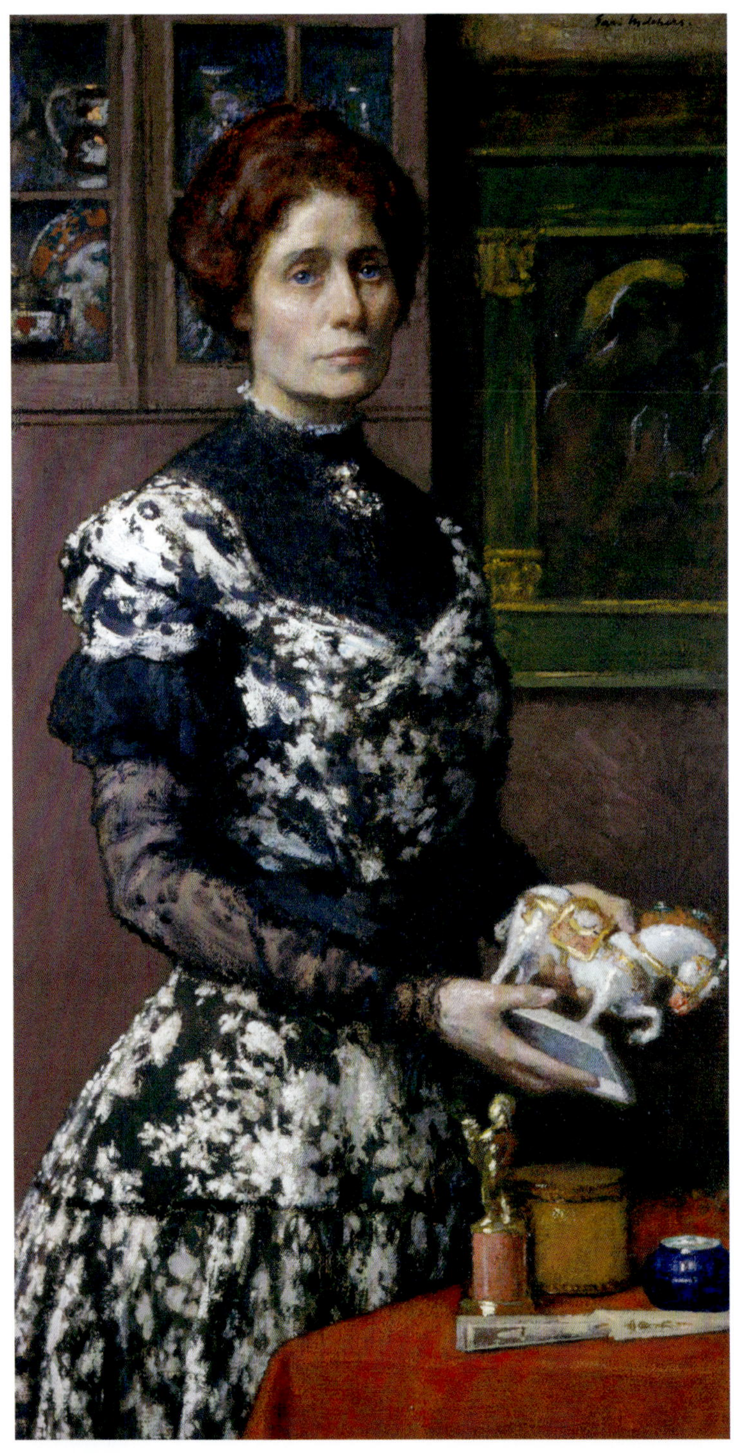

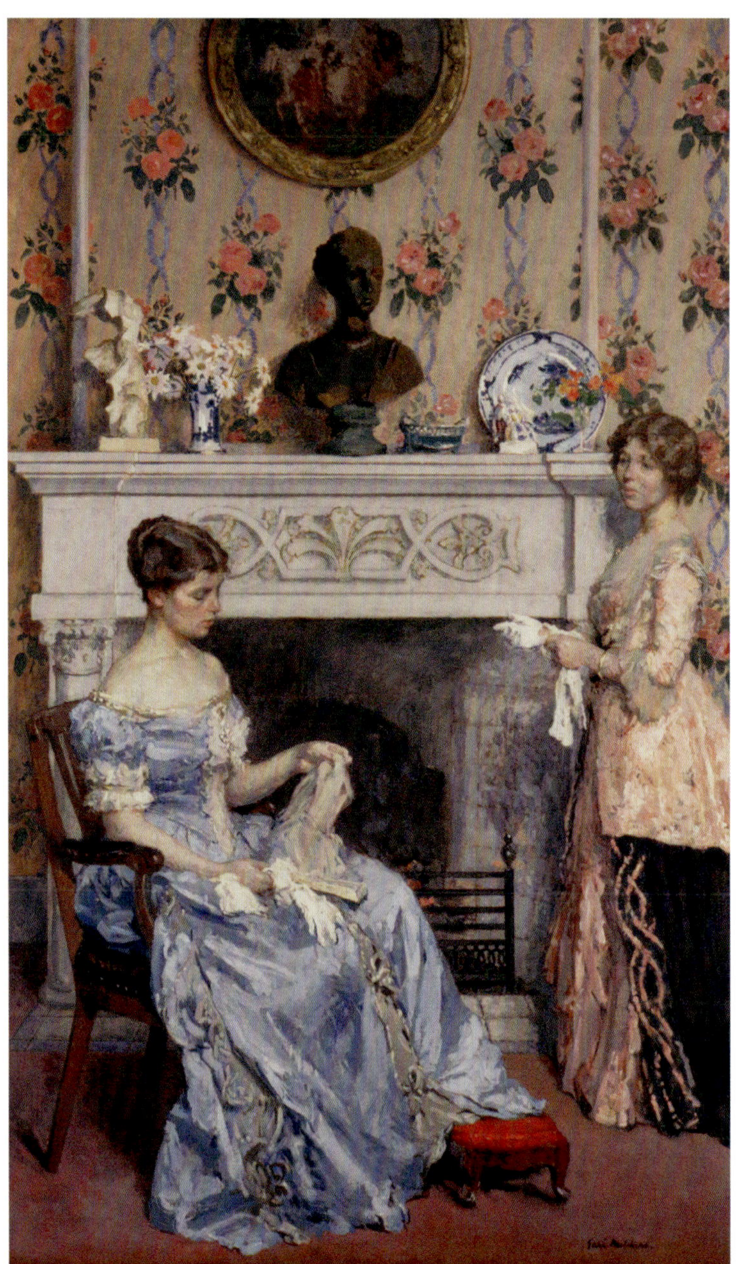

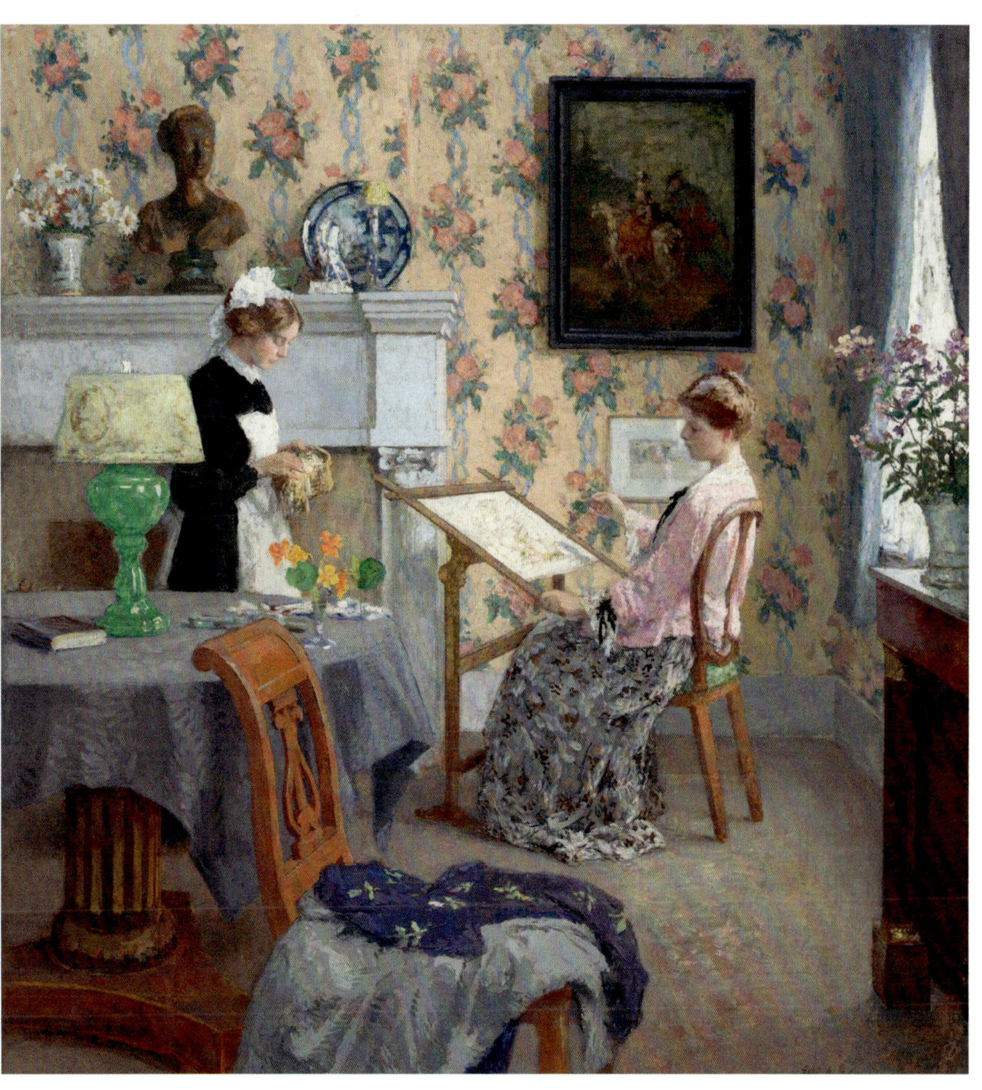

Incidentally, *The Grove*, "[...] a delightful work by Mr. Gari Melchers, which also depicts a mother and young children sheltered under a grove pierced by sunlight," was, acquired by the French National Museum.[389]

Alongside these deftly limned, colorful works, Melchers now created paintings of stylish, decorative interiors – made in Schuijlenburg – featuring fashionable women, for which Henrietta and Corinne regularly modelled. One of the first was *The Delft Horse* – a portrait of Henrietta Hitchcock – and the likewise somewhat dark painting *The China Closet* [see figs. 77 and 118]. This was followed by *At Home (Winged Victory)* and *Penelope*, for which Melchers used the same wallpaper in the background each time [figs. 119 and 120]. Melchers painted *At Home (Winged Victory)* in Schuijlenburg's drawing room, near the magnificent, still extant, fireplace. The title refers to the figurine on the mantlepiece at the left. It is a small replica

of one of the most famous statues from antiquity: the *Nike of Samothrace* (ca. 190 BCE). The life-size statue of the Greek goddess of victory was displayed in the Louvre from 1884 and has been admired by many ever since.

In a completely different way, Melchers also referenced Greek antiquity in *Penelope*. According to the Greek poet Homer, Penelope was married to Odysseus, the king of Ithaca. After her husband's prolonged absence, she promised under pressure to marry one of her many suitors once her embroidery was finished. Every night, however, she unraveled her handiwork so that she could wait longer for her husband to return, eventually successfully. Corinne may have been referring to this painting, when she wrote: "Gari is still working daily at Schuilenburg [sic] and Kierie is here also to pose. Two beautiful pictures are in progress, interiors like the one of Kierie and me threading the needle."[390]

←118 Gari Melchers, *The Delft Horse*, ca. 1900, oil on canvas, 112.4 x 57.8 cm. Gari Melchers Home and Studio, University of Mary Washington, Fredericksburg
←119 Gari Melchers, *At Home (Winged Victory)*, ca. 1905–1910, oil on canvas, 250.2 x 150.5 cm. Gari Melchers Home and Studio, University of Mary Washington, Fredericksburg   120 Gari Melchers, *Penelope*, 1910, oil on canvas, 138.4 x 129.2 cm. National Gallery of Art, Washington

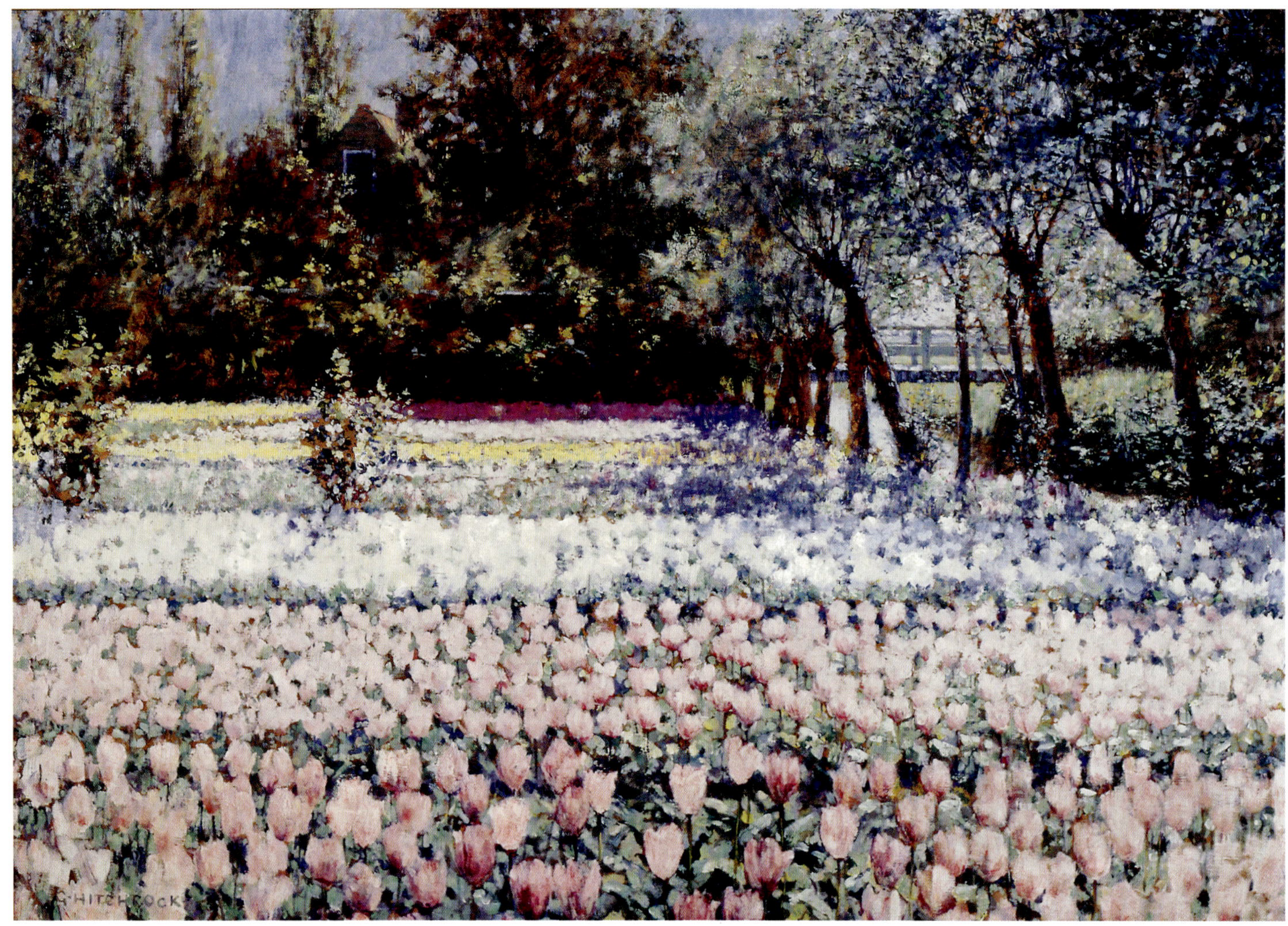

New Studios: New York and Weimar

Notably, Melchers did not send any of these fine interior pieces to the Salon in Paris.[391] For various reasons, from around 1905 he increasingly focused on the United States, where he was still relatively unknown to the general public. The subtitle of an article devoted to Melchers in an American magazine read: "Gari Melchers, A great American painter who has received more recognition abroad than at home."[392] Among artists, Melchers was of course no stranger, due to his lauded submissions to American exhibitions and his tireless promotion of American artists living in Europe. Beginning in 1906, Melchers could therefore call himself a National Academician, an honorary title given to artists nominated or elected by the National Academy of Design.

In that same year, Melchers was appointed by Alexander Rudolph Lawton – Corinne's maternal uncle – as an advisor to the Telfair Museum of Art in Savannah, a position he would hold for ten years.[393] Melchers' trait of "[his] readiness to recognize the good work of others, even when it did not conform with his own artistic standards," made him well suited for that.[394] Among the 70 works that the museum acquired thanks to his efforts were paintings by European artists such as Jan Toorop (1858-1928), François Bonvin (1817-1887), and Jean-François Raffaelli (1850-1924), as well as American ones, including Childe Hassam, James Jebusa Shannon, and George Hitchcock. However, Melchers did not purchase Shannon's *Portrait of Hitchcock* or Hitchcock's *Early Spring in Holland* from Hitchcock himself, but rather from the latter's ex-wife Henrietta [see figs. 53 and 121]. She had remarried on 18 November 1907, to the British writer and art expert Charles Lewis Hind (1862-1927), who had worked as an editor for *Scribner's Magazine*.[395] The fact that Melchers did not buy paintings directly from Hitchcock suggests that the bond between Hitchcock and Melchers had been broken since the divorce.[396]

The periods Melchers spent in America became more frequent and longer. Very deliberately, in May 1906, he rented a studio with an apartment at Bryant Park Studios in New York. He did so in the hope of exhibiting there more often and gaining

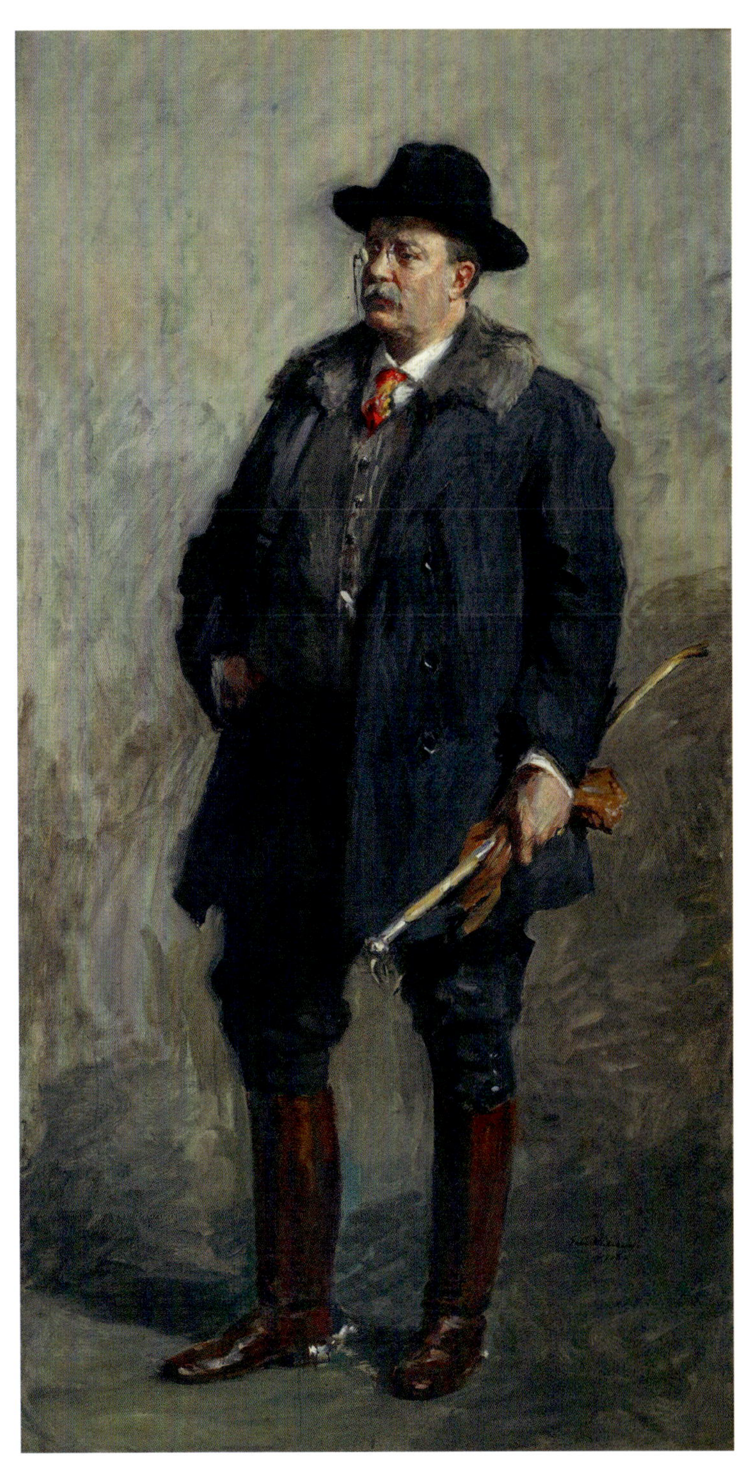

more exposure to American clients, including through portrait
commissions.[397] Both goals were quickly achieved. In 1908,
he worked on the prestigious commission to paint a portrait
of President Roosevelt [fig. 122].[398] Furthermore, after several
exhibitions at galleries, that year he had his first retrospective at
the renowned art dealer Cottier and Co. On display were recent
works made in New York, as well as his first major successful
painting *The Sermon* and the earliest interior pieces from
Egmond: *The Delft Horse* and *The China Closet* [figs. 29, 77
and 116.[399]

   122 Gari Melchers, *Portrait of President Theodore Roosevelt*, 1908, oil on canvas, 214.4 x 112.5 cm. Smithsonian, National Museum of Asian Art, Gift of Charles Lang Freer

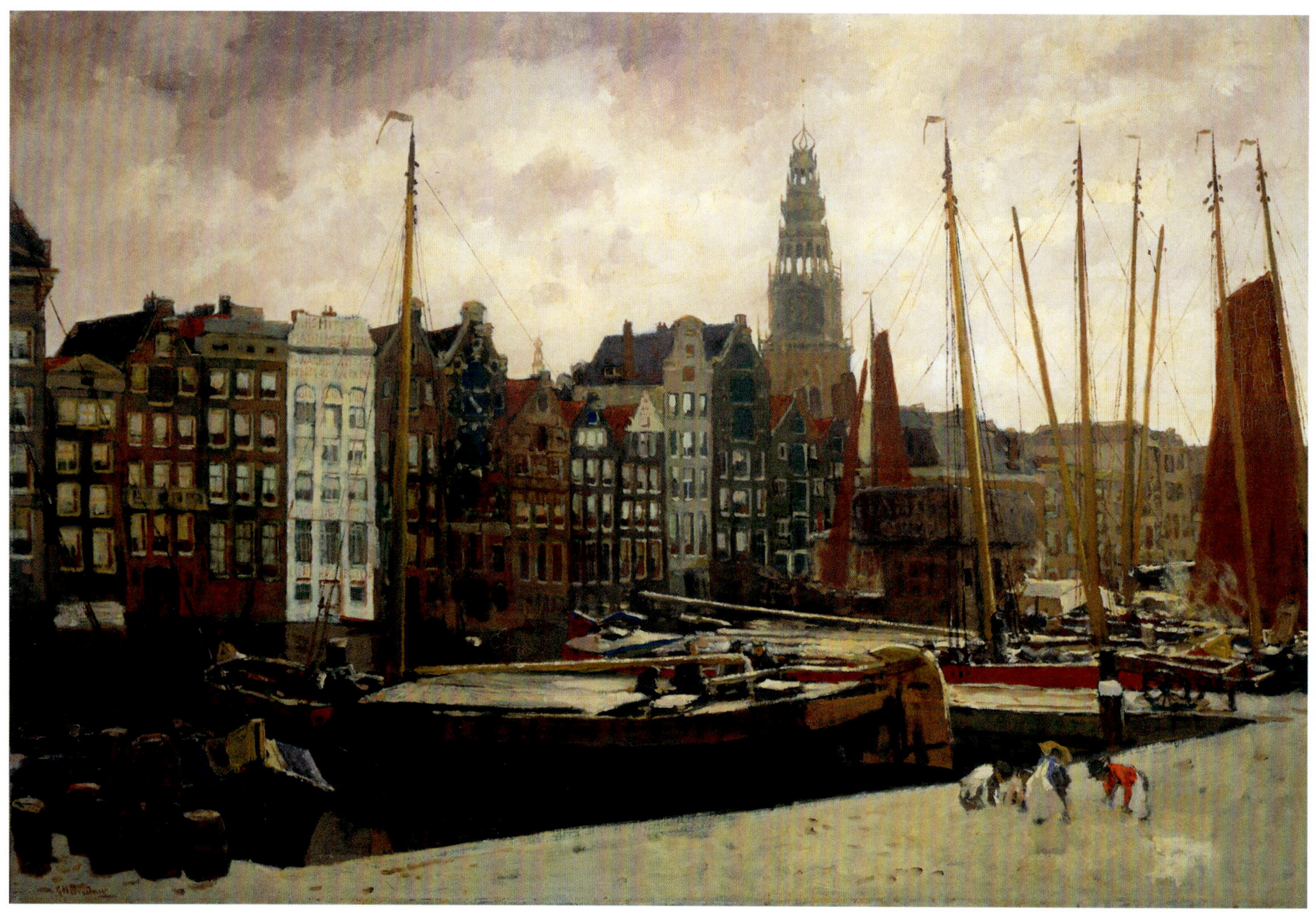

Despite the focus on career opportunities in America, the Netherlands and Egmond remained fully in the picture for Melchers. From 1905 to 1914, he and his Dutch confreres Hendrik Willem Mesdag, Bernardus Johannes Blommers), and George Hendrik Breitner (1857-1923) formed the advisory committee responsible for selecting the Dutch entries for the annual international exhibitions at the Carnegie Institute in Pittsburgh [fig. 123].[400] He himself also exhibited there under the Dutch flag. Although Melchers rarely exhibited in the Netherlands, he was definitely in contact with the leading Dutch artists. In addition, Melchers sent his decorative interior pieces to Pittsburgh: in 1907 he showed *The Delft Horse*, in 1908 *The China Closet*, and in 1914 *The Open Door* [fig. 124].[401]

As usual, Melchers continued to spend his summers in Egmond, where in 1907 the German collector Hugo Reisinger, who had emigrated to America, visited one day to select a fine work from his "talented friend."[402] Other artists still found their way to Egmond as well; the artist couple Fokko Tadama (1871-1937) and Thamine Tadama-Groeneveld (1871-1938) lived in Huize Wimmenum for several years, and Ernest Robert Salmon Noir (1864-1931) painted Egmond children in 1908: "Yesterday the house was full of kids to be painted and amused," Corinne sighed.[403]

In 1908, Melcher's considerable reputation in Europe led to a request from Wilhelm Ernest, Grand Duke of Saxony-Weimar-Eisenach, for him to become a professor at the Grand Ducal Academy of Art in Weimar.[404] Melchers worked there from 1909 to 1914, but reportedly only had to grade students' work once a week, had a spacious studio at 35 Cranachstrasse, and enjoyed enough freedom to travel with his wife. In 1910, for example, the couple visited Athens for the first time.[405] Corinne, however, did not enjoy being in Weimar; she struggled to learn the language and had difficulty finding her place.[406] She preferred to live in Egmond.[407]

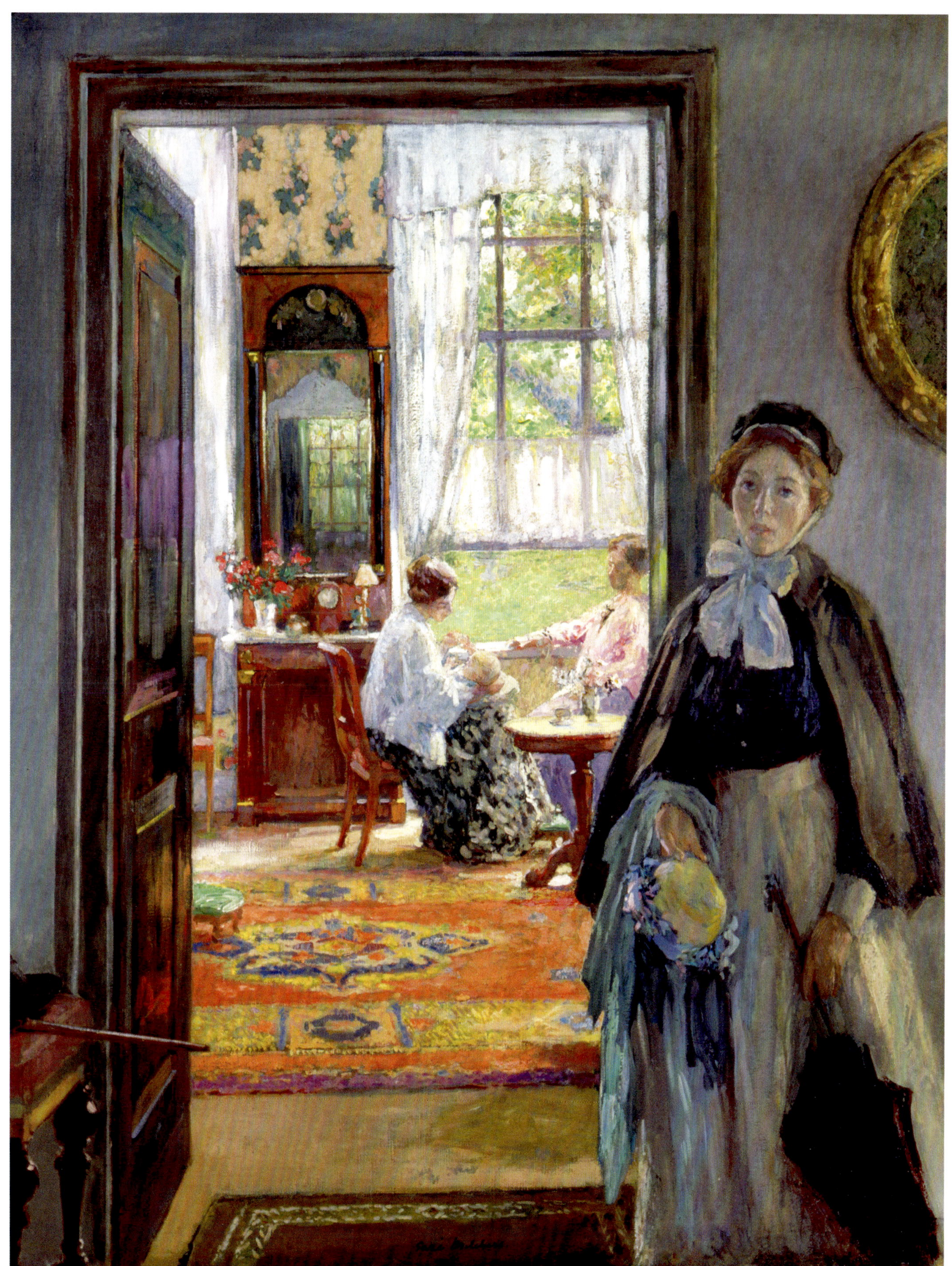

121   **124** Gari Melchers, *The Open Door*, ca. 1905–1910, oil on canvas, 160 x 125.7 cm. Gari Melchers Home and Studio, University of Mary Washington, Fredericksburg

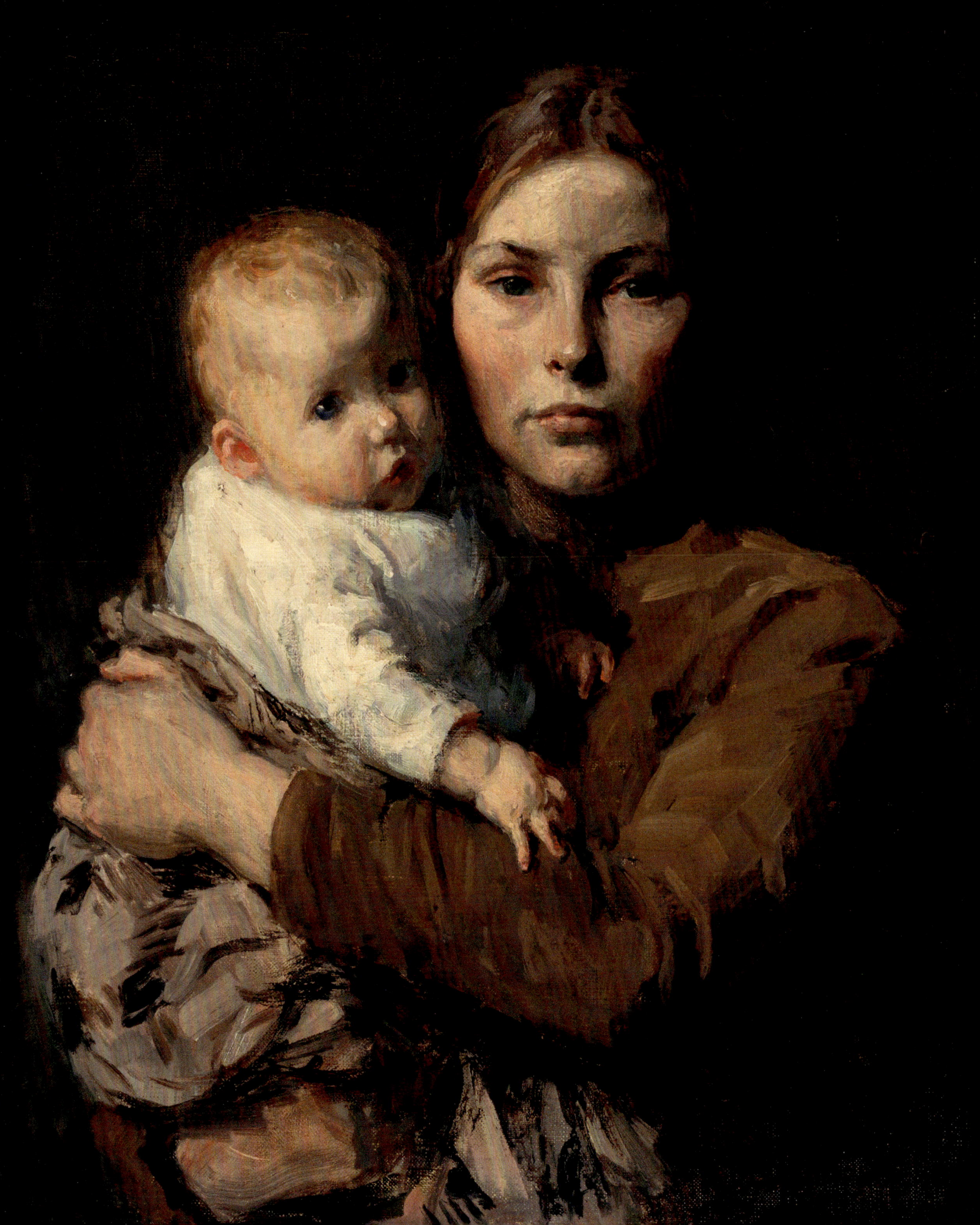

Hitchcock Dies and Melchers Leaves Europe

The Melchers' final years in Egmond were spent without Henrietta's company. Although she and her second husband Lewis Hind officially registered in Egmond on 16 June 1908, the newlyweds soon left for England with Kierie Blok.[408] Melchers was still allowed to use the studio at Schuijlenburg: "for a while, at least."[409] The artist continued to come to Egmond to work, although Corinne wrote: "We are here you know to work but we are enjoying ourselves for this wonderful air does act like champagne on us both and you know what effect that has."[410] In the morning, the couple left for Schuijlenburg before nine o'clock, where they worked until four in the afternoon. With Miggles gone, they spent much of their time with the Van den Arend family, who lived next to Schuijlenburg. Corinne called them their only Dutch friends.[411]

Melchers never stopped searching for suitable subjects, not only in Egmond but also in the surrounding area. For example, he wanted to paint in the church of the nearby village of Schermerhorn, but after the key broke off in the lock, he worked instead in Alkmaar along one of the canals.[412] When the weather was poor, he once again focused on interior scenes, for which Corinne served as model. However, at exhibitions he mainly displayed paintings of a (nursing) mother and child [fig. 125].[413]

Meanwhile, Hitchcock and Jay traveled from Paris to London, Spain, and the United States. Additionally, Hitchcock still sojourned regularly in the Netherlands; for example, he signed the Town Hall guest book in Veere, in the province of Zeeland, in 1910.[414] By this time, he was working from a studio boat unsurprisingly named *The Tulip*.[415] On 2 August 1913, Hitchcock unexpectedly passed away aboard this boat, which was then moored near a house in the harbor district of the island of Marken.[416] According to an obituary in *The Daily Mail*, the artist had died in harness; he collapsed from a heart attack while putting the final touches – brushstrokes – on work he intended to exhibit in America.[417]

The ten-year-younger Melchers still had a life ahead of him at the time of Hitchcock's death, but after the outbreak of World War I in August 1914, he decided to leave Europe. The Melchers' arrived in New York on the steamship *SS Finland* on 28 December 1914. This marked the end of Melchers' 30-year stay in Egmond. Initially, they lived in New York, but in 1917 Melchers purchased Belmont, a small estate in Falmouth, Virginia, on the northern bank of the Rappahannock River.[418]

However, Gari and Corinne did not completely turn their backs on the three Egmonds. During the war years – and even afterwards – the couple, along with Henrietta Lewis Hind from England, provided financial support to their friends in Egmond.[419] After the war, they returned to the North-Holland villages several times. For instance, Corinne wrote in her diary on 25 September 1922: "Gari goes to Schulenburg [sic] and finds it overgrown with vines, but everything intact. He finds a canvas begun of the mantel and goes to work immediately."[420] On 2 October of that year, they sold the "dear little house" on Schoolstraat to the artist Pierre Jean Apol (1867-1947) for 9000 guilders.[421] Two days later, Henrietta and Charles Lewis Hind arrived to clear out Schuijlenburg; letters were burned and, together with Kierie Blok, the property was cleaned.[422] During all these activities, former models like Anna Dekker and "Heritje Zwart" came by to greet their friends. Schuijlenburg was also put up for sale. On 7 June 1923, the house, outbuildings, vegetable garden, garden, grove, and meadow were sold for 8500 guilders to the Stichting Amsterdamsche Kolonieverpleging voor kinderen (Amsterdam Colony Nursing Foundation for Children).[423] A number of villagers continued to correspond with Corinne Melchers, recalling the "happy time when you were in Egmond with Mr. Melchers" and thanked her for the money she sent for the Christmas trees.[424] After his death in 1932, Melchers – "our dear friend" – was remembered in Egmond; the pastor noted, "Mr. Melchers belonged to the village, and his kind presence will be sorely missed."[425]

    125 Gari Melchers, *Mother and Child*, ca. 1906, oil on canvas, 63.5 x 54.3 cm. Art Institute of Chicago, Gift of James Deering

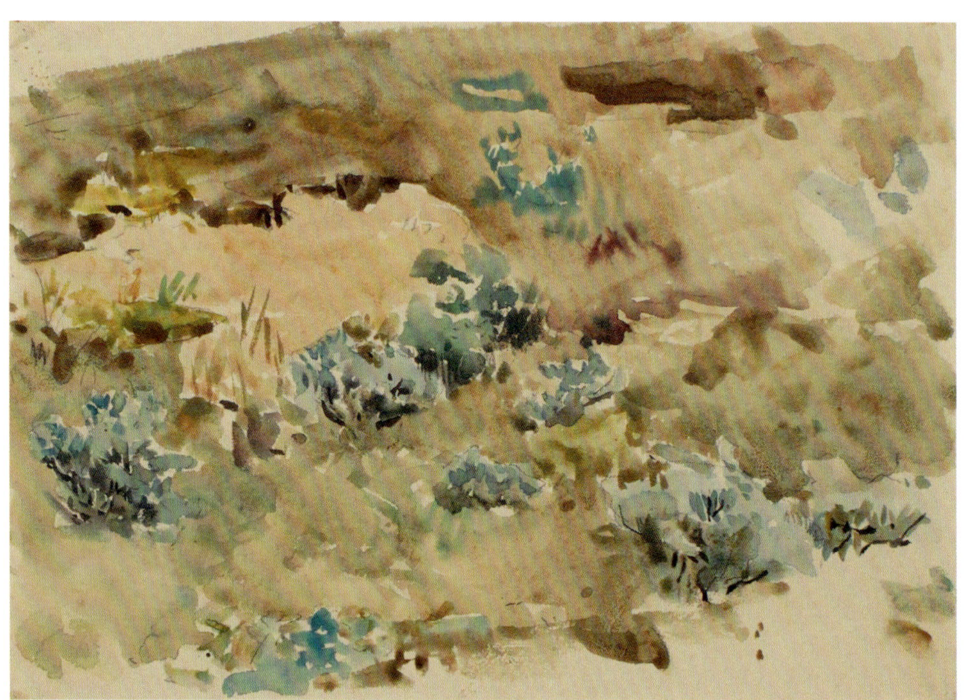

Longing for Egmond
In Conclusion
Painters of Realities and Sunlight

In 1887, three small villages on the Dutch North Sea coast, the three Egmonds, suddenly appeared on the world's artistic map. Discovered by chance by Hitchcock during the heyday of The Hague School, Egmond became a decades-long source of inspiration for two American artists: George Hitchcock and Gari Melchers. Due to the successes of Melchers' *The Sermon* and Hitchcock's *Tulip Fields*, the small fishing community and the dune and polder landscape were literally brought into the spotlight for artists and the cultural elite of Europe and America.

The large, realistically painted canvases with narrative elements that both artists laid out during the summer months in Egmond align seamlessly with the spirit of the times. Trained in the academic, naturalistic tradition of the Düsseldorf and Paris academies and inspired by the painters of The Hague School and the Dutch Old Masters, Hitchcock and Melchers depicted the life and labor of the people of Egmond as a tribute to the virtues of hardworking fishermen and farmers. In their pictures, references to a higher reality behind the ordinary world of appearances were soon incorporated. Popular biblical – and later mythological – stories were staged by the artists in contemporary Egmond. Hitchcock and Melchers used local models, regional costumes collected from the Netherlands, the varied surrounding landscape, existing landmarks such as the Protestant church and the Slotkapel, and – at least in Melchers's case – photography.

While Melchers chose to portray a variety of fair and distinctive faces, Hitchcock focused more on universally accepted ideals of beauty in his choice of models. He usually painted them in the landscape around midday, when the sun was at its zenith, earning him the title of "the painter of sunlight." "If a landscape painter is a true artist, he paints not the things, but the effects," Hitchcock mused.[426] By virtue of his articles about picturesque Holland in *Scribner's Magazine* and his long-running art classes, many artists visited the Egmonds.

This longing for Egmond was also fueled within Melchers' extensive circle of friends and acquaintances. He quickly gained fame
as "the painter of realities," an artist who excelled in painting portraits, people, and poses.[427] An artist, moreover, who championed
his confreres by serving on juries and committees. Both Hitchcock and Melchers regularly won prestigious awards, sold their
work internationally to collectors and museums, and received
various honors and knightly orders throughout their careers.
Underlying all that fame were the three Egmond villages.

Hitchcock's departure from Egmond in 1905 coincided with
its transition from a fishing village to a fashionable seaside resort.
In the years leading up to the outbreak of World War I, Melchers
shifted his focus, painting gardens and interior scenes more in
the vein of the French Impressionists. With Hitchcock's death
in 1913 and Melchers' departure in December 1914 as war swept
across Europe, the curtain fell on over twenty years of American
Longing for Egmond.

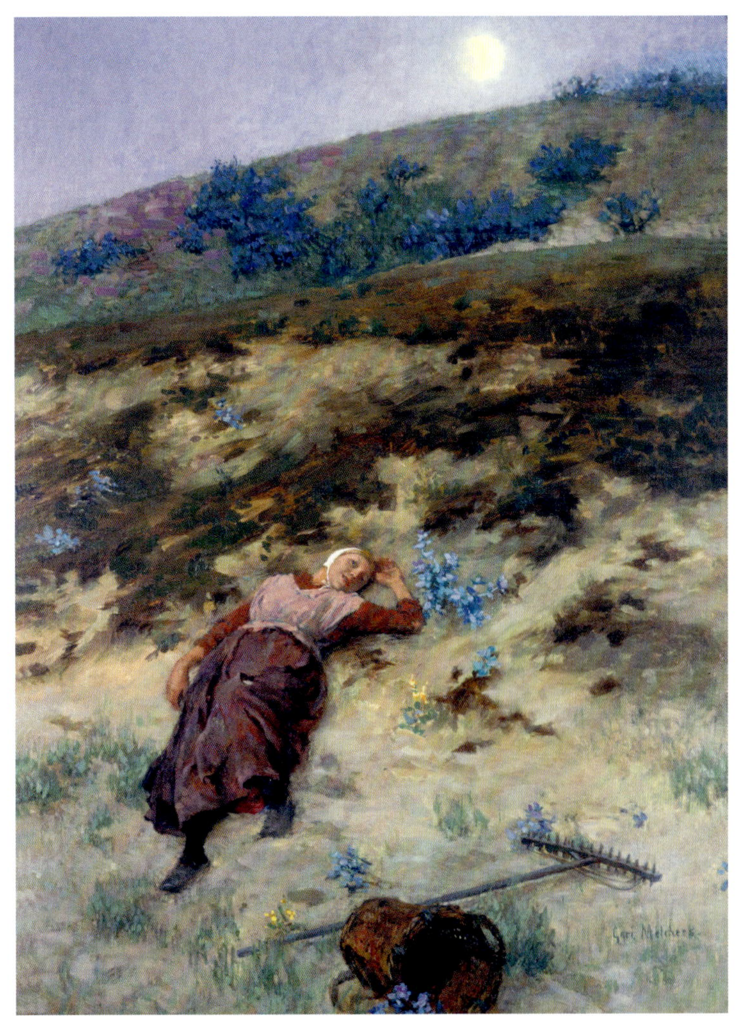

 127 Gari Melchers, *The Tired Moss Gatherer*, 1887, oil on canvas, 94 x 68.6 cm. Gari Melchers Home and Studio, University of Mary Washington, Fredericksburg

Appendix: Artists in Egmond

I could dwell at length on the life at Egmond Hoef. The visits to Schuil en Berg [sic], the home of the Hitchcocks, where so many temperaments met and discussed art [...]. The informal dinners in the vivid blue dining room of the Gari Melchers

Adeline Piper (1923)[428]

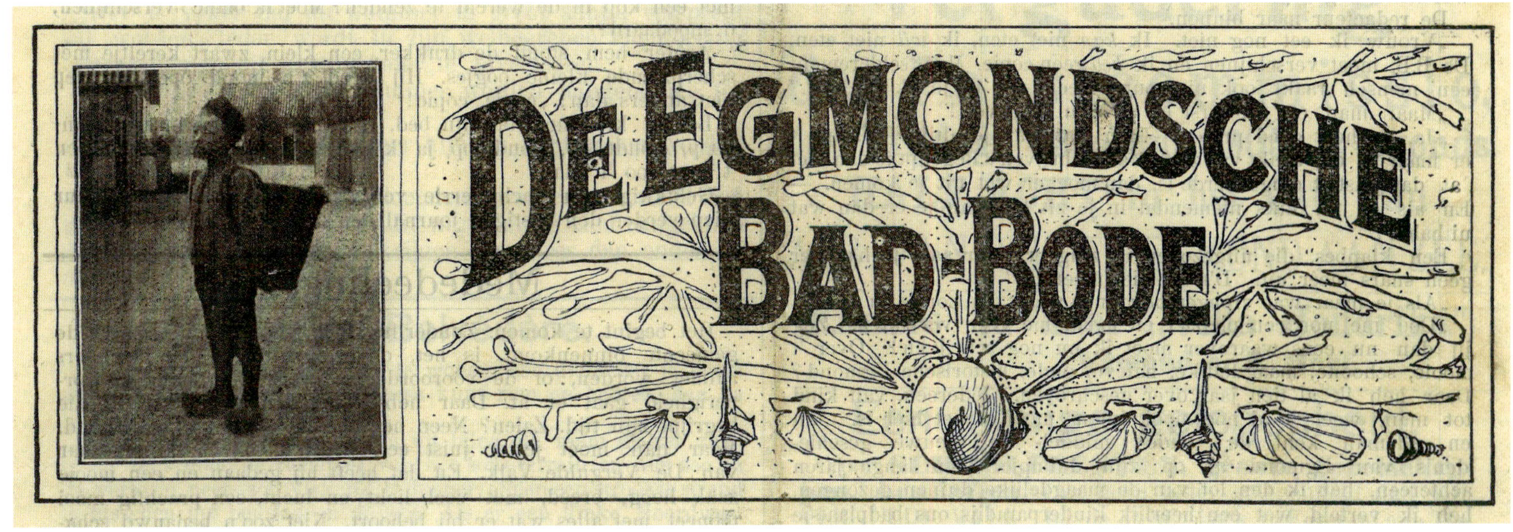

In August 1884, *De Alkmaarsche Courant* reported that 'no fewer than eight painters, including seven Germans and one American,' were staying at the Zeezicht guesthouse. This marked the first time that a visit by Hitchcock, Melchers – probably mistaken for a German – and their friends was mentioned in print. From 1888 onwards, occasional reports appeared in *The New York Herald* about artists traveling to Egmond for Hitchcock's art classes. As of 1896, records of visitors became more consistent. Between 1896 and 1940, *De Egmondsche Bad-Bode* was published biweekly by the Association for the Promotion of Tourism in Egmond aan Zee. This paper listed the names of guests staying in hotels and inns. Visitors who found accommodation elsewhere in the village were not recorded. Unfortunately, not all of the issues have been preserved in the Regional Archive of Alkmaar; editions from 1889 to 1900 are missing.

This Appendix includes artists who, according to *De Egmondsche Bad-Bode*, stayed in Egmond. Where possible, the list has been supplemented with information from other sources. It also includes people for whom it cannot fully be established whether they are visual artists, or someone else with the same name. Besides artists, we also encounter many names of people somehow involved with cultural pursuits. A notable example is Father E. Lagerwey from Amersfoort, who later founded a museum of Roman Catholic art with his colleague C. Deelder. This collection is now housed in the Catharijneconvent Museum in Utrecht. The composer Julius Röntgen, a founding figure of the Concertgebouw in Amsterdam, also visited Egmond aan Zee in the summer of 1905 with his family. The Plate family from Rotterdam, too, regularly stayed with groups of ten to twelve people: Sophie Plate, an art collector and member of the Rotterdam Art Circle, may have been among them. The writer and poet Miss H. Haitsma Mulier, who married the painter Simon Moulijn in 1902, appears in several issues. There are many more such examples.

Some of the individuals here cannot be identified with complete certainty as artists, but have been included nonetheless. Names and accommodations have been taken, to the extent possible, from *De Egmondsche Bad-Bode*. Information in square brackets indicates additions. Gender is noted with (m) for male or (f) for female. This Appendix also benefits from earlier research by Annette Stott and Peter van den Berg. Although extensive, the list is undoubtedly incomplete, and future discoveries may bring new names to light.

Olga Kruisbrink

Sources
1 *De Egmondsche Bad-Bode*
2 Gari Melchers Home and Studio Archives
3 Stott 1983 (P. van den Berg Archive)
4 Stott 1998
5 Stott 2009-2010
6 *The New York Herald: European Edition, Paris*
7 Shannon 1933
8 Van den Berg 2010

Name	Origin	Adress in Egmond	Sources	In Egmond
Anderson, Karl (1874–1956)	[New York]	*Pension Belvédère*	4–8	1901, 15 Aug.
Ansoul, S. (?–?) (f)	Moscow	*Egmond aan Zee*	3	1898, 15 Aug.
Ball, Alice [Worthington] (1869–1929)	America	*Egmond aan den Hoef*	2–3–4–5	1903, 3, 17 Aug., 3 Sept. 1906, 4 Sept.
Barrie, Alice H. (1870–1950)	America	*Egmond aan den Hoef*	1–3–4–5	1903, 3, 17 Aug., 3 Sept.
Bendemann (?–?) (m)	Dresden	*Belvédère Pension*	3	1902, 10 Sept.
Bogaert, [Albert] (1838–1921)	Maastricht	*Belvédère Pension*	1	1902, 1, 15 Aug.
Broeksmit, [Frederika Henriëtte] (1875–1945)	Charlois [Rotterdam]	*Zeezicht Hotel*	1	1897, 1 Sept.
Breslau, Louise Cath. (1856–1927)	Paris	*Zeezicht Hotel*	1	1897, 1 Sept.
Buell, Alice (?–?)			5	1888
Clarenbach, Max (1880–1952)			8	
Cochrane, Josephine Granger (1864–1953)	America	*Egmond aan den Hoef*	3–4–5–8	1903, 3, 17 Aug., 3 Sept.
Conner, J[ohn] R[amsey] (1869–1952)	America	*Egmond aan den Hoef*	1–3	1897, 1 July, 1 Sept.
Crocker, Marion E[liza] (1868–1951)	America	*Egmond aan den Hoef*	1–3–5–8	1897, 1 June, 1 July, 1 Aug., 1 Sept.
Cutler, C.J. [Carl Gordon] (1873–1945)	America	*Egmond aan den Hoef/ Belvédère Pension*	1–3–4–5	1897, 1 July, 15 July, 1 Sept. 1901, 15 Aug., 7 Sept.
Dey, H.E. (1865–1942) (m)	Montreal	*Egmond aan den Hoef*	1–3–4	1896, 19 Aug. 1897, 1 June, 1 July
Doermann, Felix (?–?)	Berlin	*Belvédère Pension*	3	1902, 1, 15 Aug., 10 Sept.
Voley [Foley], D[orothea] (?–?)	Chicago	*Welgelegen Hotel*	1–2–3–4	1902, 1 July
Frieseke, Frederick Carl (1874–1939)			2	1900, ca.
Fuch, Clara (?–?)	Düsseldorf	*Welgelegen Hotel*	3–5	1903, 3, 17 Aug.
Funck, [Theodor] (1867–1919)	Düsseldorf	*The Three Egmonds*	3	1902, 1 July
Gildenmeister, Gusta (?–?)	Düsseldorf	*Egmond aan den Hoef*	3	1903, 3 Aug.
Gruijter, Jacob W[illem], (1856–1908)			8	
Haskell, William H[omer] (1875–1952)	America	*Belvédère Pension*	3–4–5	1901, 15 Aug., 7 Sept.
Heimes, Heinrich (1855–1933)	Neuenahr, Germany	*Egmond aan den Hoef*	3	1884, 1897, 1 July, 15 July, 1 Sept.
Hermann, Hans (1858–1942)			5	1884, 1887
Gewin [Hind], [Charles] Lewis (1862–1927)	America	*Egmond aan den Hoef*	2–3	1903, 17 Aug., 3 Sept.
Hitchcock, George (1850–1913)	America	*Egmond aan den Hoef*	1–3–4	1897, 1 July, 15 July, 1 Sept.
Hitchens, Alfred (1861–1942)			8	
Homans, Nannie (1861–?)	America (Springfield, MA) (AS)	*Egmond aan den Hoef*	3–4–5	1903, 3, 17 Aug., 3 Sept.
Homelberg, M. (?–?) (m)	America	*Egmond aan den Hoef*	3–5	1903, 3 Aug.
Hopkins, Pery [sic] R. (?–?)	America	*Belvédère Pension*	3–4	1901, 15 Aug., 7 Sept.
How, [Julya] Beatrice (1865–1932)	England	*Zeezicht Hotel*	1	1897, 1 Sept.

Name	Origin	Adress in Egmond	Sources	In Egmond
Howe, [William] Henry (1846–1929)			5	ca. 1888, 1889
Hubbard, Mary W[ilson] (1871–?)	America	*Egmond aan den Hoef*	1–3–4	1897, 1 June, 1 July, 15 July, 1 Sept.
Jay, Cecil (1880–1954)	America	*Egmond aan den Hoef*	3–4–5	1903, 3, 17 Aug., 3 Sept.
Jones, Jessie Barrows (1865–1944)	America	*Egmond aan den Hoef*	3–4–5	1903, 3, 17 Aug., 3 Sept.
Keller/Heller, (m) *	Germany	*Kraakman*	3	1902, 1 July, 1 Aug.
Keil, [Richard] (1864–1933)	Munich	*Belvédère Pension*	3	1902, 10 Sept.
Kirberg, Otto (1850–1926)	Munich	*Zeezicht Hotel*	1	1896, 19 Aug.
Klein, Philipp (1871–1907)	Munich	*Welgelegen Hotel*	1	1901, 15 July
Koning, Arnold (1860–1945)	Ede	*Catharina Pension*	1	1903, 1 July
Labouchère, [Norna Susan] (1871–1940)	London	*Belvédère Pension*	1–3	1902, 1, 15 Aug.
Lamers, Rudolph (?–?)	Düsseldorf	*Belvédère Pension*	3	1902, 10 Sept.
Lawrenson, Edward Louis (1868–1940)			8	1902, 3 Aug.
Lemon, Arthur (1850–1912)	London	*In the village*	3	1901, 7 Sept.
Liesegang, [Helmut] (1858–1945)	Düsseldorf	*Belvédère Pension*	3	1902, 10 Sept., 3 Aug. 1903, 3 Sept.
Loman, Rudolph (1861–1932)	London	*In the village*	3–5	1901, 7 Sept. 1903, 17 Aug., 3 Sept.
van Maarseveen [Knipscheer, Margot] (1865–1951)	Amsterdam	*Belvédère Pension*	1	1902, 1, 15 Aug.
J.T. Mockall [Mackall, Corinne Lawton] (1880–1950)	America	*Egmond aan den Hoef*	2–3	1902, 25 July 1903, 17 Aug., 3 Sept.
Massau, Edmund (1860–1935)	Paris	*Welgelegen Hotel*	1	1903, 3 Sept.
Mees **	Rotterdam	*In the village*	1	1905, 15 Aug.
Melchers, Gari (1860–1932)	Detroit/Paris/America	*Egmond aan den Hoef / Belvedere Pension / The Three Egmonds*	1–3–4	1897, 1 July, 15 July, 1 Sept. 1901, 15 Aug., 7 Sept. 1902, 1 Aug., 10 Sept.
Minis, J.T. (?–?) (f)	America	*Egmond aan den Hoef*	3	1903, 17 Aug., 3 Sept.
Noir, Ernest (1864–1931)	Paris	*The Three Egmonds*	1–2–3–8	1902, 1 July, 1 Aug. 1908, 19 Aug.
O'Halloran, Agnes (1862–1960)			5–6	1888, 1 July
Pepper, Charles Hovey (1864–1950)	America	*Egmond aan den Hoef*	1–3–4–5	1897, 15 July, 1 Sept.
Petersen Angeln, Heinrich Wilhelm (1850–1906)			8	1884, 1893
Piper, Adeline (?–?)	America	*Egmond aan den Hoef*	2–3–5	1903, 3, 17 Aug., 3 Sept. 1906, 16 July
Pflümer, Magda (?–?)	Hamelen	*Belvédère Pension*	3	1902, 10 Sept., 3 Aug. 1903, 3 Sept.
Plimsoll, J.G. [Fanny Grace] (1841–1918)	Scotland	*Egmond aan den Hoef*	1–3–5	1897, 1 July, 15 July, 1 Sept.
Putmann (?–?) (f)	Leeds	*Egmond aan den Hoef*	1–3	1897, 1 June, 1 July
Putnam, I.N. (?–?)	America	*Egmond aan den Hoef*	1–3	1897, 1 July, 15 July, 1 Sept.

Name	Origin	Adress in Egmond	Sources	In Egmond
Rauws, C[lara] J. (1861–1940)	The Hague	*Catharina Pension*	1	1902, 1 Aug.
Ring, Alice Blair (1869–1947)	Egmond aan de Hoef		4–8	1907, 28 June
Rose, Emmy (?–?)	Berlin	*Egmond aan den Hoef*	2–3–5	1903, 3, 17 Aug., 3 Sept.
Rünge, Waldemar (?–?)	Berlin	*Belvédère Pension*	3	1902, 10 Sept.
Schreuder, [Oene] (1869–1937)	Leeuwarden	*Egmond aan Zee: Zeezicht*	1	1897, 1 Sept.
Sewell, Robert van Vorst (1860–1924)			6	1888, 20 Aug.
Sewell-Brewster, Lydia Amanda (1859–1926)			6	1888, 20 Aug.
Serton, Piet (1888–1924)	Utrecht	*In the village*	1	1902, 1 Aug.
Shannon, J[ames] J[ebusa] (1862–1923)		*Welgelegen Hotel*	4–7	1901, 7 Sept. ca. 1890–1905
Silsbee, Martha (1850–1928)	[Salem (MA) US]		5	
Slaber, M (?–?) (f)	Rochester	*Gruno Pension*	3	1904, 1, 15 Aug., 1 Sept.
Smith L. Carpo, [Letta Crapo] (1862–1921)	America	*Kraakman*	3–4–8	1902, 1 Aug., 10 Sept. 1911, 15 Aug.
Smyth (?–?) (m)	America	*Egmond aan den Hoef*	3	1897, 1 June, 1 July
Stewart, M. Louisa (?–?)	America	*Egmond aan den Hoef*	3	1903, 17 Aug., 3 Sept.
Stone, E. Bristol (1875–1913)	America	*Egmond aan den Hoef*	3–5	1903, 3, 17 Aug., 3 Sept.
Stoney, Eleanor E. (?–?)	America	*Egmond aan den Hoef*	1–3	1897, 1 Sept.
Strobentz, F[riedrich/ Fritz/ Frigyes] (1856–1929)			2	ca. 1892
Tadama, Fokko (1871–1937)	Amsterdam	*Egmond aan den Hoef*	1–3–8	1897, 1 June, 1 July, 15 July, 1 Sept.
Tadama-Groeneveld, T(h)amine] (1871–1938)	Amsterdam	*Egmond aan den Hoef*	1–3–8	1897, 1 June, 1 July, 15 July, 1 Sept.
Tilanus, [Cornelia] (1861–1956)	Amsterdam	*Zeezicht Hotel*	1	1896, 19 Aug.
Tilman, R. (?–?)	Munich	*Zeezicht Hotel*	1	1896, 19 Aug.
Upton, J.K. [Florence Kate] (1873–1922)	America (NYC) (AS)	*Winkel Pension (1902)* *Welgelegen Hotel (1903)*	2–3–4–5–8	1902, 1 July, 1 Aug., 10 Sept. 1903, 3, 17 Aug., 3 Sept.
Valentine, J[ane] H. (1866–1934)	America	*Egmond aan den Hoef*	3–4–5	1903, 17 Aug., 3 Sept.
Ward, Reginald P[hilips] (1876–1929)	Boston	*Welgelegen Hotel /* *Belvédère Pension*	1–2–3	1901, 7 Sept. 1902, 15 July, 1, 3, 8, 26 Aug., 28 Sept.
Webster, [Edwin] Ambrose (1869–1935)	America	*Egmond aan den Hoef*	1–4–5–8	1897, 15 July, 1 Sept.
Whittlesey, Carolina H. (?–?)	Cleveland (Ohio)	*Egmond aan den Hoef*	1–2–3	1897, 1 July, 15 July, 1 Sept. 1906, 4 Sept.
Wijsmuller, Jan Willebrand (1855–1925)	Amsterdam	*Duinryck Family Pension*	1	1905, 27 July, 15 Aug.
Woodward, Anna (1868–1935)	America	*Egmond aan den Hoef* *and Welgelegen Hotel*	1–2–3–4–5	1897, 1 Sept. 1903, 3, 17 Aug., 3 Sept 1904, 18 Sept. 1905, 8 July

* possibly:
Ferdinand Keller (1842–1922
Gustav Keller (1860–1911)
Louis Herman Heller (1839–1928)
Adolf Heller (1874–1914)

** possibly:
Margaretha Agatha Mees (1870–1952)
Anna Mees (1847–1928)
Nora Mees (1882–1960)
Herman Mees (1880–1964)

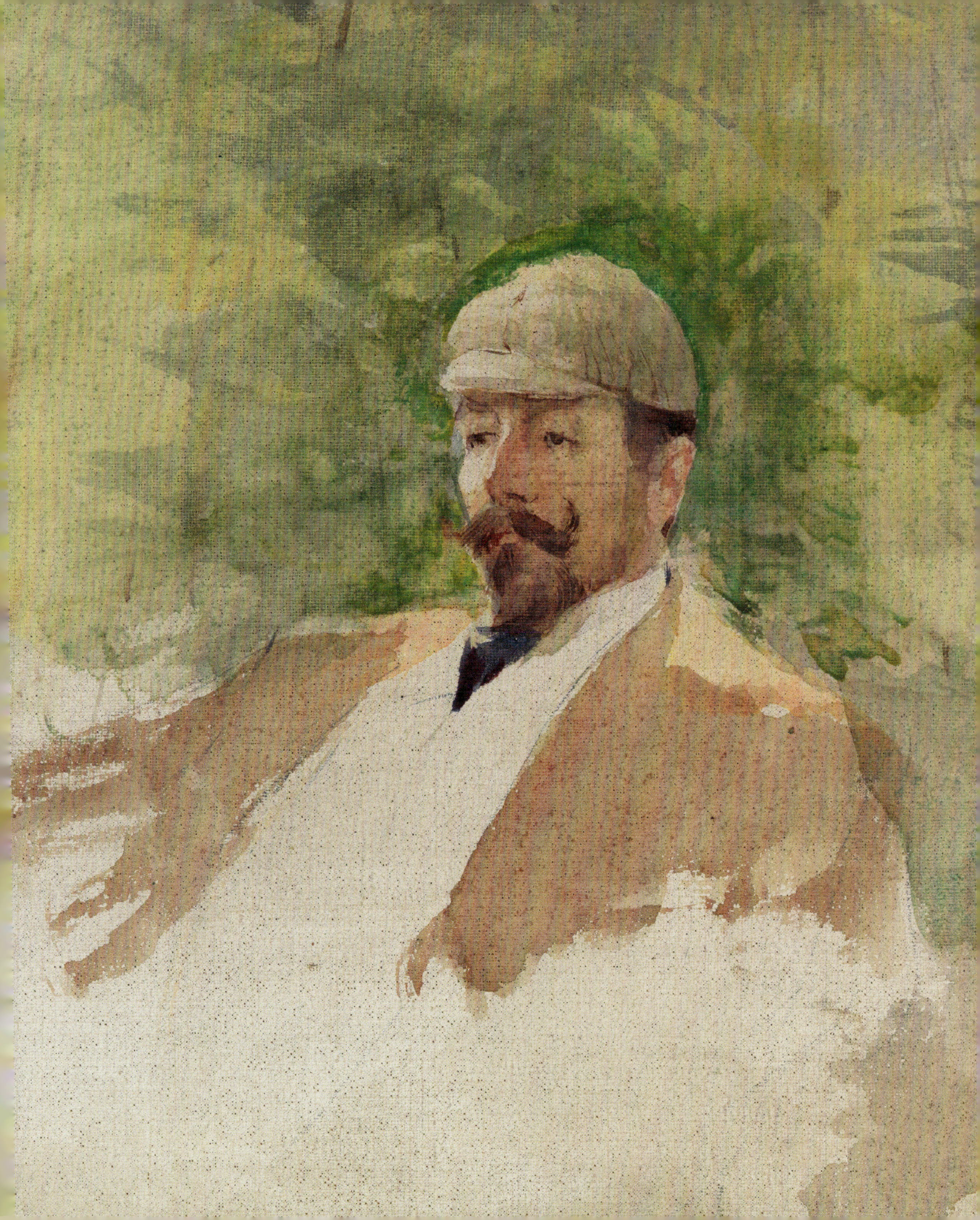

Notes

1   Leroi 1886, p. 18: "La Hollande m'attire entre tous les pays. Convaincu que pour bien faire une chose il faut la connaître à fond, je me suis installé à demeure, il y a quelques annaées, à Egmond aan Zee, avec un confrère [Hitchcock] qui partage ma passion pour ce pays."

2   Lewis-Hind 1928, n.p.

3   http://rkddb.rkd.nl/rkddb/digital book/201503542.pdf, accessed 30 October 2024. Hitchcock, G., *Egmond aan Zee*, no. 107; *Egmond Pinks*, no. 108; *Souvenir of Scheveningen*, asking price 200 and 150 guilders, respectively. Gari Melchers, G. J., *Egmond aan Zee*, no. 71; *Grandfather*, no. 72; *Looking at the Neighbor Woman*. Asking price for both, 350 guilders.

4   Their whereabouts are unknown.

5   Regionaal Archief Alkmaar, Notarial Archives 0878, file 1443: archive no. 10.3.003, Notary W. F. G. L. Gouwe, inv. no. 1449A, deed no. 297, Municipality: Alkmaar, Period: 1869-1892.

6   Regionaal archief Alkmaar, Notarial Archives, 0878, file 1471, archive no. 10.3.003, Notary W. F. G. L. Gouwe, inv. no. 1449A, deed no. 312. Municipality: Alkmaar, Period: 1869-1892.

7   Kraandijk 1875, vol. 1, p. 180.

8   Kraandijk 1875, vol. 2, p. 203.

9   Kraandijk 1875, p. 195.

10   Kraandijk 1875, vol. 2, p. 213.

11   Dumas 1983, pp. 125-136.

12   Kraan 2002, p. 242.

13   Hitchcock would have been in contact with Mesdag around 1880, considering the statements he later made, and Melchers received personal congratulations after receiving the reward in 1886. Gari Melchers Home and Studio Archives.

14   Anonymous, "Parijse Kroniek," Algemeen Handelsblad, 5 May 1888: "Een schilder kan zich, nadat het teekenen en verf gebruiken geleerd heeft, zelden alleen verder vormen."

15   Kraan 2002, p. 111.

16   Kraan 2002, p. 111.

17   Mahoney 2011, p. 91.

18   Julius Garibaldi Melchers was the second child, the eldest son, born on 11 August 1860 to Julius Theodore Melchers and Marie Bangetor, who were married on 5 May 1858; see Lewis-Hind 1928, n.p., among others.

19   Mesman 1990 (2), p. 6.

20   Mesman 1990 (2), p. vii. Julius Theodorus Melchers (1829-1909) studied in Paris at the École des Beaux-Arts under Jean-Baptiste Carpeaux (1827-1875) and Antoine Etex (1808-1888). In 1852, he settled in Detroit, United States. As a sculptor, he is primarily known for his life-sized, polychrome wooden figures of Native Americans for tobacco shops. For additional information, see Kraan 2002, p. 112.

21   Lewis Hind 1928, n.p.

22   Donaldson 1938, p. 14. Mesman 1990 (2), pp. 12, and 19. For admission, a recommendation from the embassy or consul was required, you had to pass an exam in anatomy, perspective, modeling, and general history, and you also needed to be proficient in French.

23   Mesman 1990 (2), p. 12.

24   "Figurenmahler" (Figure Painter) Certificate of the Preparatory Class of the Königlich Preussische Kunst-Akademie zu Düsseldorf, 1 July 1880, GMHS 1880. Neither Melchers' nor Hitchcock's registration cards have been preserved in the Stadtarchiv Düsseldorf; information kindly provided by Heike M. Blumreiter.

25   Landes Archiv Nordrhein Westfalen, abteilung Rheinland, Schülerlisten der Kunstakademie Düsseldorf, Regierung Düsseldorf Präsidialbüro BR 0004, no. 1561, Bl. 201V.

26   Mesman 1990 (1), p. 50.

27   Landes Archiv Nordrhein Westfalen, abteilung Rheinland, Schülerlisten der Kunstakademie Düsseldorf, Regierung Düsseldorf Präsidialbüro BR 0004, no. 1561, Bl. 204V, 206V for 1877, Bl. 227V in 1878, 253V in 1879 .

28   Beavington Atkinson 1880, p. 99.

29   Landes Archiv Nordrhein Westfalen, abteilung Rheinland, Schülerlisten der Kunstakademie Düsseldorf, Regierung Düsseldorf Präsidialbüro BR 0004, Bl. 257V (1879) and 297V (1880). The old academy building was destroyed by a large fire in 1872. Between 1872 and 1879, the students were trained in various buildings.

30   Beavington Atkinson 1880, p. 100.

31   Mesman 1990 (2), pp. 15 and 16.

32   George Hitchcock was the second son of Charles Hitchcock (1825-ca. 1855), a portrait painter who died young, and Olivia George Hitchcock-Cowell (1828-1865). George, his brother Charles (1848-?), and sister Amalia W. (1852-?) were raised by his maternal grandparents and aunts. Van den Berg 2008, p. 19, and Robinson 1891, p. 290.

33   Hitchcock graduated from Brown University in 1872 and earned his Bachelor of Law degree from Harvard Law School in 1874. On 2 June 1875, he was admitted to the Rhode Island Bar. Letter from G. Hitchcock to M. A. Vaughan, Providence, 27 November 1904, on Schuil and Burg letterhead. Brown University Special Collections, Hitchcock 1872, John Hay Library, Providence, Rhode Island, USA.

34   G. Herdle, "Picture Study - Flower Girl in Holland," n.d. Clipping in the John Hay Library. Meltzer 1912, p. 131, also writes that Hitchcock assisted the art dealer Waters for some time in selling watercolors.

35   *San Francisco Call* 87 (1901), no. 68, 7 August 1901: "George Hitchcock, the artist, though now living handsomely on the proceeds of his art in Holland, once made a living by running a small bric-a-brac shop in Chicago."

36   Fish 1898. The watercolors Hitchcock sold during these years were rather amateurish, and later he tried to buy them all back; see Boswell 1921, p. 297.

37   *The American Register for Paris and the Continent,* 31 May 1879.

38   Fish 1898, p. 577: "If I succeed, I shall not return." *Brown Herald,* 2 November 1898.

39   Robinson 1891, p. 290 and Fish 1898, p. 587.

40   Mesman 1990 (2), p. 43, note 12. Unfortunately, the student registers at Heatherley's only began in 1906. With thanks to Stephen Bartley, Hon. Archivist of the Chelsea Arts Club Archive/Heatherley's.

41   Eva 1996, pp. 5, 6.

42   Eva 1996, p. 7, and Thomas Heatherley | Works of Art | RA Collection | Royal Academy of Arts, accessed 15 November 2024. Heatherley was described as a "medieval necromancer" and a "slinking Jesus," with a high forehead, straight nose, deep-set eyes, hollow cheeks, long hair, and a beard.

43   Robinson 1891, p. 290.

44   Cope 2011, p. 134.

45   Fink 1973, p. 32.

46   Mesman 1990 (1), p. 51.

47   Fink 1973, p. 35, and Weinberg 1981.

48   Fink 1973, p. 36, and Mesman 1990 (1), p. 51.

49   Weinberg 1981, p. 73, and Mesman 1990 (2), pp. 23-24.

50   Hoeber 1907, p. 16 and Brenchley 1900, p. 146.

51   Adolphe Yvon - Wikipedia, accessed 26 January 2025.

52   Weinberg 1981, p. 68.

53   Fehrer 1989, p. v.

54   Anonymous, "Fransche brieven. Parijs 22 maart 1903," *Soerabaijasch handelsblad,* 23 March 1903.

55   Anonymous, "Fransche brieven. Parijs 22 maart 1903," *Soerabaijasch handelsblad,* 23 March 1903.

56   Fehrer 1989, p. v.

57   Fehrer 1989, p. iv.

58   Cope 2011, p. 147.

59   Fink 1973, p. 37, and Fehrer 1989, p. iv.

60   Cope 2011, p. 147.

61   Fehrer 1989, p. 3.

62   Anonymous, "Fransche brieven. Parijs 22 maart 1903," *Soerabaijasch handelsblad,* 23 March 1903.

63   Letter from J. B. Fairbanks to L. Fairbanks, 12 October 1890, in Cope 2011, p. 147.

64   On this, see Fonds de l'académie Julian, Nationalités, Ancien Livre, Archives Nationales, Paris, inv. no. 63AS/22

65   Atelier Boulanger & Lefèbvre, Fonds de l'académie Julian, Archives Nationales, Paris, inv. no. 63AS/1-8.

66   Fehrer 1989, n.p., gives 1879 and 1882, in the microfiches with lists of names of the Académie Julian only 1882 is mentioned. Fonds de l'académie Julian, Archives Nationales, Paris, inv. no. 63AS/1-8.

67   Robinson 1890, p. 291.

68   Fonds de l'académie Julian, Nationalités, Ancien Livre, Archives Nationales, Paris, inv. no. 63AS/22, Enrollment by country, and 63AS/12-24 Enrollment in the ateliers. See also the *Alkmaarsche courant,* 1 September 1886, which mentions that Melchers established himself in Paris in 1880.

69   Fehrer 1989, n.p., and the microfiches with the lists of names of the Académie Julian, see Fonds de l'académie Julian, Archives Nationales, Paris, inv.no. 63AS/1-8 mentions 1880-1886. Mesman 1990 (2), pp. 20-21 mentions 1881-1883.

70 Dreiss 1984, p. 9. Based on an undated newspaper clipping "Melchers told phase of life in painting" in the Gari Melchers Home and Studio Archives.

71 *Illustrated Catalogue Thirteenth Annual Exhibition of the American Water Color Society Held at the Galleries of the National Academy of Design,* New York, 1880; no. 97 *Scene on the Thames,* 50 dollar, Geo Hitchcock. Unfortunately, there is no mention of his place of residence.

72 Stott 1998, p. 270, Hitchcock made his first visit to the Stedelijk Museum in Haarlem in September 1880.

73 With thanks to Adrienne Quarles van Ufford (Museum Panorama Mesdag), Renske Suijver and Djalma Taihuutu (De Mesdag Collectie), who found no traces of Hitchcock in Mesdag's archives and correspondence. Robinson 1891, p. 291 writes: "he reached The Hague, ostensibly to place himself under the guidance of Mesdag, or at least to see if Dutch Art could stimulate in him that power of expression."

74 See the reporting on this in *Het Vaderland,* 28 April 1880. The panorama can still be viewed in Museum Panorama Mesdag, The Hague.

75 See the reporting on this in the *Nieuwe Groninger Courant,* 21 June 1880.

76 Robinson 1891, p. 291, and Anonymous, "Beeldende Kunst te Egmond aan Zee," *In en Om Kennemerland,* 1 January 1905.

77 Robinson 1891, p. 291. Boswell 1921, p. 297, writes: "but remained as an attentive observer of Mesdag's mastery over material […]'."

78 Meltzer 1912, p. 133.

79 Fish 1898, p. 578, and Anonymous 1905.

80 *Illustrated Catalogue Fourteenth Annual Exhibition of the American Water Color Society Held at the Galleries of the National Academy of Design,* New York, 1881. George Hitchcock, 61 West 36th Street, submitted the following pieces: no. 237 *Signaling the Returning Herring Boat, Scheveningen,* 200 dollar; no. 243 *From my Window (Scheveningen),* 225 dollar; no. 269 *On the Dunes, Scheveningen,* 50 dollar; no. 317 *A Dutch Town,* Mrs. S. W. Allerton collection; no. 338 *Morning Scheveningen;* 525 *At Anchor – Scheveningen,* 130 dollar; no. 691 *Scheveningen Fishergirl* – a study 50 dollar.

81 Benjamin 1881, p. 189.

82 New York, Castle Garden Immigration Index 1820–1913, mentions that George Hitchcock arrived in the United States on the *SS Elysia* on 22 November 1880, www.findmypast.com. In the catalog, his address is 61 West 36th Street, the same one Melchers used in 1885 for his submission to the American Water Color Society.

83 Stott 1998, p. 270.

84 Divorce certificate, 31 July 1905, Noord-Hollands Archief, Haarlem, civil registry of the municipality of Egmond-Binnen, 358.38, inv. no. 21905 and Henriette Walker Richardson Hitchcock Hind (1862-1938) - Find a Grave-Memorial, accessed 20 January 2025.

85 *Illustrated Catalogue of the Sixteenth Annual Exhibition of the American Water Color Society Held at the Galleries of the National Academy of Design,* New York, 1883, p. 37.

86 Landes Archiv Nordrhein Westfalen, abteilung Rheinland, Schülerlisten der Kunstakademie Düsseldorf, Regierung Düsseldorf Präsidialbüro, BR 0004, no. 1561, p. 427V.

87 Boswell 1921, p. 297: "He learned a lot more about how to paint."

88 Base salons, accessed 2 December 2024.

89 Bienenstock 1990, p. 77.

90 *Pater noster....,"* Painting, no. 1655, and *A Woman from d'Atina,* Painting, no. 1654. https://salons.musee-orsay.fr/Detail/entities/281203.

91 Salon de la Société des Artistes Français, Paris, 1882, no. 1830, Salon Triennal d'Anvers, Antwerp, 13 August-early October 1882, 58th Annual Exhibition, National Academy of Design, New York, 2 April-12 May 1883, Detroit Art Loan Exhibition, September 1883.

92 Hitchcock 1887, p. 168.

93 Stott 1998, p. 43. Since the beginning of the 19th century, American artists visited the Netherlands for a few days as part of the Grand Tour of Europe.

94 Barrett 2008, p. 125.

95 Stott 1998, pp. 10, and 26.

96 Stott 1998, p. 11, and 21. Interest was also very high among collectors, who purchased large numbers of works by 17th-century Dutch masters.

97 Stott 1998, p. 101.

98 Stott 1998, p. 25.

99 Collins 1895, p. 86: "I like Americans. I have reason to. They have bought a great many of my pictures. To tell you the truth, I can't paint them fast enough for them."

100 Stott 1998, pp. 12, and 38.

101 Stott 1998, p. 43.

102 Hitchcock 1889, p. 163.

103 Stott 1998, p. 270. Hitchcock also visited the Stedelijk Museum in Haarlem on [20] May 1881, [6 May 1884], 4 and 29 July 1887, 28 June 1901, 31 March 1903, and 28/29 June 1904.

104 Stott 1998, pp. 270, and 273. It is striking that neither of these two gentlemen appear in the archives of the Spaander Hotel, the copyist books of the Rijksmuseum, nor the visitor books of the Dordrechts Museum, all of which were popular destinations for many American artists at the time.

105 Mesman 1990 (2) p. 41.

106 Collins 1895, p. 86.

107 Stott 1990, p. 61.

108 Dake, C.L., "Het Hollandsche binnenhuis," *De Maasbode,* 27 August 1910: "Jullie, Hollanders, schilderen allen als Israëls."

109 *Illustrated Catalogue of the Seventeenth Annual Exhibition of the American Water Color Society Held at the Galleries of the National Academy of Design,* New York, 1884, no. 47, *Up from the Beach.* Present whereabouts unknown. The other works relate to Zaandam and Scheveningen.

110 Fish 1898, p. 578, and Anonymous, "Beeldende Kunst te Egmond aan Zee," *In en Om Kennemerland,* 1 January 1905.

111 Anonymous, "Beeldende Kunst te Egmond aan Zee," *In en Om Kennemerland,* 1 January 1905: "Op een goeien Zomerschen dag arriveerde in Zeezicht een Engelsch sprekend paar, heer en dame. Hun uiterlijk en bagage verraadden aanstonds al dat het artisten waren. De lange, rijzige, gentlemen-like figuur van den Heer maakte een prettigen indruk en gaf geheel den kunstenaar te kennen. Dit echtpaar installeerde zich op een paar kamers, met uitzicht op zee en begon al dadelijk met het nauwkeurig opnemen van het strand, de duinen, de straten en steegjes van het dorp. Dagelijks trokken de heer en de dame er op uit, gewapend met allerlei schilderbenoodigheden en bleven heele dagen in of rond het dorp bezig, met het schetsen of schilderen van personen, straatjes en huisjes maar meest van strandtafereeltjes […]. Het Hollandsch kende hij niet, maar spoedig was hij in staat aan de bevolking duidelijk te maken wat hij verlangde."

112 Meltzer 1913, p. 5. "I was on my way to Italy, when the cholera broke out there. Not wishing to run needless risks, I came up north. At Egmond I found friends, drawn, like myself, to the Dutch life and landscape." The article, based on an interview in Egmond, gives this as 1887. This must be a mistake; see 1881–1896 cholera pandemic - Wikipedia and 1884 in Italy - Wikipedia, accessed 16 December 2024.

113 Hermann exhibited his work at Arti in 1884, and the catalog gives his address as Egmond aan Zee. On Petersen-Angeln, see Schulte-Wülwer 1993-1994, p. 31. *The Alkmaarsche Courant* of 20 August 1884 lists seven Germans and one American, presumably Melchers was mistaken for a German.

114 In the *Algemeen Handelsblad,* 7 June 1884, mention is made of Heimes' stay in Egmond. Heimes had enrolled in the academy in Düsseldor in 1880, 1881, and 1883, see Landesarchiv NRW Abteilung Rheinland Bl 285V, Bl 336V, Bl 383V Bl 426V, and Bl 434V. BR 0004 / Regierung Düsseldorf Präsidialbüro BR 0004, no. 1561. In 1883 is mentioned that he went on a study trip immediately after enrolling. His level of skill was described as "unbestimmt" (indeterminate) and "leidlich" (passable).

115 Cross 2009, pp. 6-9.

116 Stott 2009-2010, p. 160.

117 Lannoy and Denneboom 1969, p. 128: "ledenbreker," "maagbederver," and "hoofdpijnschepper," and as "de verbinding tussen het eenzaam en verlaten Egmond en de wereld." Moreover, the transport improved significantly afterwards, see Blokker 2018.

118 Anonymous, "Beeldende Kunst te Egmond aan Zee," *In en Om Kennemerland,* 1 January 1905.

119 Shannon 1933, p. 27.

120 See the *Opregte Haarlemsche Courant*, 16 May 1884.

121 Robinson 1891, p. 292, Meltzer 1912, p. 132, and *Dagblad van Zuidholland en 's Gravenhage*, 7 June 1884. The painting was likely part of the empress' private collection and is not housed in any of the museums in Vienna.

122 http://rkddb.rkd.nl/rkddb/digital book/201502252.pdf, Catalogus van de tentoonstelling van Kunstwerken van Levende Meesters in de kunstzalen der maatschappij Arti et Amicitiae 1884. Melchers also exhibited *The Sermon* in 1886; however, that painting was not for sale, see http://rkddb.rkd.nl/rkddb/digital book/201502284.pdf.

123 Hitchcock 1887, pp. 165-166.

124 On this, also see Lübbren 2001.

125 Hoeber 1907, p. 17.

126 On November 10, Hitchcock signed the lease agreement with Messrs. Gulcher, the owners of the Herrschaft of Egmond, Van den Berg 2010, p. 42. On 20 November, Hitchcock, his wife, and Melchers appeared before notary W. F. G .L. Gouwe regarding the repayment of a plot of dune Section A, no. 1084, with a house under construction. Gemeentearchief Alkmaar, 0878 Notarial Archives, archive no. 10.3.003, Notary W. F. G. L. Gouwe, inv. no. 1449A, deed no. 292.

127 It is likely that the fisherman's cottage was expanded, as the following description mentions "nog een brok huis" (another part of the house).

128 The man-about-Town, "The Royal Academy," *Dagblad van Zuidholland en 's Gravenhage*, 9 May 1892.

129 Anonymous, "Een vissersliedje," *Het nieuws van den dag: kleine courant*, 16 August 1903: "Naar het zuiden en naar het noorden, zoover het oog reikt, de golvende lijn der hooge, helmbegroeide duinen. [...] En het meest naar het zuiden, hoog op het duin, een van de mooiste dingen van Egmond, het witte huisje, [van den] Amerikaanschen schilder Hitchcock, vroeger zijn atelier en nu dikwijls zijn vriend Gari Melchers tot atelier dienende. Aan den zeekant een helwitte muur, bij de trapjes van het geveltje alleen wit tusschen de voegen der steenen, drie ramen gewoonlijk met groene luiken gesloten, aan de noordzijde een onder het bruinroode dak grauw verweerde muur met een raam, ook meestal achter ruwe planken verborgen. En naar den zuidkant, in het midden vooruitspringend, nóg een bruin-roodgedakt brok huis, ook met witte muren en groene luikjes. Altijd, bij mooi weer of bij stormluchten, wordt het oog getrokken door dit prachtig 'witte huis'."

130 Gemeentearchief Alkmaar, 0878 Notarial Archives, archive no. 10.3.003, Notary W. F. G. L. Gouwe, inv. no. 1449A, deed no. 312.

131 Regionaal Archief Alkmaar, Civil Registry Egmond aan Zee, page 409, 19 December 1884. The register shows that Hitchcock and his wife were registered for that purpose in Düsseldorf, and Melchers in Paris.

132 She exhibited at the American Water Color Society in New York, the Gladwell Brother's Gallery, 14 Gracechurch Street in London, and Melchers at the Salon in Paris showed *Kniertje, the Dutchwoman* and *Poor Men of the Sea*.

133 *Alkmaarsche Courant*, 1 September 1886.

134 Anonymous, "Art in the City," *The Echo*, 2 November 1885.

135 Anonymous, "The American Water Color Society Exhibition," *The Art Amateur* 12 (1885) 4, p. 80.

136 *A Dutch Bachelor's Breakfast*.

137 Anonymous, "The American Water Color Society Exhibition," *The Art Amateur* 12 (1885) 4, p. 80.

138 *The Sea Beggars*, see Base salons: Exposant: Melcher (J. Gari) [61708], accessed 6 January 2025, see the *Alkmaarsche Courant*, 1 September 1886.

139 Hitchcock 1887, p. 163.

140 Mesman 1990 (2), p. 92.

141 Mesman 1990 (2), p. 92.

142 *Alkmaarsche Courant* 1 September 1886.

143 Bienenstock 1990, p. 83.

144 Mesman 1990 (2), pp. 93-94. He refers to an interview with Malcolm Vaughan in *The New York Herald Tribune*, 30 December 1928.

145 Meltzer 1913, pp. 6 , 7.

146 Lepage was also an important model for Hitchcock. See "Tardy Honor for George Hitchcock. Finally Chosen a Member of the New York National Academy of Design," *The New York Times*, 12 September 1909.

147 Meltzer 1913, p. 6.

148 Anonymous, "Driejaarlijksche Tentoonstelling van Kunstwerken, in het Rijksmuseum te Amsterdam," *Dagblad van Zuidholland en 's Gravenhage*, 20 October 1886: "Geen sprake is er van modellen, die op het schildersatelier met deze of gene kleederdracht – in dit geval een Noord-Hollandsch pakje – toegetakeld, in een of ander pittoresk licht worden geplaatst, om aldus geschilderd te worden. Blijkbaar heeft deze kunstenaar de figuren, die hij voor zijne prediking behoefde, op de plaats zelve gezocht, ze bij elkaar in het kerkje gerangschikt, en hetzij daar, hetzij op zijn atelier, met zijn gevoelig penseel dit alles op het doek gebracht, zonder zich om een groot licht en bruin te bekommeren."

149 Letter from Burgomaster Tienhoven to G. Melchers, 9 November 1886, Gari Melchers Home and Studio, inv. no. 1886.3.

150 Leroi 1887, p. 20:"Je ne vois guère à blâmer que les proportions adoptées par M. Gari Melchers pour une simple étude, car En Hollande n''est autre chose. M'est avis qu'après son si légitime succès de l'an dernier, on était en droit dáttendre quelque chose de plus important, de plus sérieux, de la part d'un jeune homme de cette Valeur."

151 Mesman 1990 (2), pp. 78, 80.

152 Bienenstock 1990, p. 89.

153 Leroi 1887, p. 20: "M. Hitchcock [...] est l'un des victorieux de cette exposition. Dès le premier jour, sa *Culture des tulipes* est allée aux nues parmi les raffinés qui prisent par-dessus tout une note orginale. Le choix très osé du motif, la largeur et, en même temps, la finesse de la touche, une exécution féconde et délicatesses infinies, la perfection du fond de paysage, l'esprit, la grâce, l'élégance, le goùt de la charmante figure de femme, ont accaparé tous les suffrages qui comptent."

154 Robinson 1891, p. 292. According to Gérome, the painting was the best of all the American entries.

155 Postlethwaite 1893-1894, p. 115 and Fish 1898, p. 579.

156 P. B., "Algemeene tentoonstelling van beeldende kunsten te Brussel in 1887," *De Vlaamsche School* 33 (1887), pp. 159-160: "smaakvol gekleede vrouw, temidden van het 'bloemtapijt' in haar tuin."

157 "Deux peintres, hollandais tout deux et ayant un air de famille, Hitchcok [sic] et Gari Melchers nous donnent, le premier *la Culture des Tulipes*, une vraie perle empreinte d'une réelle poésie et d'un charme pénétrant; le second, *Le prêche*, qui et tres admire," Anonymous, "Expositions Étrangères, Bruxelles (Suite)," *Journal des Artistes*, 11 September 1887.

158 Hitchcock1887, p. 167.

159 "..des champs énormes et pleines fleurs; c'est du rest admirable, mais à rendre fou le pauvre peintre; c'est inrendable avec nos pauvres couleurs." Letter from Claude Monet to Théo Duret, 30 April 1886, Van de Wetering 1986-1987, pp. 60, 181.

160 Stott 2009-2010, p. 71.

161 "Mr George Hitchcock, the artist and Mrs Hitchcock [...] arrived in Paris yesterday from Rome and are stopping at the Hotel de St. Petersbourg, rue Caumartin. Mr Hitchcock intends taking a studio in Paris for the purpose of completing his Salon picture," *The New York Herald: European Edition-Paris*, 22 February 1888.

162 *Galignani's Messenger*, 9 March 1888; and, "Mrs Hitchcock appeared in black silk, a light cover coat, and a black lace Directoire hat," "'Varnishing,' Fashion and Bohemia at the Opening of the Salon, Very Damp delight, Pretty saints in prettier dresses review the pictures," *The New York Herald, European edition – Paris*, 1 May 1888.

163 See "Protecting the American Interest at the 1889 Exhibition," 8 April 1888, Gari Melchers Home and Studio Archive 1888.1, and "The Jury of Admission for the Exposition of 1889," *The New York Herald: European Edition-Paris*, 12 December 1888.

164 A. Michel, "Salon de 1888 (premier article)," *Gazette des Beaux-Arts* 37 (1888) 2, 1 June 1888, pp. 441-454: "superieure à tout ce qu'il a encore peint."

165 Melchers likely saw a similar scene and subsequently asked a few gentlemen to pose for him. See, for example, a preliminary study in Dreiss 1984, p. 82. One of the models was probably Albert van Pel, innkeeper of Zeerust. See Kager 2015, p. 81.

166 Letter from Hendrik Willem Mesdag to Gari Melchers, Gari Melchers Home and Studio Archive, letter 1888.3a.

167 In that year, Hitchcock exhibited the painting in Paris, Base salons: Exposant: Hitchcock (George) [139692] and in Munich, see *Offizieller Katalog der III. Internationalen Kunst-Ausstellung (Münchener Jubiläums-Ausstellung) im Königl. Glaspalaste 1888*, no. 1246. Anonymous, "Beeldende Kunst te Egmond aan Zee," *In en Om Kennemerland*, 1 January 1905; Hitchcock 1888.

168 Quick 1976, p. 106.

169 Fish 1898, p. 579, and The exhibition of the Royal Academy, 1886. The 118th. | Exhibition Catalogues | RA Collection | Royal Academy of Arts, no. 636, accessed 16 January 2025.

170 In the Netherlands the painting was known as *De Maria boodschap* (The Annunciation), Anonymous, "Beeldende Kunst te Egmond aan Zee," *In en Om Kennemerland*, 1 January 1905.

171 "George Hitchcock", *The Art Amateur* 22 (1890) 3, pp. 54-55, and Fish 1898, p. 579.

172 "The Paris Salon [fourth notice]," *Galignani's Messenger*, 11 May 1888.

173 Leroi 1888, pp. 192-194: "C'est d'une criante injustice et j'en suis affligé."

174 Also see Anonymous, "Beeldende Kunst te Egmond aan Zee'," *In en Om Kennemerland*, 1 January 1905.

175 Hitchcock 1888, p. 713.

176 Lewis Hind 1928 also mentions Melchers's admiration of Botticelli, a copy of whose work he made in the Louvre.

177 "Art for Chicago, Selections for the Autumn Exhibition of the Western Metropolis," *The New York Herald*, 14 May 1889, and *Chicago, Sixteenth Annual Inter-State Industrial Exposition, Sept. 5-Oct. 20, 1888*, no. 203.

178 Hitchcock 1891, p. 627.

179 Letter from O. V. Calder to F. A. Sweet, 17 March 1956, in the Hitchcock documentation of the Art Institute of Chicago, 1930.1289.

180 *Galiganani's Messenger*, 19 September 1889. In 1930, ten paintings "which are not of sufficient interest for the collection," including *Annunciation Lillies*, were given by Potter Palmer to the Art Institute of Chicago with the idea that they could be sold to reduce the institution's debt. Letter from Potter Palmer to R. B. Harshe, 16 May 1930, object documentation, the Art Institute of Chicago.

181 "Les fermières hollandaises," *The American Register for Paris and the Continent*, 18 May 1889, historicalstatistics.org/Currencyconverter.html, accessed 20 January 2025.

182 Child 1889, p. 508: "A late comer in art."

183 The sieve was also described as a fishing net, see Anonymous 1890, p. 55.

184 With thanks to Frans Smeding, who places *the Madonna in* the inner dunes in early summer, with, thistles and bindweed.

185 Child 1889, p. 508, and *The New York Herald*, European edition – Paris, 7 May 1889.

186 Von Jagow 1888, p. 24. Letter from George Hitchcock to Mr. Keelen, 3 March 189[?], John Hay Library/ Brown University, special collections, Biographical Files Hitchcock, Volume/Box: 31236073812409.

187 Child 1889, p. 510.

188 Child 1889, p. 510.

189 Sheldon [1890], p. 125.

190 *The New York Herald: European Edition - Paris*, 28 December 1888.

191 "Our Strongest American Artist," *Galignani's Messenger*, 15 June 1889.

192 *The New York Herald: European Edition*, Paris, 12 May 1888

193 Letter from George Hitchcock to Mr. Keelen, 3 March 189?, John Hay Library/ Brown University, special collections, Biographical Files Hitchcock, Volume/Box: 31236073812409. Melchers worked in a studio at 3 Rue Viète in Paris.

194 "Painter and Critic, an American Artist on the Salon and Salons," *The New York Herald: European Edition*, Paris, 12 May 1888.

195 "Under Artistic Counsel," *The New York Herald: European Edition*, Paris, 16 and 22 September 1888.

196 *The New York Herald: European Edition*, Paris, 1 July 1888

197 "American Art Notes, Whereabouts of Paris American Artists," *The New York Herald: European Edition*, Paris, 20 August 1888.

198 *The New York Herald: European Edition*, Paris, 7 November 1888.

199 Meltzer 1912, p. 134, mentions 300 students.

200 Veldheer 1899, p. 186: "Het dorp schijnt een zekere vermaardheid gekregen te hebben bij Amerikaansche schilders. Des zomers vestigt zich hier een geheele kolonie en 't is een allergrappigst gezicht als men zoo'n troepje Amerikanen of Amerikaanschen, want de vrouwelijke artisten zijn ook ruim vertegenwoordigd, onder hunne witte zonneschermen als een verzameling reusachtige paddestoelen, ijverig ziet werken. Dat allen ongeveer hetzelfde sujet op het doek krijgen en dat de originaliteit hierdoor verloren gaat, schijnt hun al weinig te deren."

201 *The Toronto Daily Mail*, 25 June 1889.

202 "A Heartless Villain, George Hitchcock Cynically Murders his Wife's Happiness," *Herald Tribune*, 25 June 1889.

203 At the opening of the Exposition Universelle, both ladies were spotted and their clothing described: "Mrs George Hitchcock wore brown cloth and gold embroidery. Miss O 'Halloran was in gray blue silk with full white vest and a large black hat trimmed with black lace," *The New York Herald*, 7 May 1889.

204 "D'un jeune Américaine," *Gil Blas*, 26 June 1889.

205 "A Paris Elopement," *The Toronto Daily Mail*, 25 June 1889.

206 "A Paris Scandal, Elopement of an artist, some extraordinary letters," *The Salisbury Times*, 29 June 1889, there may even have been talk of a pregnancy.

207 Among others, see *Sacramento Daily Union*, 61(1889) no. 127, 22 July 1889.

208 *Galignani's Messenger*, 11 July 1889.

209 *The New York Herald: European Edition*, 21 June 1889.

210 *The New York Herald: European Edition*, 3 October 1889.

211 Havard 1875 and Boughton 1885.

212 Most artists' colonies vanished with the outbreak of World War I.

213 Regarding artists' villages, see Lübbren 2001 and Barett 2008, among others.

214 Barrett 2008, p. 10.

215 Stott 1998, p. 62.

216 Lübbren 2001, p. 20.

217 Lannoy and Denneboom 1969, p. 86.

218 Shannon 1933, p. 26.

219 Various painted panels are in the upstairs room of Zeezicht Hotel, described in Anonymous 1905.

220 Barrett 2008, p. 250.

221 *The New York Times*, 31 December 1900.

222 In the *Egmondse Badbode* ever more guesthouses were being mentioned: from 1896, Zomerlust Hotel; in 1900, Zeerust; in 1901, Pension de Boer; in 1902, Pensions Catharina and Belvedere, Tates, and Bos; and in 1903, Pension Huize Gruno. Additionally, in 1906, the Kurhaus was built on the new seaside boulevard with 50 rooms, but it went up in flames as early as 1914.

223 Davis 1992, p. 51.

224 Advertisement in the *Egmondse Badbode* 7 (1902) 1, see Belleman-Beentjes 2005, p. 23.

225 Advertisement in the *Egmondse Badbode*, 13 July 1903, see also Van den Berg 2010, p. 58.

226 In Anonymous 1905, mention is made of Simson and Square's Hitchens along with a host of other artists.

227 Schulte-Wülwer 1993-1994, p. 31.

228 Shannon 1933, p. 18.

229 Postlethwaite 1893-1894, p. 114 and Shannon 1933, p. 18.

230 In that year, Howe submitted *Surroundings of Egmond, Holland* to the Salon, cat. no. 1365. See also: *On the Beach, Egmond, Holland*, 1889. Sale Detroit (Dumouchelles), 20 May 2003, lot 2070.

231 See Van Heteren & Stolwijk 2023.

232 "Art Notes," *Brush and Pencil*, 2 (1898) 3, p. 137; see, for instance, *The American Art News* 4 (1906) 32, p. 7, in which various advertisements were placed for courses being offered in Europe.

233 Barrett 2008, p. 218.

234 Stott 1998, p. 69.

235 Stott 1998, pp. 68-69.

236 Stott 2009-2010, p. 77.

237 "Most of them have been here several seasons." Letter from Louisa Lawton Mackall to Mollie, 25 August 1902.

238 Lübbren 2001, p. 168 mentions a percentage of 49, while other colonies did not reach higher than 20 per cent.

239 "Corinne leaves here after an early breakfast for the Hoef where she gets her things from her studio, & goes out sketching – sometimes she lunches there at a little Inn or carries it with her from here – but generally she rides back here for lunch. 11 o'c Then she goes back & sketches again, & does not get home till 5 or 6 o'c, or later, then is tired. We dine at 7 or later & she goes early to bed – so she has no time for much else." Letter from Louisa Lawton Mackall to her family, August 1902, Gari Melchers Home and Studio Archives.

240 "Mr. Hitchcock wants C. to paint always out of doors – & not even when it rains to do indoor work […] He makes them do large canvases & is said to be a very fine teacher. & fine on colour & atmosphere." Letter from Louisa Lawton Mackall to an unknown recipient, 3 August 1902, Gari Melchers Home and Studio Archives.

241 "Am at the studio at about 8 am. Fail utterly at Dutch girl who poses for a couple of hrs [hours]. Mr Hitchcock comes and gives an outline of what he wants done," and "Had criticism in the morning." Diary Corinne Lawton Mackall, 2 and 30 August 1902, Gari Melchers Home and Studio Archives.

242 Diary Corinne Lawton Mackall, 6 September 1902, Gari Melchers Home and Studio Archives.

243 Diary Corinne Lawton Mackall, 7 and 14 August 1902, Gari Melchers Home and Studio Archives.

244 Lyttelton 1926, p. 21.

245 Newspaper article in *Baltimore Morning Sun*, 5 March 1911, cited in Stott 2009-2010, p. 76.

246 Letter from Louise Lawton Mackall to an unknown recipient, 3 August 1902, Gari Melchers Home and Studio Archive.

247 *The Herald Tribune*, 26 June 1889.

248 Diary Corinne Lawton Mackall, 30 July 1902, Gari Melchers Home and Studio Archive, and Shannon 1933, p. 18.

249 Shannon 1933, p. 18.

250 Meltzer 1913, p. 6.

251 Hoeber 1907, pp. 11-12 and Stott 2009-2010, p. 184.

252 Anonymous, "Gari Melchers' Great Painting, 'The Supper at Emmaus,'" *San Francisco Call* 87 (1900) no. 101, 11 March 1900.

253 Shannon 1933, p. 26: "A most amusing person," "he was quite indifferent to comfort, and his clothes were a joke"; and Hoeber 1907, p. 11: "Cheerful, optimistic temperament with a generous, sympathetic nature."

254 Lesko 1990, p. 15.

255 Stott 1990, p. 60.

256 Diary Corinne Lawton Mackall, 21 April 1902, Gari Melchers Home and Studio Archives.

257 "Mr. Melchers had stopped a long time where she was sketching, giving her a regular lesson – & said if she would like it, he would come often to her studio & give […] criticisms. She was 'talked to death' she said, as he never takes scholars." Letter from L. Lawton Mackall to an unknown recipient, 3 August 1902, Gari Melchers Home and Studio Archive.

258 Corinne Lawton Mackall and Gari Melchers were wed on the island of Jersey on 14 April 1903.

259 "Around the studios," *American Art News*, 3 (February 1905), no. 67, pp. 1-8.

260 Meltzer 1913, p. 5.

261 *The New York Herald: European Edition*, Paris, 7 June 1891.

262 "The Fourth Exhibition of American Oil Paintings in Chicago," *The American Register for Paris and the Continent*, 5 December 1891.

263 After selecting the participants, MacEwen and Melchers traveled to Berlin, where they set up the American section. Melchers won the Grand Diploma of Honor with his entries *The Last Supper*, *Shepherdess*, and *Child in the Church*, *Internationale Kunst-ausstellung veranstaltet vom Verein Berlinre Künstler*, no. 2051a, b, c; and *The New York Herald*, 19 March 1891.

264 *The American Register for Paris and the Continent*, 9 May 1891.

265 Leroi 1890, p. 37.

266 Shannon 1933, p. 26: "known all over the world except in England."

267 The exhibition was mounted by H. Wunderlich & Company in New York, see: "Atmospheric Notes," *The New York Times*, 4 November 1890, Peter van den Berg Archive and Sacramento daily Union 2 (1890) no. 28, 23 November 1890.

268 See *The New York Herald: European Edition*, Paris, 11 February 1890, *The Morning Post*, 19 December 1890, and *The Graphic*, 27 December 1890. Fish 1898, p. 580 mentions that these were studies and figure sketches.

269 Robinson 1891, pp. 293 and 295.

270 Compare Robinson 1891, p. 293 with *The Blessed Mother*. The painting was sold in 1893 by Boussod Valadon to Mr. and Mrs. J. H. Wade. According to an old clipping, the painting was "the fruit of effort concentrated during three years," object documentation of The Cleveland Museum of Art.

271 The young woman's clothing is anything but the daily costume of Egmond folk. The cap, for instance, more closely resembles a Brabant or Zeeland *poffer*.

272 With thanks to Frans Smeding for identifying the flowers.

273 Van den Berg 2008, pp. 110-112 and <u>The Correspondence of James McNeill Whistler :: People Search - Single Document Display</u>, accessed 4 February 2025. For the exhibition, see: <u>Whistler Paintings: Management - names matching paintings</u>.

274 Shannon 1933, p. 101.

275 *Maternity* was sold to the Scottish collector George McCulloch, who amassed a fortune through the mining industry. For the entries to *The Royal Academy*, see: <u>Exhibition catalogues | RA Collection | Royal Academy of Arts</u>, accessed 4 February 2025. See *The American Register for Paris and the Continent*, 5 December 1891 and <u>The McCullough Collection of Modern Art at 184 Queens Gate, London | Home Subjects</u>, accessed 4 February 2025.

276 "Het mooiste doek in de zalen is van een mij tot hiertoe onbekend schilder Hitchcock", The man-about-Town, "The Royal Academy," *Dagblad van Zuidholland en 's Gravenhage*, 9 May 1892.

277 *The American Register for Paris and the Continent*, 5 December 1891. In 1895 Melchers also painted some large decorative pieces for the walls of the Library of Congress.

278 Both canvasses have been preserved and are on display in the library of the University of Michigan, Ann Arbor.

279 *Le Génie Cicil: Revue générale des industries francaises et étrangères*, 15 October 1892, mentions that MacEwen and Melchers painted the decorations.

280 *The American Register for Paris and the Continent*, 16 November 1895.

281 Oresman 1980, p. 22.

282 In addition, he showed: *The Annunciation* and *The Wedding*. *World's Columbian Exposition, 1893: Official Catalogue. Part X. Department K. Fine Arts*, nos. 712-718. Moreover, Melchers lent a painting by Troyon in his own collection (no. 2984).

283 <u>The Statue of Liberty & Ellis Island</u>. Hitchcock and his wife arrived in New York on 4 February 1893. *World's Columbian Exposition, 1893: Official Catalogue. Part X. Department K. Fine Arts*, nos. 550-560. Hitchcock also submitted works on paper from *Scribner' Magazine*'s collection, nos. 2258-2260. Hitchcock received a medal with a diploma for the oil paintings emphasizing their merits, *The American Register for Paris and the Continent*, 2 September 1893.

284 *Art of the World* 6 (1893), p. 53.

285 "Zeeuws boerenmeisje", The man-about-Town, "The Royal Academy," *Dagblad van Zuidholland en 'Gravenhage*, 9 May 1892.

286 With thanks to Jacco Hooikammer, Openluchtmuseum Arnhem. It concerns the traditional clothing of the islands of the Province of South-Holland.

287 Melchers visited Katwijk, Nunspeet, Volendam, Brabant, and Zeeland, among others, see Stott 1990, pp. 63-64. Corinne Melchers adjusted the costumes where necessary.

288 Letter from Naatje, Sijtje, and Jan Bult, 9 January 1938, Peter van den Berg Archive: "het goed van de modellen is erg oud in de oude houten koffer" (The clothing for the models in the wooden chest is old).

289 Stott 1990, p. 58, and Stott 2009-2010, p. 180.

290 Shannon 1933, p. 25.

291 Hitchcock 1891.

292 Hitchcock 1891, p. 622.

293 Blaauboer 1941 (1), Corinne Melchers calls the model in his red baize breeches for *The Family* Job.

294 Melchers 1922, n.p.

295 Research using oral history of, among others, Ron van Vleuten and Carla Kager, have made it possible to link some names to paintings. However, there is not always consensus; for example, the models for *The Sailor and His Sweetheart* are referred to as Arie Stam and Marijtje de Jong, while Mrs. Melchers mentioned the names Job and Gerritje in 1941. One of the models for *Skaters* is believed to be Andries Duinmeijer, but elsewhere Arie Stam is mentioned. For *The Shipwright*, Jan Stoker – who was not himself a shipwright – is said to have been the model. See, among others, Blaauboer 1941 (1) and 1941 (2), Mesman 1990 (2), Van Vleuten 1990, and Kager 2021.

296 With thanks to Jacco Hooikammer, Openluchtmuseum Arnhem. Blaauboer 1941 (2) mentions the North-Holland cap, two women with a farmer's bonnet and the rest wearing a "bazuin."

297 Van Vleuten 1990, pp. 162-163. The woman in the second row with the little hat has been identified as Jansje Zwaan.

298 L. Groen, "Opa fake getrouwd in de Slotkerk?," *Noord-Hollands Dagblad*, 12 April 2021.

299 Shannon 1933, p. 22.

300 Dreiss 1984, p. 32.

301 Van Vleuten 1994, p. 42. According to Dreiss 1984, p. 32, Melchers used self-portraits for the face of Christ.

302 Van Vleuten 1990, p. 163.

303 Letter from Corinne Melchers to her mother, May 1903, Gari Melchers Home and Studio Archives.

304 Roland Holst-van der Schalk 1977, p. 34.

305 Van Vleuten 1990, p. 162.

306 Regionaal Archief Alkmaar, Notarial Archives 312 10.3.003, Notary M. Gouverne, inv. no. 1473, deed 140. For the purchase, see Van den Berg 2008, p. 90. Hitchcock had already moved earlier to Egmond Binnen, first residence 265, later 334, Regionaal Archief Alkmaar, Civil Registry, archive no. 77.1.2.029, inv. no. 239, page 502.

307 Letter from George Hitchcock to Mr. Keelen, 3 March 189?, John Hay Library/ Brown University, special collections, Biographical Files Hitchcock, Volume/Box: 31236073812409. The horses provided entertainment for Hitchcock. Letter from Corinne Melchers to her mother, 17 April 1904, Gari Melchers Home and Studio Archives.

308 Shannon 1933, p. 19.

309 Shannon 1933, p. 25, and *Alkmaarsche Courant*, 7 June 1895.

310 Letter from Louisa Mackall to her family, August 1902, Gari Melchers Home and Studio Archives.

311 Schulte-Wülwer 1993-1994, p. 32 quotes a letter from Catharina Petersen-Angeln to her sister, 27 September 1893, in which Hitchcock is called "der Ritter von der Burg." In America, his nickname was "The Tulip," see Postlethwaite 1893-1894, p. 115.

312 Letter from Corinne Melchers to her mother, 17 April 1904, Gari Melchers Home and Studio Archives.

313 "George Hitchcock Coming," *The New York Times*, 6 November 1910.

314 Shannon 1933, p. 20: "Miggles ran her home so well. She only had the rough fishergirls, and she made them into efficient maids."

315 Shannon 1933, p. 22.

316 According to a conversation between R. van Vleuten and J. Blok (Kniertje's brother) on 20 February 1965, Kniertje was Henrietta's housekeeper and George's secretary, George, Peter van den Berg Archive.

317 Hitchcock showed *Notes from Spain* at Wunderlich in New York, in de winter of 1892.

318 "Mr M is only here a few months each year. He has studios in four or five places, & no one ever sees him here." Letter from Louisa Mackall to a member of her family, August 1902, Gari Melchers Home and Studio Archives.

319 Due to the long shutter speeds, curious cutoffs occurred as moving people approached the camera. These individuals are also not sharp in the image. In the Netherlands, George Hendrik Breitner made use of photography, both as a memory aid and for compositional purposes.

320 Lewis-Hind 1928 notes that his sketches were particularly spot-on.

321 Melchers 1922, n.p.: "The ever changing aspect of nature, be it man or landscape, makes the first impression quickly recorded in the thumb-box sketch, or with a dozen lines on the back of an envelope, an invaluable document. Again and again in the painting of a picture we refer with respect to this first strong impression of nature."

322 "Then he wanted to begin one [picture] of a Dutch girl like a tiny sketch he had made years ago. So we had a couple of girls to come and try for the pose but they didn't look the part for a bit – not Dutch enough. Then I in trying part of the dress on was found to be the very Dutchiest thing imaginable. So your daughter is now sitting as a Holland peasant like this – with a white cap tied tight under her chin." Letter from Corinne Melchers to her mother, May 1903, Gari Melchers Home and Studio Archives.

323 Stott 1990, p. 65.

324 Hoeber 1907, p. 15: "he has no *parti pris*, he may use his brush, his thumb or a palette knife."

325 Letter from Gari Melchers to Corinne Lawton Mackall, 1903, Gari Melchers Home and Studio Archives.

326 Letter from George Hitchcock to Mr. Keelen, 3 March 189?, John Hay Library/ Brown University, special collections, Biographical Files Hitchcock, Volume/Box: 31236073812409.

327 Hitchcock 1887, p. 161.

328 With thanks to Frans Smeding.

329 With thanks to Frans Smeding.

330 *Offizieller Katalog der Internationalen Kunst-Ausstellung Dresden*, 1897, no. 241 *Flight into Egypt*, ill. p. 135. Digitale Sammlungen: Offizieller Katalog der Internationalen Kunst-Ausstellung Dresden 1897.

331 *Große Berliner Kunstausstellung*, 1902, no. 500, ill. p. 102.

332 See *The Royal Academy* 1894, no. 577, and Stott 2009-2010, p. 148 (incorrectly as 1895).

333 Hitchcock 1891, p. 629.

334 *Offizieler Katalog der Internationalen Kunstausstellung München*, 1900, no. 115.

335 With thanks to the Stichting Historisch Egmond.

336 The painting was originally called *Her First Communion*, but to avoid confusion with *The Communion* its title was changed, see letter from J. S. Swift to Mr. Springer, 15 July [1968], object documentation, The Detroit Institute of Arts.

337 Lesko 1990, p. 201.

338 *Catalogue of the 13th Annual Exhibition of Oil Paintings and Sculptures by American Artists*, 1900, no. 164, and *Offizieller Katalog der Internationalen Kunstausstellung Dresden*, 1901, no. 469.

339 *Katalog Grosse Berliner Kunst-Ausstellung*, 1900, Katalog, Grosse Berliner Kunst-Ausstellung, 1900: Grosse Berliner Kunst-Ausstellung (1900): Free Download, Borrow, and Streaming: Internet Archive. According to Mesman 1990 (2), p. 177, rarely was an entirely gallery made available.

340 Mesman 1990 (2), p. 176.

341 Mesman 1990 (2), p. 170.

342 "Subliem is zijn *Christus in Emmaus*; waarover om de ideale, reine, haast etherische gestalte van Christus een waas van teere geheimzinnigheid gesluierd ligt, die hem anders maakt dan een gewoon mensch, terwijl bij de twee naast hem aanzittenden, een vage gewaarwording ontwaakt der heiligheid van den Heiland. De geheele gelaatsuitdrukking van die twee eenvoudige zielen is zoo treffend en zoo vol waarheid weergegeven, dat men hun gedachtengang haast volgen kan." N., "Uit Duitschland, (Particuliere correspondentie.) Berlijn, 7 Juni," *Dagblad van Zuidholland en 's Gravenhage*, 9 June 1900.

343 Lesko 1990, p. 167.

344 Base salons: Entrée catalogue: Maternité [296934].

345 Dreiss 1984, pp. 35-36.

346 Dreiss 1984, p. 33.

347 Piper 1924, p. 79. Previously, she had already referred to "the heavy headed, stupid Dutch baby."

348 *Offizieller Katalog der VII. Internationalen Kunstausstellung im Kgl. Glaspalaste zu München*, 1897, no. 739, and The exhibition of the Royal Academy, 1897. The 129th. | Exhibition Catalogues | RA Collection | Royal Academy of Arts, no. 954.

349 L. S., "Uit Engeland, Een Engelschman over Transvaal – Royal Academy," *Opregte Haarlemsche Courant*, 5 May 1897: "een feeën-bosch in blauw groenigen nevel; de ridder, achter boomen, te paard naderend; op den voorgrond de jonkvrouw op het mos."

350 Base salons: Exposant: Hitchcock (George) [194065].

351 Jean B. Cyrane, "Les Etats-Unis a l'exposition," *Revue Franco-Allemande*, 1 January 1900, p. 182: "George Hitchcock expose à nouveau le Vaincu qui avait plu, voici quelques années, par l'antithèse des tulipes fraîches presque raidies dans l'éclat brutalement nuancé de leurs pétales, la fatigue très sobre du cheval et la lassitude découragée du guerrier dont l'oriflamme traîne à terre" (George Hitchcock again exhibited *The Defeated*, which had been appreciated a few years ago, for its antithesis of almost rigid tulips and the brutally nuanced brightness of their petals, the very sober fatigue of the horse, and the discouraged weariness of the warrior whose banner drags on the ground). *The New York Herald: European Edition*, Paris, 1 May 1898: "*Vaincu* fine colour scheme, it is an armor clad warrior on horseback, trailing his banner through a field of white violet and pink tulips."

352 Unfortunately, no illustrations of these works were included in the illustrated catalogs of these salons. According to *The Bulletin of The Art Institute of Chicago*, January 1911, *The Last Moments of Sappho* was part of the collection of *The Chicago Tribune*, which had lent it to the museum for many years.

353 "Tardy Honor for George Hitchcock. Finally Chosen a Member of the New York National Academy of Design," *The New York Times*, 12 September 1909.

354 Lorguet 1901, p. 182: "C'est d'Amerique nous viennent les savoureuses audaces de George Hitchcock, ce *Cavalier vaincu*, vu de dos, traînant mélancholiquement son étendard violet dans l'éblouissement violet, blanc et rouge d'un champ de pavots, ou, dans les mêmes plates-bandes polychromes, cette *Fiancée Hollandaise* cueillant un bouquet, puis cette *Fuite en Egypte* ou cette *Jeanne d'Arc* dans une claire symphonie de blés et de bleuets" (It is from America that the delicious boldness of George Hitchcock comes to us, this *Defeated Knight*, seen from behind, dragging his violet banner melancholically in the violet, white, and red dazzle of a poppy field, or, in the same polychrome flowerbeds, this *Dutch Fiancée* picking a bouquet, then this *Flight into Egypt* or this *Joan of Arc* in a clear symphony of wheat and cornflowers).

355 *The New York Herald: European Edition*, Paris, 6 May 1902.

356 Base salons: Exposant: Melchers (Gari) [167257], accessed 14 February 2025.

357 Lewis-Hind 1908, p. 10093, Lewis-Hind 1928 mentions that the motto was above the door.

358 Bienenstock 1990, pp. 92-116.

359 Letter from Corinne Melchers to her mother, 8 July 1905, Gari Melchers Home and Studio Archives.

360 "Een visschersliedje," *Nieuws van den dag*, 16 August 1903.

361 *De Egmondse Bad-bode*, 1 May 1902.

362 For information on Lawton Mackall's background, see Dreiss 1984, p. 36.

363 Corinne Lawton Mackall also stayed in the blue room, see the letters from Naatje, Sijtje, and Jan Bult to Corinne Melchers, 6 September and 19 December 1933, respectively, Peter van den Berg Archive.

364 Letter from Gari Melchers to Corinne Lawton Mackall, 16 January 1903, Gari Melchers Home and Studio Archives.

365 20 May 1903, registration of Gari Melchers and Corinne Melchers in the civil registry of Egmond-Binnen, Regionaal Archief Alkmaar, Civil Registry, archive no. 77.1.2.029, inv. no. 242, page 463. The mortgage for the Schoolstraat property was closed on 28 April 1906.

366 Meltzer 1913, p. 5.

367 Shannon 1933, p. 26: "So he might come over […] in the morning and be gone in the afternoon and not return till the next year."

368 Brinton 1907, p. 439.

369 Letter from Gari Melchers to Mrs. L. Mackall, 19 December 1903, Gari Melchers Home and Studio Archives.

370 "Society Events in Paris," *The American Register for Paris and the Continent*, 16 January 1904. Letter from Corinne Melchers to her mother, 16 January 1904, Gari Melchers Home and Studio Archives.

371 "…she would be a great help at the dressmakers and then we could stay comfortably in Gari's apartment and go out and have meals together." Letter from Corinne Melchers to her mother, 18 September 1904, Gari Melchers Home and Studio Archives.

372 *The New York Herald: European Edition-Paris*, 17 March 1903.

373 "He is so much pleased that his two pictures to be at the Salon are to be published on post cards. The gossips (two seized girls he was painting last summer) and The flight into Egypt." Letter from Corinne Melchers to her mother, 17 April 1904, Gari Melchers Home and Studio Archives.

374 Regionaal Archief Alkmaar, Civil Registry of the Municipality of Egmond-Binnen, archive no. 358.38, inv. no. 21905. The divorce decree was issued on 31 July 1905. The judgment had been delivered at the court in Alkmaar on 25 July.

375 Letter from Corinne Melchers to her mother, 27 August 1905, Gari Melchers Home and Studio Archives.

376 "She is to live on here & the house is to be hers." Letter from Corinne Melchers to her mother, 16 July 1905, Gari Melchers Home and Studio Archives. Hitchcock had 49,300 guilders in joint ownership. The *Annunciation* was worth 5000 guilders, other works over 36,000 guilders. Schuijlenburg was sold on 18 July to J. J. Shannon for 5000 guilders (cadastral register art 337, part 599, no. 40), who sold it on 5 August to Henrietta Walker Richardson for 5000 guilders (cadastral register 338, part 588/102 / Haarlem Archive for Leasehold A 1116 art 140). The studio on the dunes was also sold for 900 guilders, Provinciaal Archief Haarlem, Mortgage Register no. 140, see Van den Berg 2008, p. 101.

377 Regionaal Archief Alkmaar, Notarial Archives 0878, file 1499, archive no. 10.3.003, Notary A. P. H. de Lange, inv. no. 1501, deed no. 502. Kniertje Blok would inherit 500 guilders, in addition to 100 guilders per year of service as of 1905, up to a maximum of 2000 guilders.

378 The marriage was performed at the registry office in Kent, Peter van den Berg Archive.

379 "Maartija and Kraakman divide the only four painters spending the summer here", Letter from Corinne Melchers to her mother, 27 August 1905, Gari Melchers Home and Studio Archives.

380 Mesman 1990 (2), p. 86, and Letter from Henrietta to Gari Melchers, 17 August 1911, Gari Melchers Home and Studio Archives.

381 "Letter from Corinne Melchers to her mother, 13 August 1906, Gari Melchers Home and Studio Archives.

382 *Sesta esposizione Internazionale d'arte della Città di Venezia* 1905, Gallery 5, no. 8. Other members of the international committee were Constantin Meunier, Philipe Zilcken, and Gustave Klimt, see *Architectura; orgaan van het Genootschap Architectura et Amicitia* 13 (1905) no. 1, 7 January 1905.

383 "Modern Art of All Nations at the Venice Exhibition," *The New York Herald: European Edition-Paris*, 7 May 1905.

384 Base salons: Exposant: Hitchcock (Georges) [241053].

385 Base salons: Exposant: Hitchcock (George) [244535].

386 *American Art News*, 4 (1906) no. 32, 16 June 1906, p. 3.

387 *American Art News*, 4 (1906) no. 32, 16 June 1906, p. 3.

388 Lewis-Hind 1908, p. 10104.

389 Base salons: Entrée catalogue: "Le bosquet" [393598]. Saunier 1908, p. 18: "C'est là une oeuvre délicieuse de M. Gari Melchers, qui groupe d'autre part une mère et de jeunes enfants abrités sous un bosquet transpercé de soleil."

390 Letter from Corinne Melchers to her mother, 25 August 1908, Gari Melchers Home and Studio Archives.

391 Melchers submitted works to the Salons of 1902, 1905, 1906, 1908, and 1913. The last two submissions were sent via M. P. Navez, 76 Rue Blanche, who also served as a contact person for other artists. It is likely that Melchers no longer had a permanent address in Paris.

392 Brenchley 1900, p. 145 and Lewis-Hind 1908.

393 Shellman Coleman 1990, pp. 125-150.

394 See "Gari Melchers," *The New York Times*, 1 December 1932, p. 20 and https://www.telfair.org/article/the-paradox-of-gari-melchers.

395 See Shellman Coleman 1990, pp. 149-150. Lewis-Hind was first in Egmond in 1903. See Van den Berg 2008, pp. 166-177.

396 It is also notable that Hitchcock is nowhere mentioned as one of Melchers' friends in Brinton 1907.

397 Dreiss 1990, pp. 111 and 113.

398 Letter from Gari Melchers to Corinne Melchers, 28 February 1908, Gari Melchers Home and Studio Archives, 1908.30.

399 Dreiss 1990, p. 115.

400 See *Catalogues of The .. Annual Exhibition at the Carnegie Institute*, Pittsburgh.

401 *Catalogue of the Eleventh Annual Exhibition at the Carnegie Institute*, Pittsburgh, no. 315, *The Delft Horse*; *Catalogue of the Twelfth Annual Exhibition at the Carnegie Institute*, Pittsburgh, no. 216 *The China Closet*; *Catalogue of the Seventeenth Annual Exhibition at the Carnegie Institute*, Pittsburgh, no. 206, *The Open Door*.

402 *The New York Herald: European Edition-Paris*, 29 July 1907.

403 In a newspaper clipping, Fokko Tadama, born in Egmond aan Zee, refers to himself as a student of Hitchcock. The couple left for Katwijk aan Zee in 1908. Letter from Corinne Melchers to her mother, 19 August 1908, Gari Melchers Home and Studio Archives.

404 Letter from Corinne Melchers to her mother, 16 July 1908, Gari Melchers Home and Studio Archives, and *Het nieuws van den dag: kleine courant*, 25 July 1908.

405 "Notes from Athens," *The New York Herald: European Edition-Paris*, 18 April 1910.

406 Letter from Corinne Melchers to her mother, 18 January 1910, Gari Melchers Home and Studio Archives.

407 Moreover, Melchers no longer had a studio in Paris. In 1908 and 1913, the address listed was P. Navez, 76 Rue Blanche, an address that frequently appeared in catalogs. It is likely that Navez provided services such as packing, possibly framing, and selling art supplies.

408 Regionaal Archief Alkmaar, Civil Registers, archive no. 77.1.2.029, inv. no. 242, page 424.

409 Letter from Corinne Melchers to her mother, 19 August 1908, Gari Melchers Home and Studio Archives.

410 Letter from Corinne Melchers to an uncle, 28 February 1912, Gari Melchers Home and Studio Archives.

411 "You know we are off every morning before nine o'clock to go to Schuilenburg [sic] and stay there till four in the afternoon when we have a very substantial tea." Letter from Corinne Melchers to an uncle, 28 February 1912, Gari Melchers Home and Studio Archives.

412 Letter from Corinne Melchers to her mother, 29 July 1912, Gari Melchers Home and Studio Archives.

413 See for example, *Ausstellung Amerikanischer kunst: Königliche akademie der künst zu Berlin*, 1910, *Catalogue of the Sixteenth Annual Exhibition at the Carnegie Institute*, Pittsburgh, no. 219 and Paris, *Salon de la Société nationale des Beaux-Arts*, Grand Palais 1913, no. 868.

414 Van den Berg 2008, p. 135.

415 The boat was already mentioned in *The New York Times*, 3 December 1911.

416 Gemeente Marken, Civil Registry no. 358.75, Archive section of (duplicate) registers of inv. no.: <u>31913</u>. This was incorrectly reported in the international press.

417 *The Daily Mail*, 5 August 1913.

418 See Reid 1990, p. 151.

419 During Melchers' stay in Egmond, he was actively involved in the community; he donated 25 guilders for the new organ in the Slotkapel (see *Geestgronden* 6 [1999] 4, p. 105). Letter from K. A. Cohen Stuart to G. Melchers, 3 November 1917, and letters from Naatje, Sijtje, and Jan Bult to Corinne Melchers, 20 February, 19 December 1933, and 24 January 1937, Peter van den Berg Archive.

420 Diary of Corinne Melchers dated 25 September 1922, Gari Melchers Home and Studio archives.

421 "Accept Apol offer of 9000 fls for the house" and "at 11 o'c I sell my dear little house to Peet Apol for 9000 fl, 1500 being technically 'rent.'" Diary Corinne Melchers, 2 and 9 October 1922, Gari Melchers Home and Studio Archives. The house with barn, yard, and garden on Schoolstraat, Egmond aan den Hoef, 15 ares (1500 square meters) and 80 centiares (80 square meters) (±0.39 acres), was sold for 7500 guilders. The sellers obtained the mortgage in Alkmaar on 28 April 1906, through a private mortgage, and part of it on 18 February 1907, through a private deed of exchange. See Regionaal Archief Alkmaar, Notarial Archives, inv. no. 0881, archive no. 15.3.010, Notary F. W. A. van Riet, inv. no. 27, deed no. 310 Bergen 1921-1925.

422 Diary of Corinne Melchers, 8 and 26 October 1922, Gari Melchers Home and Studio Archives.

423 On 9 March 1923, H. Hind signed the power of attorney for Karel Anthonis Cohen Stuart in Alkmaar to sell Schuijlenburg, with outbuilding, kitchen garden, garden, grove, and meadow, Egmond Binnen cadastral section E, nos. 130, 132-133-134, 2929, 293, 295, 296, 393, and 392, totaling 1 hectare (10,000 square meters), 3 ares (300 square meters) and 20 centiares (20 square meters) (±0.079 acres), see Van den Berg 2008, p. 100.

424 Letter from Naatje, Sijtje, and Jan Bult to Corinne Melchers, 21 December 1937, Peter van den Berg Archive.

425 Letter from Naatje, Sijtje, and Jan Bult to Corinne Melchers, 19 December 1933, object documentation Detroit Institute of Arts, and Letter from R. Fischer [?] to Corinne Melchers, 2 Januari 1933, object documentation Detroit Institute of Arts.

426 Stott 2009-2010, p. 76.

427 Meltzer 1913.

428 Piper 1923, p. 490.

Bibliography

Anonymous 1890
Anonymous, 'George Hitchcock', *The Art Amateur* 22 (February 1890) 3, pp. 54-55

Barrett 2008
B. D. Barrett, *North Sea artists' colonies 1880-1920, their development and role in marketing modernism with particular reference to the coast of Denmark, Germany and the Netherlands*, PhD diss., Rijksuniversiteit Groningen 2008

Beavington Atkinson 1880
J. Beavington Atkinson, "Dusseldorf: Its Old School and Its New Academy," *The Art Journal* (1875-1887), New Series, vol. 6 (1880), pp. 97-100

Belleman-Beentjes 2005
T. Belleman-Beentjes, "Het winkeltje van Belleman," *De Geestgronden* 1 April 2005, pp. 19-27

Benjamin 1881
S. G. W. Benjamin, "Fourteenth Annual Exhibition of the American Water Color Society (Opened Jan. 24. Closed Feb. 23)," *The American Art Review* 2 (1881) 5, pp. 193-201

Van den Berg 2008
P. van den Berg, *De uitdaging van het licht. George Hitchcock, 1880-1913. Een kroniek in beelden en teksten over de Egmondse kunstenaarskolonie*, Egmond 2008

Van den Berg 2010
P. van den Berg, *De Egmondse School, George Hitchcock en zijn Art Summer School 1890-1905*, Westzaan 2010

Van den Berg 2021
P. van den Berg, *De schilders van Egmond*, Zwolle 2021

Bienenstock 1990
J. A. M. Bienenstock, "Gari Melchers and the Belgian Art World 1882-1908," in Lesko 1990, pp. 75-110

Blaauboer 1941 (1)
J. Blaauboer, "Een herinnering aan Gari Melchers. De schilder van Egmond, die in Amerika woonde," *Alkmaarsche Courant* 4 January 1941

Blaauboer 1941 (2)
J. Blaauboer, "Een schilder uit Egmond, die in Amerika grooten naam maakte," *Nieuwe Haarlemsche Courant* 27 February 1941

Blokker 2018
L. Blokker, "De Alkmaarse stadstram. Van paardenvoetjes tot benzinedampen," *Oud Alkmaar* 1 September 2018, pp. 37-43

Boswell 1921
P. Boswell, "The George Hitchcock Memorial Exhibition to be held at a New York Gallery," Arts and Decoration 14 (February1921), p. 297

Boughton 1885
G. H. Boughton, *Sketching Rambles in Holland*, New York 1885

Brenchley 1900
J. Brenchley [H. Hitchcock], "Gari Melchers and his work", *The magazine of Art* 24 (1900), pp. 145-151

Brinton 1905
C. Brinton, "George Hitchcock – Painter of Sunlight," *International Studio* 24 (July 1905), pp. i–vi

Brinton 1907
C. Brinton, "The Art of Gari Melchers," *Harper's Monthly Magazine*, February 1907, pp. 430-439

Brinton 1908
C. Brinton, *Modern Artists*, New York 1908

Brinton 1915
C. Brinton, *George Hitchcock*, Rochester/New York (The Memorial Art Gallery) 1915

Child 1889
T. Child, "American Artists at the Paris Exhibition of 1889," *Harpers New Monthly Magazine* LXXIX (September 1889), pp. 508-510

Collins 1895
F. M. Collins, "A Visit to Joseph Israëls by Two Young American Painters," *The Art Amateur* 33 (1895) 5, p. 86

Cope 2011
R. Cope, "'With God's Assistance I Will Someday Be an Artist': John B. Fairbanks's Account of the Paris Art Mission," *Brigham Young University Studies*, vol. 50, no. 3 (2011), pp. 133-159

Cross 2009
R. K. Cross (B.A.), *Walter MacEwen: A Forgotten Episode in American Art*, M.A. thesis, University of North Texas, May 2009

Davis 1992
N. S. Davis, *A Lark Ascends. Florence Kate Upton, Artist and Illustrator*, London 1992

Donaldson 1938
B. M. Donaldson, *Gari Melchers: A Memorial Exhibition of his Works*, Richmond (Virginia Museum of Fine Arts) 1938

Dreiss 1984
J.G. Dreiss, *Gari Melchers. His works in the Belmont Collection*, Charlottesville 1984

Dreiss 1990
J.G. Dreiss, 'Gari Melchers in New York', in Lesko 1990, pp. 111-124

Dumas 1983
C. Dumas, "Haagse School verzameld," in R. de Leeuw, J. Sillevis & C. Dumas, *De Haagse School. Hollandse meesters van de 19de eeuw*, Paris (Grand Palais), London (Royal Academy of Arts), The Hague (Gemeentemuseum) 1983

Eva 1996
R. Eva, *The Heatherley School of Fine Art. 150th Anniversary Exhibition*, London 1996

Fehrer 1989
C. Fehrer, *The Julian Academy*, Parijs, 1868-1939, New York 1989

Fink 1973
L. Fink, "Artists in France 1850-1870," *The American Art Journal*, vol. 5, no. 2 (November 1973), pp. 32-49

Fink 1991
L. M. Fink, "American Art at the 1889 Paris Exposition: The Paintings They Love to Hate," *American Art*, 5 (1991) 4, pp. 34-53

Fish 1898
A. Fish, "George Hitchock: Painter," *The Magazine of Art* 21 (1898), pp. 577-583

Gallati 2014
B. D. Gallati, *Seeking Beauty: Paintings by James Jebusa Shannon*, New York (Debra Force Fine Art) 2014

Havard 1875
H. Havard *The dead cities of the Zuyder zee, a voyage to the picturesque side of Holland*, London 1875

Van Heteren & Stolwijk 2023
M. van Heteren & C. Stolwijk, *Van Gogh, Cézanne, Le Fauconnier & The Bergen School*, Alkmaar (Stedelijk Museum Alkmaar) 2023

Hitchcock 1887
G. Hitchcock, "The Picturesque Quality of Holland," *Scribner's Magazine* 2 (August 1887) no. 2, pp. 160-168

Hitchcock 1888
G. Hitchcock, "Sandro Botticelli," *Scribner's Magazine* 4 (December 1888), pp. 711-718

Hitchcock 1889
G. Hitchcock, "The Picturesque Quality of Holland. Interiors and Bric a brac," *Scribner's Magazine* 5 (February 1889), pp. 162-171

Hitchcock 1891
G. Hitchcock, "The Picturesque Quality of Holland. Figures and Costumes," *Scribner's Magazine* 10 (November 1891), pp. 621-629

Hoeber 1907
A. Hoeber, "Gari Melchers," *International Studio* 31 (1907) XVI, pp. 11-18

J.B. 1895
J.B., 'Mary at the house of Elizabeth', *The Art Journal* NS (1895), pp. 221-222

Von Jagow 1888
E. Von Jagow, "The Salon of 1888," *The Connoisseur* 3 (1888) 1, pp. 24-27

Kager 2015
C. Kager, "De Loodsen, een boeiend schilderij van Gari Melchers," *Geestgronden* 22 (2015) 2/3, pp. 76-93

Kager 2021
C. Kager, "Melchers en de smederij van Karels, Wie is wie op The Smithy?," *Geestgronden* 28 (2021), no. 80, pp. 14-22

Kraan 2002
H. Kraan, *Dromen van Holland. Buitenlandse kunstenaars schilderen Holland 1800-1914*, Zwolle 2002

Kraandijk 1875
J. Kraandijk, *Wandelingen door Nederland met pen en potlood*, Haarlem 1875

Lannoy & Denneboom 1969
K. Lannoy & B. Denneboom, *Derper-Hoever-Binder: over geschiedenis en volksleven van de drie Egmonden*, 's-Gravenhage 1969

Leroi 1886
P. Leroi, 'Salon de 1886', *L'art Revue Bi Mensuelle Illustré* 12 (1886) II, pp. 15-20

Leroi 1887
P. Leroi, 'Salon de 1887 (suite XVI', *L'art Revue Bi Mensuelle Illustré* 13 (1887) II, pp. 3-24

Leroi 1888
P. Leroi, 'Salon de 1888', *L'art: Revue Bi-mensuelle illustrée* 14 (1888) 1, 1 jan 1888, pp. 192-194

Leroi 1890
P. Leroi, 'Les ouvrages de peinture, sculpture et gravure exposés au champ de Mars III (fin)', *L'Art Revue Bi Mensuelle Illustrée*, 16 (1890) nr. 2, pp. 37-40.

Lesko 1990
D. Lesko, *Gari Melchers, a retrospective exhibition*, St. Peterburg, Florida (Museum of Fine Arts) 1990

Lewis Hind 1908
C. Lewis Hind, "Gari Melchers: A Great American Painter Who Has Received More Recognition Abroad Than at Home," *The World's Work* 15 (April 1908), pp. 10092-10105

Lewis Hind 1928
H. Lewis Hind, *Gari Melchers, Painter*, New York 1928

Lorguet 1901
P. Lorguet, *Les maitres d'aujourd'hui, la peinture francaise contemporaine*, Parijs 1901

Lübbren 2001
N. Lübbren, *Rural artists' colonies in Europe 1870-1910*, New Jersey 2001

Lyttelton 1926
E. Lyttelton, *Florence Upton, painter*, London 1926

MacChesney 1911
C.T. MacChesney, "Famous American Artist … Some Remarks on Modern Art," *The New York Times*, 19 January 1913

Mahoney 2011
D. Mahoney, "Other Americans Abroad: The Lure of Paris," in J. A. Barter (ed.), *The Age of American Impressionism. Masterpieces from the Art Institute of Chicago*, New Haven & London 2011, p. 91

Melchers 1922
G. Melchers, "Introduction," in J. W. Beatty, *The Relation of Art to Nature*, New York 1922

Meltzer 1912
C. H. Meltzer, "A Painter of Sunlight," *Heart's Magazine* 12 (July 1912), pp. 131-134

Meltzer 1913
C. H. Meltzer, "Gari Melchers. A Painter of Realities," *Cosmopolitan Magazine* 55 (June-November 1913), pp. 4-9

Mesman 1990 (1)
G. Mesman, "The Student Years: Düsseldorf and Paris," in Lesko 1990, pp. 49-54

Mesman 1990 (2)
G. Mesman, *Julius Garibaldi Melchers (1860-1932). A Survey of his Dutch Paintings with an Emphasis on his Religious Work*, PhD diss., The City University of New York 1990

Nilsen Laurvik 1912
J. Nilsen Laurvik, 'Gari Melchers-Painter', *The International Studio* 48 (1912) 190, pp. 27-32

Narodny 1930
I. Narodny, 'Gari Melchers', *American Painters*, New York 1930, pp. 89-98

Oresman 1978
J.C. Oresman, *Gari Melchers 1860-1932 American Painter*, New York (Graham Gallery) 1978

Oresman 1980
J. Oresman, "Gari Melchers' Portraits of Mrs. George Hitchcock," *Archives of American Art Journal* 20 (1980) 3, pp. 19-24

Pattison 1911
J. W. Pattison, "The Art of George Hitchcock and Cecil Jay," *Fine Arts Journal* 25 (February 1911), pp. 72-83

Pene du Bois 1913
G. Pene du Bois, "George Hitchcock: Painter of Holland," *Arts and Decoration* 3 (October 1913), pp. 401-404

Piper 1923
A. D. Piper, "Florence K. Upton, an Appreciation of her Work," *The American Magazine of Art* 14 (September 1923) no. 9, pp. 487-492

Piper 1924
A. D. Piper, "Gari Melchers," *The American Magazine of Art* 15 (February 1924) no. 2, pp. 79-85

Postlethwaite 1893-1894
H. I. Postlethwaite, "Some rising stars," *The Magazine of Art* 17 (1893-1894), pp. 113-118

Quick 1976
M. Quick, *American Expatriate Painters of the Late Nineteenth Century*, Dayton (Dayton Art Institute) 1976

Reid 1979
R.S. Reid, 'Gari Melchers, an American Artist in Virginia', *Virginia Cavalcade*, spring 1979, pp. 155-169

Reid 1990
R. Reid, 'Belmont, The Gari Melchers Memorial Gallery', in Lesko 1990, pp. 151-158

Robinson 1891
L. G. Robinson, "Mr. George Hitchcock and American Art," *Art Journal* (October 1891), pp. 289-295

Roland Holst-van der Schalk 1977
H. Roland Holst-van der Schalk, *Kapitaal en arbeid in Nederland*, 4th edition, Nijmegen 1977

Saunier 1908
Ch. Saunier, *Les Salons de 1908*, Parijs 1908

Schulte-Wülwer 1993-1994
U. Schulte-Wülwer Heinrich Peteren-Angeln, *Maler der Nord- und Ostzsee (1850-1906)*, Flensburg (Städtischen Museum Flensburg) 1993-1994

Shannon 1933
K. Shannon, *For my children*, London 1933

Sheldon [1890]
G. W. Sheldon, *Recent ideals of American art*, New York/London [1890]

Shellman Coleman 1990
F. Shellman Coleman, 'Melchers and the Telfair Academy: The evolution of a collection', in Lesko 1990, pp. 125-150

Stott 1986
A. Stott, *American Painters Who Worked in the Netherlands, 1880–1914*, PhD diss., Boston University, 1986

Stott 1990
A. Stott, "The Holland Years," in Lesko 1990, pp. 55-74

Stott 1998
A. Stott, *Holland Mania: The Unknown Dutch Period in American Art and Culture*, New York 1998

Stott 2009-2010
A. Stott, "The Egmond School of American Impressionism," in *Dutch Utopia. American Artists in Holland 1880-1914*, Savanah (Telfair Museum of Art)/Cincinnati (Taft Museum of Art)/Michigan (Grand Rapids Art Museum)/Laren (Singer Laren) 2009-2010

Strahan 1881
E. Strahan, "Exhibition of the American Water-Color Society," *The Art Amateur* 1881, pp. 48-50

Vaughan 1928
M. Vaughan, "A Painter of Modern Madonnas," *New York Herald Tribune*, 30 December 1928, pp. 16-18

Veldheer 1899
J. G. Veldheer, "De drie Egmonden," *Eigen Haard. Geïllustreerd Volkstijdschrift*, 1899, pp. 182-186

Van Vleuten 1990
R. van Vleuten, "Egmond Remembers Gari Melchers," in Lesko 1990, pp. 159-163

Van Vleuten 1994
R. van Vleuten, "Amerikaanse schilders in Egmond," *De Geestgronden – Egmonden* 1 (1994) 1/2, 1 October 1994, pp. 32-43

Van Vleuten 1995
R. van Vleuten, "Amerikaanse schilders in Egmond (2)," *De Geestgronden – Egmonden* 2 (1995) 2/3, 1 July 1995, pp. 27-41

Weinberg 1975
H.B. Weinberg, "Robert Reid: Academic 'Impressionist'", 15 (1975) 1, pp. 2-11

Weinberg 1981
H. B. Weinberg, "Nineteenth-Century American Painters at the École des Beaux-Arts," *The American Art Journal* 13 (1981) 4, pp. 66-84

Van de Wetering 1986-1987
E. van de Wetering, "De Hollandse werkelijkheid en Monets schilderkunstig 'bedrog'," in L. van Tilborgh, *Monet in Holland*, Amsterdam (Rijksmuseum Vincent van Gogh) 1986-1987, pp. 49-70

Woods 1913
J. C. B. Woods, "George Hitchcock," [unknown], 1913, pp. 14-19, Peter van den Berg Archive

Photo Credits
Lenders

Cover

George Hitchcock, *The Wayfarers*, ca. 1890, oil on
canvas, 110.5 x 89.5 cm. Private collection

Gari Melchers, *The Sisters*, ca. 1895, oil on canvas,
184.2 x 133.7 cm. National Gallery of Art, Washington,
Gift of C. H. Reisinger

Image Captions

Gari Melchers (left) and George Hitchcock, Egmond
aan Zee, Holland, ca. 1890. Photo Gari Melchers
Home and Studio, University of Mary Washington,
Fredericksburg **p. 2**

Gari Melchers, *The Goat Herd*, photo Gari Melchers
Home and Studio, University of Mary Washington,
Fredericksburg **p. 3**

George Hitchcock, *The Annunciation*, 1887, oil on
canvas, 158.8 x 204.5 cm. Art Institute of Chicago,
Potter Palmer Collection **p. 4-5**

George Hitchcock, *Maternity*, 1889, oil on canvas,
179 x 251.3 cm. Aberdeen Archives, Gallery &
Museums **p. 6-7**

Gari Melchers, *Skaters*, ca. 1892, oil on canvas,
110 x 70 cm. Pennsylvania Academy of the Fine Arts,
Philadelphia, Joseph E. Temple Fund **p. 10**

George Hitchcock *Wimmenumer Mill*, oil on canvas,
42 x 34 cm. Private collection **p. 13**

John McLure Hamilton (1853-1936), *George Hitchcock*,
ca. 1890-1900, watercolor, gouache, and pencil on
fine linen, 16.2 x 21.3 cm. Pennsylvania Academy of
the Fine Arts, Philadelphia **p. 131**

George Hitchcock, *The Blessed Mother*, 1892, oil on
canvas, 160.3 x 112 cm. The Cleveland Museum of Art,
Gift of Mr. and Mrs. J. H. Wade **p. 143**

Photo Credits

Aberdeen City Council (Archives, Gallery & Museums
Collection) **fig. 43**

Album/Scala, Florence **figs. 14, 97**

Rob Futrell, courtesy of the Lightner Museum,
St. Augustine, Florida **fig. 111**

René Gerritsen, Kunst- en Onderzoeksfotografie
figs. 23, 26, 37, 42, 75, 101, 102, 103

Grand Palais Rmn (Château de Blérancourt) / Gérard
Blot **fig. 115**

Grand Palais Rmn (Musée d'Orsay)/Hervé Lewandowski
fig. 31

Grand Palais Rmn (Musée d'Orsay)/Jean Schormans
fig. 63

Grand Palais Rmn / Agence Bulloz **fig. 15**

Josse/Scala, Florence **fig. 99**

Andres Kilger **fig. 71**

Kunstpalast – Horst Kolberg Artothek **fig. 56**

Marten de Leeuw **fig. 24**

The Metropolitan Museum of Art/Art Resource/Scala,
Florence **fig. 93**

Museum of Fine Arts, Boston **fig. 4**

Courtesy Parrish Art Museum **fig. 21**

Scala, Florence/bpk, Bildagentur für Kunst, Kultur und
Geschichte, Berlin. Andres Kilger. Nationalgalerie,
Staatliche Museen zu Berlin **fig. 11**

Scala, Florence/bpk, Bildagentur für Kunst, Kultur
und Geschichte, Berlin. Elke Estel / Hans-Peter Klut.
figs. 69, 70

Brandon Scott, Courtesy the Mint Museum **fig. 76**

Travis Fullerton © Virginia Museum of Fine Arts **fig. 72**

Lenders

Amsterdam – Rijksmuseum

Dordrecht – Dordrechts Museum

Egmond – Museum van Egmond

Paris, FR – Fondation Custodia

London, UK – National Gallery

Florida, US – The Thomas H. and Diane DeMell
Jacobsen PhD Foundation

Fredericksburg, US – Gari Melchers Home and Studio

Savannah, US – Telfair Museums

Washington, US – National Gallery of Art Washington
– Smithsonian American Art Museum

New York, US – Lawrence Steigrad Fine Arts

Private collections

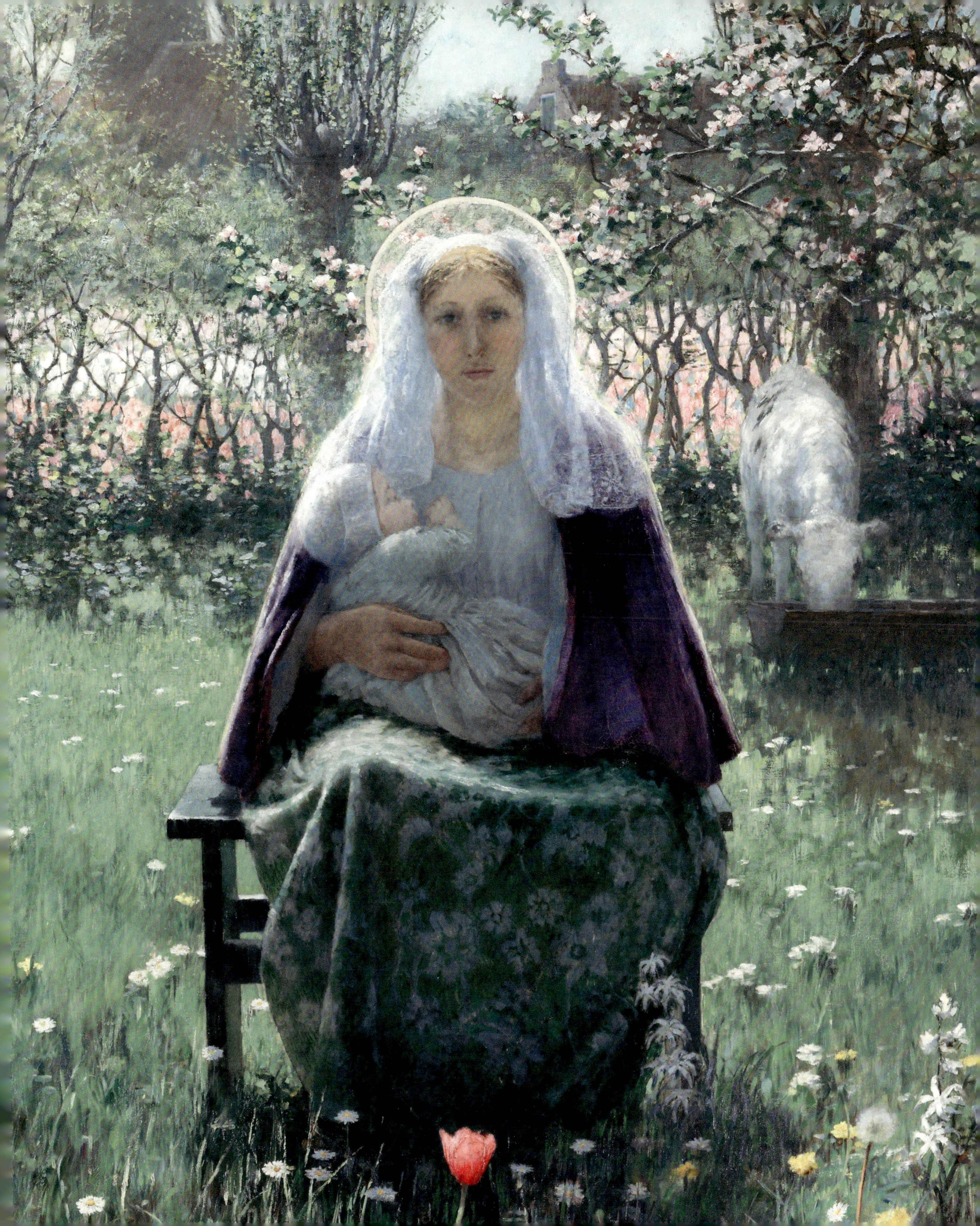

Credits

This publication has been published on the occasion of the exhibition: *Longing for Egmond. From Source of Inspiration to Artists' Village* in Stedelijk Museum Alkmaar (June 28 – November 2, 2025)

Publishers
Waanders Publishers, Zwolle
Stedelijk Museum Alkmaar

Author
Marjan van Heteren

Translation
Kist & Kilian (Dutch–English)

Image editing
Olga Kruisbrink

Design
Studio Berry Slok, Amsterdam

Lithography
Benno Slijkhuis, Wilco Art Books

Printing
Wilco Art Books, Amersfoort

© 2025 Waanders Uitgevers b.v., Zwolle;
Stedelijk Museum Alkmaar

ISBN 9789462626317
NUR 644

This publication has also been published in a Dutch edition.
ISBN 9789462626171

www.waanders.nl
www.stedelijkmuseumaalkmaar.nl

The publication and exhibition have been made possible thanks to:

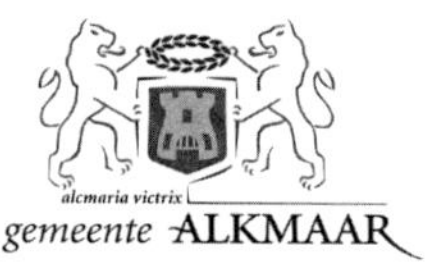

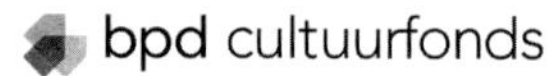

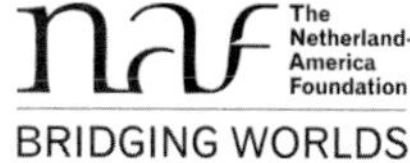

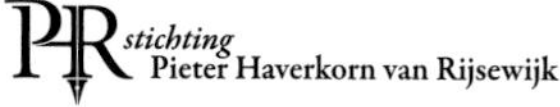

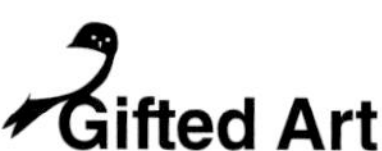

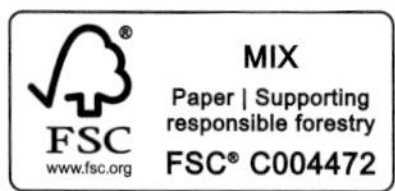